District Primary Education Programme

जिला प्राथमिक शिक्षा कार्यक्रम
District Primary Education Programme

District Primary Education Programme

Editor
Dr. Digumarti Bhaskara Rao
M.Sc., M.A., M.A., M.Ed., Ph.D.
R.V.R. College of Education
Guntur-522006, Andhra Pradesh,
India

1998
DISCOVERY PUBLISHING HOUSE
NEW DELHI-110002

First Published—1998

ISBN 81-7141-396-X

Published by :

Discovery Publishing House
4831/24, Ansari Road, Prahlad Street
Darya Ganj, New Delhi-110 002 (INDIA)
Phone : 327 92 45
Fax. : 91-11-3253475

Laser Typeset by :

Innovative Processors
4819/24, Ansari Road, Darya Ganj, NewDelhi

Printed at :
Taruna Offset Press, Delhi

Preface

The District Primary Education Programme is one of the home grown innovative educational programmes with three main goals—universal access, retention and achievement. It is an ambitious national programme firmly rooted in the National Policy on Education and Programme of Action, aiming to achieve Education for all by 2000 A.D. It is an exercise in decentralised planning which puts local communities in charge of education. The districts chosen under it represent those where female literacy is below the national average of 52.21 per cent. It covers 42 districts of Assam, Haryana, Karnataka, Kerala, Madhya Pradesh, Maharashtra and Tamil Nadu in Phase I; 79 districts of Andhra Pradesh, Gujarat, Himachal Pradesh, Orissa, Uttar Pradesh and West Bengal in Phase II and 17 districts of Bihar in Phase III. The DPEP is inaugurated formally on November 8, 1994.

The main thrusts under DPEP are—District level planning; Community participation and Decentralised management; focus on education for girls, scheduled castes and scheduled tribes; improving effectiveness in education through training of teachers; improvement of learning materials; and upgrading of infrastructural facilities.

The DPEP is a sustainable, cost-effective and replicable one on a national scale. The programme thus focuses on—providing all children with access to primary education either in formal system or through non-formal education programme; reducing differences in enrolment, drop-out and learning achievement to less than five per cent between boys and girls, as also for disadvantaged social groups; a reduction in the overall drop-out rate in primary education to less than ten per cent for all students; an increase of atleast twenty five percent in average primary learning achievement levels measured against benchmark surveys; facilitating access for disadvantaged groups such as girls, socially backward communities and the handicapped; improving the quality of education through a process of demand creation for better service; recruitment and regular upgrading of teachers' skills; involvement of community in programme planning as district from project planning; strategies for convergence with related services such as health care, early childhood care and education and other government welfare schemes; improvement of infrastructural facilities; effective decentralised school management; and achievement of minimum levels of learning.

The DPEP attempts little less than a complete overhaul the system of educational planning in the country and to implement interventions in primary education in a holistic and coordinated fashion. The programme is under implementation in a mission mode through registered autonomous societies in each state. The district and sub-district structures, however, evolved and would evolve in congruence with the needs of the communities and the panchayati raj institutions. At the national level, the NCERT, NIEPA and EdCIL along with DPEP Bureau are facilitating planning and capacity building at the state and district level. The district level planning is distinct in its emphasis on participation of all major actors in the education system, such as parents, guardians, teachers, educational administrators and voluntary organisations.

The DPEP has attracted the attention of educationists, educational administrators, educational policy makers, educational researchers alongwith the international educational institutions and financial organisations and received their appreciation alongwith technical and financial assistance. This programme is marching ahead with great conviction and we can expect that this programme alongwith other educational programmes will achieve the goals of EFA in India by the turn of the century.

Wishing all success

Dr. Digumarti Bhaskara Rao
Independence Day, 1997

Primary Prattle

Pro was in high spirits when Con called on him one evening.

'What's it?' asked Con.

'DPEP', said Pro.

'D-Pep? sounds good. Pour me one, too.'

'No, no,' said Pro. 'It is not that kind of pep. This is a pep for children's education. The District Primary Education Programme. It's for improving the quality of primary education.'

'What's wrong with it now?' asked Con.

'Everything', said Pro. 'Schools are ill equipped, teaching is apologetic, and the children are overburdened with books. Little wonder they drop out. Or don't join up at all. And for those who remain, learning achievement is practically nil. It's a bleak scenario.' Con shrugged. 'Why bother with the small fry? Quality education can be imparted at higher levels.'

Pro drew himself up sharply. 'Primary Education,' he proclaimed 'is the foundation on which children build up their lives. And like all other buildings, if the foundation is weak the whole structure will collapse.' Con collapsed with a sigh into the nearest chair.

Pro continued, 'DPEP ushers in a new era of primary education centred around the child's needs and thoughts. It provides functional schools where children can happily go to. The class rooms are cheerful, the textbooks are revealing and the learning process is filled with fun and frolic. The idea is to spark children's interest so that they develop a genuine desire to learn.'

Con chuckled 'Why don't you try whacking them on the bottom?'

'That will only make their bottom smart,' retorted Pro. And pink bottoms certainly don't make for a rosy future. It's young minds draped with understanding, problem-solving abilities, skills and values that can lead us to a better tomorrow.'

'How nice,' said Con. 'But do you really believe that things will change?' 'Heroditus once said that nothing is permanent except change. I believe that,' said Pro.

'Obviously, Heroditus didn't believe it himself. Or did he change his opinion?'

'Look,' said Pro. 'Let's not be argumentative. DPEP may or may not change things. But at least it is a step in the right direction.'

'Watch out for the fitfalls!'

'Oh, surely. We'll make an attempt to level it up. After all, children's education is our collective responsibility.

'Then what are parents for?'

'A child's world is not restricted to it's parental home, rather the whole world is the child's home. And we, as part of the larger household, have an inherent duty to put it in order.'

'So the old flesh and blood can get off lightly?' 'I didn't say that', protested Pro.' Parents have a key role to play in the development of a child. It's their duty to initiate the child. Their concern, their understanding, their notion of what is good and bad for the child, will go a long way in motivating the child.' 'How well they play their role!' Con observed. 'It varies from ceaselessly exhorting the children to study hard and get marks to gross neglect of their education.'

'Spare the sarcasm,' said Pro, 'I agree that that there are parents who are not the most sensible in their handling of children. So we'll educate them.'

'What do you suggest - a bachelor's degree in parenthood?'

'Ha, ha.' said Pro.' Awareness programmes will do quite well thank you.'

'Now you are talking about moulding mature minds,' pointed out Con.

'Young minds can easily be got at... but how do you crack the older nuts?'

'Reason is a powerful tool,' said Pro. 'It's simple. When education is imparted as a bitter drug, children find it hard to swallow. So what we should do is make it as sweet as possible.' 'Diabetes through primary education 'that's a new one,' laughed Con. 'And what reason will you use with parents who don't send their children to school?'

'We'll simply ask them why they want to suffer the brats at home all day long when they can always be packed off to school. Good enough reason, what?' smirked Pro. 'But seriously,' he added 'Neglect occurs due to various reasons. It could be traditional habits, or religious inhibitions, or cultural taboos, maybe the imperatives of child labour, or just plain indifference which dictates whether or not parents send their children to school.'

'So?'

'So we point out to them the inadequacies of their ways. Today's world is much more complex than the days of yore. What was good for the parents is not good enough for the child. Under these circumstances, education is a must for both boys and girls. So off to school with them!'

—Dr. Roy Ommen

Acknowledgements

I am grateful to Dr. R.V. Vaidyanatha Ayyar, Mr. R.S. Pandey and Ms. Sujaya Krishnan, Department of Education, Ministry of Human Resource Development, Government of India for their cooperation by sending the DPEP documents on request.

I am thankful to Prof. Kuldeep Mathur, Director, National Institute of Educational Planning and Adminstration, New Delhi for giving me permission to reprint the Report of NIEPA-IIEP workshop on District Level Plan Implementation Strategy with particular reference to School Improvement, August 18-20, 1994.

I am also thankful to Ms. S. Krishnan, Editor, DPEP CALLING Newsletter, for extending her kind support by permitting to reproduce the articles on DPEP from the newsletter.

I extend my appreciation to Dr. R.V.V. Ayyar, Mr. R.S. Pandey, Dr. N.V. Varghese, Dr. M.K. Mishra, Prof. G.L, Arora, Dr. Ajit Singh, Dr. S.K. Yadav, Dr. Yash Aggarwal, Prof. M.A. Khader, Dr. Subir Shukla, Dr. Amita Sharma and Dr. S.C. Girotra for their valuable contributions, and I also extend the same sense of appreciation to the staff of DPEP Bureau, members of DPEP CALLING and personnel of Department of Education for their continuous efforts to put the facts before the readers and other interested parties.

I deem it a privilege to dedicate this work to the personnel of DPEP Bureau for their excellent service to the nation in the field of education.

D.B. Rao

Contents

District Primary Education Programme

DPEP—A Programme for Educational Transformation

DPEP was launched in 1994. It seeks to operationalise decentralised planning and management, identified by the National Policy on Education, 1986 and the Programme of Action (PoA) 1992 to be the main strategy for Universalisation of Elementary Education (UEE). This is done through district and population-specific planning.

DPEP emphasises on

- contextuality, i.e., giving primacy to local needs
- reduction of existing gender and social disparities in educational access
- provision of alternative schooling of comparable standards to the disadvantaged groups
- obtaining genuine community involvement in the running of schools
- empowerment and capacity building at the local level
- addressing access, retention and quality issues
- devising an appropriate fund flow mechanism from Centre to the States.

Ownership is the Key

DPEP is an attempt to initiate a process of planning from the grassroots. Districts identify their needs and formulate a plan. State level interventions are meant to provide support to the district level. The programme has drawn inspiration from earlier experiences in community participation such as the Bihar Education Project and the Lok Jumbish Project in Rajasthan.

Strategies and interventions which include, amongst others, construction of school buildings, improvement of teaching-learning materials and teacher training practices, as well as capacity building for academic and management support, are designed through wide ranging consultations with grassroot level functionaries, NGOs, teacher representatives and support institutions.

DPEP effectively builds on the groundwork that has been done by the Total Literacy Campaigns and the Panchayati Raj Constitutional Amendments to ensure popular participation in primary education.

The programme has definitely kindled a feeling of ownership among the officials, teachers and the community.

Equity Focus

A gender perspective has been incorporated into all aspects of planning and implementation of DPEP. Pertinent lessons have been drawn from the Mahila Samakhya Project DPEP targets low female literacy districts. Apart from specific strategies designed to enhance girls' access, enrolment and retention in the school system, DPEP recognises the crucial importance of enabling communities, particularly women, in the activities of the programme through—

- formation of village level women's collective and training of local women activists
- empowerment of local bodies such as VECs, mother-teacher associations and women's groups
- intensive capacity building for community and women's groups
- involvement of community and women's organisations in mobilisation, school management and monitoring.

Tribal education has received a boost with DPEP giving priority to the opening of schools in tribal areas. Some of the interventions include setting up of residential schools, providing alternative schooling, creating a cadre of parateachers within the community, involvement of NGOs, teaching in local dialects and developing culturally sensitive education material.

Pedagogical Renewal

Pedagogical renewal which includes teacher motivation and competence is the key to UEE, DPEP strives to link pedagogical necessities with broader educational concerns with the ultimate objective of improving the school processes and classroom practices. The APPEP and Shiksha Karmi Projects, forerunners to the DPEP, have provided valuable lessons in this area.

The multi-pronged strategy to improve pedagogy include—

- MLL bases teaching/learning practices

- improving textbooks
- changing teaching styles and practices
- enhancing teacher motivation and competence
- strengthening academic support to teachers
- supporting educational evaluation at district and school levels
- developing strategies for multigrade schools
- promoting educational research
- promoting joyful and child-centred learning.

This programme has created local-specific and favourable conditions to improve teacher competencies through frequent in-service training programmes at decentralised levels in block and cluster resource centres.

Building Capacity for Sustainability

Building institutional capacities at all levels is the *sine qua non* for proving sustainability to the system. This assumes greater significance in view of the Panchayati Raj legislations transferring responsibilities, including that of primary education, to local bodies. The experience gained in the UP Basic Education Project served as a starting point.

DPEP seeks to strengthen District Institutes of Education and Training (DIETs), State Council of Educational Research and Training (SCERTs) and State Institute of Educational Management and Training (SIEMTs) and make them vibrant, optimal functioning institutions: National level apex institutions such as the National Council of Educational Research and Training (NCERT) and National Institute of Educational Planning and Administration (NIEPA) are supported so that they can in turn lend their expertise to state and district level institutions. Expertise is also being developed in crucial areas such as planning, management and action research.

A Responsive System

What perhaps sets DPEP apart from earlier attempts at UEE is the efforts towards demand based interventions, systematic planning, empowerment and accountability at all levels. Well defined activities and goals are specified and taken up for implementation in a time-bond manner. Clearcut responsibilities are assigned to various agencies.

Empowered management mechanisms have been set up for project management and implementation at all levels which facilitate flexibility, quick administrative decision-making and smooth flow of funds. These bodies also provide for partnership between central and state governments as well as between the voluntary sector and educational experts.

Necessitated by this orientation and integral to DPEP is a regular system of monitoring and evaluation. This system provides continuous and timely information required to fine tune the programme. A Project Management Information System has been developed.

Supervision missions are mounted frequently. Subject specialists' and experts visit states, districts and field level institutions in all DPEP areas to get a first hand view of the progress and support the implementation.

2

District Primary Education Programme: Philosophy and Approach

DPEP: A Home Grown Idea

- Not something suggested from abroad.
- Gadgil (1930s) - Vardah District Planning of Universal Elementary Education (UEE).
- Seeks to operational Para 7.2 of Plan of Action (POA), 1992
- Extend to UEE the district approach of Total Literacy Campaign (TLC).
- Contexulity

DPEP: A National Programme

- External funding happy concidence.
- Equal partnership to plan and manage a National Programme
- A centrally sponsored scheme with broad, flexible parameters.

Capacity Building

- We should plan
- We should implement
- We should manage
- We should evaluate
- Networking
  - among Insititutions within States
  - with National Insititutions
  - with other States
- No short cuts; self-learning

Planning Process

- A stitch in time saves nine
- Proper planning the foundation for successful project

DPEP: Not Finance Driven

- False premise
  - ❑ Rs. 40 crores given; what to do
- Correct premise
  - ❑ What is it that we require to achieve Universal Primary Education (UPE).
  - ❑Allocation a budgetary ceiling to trim the programme.

DPEP is only about

- Process
- Outcomes
- four dimensions of UPE
  - ❑ Access
  - ❑ Retention
  - ❑ Equity
  - ❑ Achievement

Nine Pillars of DPEP

- Mobilisation for UEE
  - ❑ Village Education Committees (VECs)
  - ❑ Teachers
  - ❑ Parents
  - ❑ Linkage with TLC
- Primary Education not Primary Schooling
- Quality
  - ❑ School effictiveness
  - ❑ Curriculum, textbooks
  - ❑ Minimum levels of learning (MLL)
  - ❑ Multigrade Teaching
  - ❑ Single Reading-learning skill

- Innovations
  - Change
  - Testing
  - Open mind
  - No NIH Syndrome
- Gender
- Evaluation, Monitoring and Research
  - Role of students
  - Ultimate objectives
- Management of change
  - Improvement of the system
- Convergence
  - Primary Education
  - Primary Health
  - Early Childhool Care and Education (ECCE)
- Training
  - Teaching Training
  - Role change of management

Role of DIETs, IASEs and CTEs in DPEP

- Environmental building activities
- Survey
- Training
- Assessing training needs of the teachers of formal and non-formal systems
- Planning Activities
- Studies
- Support.

3

District Primary Education Programme: Guidelines

INTRODUCTION

The District Primary Education Programme guidelines were formulated in April 1993; since then there have been major developments in the evolution of DPEP. In December 1993 the Cabinet accorded its approval for the scheme in principle: in January 1994 the full Planning Commission approved DPEP as a centrally sponsored scheme. District projects were prepared in 42 districts spread over the seven states of Assam, Haryana, Madhya Pradesh, Karnataka, Maharashtra, Tamil Nadu and Kerala. The Planning process in these districts has been intensive and participative; the process has conflated theory and practice and extensively drawn up organisations like NCERT, NIEPA and IIMs. It would be a truism to say that DPEP planning processes have provided a valuable opportunity for NCERT/ NIEPA to field test many of the pedagogical and management concepts that they have been developing over the years. The studies conducted as a part of the planning process have been of a path breaking nature; and learning levels of over sixty thousand students were tested as part of a baseline study with a rigorous sampling and pedagogic design, with a veiw to identify area-specific interventions in each of these districts. The expenditure Finance Committee of the Government of India met in May 1994 and has approved details of the DPEP proposals and its financial parameters. The DPEP was primarily launched on November 8, 1994.

The loftiness of the objectives, the nature and intensity of the planning process, the integration of professional inputs, participative planning and management, and the emphasis on capacity building have together rendered DPEP an exciting idea not only in the country but all over the world. DPEP has broken new paths in international cooperation, in that it belongs to the new genre of the developmental cooperation which emphasises sustainability, equity, local ownership and execution and is supportive of national policies in the education sector, DPEP is a homegrown idea in keeping with CABE guidelines, and its distincitveness lies in that in spite of diversity of sources of funding, it is a national programme intending to achieve UEE in a contextual manner with emphasis on participation and capacity building . Furthermore, many functions peformed by funding agencies in the past like supervision and appraisal missions, have been vested with DPEP at the national level—in fact DPEP seems likely to emerge as an intermediary financial, technical and resource organisation which may well develop into an educational fund/bank for primary education development in the country. DPEP is not an enclave project: it is a major and multifaceted programme seeking to overhaul the primary education system in the country.

District Primary Education Programme: Basics

1.1.1 The National Policy of Education, 1986 (as updated in 1992) and the Programme of Action, 1992 (POA) reaffirm the national commitment to Universalisation of Elementary Education (UEE), Para 5.12 of NPE resolves that free and compulsory education of satisfactory quality should be provided to all children upto 14 years of age before we enter the 21st century. The NPE also specifies in Para 5.5 that UEE has three aspects:

(i) universal access and enrolment;

(ii) universal retention of children upto 14 years of age; and

(iii) a substantial improvement in quality of education to enable all children to achieve essential levels of learning.

1.1.2 Right from independence India has persevered with the goal of UEE; even though substantial progress has been achieved, the goal still remains elusive. The additional participation in elementary education has to come from social strata and regions which are more difficult to reach. Therefore, the path that lies ahead in the march to UEE is more ardous; the journey ahead is a marathon calling for a higher intensity of effort and more systematic planning and implementation.

1.1.3 National experience with the pursuit of UEE had established the following:

(i) *UEE is contextual.* The contextuality varies widely across the country. Even in States like Kerala where participation is near-universal much requires to be done in respect of quality and achievement. In such States the pursuit of UREE would be mainly in the areas of quality, facilities and achievement. In other States participation and demand aspects need more attention.

(ii) *Contextuality entails local area-planning with disaggregated targets and decentralised planning and management.* Planning for UEE had hitherto been mainly at the national and state-level. Barring some States and Union Territories, these entities are too large and heterogeneous for effective planning; they cannot provide contextuality. Ideally the planning should be from below, right from the village upwards but given the objectives conditions, a beginning has to be made with district as the unit of planning. The district plans are to be prepared through an intensive process of interation with the local bodies, teachers and NGOs so that it is "owned" by all who are to be associated in implementation and it reflects the ground-level realities.

(iii) *Resources are an important but not sufficient condition for achieving UEE.* A host of measures both financial and non-financial, both on the supply side and on the demand side, need to complement higher allocation of resources.

(iv) *The strategies for UEE* have hitherto emphasised, mainly access in terms of construction of class rooms and appointment of teachers. This has been inadequate and *need to be augmented by:*

(a) a holistic planning and management approach which goes beyond implementation of a disjointed set of individual schemes, perceives the task of UEE in its totality, integrates all the measures needed to achieving UEE in the specific context of the district;

(b) this holistic planning should incorporate a gender perspective in all aspects of the planning and implementation process and be an integral part of all measures needed to achieve UEE;

(c) addressing the more difficult aspects of access, particularly access to girls, disadvantaged groups and out of school children;

(d) improving school effectiveness:

(e) strengthening the alternatives to schooling, particularly the non-formal education system;

(f) stressing the participative processes whereby the local community facilitates participation, achievement and school effectiveness;

(g) toning up teacher competence, training and motivation;

(h) stressing need for improved teaching/learning materials;

(i) streamlining of planning and management in respect of both routine and innovative areas; and

(j) Convergence between elementary education and related services like ECCE and school health.

1.1.4 The District Primary Education Programme (hereafter referred to as the Programme) is based on the above national experience and seeks to operationalise para 7.4.6 of the POA, 1992 which reads as follows:

"Further efforts would be made to develop district specific projects, with specific activities, clearly defined responsibilities, definite time-schedule and specific targets. Each district project will be prepared within the major strategy framework and will be tailored to the specific needs and possibilities in the district. Apart from effective UEE, the goals of each project will include the reduction of existing disparities in educational access, the provision of alternative systems of comparable standards to the disadvantaged groups, a substantial improvement in the quality of schooling facilities, obtaining a genuine community involvement in the running of schools, and building up local level capacity to ensure effective decentralisation of educational planning. That is to say, the overall goal of the project would be reconstruction of primary education as a whole in selected districts instead of a piecemeal implementation of schemes. An integrated approach is more likely to achieve synergies among different programme components."

1.1.5 The Programme also builds upon the experience gained in—

(i) the implementation of the Bihar Education Project (with UNICEF assistance) and the Lok Jumbish Project (with SIDA assistance);

(ii) the planning of basic education project in Uttar Pradesh (with IDA) assistance);

(iii) the implementation of the Andhra Pradesh Primary Education Project (with ODA assistance), Shiksha Karmi Project (with SIDA assistance) and Mahila Samakhya (with Dutch assistance).

In BEP and UP projects too, investment is concentrated in the chosen districts and district specific investment is complemented by a few State level interventions such as strengthening of State level institutions. Where the Programme goes beyond the Uttar Pradesh and Bihar projects, is in

(i) the emphasis of local area planning with the district plans being formulated in their own right rather than being derived from a state plan project document.

(ii) Greater rigour and infusion of professional inputs in planning and appraisal.

(iii) More focussed targeting in that the districts selected would be:

(a) educationally backward districts with female literacy below the national average; and

(b) Districts where TLCs have been successful leading to enhanced demand for elementary education.

(iv) More focussed coverage in that the Programme would focus on primary stage (Classes I-V and its NFE equivalent), with stress on education for girls, and for socially disadvantaged groups. In States where enrolment and rentention is near universal in the primary stage, support can be considered for the upper primary stage.

1.1.6 The District Primary Education Programme has been approved as a Centrally Sponsored Scheme of the Government of India for primary education development. As of now the process of planning has been completed for 42 districts in the states of Madhya Pradesh, Assam, Haryana, Maharashtra, Karnataka, Tamil Nadu and Kerala. Ten districts in West Bengal and Andhra Pradesh have initiated the project planning process recently. The objective of the programme is to gradually extend the coverage to all the districts which satisfy one of the twin criteria referred to in para 1.5 (iii). The pace of expansion would depend upon the availability of resources and in states where the Programme is now being started on the pace and quality of implementation in the districts now chosen. The attempt would be to start the Programme in at least 110 districts in the Eighth Five Year Plan with an estimated outlay of Rs. 1950 crores of which Rs. 1720 crores are proposed to be drawn from external sources.

1.1.7 The Programme would develop and implement in the districts selected a replicable, sustainable and cost-effective programme:

(i) to reduce differences in enrolment, dropout and learning achievement among gender and social groups to less than five per cent.

(ii) to reduce overall primary dropout rates for all students to less than 10 per cent.

(iii) to raise average achievement levels by atleast 25 per cent over measured baseline levels and ensuring achievement of basic literacy and numeracy competencies and a minimum of 40 per cent achievement levels in other competencies, by all primary school children.

(iv) to provide, according to national norms, access for all children, to primary education classes (I-V), i.e. primary schooling wherever possible, or its equivalent non-formal education.

The programme would also strengthen the capacity of national, state and district institutions and organisations for the planning, management and evaluation of primary education.

1.1.8 The Programme would be implemented in a mission mode through registered state level autonomous societies. Each society would have two organs:

(i) a General Council with Chief Minister as ex-officio president; and

(ii) Executive Committee under the chairmanship of Chief Secretary/Education Secretary of the State.

The executive responsibility will vest with the State Programme Director being the Member-Secretary of the Executive Committee and the Council. Government of India would be represented in the General Council and the Executive Committee. The plans would be formulated and implemented with the active association of the community, NGOs, teachers and educationists. Therefore, all these groups would have to be provided adequate representation and voice in the management of the project at all levels; state, district, block and village. The Memorandum of Association and bye-laws of Association of UP would serve as a model; however, district and sub-district structures would have to be developed by states to suit their administrative patterns and ethos.

1.1.9 The district plans would be regorously appraised and their implementation systematically monitored.

1.1.10 Funds would be released from the Government of India to the State-level societies. GOI contribution is expected to be of the order of 85 per cent and is likely to follow the existing pattern for releases to IDA projects.

1.1.11 States would need to at least maintain the 1991-1992 expenditure levels on elementary education in real terms, excluding funds earmarked for DPEP as State share.

TABLE I

Programme Criteria and Evidence

Criteria	*Evidence*
Equity focus	Focus on districts with low female literacy rates. Baseline beneficiary studies.
	Specific strategies for girls, SC/ST students.
Decentralisation	Action plans and budgets developed at the district level.
	Investment in district-level institutional capacity.
Participatory Planning	Village leadership, NGOs, District, Block and School level personnel involved in programme planning through consultations and workshops.
Technical Feasibility	Strategies are based on empirical evidence or experience, preferably in India.
Managerial Feasibility	Implementation by a registered society empowered to make financial, staffing and project design decisions.
	Plan for MIS development that meets GOI requirements.
	Acceptable plans for development of enhanced State capacity for textbook development, teacher training, management training, student learning assessment, and programme evaluation.
Financial Feasibility	States would need to at least maintain the 1991-92 expenditure levels on elementary education in real terms, excluding funds earmarked for DPEP as State share.
	State share of annual programme costs are included in annual State budgets. Annual recurrent costs of the investment are shown to be sustainable on State Non-Plan budgets at the end of the project.

1.1.12 While the quantum of funding would depend upon the district plan and its appraisal, the over-all investment per district is expected to be within a ceiling of 30-40 crores per district. This is only a normative figure and the requirement of each district will vary. It must be borne in mind that DPEP is not a finance driven programme but seeks to build systems that are cost-effective, replicable and sustainable. The construction component would be limited to 24% and management cost to 6%. The recurring liabilities at the end of the Programme would be the exclusive responsibility of the State Government.

1.1.13 Appraisal would be with reference to the criteria of equity, participative process, feasibility, sustainability and replicability. Details are spelt out in Table I (see p. 14).

Financial Parameters

2.1 DPEP financing would be covered as per parameters set out below:

Additionality of DPEP Resources

1. As DPEP is externally funded it is subject to the parameters of external assistance approved by CABE at its 46th meeting held on March 8-9, 1991 and reiterated by its 47th meeting held on August 5-6, 1992. One of these parameters is that external funding should be additional to the resources for education. This would, in operational terms, mean that DPEP cannot finance:

   (i) Salaries of sanctioned but unfilled posts.

   (ii) Salaries of posts that should have been created as per the State Government norms such as teacher posts that ought to be created as per the teacher-pupil ratio.

   (iii) Salaries of posts transferred to DPEP, e.g., if some of the functions relating to textbook development are transferred along with posts to a Textbook Development Board to be financed by DPEP, the posts transferred would not be financed.

   DPEP would finance coverage under State Government schemes only over and above the level that the state would itself cover each year.

Safeguard of Investment in Elementary Education

2. Inextricably linked to and flowing from the principle of additionality, is the need to safeguard existing expenditure on elementary education. This would help enable DPEP resources to remain an additionality. It is therefore a basic requirement of DPEP that at least 1991-92 levels of expenditure on elementary education are maintained in real terms.

Utmost Parsimony in Expenditure

3. The DPEP seeks to operationalise Para 7.4.6 of the Programme of Action 1992 which enjoins that an ethos of cost effectiveness and accountability should permeate every part of the education system. This ethos is all the more necessary for DPEP as it is largely financed by external debt. In operational terms this would mean, *inter-alia,* that administrative overheads should be a bare minimum (the 6% ceiling on administrative cost is a ceiling and not an entitlement). DPEP would not finance expansion of supervisory cadres, or activities having no proven direct educational salience.
4. The cardinal principle is that every proposal has to be appraised and found to conform to the criteria of relevance, feasibility and sustainability.

Incentives

5. DPEP would not finance non-educational incentives such as free uniforms, incentives for attendance, nutrition, etc. Only provision of free textbooks to girls, SC/STs would be financed in project districts in States which do not have such a scheme.

Convergence

6. A central concern of the POA of 1992 is the convergence of the services such as primary education, health, ECCE etc. DPEP would prefer measures to promote convergence wherever such services exist rather than replicating the services. Thus DPEP would not finance setting up of ECCE Centres in villages covered under ICDS. Instead, it would seek to bring together the ICDS and the primary school. Likewise it would not seek to replicate medical services or supplies in schools but would facilitate diagnosis of learning disabilities through medical check-up of students and better linkages between PHCs and the schools. Activities and processes which would promote these convergence would be financed.
7. At another level convergence would be attempted amongst the various DPEP programme components and processes. An example is the convergence of reduction of academic burden (cf. Yashpal Committee); MLL, multigrade teaching, gender sensitivity, training, development of instructional materials and learners evaluation. Another is involvement of VECs in the setting-up, facilitation and supervision of NFE centres.

Phasing and Innovation

8. Basic to the DPEP is the premise that there are large "unknown" areas that are crucial to the achievement of UEE. Innovation, which is critical to DPEP, entails systematic trial, evaluation, scaling and phasing. It would be expedient to move systematically and in a phased manner. Programme implementation can begin with core known programme components and progressively add on more and more components. All new programmes and strategies that have been either untested or are still at a nascent stage need to be systematically planned and their implementation staggered.

Local Area Planning

9. DPEP stresses participative process whereby the local community would play an active role in promoting enrolment, retention, achievement and school effectiveness. This process would be institutionalised through the Village Education Committee and bodies like Mother-Teacher Associations. In line with this approach of participative decentralised planning DPEP would not fund supply of standardised packages of teaching-learning equipment, furniture and other materials to schools. Instead VEC and the school would be facilitated to improve the school facilities according to locally felt needs and priorities, through provision of an amount of Rs 2000 per school per annum to be jointly operated by the VEC and school. In addition the school will be provided an amount of Rs 500 per teacher to procure consumables and to develop, prepare and acquire low cost teaching aids.

State and District Component

10. The State Component is intended to provide the resource and management backup for the implementation of the district components. The state component should therefore comprise activities having direct relevance to the district components. As already spelt out the state component would comprise, inter-alia, development of MIS, training modules and instructional material. The financing of the end-products of these developments would be limited to DPEP districts.

Inter-District Disparities

11. The basic premise of DPEP is contextuality. Therefore the relative emphasis on access, equity, quality and achievement would vary from district to district. Therefore in appraisal

the DPEP National Management Structure expects inter-district variations in programme components and investment patterns.

Systematic Preparation

12. The first year of implementation would focus on putting systems in place and setting processes in motion. This would include:

- formation of bodies like VECs, Mother Teacher Associations;
- awareness building campaigns for providing the necessary institutional infrastructure for stepping up enrolment, retention and for facilitating performance of schools and NFE centres;
- building up the training infrastructure by strengthening capacity of DIETs, setting up Block Resource Centres and school clusters;
- setting in motion processes such as development of training modules and materials, reduction of academic burden and improving the efficiency in production and distribution of learning materials.

National Components

13. Greater clarity has emerged on the national component and on the overall programme design. The national components are now perceived to comprise:

(i) setting up of management structure at the National level

(ii) Development of MIS

(iii) Technical assistance to DPEP States in Project Planning and Management

(iv) Technical assistance in Pedagogy. This will include among other things

- rationalization of academic burden (as per Yashpal Committee)
- development of prototype training modules,
- programme for teaching numeracy and reading skills, etc.

(v) Programme Evaluation and Research

(vi) Appraisal, Supervision and Monitoring arrangements for DPEP.

Programme Design

14. The programme design broadly encompasses the following inter-related and mutually reinforcing areas:
    - (i) Building institutional infrastructure for action research, training and academic supervision through augmenting/networking/setting up of institutions as the national, state, district and sub-district levels;
    - (ii) Building community support for primary education through institutions like VEC, MTA and setting in processes such as awareness, micro-planning and training of the functionaries of VEC, MTA;
    - (iii) Enhancing school effectiveness in terms of its reach (enrolment), grasp (retention), classroom transaction and learning achievement;
    - (iv) NFE systems to reach out to those who would be still left in spite of efforts to enhance school effectiveness;
    - (v) Convergence of ECCE, primary schooling and health;
    - (vi) Programmes and process with a focus on girls, SCs and STs.

ECCE

15. DPEP would finance expansion of ECCE through establishment of ECCE centres in villages not eligible to be covered by ICDS. In states with limited experience of ECCE, new ECCE centres would be financed initially on a limited scale only, in one district, or in one block per district, where inter-district variations are substantial. This activity could be scaled up gradually over the project period. The DPEP would not finance nutrition.

16. In order to improve the quality of ECCE, DPEP would fianance development of pre-school materials and training of functionaries in the ECCE centres set up under DPEP. It would also finance the training of ICDS Anganwadi/Balwadi workers in forging linkages with schools.

NFE

17. DPEP would strive for the development of an effective NFE system which can meet the diverse educational needs of

children whom the school, in spite of all the measures designed to improve its effectiveness, would not reach. To this end, DPEP would finance:

(i) to begin with, NFE centres as per the GOI scheme in states which are not covered by that scheme.

(ii) development of a variety of NFE models;

(iii) extension coverage of viable and scalable NFE models and instructional material;

(iv) production and distribution of material for NFE programmes financed by DPEP in project districts.

(v) training related to NFE financed by DPEP.

Educational Planning and Management

18. DPEP would finance, subject to a ceiling of Rs 3 crores, strengthening of state capacities in the area of educational planning and management which could include inter-alia, setting up of a separate SIEMT, augmenting state level structures such as SCERTs by creation of additional units for this purpose or contracting services of existing resource institutes in the state such as IIMs for training, research and related activities.

Salaries

19. Financing of salaries would be on a declining basis, that is to say begining with 90% in the first two years, declining to 80% for the third, fourth and fifth year, and 65% in the sixth and seventh year of the project. The average works out to 75% of the salaries.

In terms of these guidelines DPEP would finance teachers' posts in new schools being financed by DPEP. Depending on the practice in a State, construction of school building can either precede or follow the opening of a school. It is expected that as a result of the intervention in DPEP there would be substantial improvement in enrolment. Therefore, with effect from third year of the project, teacher posts would be financed on a school to school basis where the extra enrolment and the teacher-pupil ratio (with reference to the first year of the project) warrant such appointment.

20. DPEP would finance new posts created in institutions set up under DPEP such as ECCE centres, Block Resource Centres, school clusters and State Institutes of Education and

Management, and in the State level societies and their units in the districts.

21. DPEP would also finance extra posts created in existing institutions such as DIET, SCERT for assisting DPEP.

22. However the salaries of existing state government officials holding positions in DPEP on an ex-officio basis and salaries of supervisory and administrative staff at secretariat, district and sub-district level will not be financed by the DPEP. Wherever amalgamation or upgradation of existing structures is proposed, state government's commitment towards meeting salaries of existing posts would be carried over so that DPEP finances salaries of only additional staff.

Civil Works

23. DPEP will finance civil works (limited to 24% of project cost) such as construction of new primary schools, new class rooms, major repairs and rehabilitations of schools, construction of toilets, residential schools, rooms at ECCE centres, water supply and electrification, SIEMT, and other state educational facilities as approved by DPEP, Maintenance would be financed as per state norms and be within the 24% ceiling.

24. DPEP would not finance construction activities in aided or private schools, NGOs, other associations or groups.

25. Construction of offices would not be funded under DPEP barring office space for the State Society on a small scale within the SIEMT or SCERT only.

26. DPEP would finance construction of residential schools for Scheduled Tribes from the second year of the project onwards following proven evidence of demand from the community and independent evaluation of similar schools.

School Facilities

27. Grants of Rs 500 per teacher per annum would be provided to the schools for teaching learning aids and consumables. Further, a grant of Rs 2000 per annum would be provided jointly to each school and VEC for improving school facilities such as books and journals (other than textbooks), furniture, health check up, and bettering school environment, etc. No other financing would be provided to schools for equipment.

28. All new schools constructed under DPEP in the first instance would be provided with furniture as per state norms. Once

established and functioning, they would also qualify for the grant for teaching learning aids and facilities as above.

Furniture and Equipment for other Institutions

29. DPEP will fianance equipment needed for state society offices, the district units of societies, MIS cells in state and project districts, in SIEMT, SCERT, BRC, school clusters and other educational facilities as justified in the proposals and approved by the DPEP. To begin with, no TVs/VCRs and audio visual equipments would be provided to institutions below the level of DIET.
30. Procurement procedures for all equipment to be acquired under DPEP have to conform to approved procedures, which would be spelt out shortly.

Improvement and Upgradation of Learning Content, Process and Materials

31. DPEP will finance a design for learning processes and materials based on rationalization and reduction of academic burden (as recommended by Yashpal Committee Report); principles of minimum Levels of Learning; and multi-grade teaching concepts. DPEP financing for this purpose would be limited to development of a design upto camera ready stage, only. Financing of printing of learning materials would be for the purpose of field trials only. Costs of distribution of learning materials would not be borne by DPEP.

DPEP would also finance:

- improving efficiency in the process of production and distribution of teaching/learning materials.
- provision of free learning materials to SCs/STs and girls in project districts (if not already fiananced by State Government).
- printing and distribution (in project districts) of teachers handbooks and student workbooks (if not already financed by State Government).

Awards/Incentives, etc.

32. DPEP would not finance non-educational incentives for improving school attendance and retention such as mid-day meals, nutrition, free uniforms. It would also not finance cash scholarships/awards except an awards programme for schools that could be organised at block level with a view to

promote competition amongst schools in areas such as enrolment and retention of girls, SCs/STs. The award winning school can use the award for acquiring educational material or facilities in the schools.

Vehicles

33. Vehicles can be provided under the project as follows:

State level: One vehicle for State Project Director, two vehicles for common pool, one for Director of SIEMT and one for common pool of SIEMT.

District level: One vehicle for District Programme Coordinator and vehicles for common pool calculated at the rate of one vehicle for every four blocks;

One vehicle for DIET for academic supervision through BRCs and school clusters.

Procurement of vehicles should be staggered as per need.

Teacher Training

34. DPEP would finance in project districts training of:

- teachers of primary schools including private and aided schools;
- pre-primary teachers/workers other than those under ICDS;
- administrative staff;
- VEC/MTA members and NGOs.

35. It would also finance, for use in DPEP districts, development and printing of training materials, development of training modules for teacher training, ECCE and educational management.

36. All pedagogic training modules should integrate as far as possible the MLL, multigrade teaching, gender sensitivity, environmental and other relevant concerns.

Innovations

37. In order to encourage innovations at all levels, innovation funds would be set up at the district, state and national levels. Innovation fund would be provided according to the following scale:

In each DPEP district level, a fund of Rs 1 lakh per annum. The cost of a single project should not exceed Rs 1 lakh; its duration should not exceed one year. This fund would be administered by the district unit of the State society.

At the State level, a fund of Rs 20 lakhs would be provided per annum. The cost of a single innovative project should not exceed Rs 5 lakhs and its duration should not exceed two years.

At the national level, a fund of Rs 100 lakhs would be provided per annum. Each individual project should not cost more than Rs. 20 lakhs.

38. No diversion from these funds to other activities would be permissible. Innovative projects could be taken up from the second year onwards. NGOs, institutions like SCERTs, SIEMT, DIETs, BRCs, school clusters can be financed.

Other Programme Costs

39. DPEP would also finance other programme costs, such as Consultant services, professional fees;

Grants to NGOs and institutions like IIMs for support to programme activities;

Research, evaluation studies, impact studies;

Fellowships.

Caveat

40. The above list is not exhaustive. As programme evolves and new activities come up, the eligibility for DPEP financing will be decided by the project approval board at the national level.

Planning Process

3.1 Planning process and project formulation under DPEP is of great significance. DPEP emphasises location-specific planning in a participatory manner. In a sense there are some basic postulates which need to be borne in mind for DPEP planning process, namely the "nine pillars". DPEP planning should include:

(i) Mobilization for UEE by activating village education committees, teachers, parents/guardians and linking up with efforts under the Total Literacy Campaign.

(ii) Planning for primary education and not merely primary schooling. Alternative methods have significance and a holistic view be taken.

(iii) Cover all qualitative aspects such as school effectiveness, textbooks, teacher training and improvement in simple reading and learning skills.

(iv) Convergence of services, such as primary education, primary health and ECCE to provide synergistic development.

(v) Provision for trainings to improve teacher motivation and classroom transactions, as also in management of education.

(vi) Openness to innovations which thrown up new solutions and once tested can be scaled up, or aborted if unsuccessful.

(vii) A marked gender focus to provide for improvement in access, retention and achievement levels of girls education, as also to permeate gender sensitivity through all aspects of DPEP planning, including teacher training/ recruitment, textbooks other educational facilities and incentives.

(viii) The canvas of DPEP is systemic where the issue is one of management of change and improving of the system.

(ix) Evaluation, monitoring and research are interactive and supportive of DPEP. Studies and evaluations will play a major role in project planning and action research to facilitate decision-making.

3.2 The preparation of detailed district and state projects is the responsibility of the State Government under the programme. The projects should provide details of activities envisaged in the districts over the period of 7 years. The process by which the district/state proposals would be drawn up and approved for DPEP is indicated as follows:

A. Identification of districts according to DPEP criteria

B. Approval of district selection by DPEP

C. Appointment (if not in place) of District Planning Teams

D. Appointment (if not in place) of State Planning Teams

E. Preparation of preliminary district plans/proposals and cost estimates for eligible activities according to DPEP criteria and guidelines.

F. Preparation of state proposals for capacity building.

G. Preliminary appraisal of district/State proposals by DPEP

H. Once State/district proposals are ready they would be appraised and later monitored by GOI.

Components of the Programme

3.3.The following activities could form the components of the Programme:

(i) *Project preparation activities* illustrated above in para 2.2.1 above. The project formulation exercises, studies and surveys, training of planners as well as workshops for mobilisation of public opinion and consultations with various interested groups would be eligible for financing under this category.

(ii) *Environment building activities:* Structures and fora could be evolved for a continuous process of consultations with parent-teacher groups, teachers' associations, elected representatives. Panchayati Raj institutions, and non-governmental agencies working on educational issues. Innovative activities could be devised to mobilise public opinion and to generate a demand and concern for educational development in the district.

(iii) *Activities under Primary Formal Education:*

(a) Micro planning and school mapping to be taken up at village and block level within the district.

(b) Physical facilities for education like new school buildings and extension repair of the existing school buildings through low cost indigenous materials, vernacular design and participative construction methods, subject to the state norms being adopted. (o.7 sq.m. of space per student and a classroom of 40 students), and cost of civil construction being limited to 24% of the total project cost.

(c) Assessing the existing levels of equipments and teaching learning aids in a school and making provisions for them wherever inadequate and wherever not covered by State or central schemes.

(d) Streamlining the production and distribution of textbooks, NFE and ECCE materials and teachers' guides.

(e) Development of school libraries.

(f) Establishing the current level of MLL (Minimum Levels of Learning) within the district on a sample basis and make plans to reach prescribed MLL within a specified time frame.

(g) Assess the need for teachers, particularly in rural areas and provide for their recruitment, training and induction. Emphasis to be on lady teachers for rural areas and provide for their salaries as per DPEP financial parameters.

(h) Provision of free textbooks for the focus group of the disadvantaged (SC/ST/girl child).

(iv) *Activities under Primary Non-Formal Education:*

(a) Development of viable models of NFE for children out-of-school.

(b) Assessing the need for and location of new NFE centres.

(c) The recruitment and training of NFE instructors.

(d) The development of teaching and learning materials for NFE.

(e) To mobilise the community for the management and monitoring of NFE centres.

(v) *Activities under Early Childhood Care and Education*:

(a) Development of modules for child development and education.

(b) Convergence of ECCE facilities with ICDS and ECE programmes and primary schools in terms of coordination of timings, enrolment drives and health and immunizations services.

(c) In non-ICDS areas, opening of ECCE centres and providing for induction and training of ECCE workers as well as teaching learning materials.

(d) Actions related to preparing the child for primary schooling like school readiness programme.

(vi) *Training:*

(a) Strengthening the teachers in-service training and development of new designs for such training:

(b) selection and training of master trainers and resource persons within the district.

(c) Training of educational administrators including district and blocklevel functionaries and VEC members.

(d) Augmenting the DIETs

(e) Any other activity/facility required for continuous and updated training.

(vii) *Women's development:*

(a) Establishing specific activities for women's education.

(b) Providing for training and orientation of women functionaries and activists.

(c) Training of women VEC members.

(d) Initiation of awareness generation programmes.

(viii) *Management structures and MIS:*

(a) The setting up of a State level registered society and district and sub-district level management structures to ensure flexibility and promptitude in decision making and flow of funds.

(b) The development and installation of an MIS system and facilities for data analysis. The system should be compatiable with national system and should build upon school statistics, baseline studies and inputs monitoring.

3.4 Activities eligible at the state level for programme support would include those which seek to improve:

(a) the efficiency of State textbook preparation, publication and dissemination;

(b) effectiveness of inservice and preservice primary teacher training education;

(c) effectiveness of educational research, evaluation and monitoring and assessment.

3.5 At the district level, the eligible activities would include those which seek to improve:

(a) District capacity for programme management, supervision, monitoring and evaluation;

(b) the quality of primary education—formal and non-formal education; and

(c) targetting of support for access to and benefit from primary education for girls, SC and ST students.

3.6 The programme also offers support to States in shaping State Institute of Educational Management and Training or equivalent institutional arrangements and strengthening of the District Institutes of Education and Training through equipment and staff development.

3.7 The District plans and State proposals for Programme support shall be prepared incorporating the principles of equity, feasibility, sustainability and replicability. The final outlay for each District would be determined after appraisal.

3.8 In keeping with the objectives of the Programme the formulation of the district plans would be through a process of capacity building rather than by entrusting the job as a turnkey assignment to consultants, institution or individual. Taking cognizance of the scarcity of project formulation skills the Programme envisages particular measures for strengthening state-level resource institutions and DIETs, networking of these institutions with NCERT and NIEPA on the one hand with state level social sciences research organisations/IIMs/university departments on the other. Hitherto, the state level resource institutions were strengthened mainly with reference to teacher training. Hereafter equal emphasis would be laid on administration and management training for educational functionaries, NGOs and members of the VECs, district and sub-district project structure. One of the very first steps in project formulation would be to identify key level functionaries in the State Education Department, other State level organisations, and orient and then engage them in training state and district level functionaries. As far as possible the resource persons have to be drawn from a network of resource institutions so that they can help develop capabilities and be associated with the Programme on a long-term basis.

3.9 Each of the districts selected under the Programme would draw up a five to seven-year plan clearly spelling out:

(i) the present status of primary education;

(ii) the gap to be bridged between the present status and the Programme objectives;

(iii) the strategies;

(iv) the programme components;

(v) measures for securing convergence of primary education and related services like ICDS, ECCE and School health;

(vi) phasing;

(vii) unit costs;

(viii) the sources of funding which would comprise the ongoing State and Central schemes and the *additional educational interventions* the Programme would fund;

(ix) management structures;

(x) arrangements for monitoring with clearly specified benchmarks and indicators.

3.10 Simultaneously a state level plan would be formulated to spell out:

(i) the planning and management support for district planning and implementation;

(ii) strengthening of resource institutions;

(iii) linkages with state level social science research institutions/IIMs, university departments, NCERT and NIEPA;

(iv) training in pedagogy and management;

(v) streamlining of textbook production and distribution;

(vi) reducing the level of difficulty of language and mathematical learning materials;

(vii) management information systems.

3.11 *Project Preparation Activities*

3.11.1 The following specific activities need to be taken up by States in the initial phase.

Organisational Activities

(i) Formation of core groups at State and district levels.

(ii) Training of State and district level core group and other functionaries.

(iii) Forging linkages between SCERT, State level social science research organisations/IIMs/university departments and NCERT/NIEPA.

(iv) Identification of resource persons in this network of resource organisations.

(v) Identification of State Project Director.

(vi) Registration of State level societies.

(vii) Framing of Financial/Procurement and Service Regulations of the Society.

Planning Activities

(viii) Organisation of conventions and workshops for wide consultation on the action plan with groups of teachers, community leaders, women activists, representatives of disadvantaged section of the society, the non-governmental organisations and other stake holders in the primary education system.

(ix) Survey of school facilities, teaching-learning equipment.

(x) Identification of schools to be constructed/repaired.

(xi) Identification of the standard list of teaching-learning equipment that is to be provided.

(xii) Preparation of action plan would need to be based on:

(a) the current status of primary education in the districts selected, *based on available data*.

(b) a plan outlining the process for formulating the district projects.

(c) A programme for conducting the studies which need to be completed before pre-appraisal.

(d) An outline of the activities envisaged in the districts and at the state level with approximate unit costs, phasing, organisational arrangments for planning, implementation and monitoring.

(e) Development of management structure for the programme.

(f) Preparation of a construction manual.

(g) Development of a training plan for management, teacher training and pedagogical development.

(xiii) Local capacity building for professional inputs into the plan, preparation and assessment of plans.

(xiv) Improvement and further refinements in the first draft, based on the findings of studies conducted (see below under "Studies") and processes.

Studies

The studies to be conducted for project preparation would include:

(i) Conduct benchmark surveys on key educational indicators like enrolment, transition, retention, minimum levels of learning.

(ii) Conduct study on girls (gender perspective).

(iii) Conduct studies to develop appropriate teacher training, methodology and design.

(iv) Conduct studies on textbooks for education in areas predominantly inhabited by tribals.

(v) Conduct studies on state finances.

(vi) Studies on production and distribution of textbooks, NFE and other instructional materials.

(vii) Studies on educational needs of disadvantaged groups of society like SC/ST.

(viii) Such other studies as may be considered expedient.

Terms of reference and the methodology of the studies must be drawn up in consultation with the Government of India. The findings of the Studies would have significance for planning DPEP project interventions as well as initiating informed analysis amongst the many stakeholders in the primary education system,. Hence arrangements will have to be made at the conclusion of the studies to disseminate its results through workshops at the state and district level. Sensitization to the issues at stake would encourage debate and local solutions would emerge.

3.12 Financial as well as technical assistance would be provided for project preparation and studies based on specific, well-delineated proposals.

3.13 The source of funding for implementation of the district plan and state level interventions would be:

(i) on-going central and state schemes, and

(ii) the funds the Programme would provide.

The Programme would fund all educational activities which lead to the strengthening of the primary education in the district as well as certain State level interventions. Though the final outlay for each district would be determined after appraisal, it is anticipated that the average investment per district (inclusive of the district share of the state level interventions) would be within the ceiling of Rs 30-40 crores. Funding would be subject to a ceiling on the construction component, at 24 per cent of the total project cost and a ceiling of 6 per cent of management costs. This is to ensure that programme components receive a minimum of 70 per cent of the total project cost. The appraisal criteria would be equity, participatory process, feasibility, sustainability and replicability. States would have to clearly analyse the financial commitments involved in the project and their own ability to meet the recurring costs after the project period is over. The ability of the State Government to support the recurring liabilities of the Programme at the end of the Project period should be established.

3.14 Project Cycle

After a state is identified for being covered up under DPEP by the GOI, the State would be required to draw up State and District proposals. At the national level there would be a resource team to examine and appraise these proposals. This national resource team of appraisers would be joined by expert teams fielded by the external agency funding the programme. Appraisal Resource team will provide on-site technical assistance and appraisal for state and district proposals. Four missions would be conducted for each state: (1) Identification Mission at the identification of the State and Districts; (2) Preparation Mission at the initiation of project preparation; (3) Pre-appraisal Mission on completion of draft proposals; (4) Appraisal Mission on completion of revised proposals. The national resource team on appraisal will have expertise in educational planning and statistics, civil works, in-service training, community participation, programme management, special programmes for women/girls and SC/ST. Each visit will be for a duration of four weeks.

3.15 The process by which the district/state proposals would be drawn up and approved for DPEP is indicated as follows:

Before Identification Mission

Identification of districts by the concerned State Government according to DPEP criteria.

Approval of district selections by DPEP bureau in GOI.

Collection of a consistent set of basic information for the identified district/state in standard formats.

Identification of the District Planning teams by concerned State Government.

Identification of State Planning Team.

During Identification Mission

Identification Mission through a workshop and local visits will set the basic framework of planning;

Identify the issues and problems in the existing system;

Orient the district and state planning teams;

Set up the planning process;

Identify studies that need to be conducted;

Identify State Resource team for conduct of each study;

Prepare the terms of reference of each study planned;

Identify the local institution/human resources with a view to establish a network for use by DPEP;

Identify the broad strategies to tackle the identified issues through group work of District and State Planning teams;

Identify the management structure for the project and other relates issues.

Before Preparation Mission

Participatory planning at block, subdivision and district level, their documentation for each district and block;

Refinement of issues in the light of community participation and documentation of strategies district and block wise.

Mapping of school facilities;

Preparation of maps and information for school sitting as per format;

Completion of the field works of Studies and availability of the raw data and first findings;

Preparation of first draft districts and state proposals with quantitative targets.

During Preparation Mission

Field Visits to districts and institutions; the quantitative aspects of the proposals would be looked into with great care and detail, i.e; the targets set, the unit costs, time estimation for completion of an activity and the like;

Scrutiny of the first draft proposals with district and State Planning Teams with reference to;

Civil construction and site availability for such construction plans;

Checking of the internal consistency of the proposals—component wise;

Existing capacity available within the district and State to carry out the Tasks set for themselves;

Current utilisation of the existing institutions for betterment of the primary education system;

Additionality of the activities proposed;

Feasibility of the activities proposed;

Sustainability of the activity proposed;

Sharing of the Preliminary Findings of the studies in a workshop with local community—Preparation Mission Team to participate in one such workshop.

Before Pre-Appraisal Mission

Final report of Studies; completion of sharing of the studies in all the districts

Revision of preliminary district/state proposals and cost estimates for eligible activities according to DPEP criteria and guidelines, results of studies and recommendations of the preparation mission;

Preparation of state proposals for capacity building

Preparation in consultation with GOI, of;

Draft Memorandum of Association for the implementation Society;

Draft bye-laws of financial regulations and procurement manual;

Draft service regulations;

Draft construction manual.

During Pre-Appraisal Mission

Scrutiny of district proposals by DPEP. The quantitative

aspects of the plan and therefore the costs of the district proposals would be finalised. The focus would shift on the operational aspects of plan implementation, like;

Examination of construction process (Manual)

Examinations of draft rules and bye-laws of the Society.

Examination of the financial and service regulations of the Society.

Examination of the Procurement rules for goods and services by the Society.

Before Appraisal Mission

Finalise the proposals in accordance with earlier recommendations.

Obtain necessary approvals for project management structure.

Obtain necessary approvals for the rules, regulations and bye-laws.

During Appraisal Mission

Appraisal would be document-based and no field visits are envisaged. The documents therefore need to be self contained and comprehensive. The practice of providing supplementary information at this stage would be discouraged. At appraisal stage it is expected that interacting parties would come with the agreements to be reached amongst themselves for implementation of the programme.

NATIONAL SUPPORT AND MONITORING

National Component under DPEP: An Overview

4.0 The preparation of detailed district and state projects is the responsibility of the State Government under the programme. The projects would provide details of activities envisaged in the districts and at state level over the period of 7 years. While the decentralisation of planning and implementation of district based interventions is the starting point for DPEP, the Central Government has a responsibility to ensure the smooth implementation of the programme and render technical assistance to the states and districts as the needs emerge. As per the Constitution of India, education is a concurrent subject for the Central and State Governments. This implies a spirit of mutual support and partnership between Centre and states to further the goal of UEE. DPEP embodies this resolve and the guidelines/parameters of the programme have emerged after intensive dialogue with the States. Programme activities under DPEP will be concentrated at the district level, with supportive interventions from the state and national levels. The bedrock of the programme is to build national and local level capacities to plan, manage and implement the programme for primary education development.

4.1 The implications of the programme at the National level are several. As DPEP will cover several states and more than a hundred districts, and being a logical sequence to the externally-aided basic education projects in Bihar, Rajasthan, Andhra Pradesh and Uttar Pradesh, there is no reason to provide for a regular system of monitoring, information sharing and dissemination of experiences at the national level. It is equally important to strengthen national capacity for research and design in primary education as also to establish an effective network between resource institutions at the national and state levels.

The main functions at the National level would be as follows:

(i) Ensuring linkages between DPEP on the one hand and other areas of elementary education and adult literacy on the other.

(ii) Technical assistance to the states in preparation of projects and their implementation.

(iii) Appraisal of the projects received from States.

(iv) Consideration of Annual Work Plans and sanction of Budgets. Given the process-intensive and innovation-demanding nature of the programme, the workplans have emerged as the main instrument of programme planning and implementation. If an analogy is to be drawn, annual workplans would be to a DPEP project what the annual plan is to the Five Year Plan. This idea has been accepted by the agencies.

(v) Monitoring and Supervision. There would be two formal supervisions in a year, the second coinciding with review of annual workplans and sanction of budget for the next financial year.

(vi) Design and implementation of the national research and development programme.

(vii) Securing necessary approvals within the Government of India.

(viii) Coordination with State Governments.

(ix) Coordination with multilateral and bilateral agencies.

4.2 Structure of National Management Agency

The guiding principles of organising the National Level Structure (NLS) are as follows:

(i) The implementation to be in a Mission mode, which entails NLS having adequate financial and administrative powers commensurate with its tasks.

(ii) The role of NLS would essentially comprise facilitation, capacity building, appraisal, coordination and over all direction of the programme. Till adequate capacity building in the states it would assist the states in planning and implementation.

(iii) NLS should have a lean organisation with minimal permanent staff and with most of its work, such as technical assistance to States, appraisal, research and evaluation, being done through contractual arrangements with institutions and individual consultants.

4.3 The NLS would comprise of the Mission's General Council and a DPEP Project Board. A Bureau for DPEP would be situated in the Ministry of Human Resource Development, with a policy cell and another, programme cell. To carry out the commitment at the national level, back up and support services would be provided through consultancies both institutional as well as individual. The consultancy and support services will be required in technical tasks such as planning, appraisal, supervision, monitoring, research and evaluation.

4.4 The NLS would include the following:

(i) A Mission General Council (GC)

(ii) A Project Board (PB)

(iii) DPEP Bureau in the Ministry with two broad functions: (a) PB servicing (b) Programme.

(iv) Consultancy and support services for which, for the time being, EdCIL would be the sole source. It would assist the DPEP Bureau in technical tasks such as planning, appraisal, supervision, monitoring, research and evaluation, resource support.

General Council

The General Council has been developed along the lines of the National Literacy Mission which is managing the Total Literacy Campaigns in the country. The General Council for the Mission of DPEP will be headed by the Union Minister for Human Resource Development and will have, as members, the Ministers of Education of States which implement the programme, Education Secretaries of the participating States, Secretaries of the Central Government Departments of Education, Women and Child Development, Health etc. Some eminent educationists, NGOs and public men will also be on the council. Joint Secretary of DPEP bureau will be the Secretary of the Council.

The Council will meet annually. The Council will facilitate Centre-State coordination and promote debate on issues with policy implications for primary education development. The role of the Council will be to provide policy direction to the DPEP and to review the progress of the programme.

Project Board

4.5 The General Council will be assisted by a DPEP Project Board. This Board has been developed on the lines of the National Aids Control Programme. The DPEP Project Board will be an empowered body assigned with full financial and administrative powers to implement the programme. It will be headed by Union Education Secretary and will have representatives not below the rank of Joint Secretary of concerned departments, and Financial Adviser. The Joint Secretary of DPEP bureau will be the Member-Secretary of the PB. It will meet at least once every quarter and more frequently if required.

4.6 The basic objective of setting up the PB is to ensure that the necessary Governmental approvals are processed within the Ministry itself with the utmost expedition. Its composition is designed to facilitate this objective and is as follows:

Secretary (Edn) *Chairman*
Joint Secretary & Financial Adviser
Advisor (Education) Planning Commission
Representative of Department of Expenditure

Joint Secretary (DPEP) *Member-Secretary*

4.7 The broad functions of the PB are as follows:

(i) Recommend to the Government policies in regard to DPEP.

(ii) Consider annual workplans received from the states.

(iii) Approval of norms for new programme components and activities which emerge over the course of implementation.

(iv) Promote convergence of services.

(v) Quarterly review of DPEP.

The PB will exercise all Financial and Administrative powers necessary for programme planning and implementation. It will exercise all powers vested in Department of Education. No separate reference would be required to Department of Expenditure as their representative is in the PB and thereby all financial powers would vest in the PB also.

It will also discharge the functions of the EFC (Expenditure Finance Committee of the Department of Expenditure) in regard to DPEP projects which would be formulated in the subsequent rounds of project formulation.

The PB will be an integral wing of the Ministry and its proceedings will issue under the authority of the Ministry.

DPEP Bureau

4.8 There would be a dedicated cell in the Ministry under the Joint Secretary. Much of the background work relating to policy, servicing of PB, release of finances to states, overall review of the programme would be done within the Bureau itself through its PB servicing division. Work relating to technical support to the states, appraisal, supervision, monitoring, research and evaluation, reimbursement and procurement would be organised through the programme division.

4.9 The PB Servicing Division would have two Deputy Secretaries/Directors with appropriate support staff. This Division would be responsible for policy, coordination with funding agencies, Department of Economic Affairs, Planning Commission and different ministries and departments in Government of India such as Department of Rural Development, Department of Women and Child Development etc., so as to ensure convergence of different programmes having a bearing for servicing and implementing the decisions of PB, release and reimbursement of funds, proper maintenance of accounts and compliance with procurement norms of the external funding agencies.

4.10 The Programme Division will organise carrying out its tasks of technical assistance in planning and pedagogy, appraisal of projects, supervision, monitoring, programme evaluation and research, and civil works through consultancies. In addition the programme division would be responsible for overall coordination with States on programme implementation and for the purpose the deputy secretaries in the programme division would be assigned specific States.

4.11 The DPEP Bureau would be serviced by consultancy and support services. Tasks would be assigned by JS(DPEP) for responding to requests for professional services arising from programme planning and implementation. For the remaining 3 years of the eighth plan, professional experts would be engaged on a sole source basis by the EdCIL to facilitate recruitment of professionals and engagement of institutional and individual consultants as per need. With the approval of the JS(DPAEP), EdCIL would enter into sub-contracts with institutions and individuals for the implementation of various tasks to be discharged by it. The professionals would be contracted following norms and procedures set out in the contractual terms of reference to be entered into with EdCIL.

4.12 The Programme Division of DPEP Bureau at the national level will be the nodal point for ensuring such backup support as may be required by the Programme. The four Deputy Secretaries in the Programme Division will have specifically assigned States as well as functional areas. The Consultant (EdCIL) would be reporting to and be accountable to the Joint Secretary in DPEP Bureau but for day-to-day requirements of backup and other administrative support the respective deputy secretaries in the programme division would be constantly in touch with EdCIL and Consultants and functional areawise task forces. There will also be a larger Advisory Group to guide and review the activities of the Task Force. A resource support and institutional networking agenda will be built around this core.

4.13 The national level technical assistance will include the following:

(i) Development of State capacities for plan formulation.

(ii) MIS including school statistics, project indicators and building of data base, would be developed, tested and installed in DPEP.

(iii) Development of In-Service Teacher Training including prototype training designs and materials and competencies in multi-grade teaching and MLL.

(iv) Development of prototype materials for Teaching, Reading and Mathematics for Classes I-III and evaluations of impact.

(v) Development of prototype training materials in educational planning and management and the training and the training of teams in DPEP assisted states/districts.

(vi) A unit for programme research, studies and evaluation to organize research activities for better DPEP implementation and evaluation, as well as establish a network of research institutions for primary education.

(vii) Intervention strategies for tribal education.

(viii) Development of cost-effective designs for primary schools.

(ix) Provision for international exchanges and trainings for capacity building.

4.14 Though the states will be responsible for preparation of the district projects, a national resource team will assist state planning and management units/institutions to develop competencies in plan formulation through technical assistance. More specifically assistance in following planning areas can be given:

(i) Analysis of education statistics;

(ii) District level planning through participatory planning,

(iii) Strategy formulation,

(iv) Intervention designs,

(v) Costing,

(vi) Implementation planning, and

(vii) Training and orientation of district/state core teams.

The National Management Structure would finance and monitor

national level technical assistance and research activities through annual work plans and budgets for cooperating research organizations (NCERT, NIEPA, other national and state organizations) and commissioned research and evaluation to meet the needs of DPEP. A media unit will organise audio-visual documentation and arrange publicity and media coverage for DPEP.

4.15 Monitoring and Supervision Functions

Monitoring Unit

The monitoring resource team at the national level will receive quarterly reports from the projects and analyse them. For the purpose monitoring resource team personnel and consultants will visit each State and a sample of districts quarterly, preparing reports on all elements of programme implementation. They will present to the Ministry a quarterly review of the programme. Reports will be made available to all funding agencies. A Project Management Information System will be developed to monitor the programme inputs, the expected outcomes and the financial disbursements. School Statistics to be collected in all DPEP districts (and subsequently the as a whole) will be standardised and for that data capture formats will be developed. Data collectors (i.e. Teacher, Block and District Officials) and the Data Entry Operators will be trained. Concurrent evaluation of the programme will also be taken up at the national level as part of the monitoring programme for the project.

Supervision

There will be biannual supervision missions to assess the progress of the programme. These supervision missions would be jointly conducted by the GOI and International funding agencies. Two of the four quarterly monitoring visits will coincide with these supervision missions. The first supervision mission would be in September-October and the second would be February-March. The timing would facilitate to ensure and verify the budgetary (supplementary as well as general) provisions, and the progress being achieved on the ground. These missions will therefore comprise field visits on a sample basis. Document bases analysis of all the districts and states would however be undertaken.

*These DPEP Guidelines are issued in May 1995 by the Government of India

District Level Plan Implementation Strategy

Introduction

Universal Elementary Education (UEE) continues to be a constitutional provision and national commitment in India. In the initial stages, the effort was to expand the formal schooling facilities to achieve the goal of UEE. Limitations of such a single track approach to achieve UEE was recognised and hence alternatives to formal schooling, essentially in the form of Non-formal Education (NFE), were initiated in the seventies. By the eighties, an integrated approach to achieve UEE and adult education was evolved which later got incorporated in the broader objective of Education for All (EFA). At present, EFA in India includes formal primary schooling, alternatives to primary schooling, adult education and pre-primary education. The Jomtien Declaration of 1990 and the Delhi Declaration of 1993 further reiterate India's commitment of EFA.

Decentralised planning at the district level is envisaged to be one of the strategies to achieve the goal of EFA. Although, the idea of decentralised educational planning in India can be traced back to the Wardha District Planning for UEE in the thirties, concerted efforts to translate the idea into operational terms on a wide spread scale was initiated in the eighties. In 1982, the Planning Commission appointed a Committee on district planning which identified areas within education which can be brought under the purview of district planning. The National Policy on Education and Programme of Action (1986) envisaged setting up of District Boards of Education to strengthen and coordinate educational planning efforts at the district level. The Working Group on Early Childhood and Elementary Education (1988) set up in the context of the Eighth Five-Year Plan further reaffirmed the need to keep district as the unit for planning education.

The District Primary Education Programme (DPEP) launched in 1993-94 is yet another recent effort to translate the idea of district planning into concrete action with the accompanying financial outlays.

Under this programme, district specific educational plans are devel -oped through a participatory process. The DPEP under lines the need for reconstruction of primary education as a whole instead of piecemeal implementation of schemes and it follows an integrated approach to educational development. The programme is funded by various international agencies. At present, the programme covers 42 districts from seven selected states of India. Educationally backward district, based on the female literacy rates, are selected for the implementation of the programme. It is expected that the programme would be expanded to 110 districts by the end of the Eighth Five-Year Plan.

At present, 42 districts have already prepared the district education plans under this programme. These district plans are closely scrutinised by the National Core Team and the external funding agencies. All these district plans have clearly identified the possible areas of intervention, strategies to overcome the difficulties and management structures to implement the programme. Needless to add that the programme envisages the centrality of improving the functioning of primary schools to achieve the objectives and targets. The first phase of the programme, namely, drawing up of district plans is now complete in all the selected districts. Having prepared the district plans, the next critical step would be to formulate effective implementation strategies keeping school improvement at the central focus.

The implementation strategies should be build on the already accumulated experiences in the country. There are two sets of empirical knowledge and experience which should guide the designing of plan implementation strategies with respect to school improvement. First, in the past, a sizeable body of research evidence has been generated with regard to factors contributing to effective school functioning. Secondly, a number of innovative projects, completed as well as ongoing, provide significant insights into the dynamics of school management, particularly with respect to the role of the community in ensuring effective school functioning. The new thrust given by the Panchayati Raj legislations has further highlighted the importance of school community relationship in strengthening school management processes at the grassroot level.

A close examination of the research evidence as well as the innovative experiences available would throw significant light on the way implementation strategies at the district level are to be formulated. Apart from the general inputs that flow from such an analysis, it should have direct implications for two major dimensions, namely (i) the type of management structure at district and sub-district levels downwards upto the schools, and (ii) the monitoring mechanisms to be created at various levels to ensure effective implementation of the plan with focus on school improvement. It is in this context, that the present workshop is jointly organised by the National Institute of Educational Planning and Administration (NIEPA), New Delhi and the International Institute for Educational Planning (IIEP), Paris.

Objectives

The objectives of the workshop are:

(i) to discuss the major concerns focussed on by the district plans prepared under the DPEP;

(ii) to undertake a review of issues concerning functioning of schools as evident from various research studies as well as from baseline surveys undertaken in the context of the DPEP;

(iii) to examine the feasibility of innovative measures undertaken in different areas with respect to improving school functioning; and

(iv) to formulate strategies for effective plan implementation and monitoring at the school as well as district and sub-district levels.

The deliberations in the workshop centred around four components:

1. A brief review of the lessons learned from the district plan preparation and the tasks ahead for plan implementation;
2. A discussion of project management structure focussing on: i) structure and process; ii) monitoring framework; and iii) capacity building.
3. Analysis of current issues and innovative experiences in school management focussing on; (i) in-school management process, role of the headmaster and teachers and supervisors; and (ii) involvement of community in the school functioning;
4. To work out implications for designing implementation strategies at the district level.

The discussions on implications in the workshop focussed mainly on four major dimensions; (i) changes required in the structure and process, (ii) monitoring framework to be evolved; (iii) capacity building required to facilitate implementation of the programme; and (iv) the role of alternatives to formal schooling.

Participants

The participants of the workshop consisted of senior level administrators directly involved in the plan formulation and implementation processes in the DPEP states; selected district level officials who have participated in the formulation of district plans; representatives of the Ministry of Human Resource Development and Planning Commission; faculty members from the National Council of Educational Research and Training, NIEPA, IIEP, University departments and other resource organisations and representatives from international agencies. List of participants is given in Annexure III.

Workshop Methodology

The deliberations in the workshop essentially consisted of an exchange of experience supported by lessons derived from existing research evidence, followed by group discussions on the implications for district plan management. A brief presentation on the themes was followed by discussions in the plenary sessions. These discussions formed the basis for deliberations in the group work. The participants, based on their experience, expertise and choice were divided into four groups namely, (i) changes in management structure and process; (ii) monitoring framework; (iii) capacity building; and (iv) alternatives to formal schooling. The group reports were presented and discussed in the plenary session.

Inaugural

The workship was inaugurated by Shri Arjun Singh, Hon'ble Minister for Human Resource Development on 18th Augus+, 1994 at 1030 hrs. at Vigyan Bhawan, New Delhi.

Welcoming the Hon'ble Minister for Human Resource Development, *Professor Kuldeep Mathur*, Director, NIEPA observed that his presence on the occasion was indicative of the importance he attached to the theme of the workship and emphasized that under the Hon'ble Minister's guidance, a new momentum had been created for speedy realization of the objective of universalisation of elementary education, particularly after the adoption of the revised National Policy on Education, 1992, and more particularly, the recent summit of the nine high populated developing countries hosted by India in New Delhi in December, 1993. He expressed his gratitude to the Hon'ble Minister for agreeing to inaugurate the workshop which was being organised in collaboration with the International Institute for Educational Planning, Paris. He was glad that the Director of the IIEP, Mr. Jacques Hallak, was personally present on the occasion underlining the close cooperation that existed for the last three decades between NIEPA and IIEP.

NIEPA had been actively advocating for years the need for decentralized planning and disaggregated target setting for a achieving the objectives of UEE. It was, therefore, gratifying to see the concept of comprehensive district based projects come of age with the launching of the District Primary Education Programme. Evolving from the national experience with area-specific projects, the DPEP is indeed an ambitious nation-wide plan to put local communities in charge of education in their areas and enhance investments in primary education. Beginning with 42 districts in six states, the District Primary Education Programme is expected to cover 110 districts by the end of the Eighth Plan period. The earlier efforts such as Operation Blackboard Scheme or the Non-formal Education programme were directed towards sector-based investments and the planning for such programmes was centralised and schematic. EFA initiatives, however, are becoming more area and people specific. Moreover, the regional and inter-district disparities within various states in their development of education has been pointedly highlighted in the research studies conducted by NIEPA. It is, therefore, appropriate that the districts chosen under the DPEP represent those where female literacy is below the national average and others where the Total Literacy Campaigns have successfully generated a demand for elementary education. Spread over six states, they provide a flavour of the entire country.

It is equally appropriate that the main strategies under the DPEP include district-level planning; community participation and decentralised management; focus on education for girls, Scheduled Castes and Scheduled Tribes; and improving effectiveness of education through training teachers, improvement of learning materials and upgrading infrastructure facilities.

The country today is at a critical stage in the implementation of the DPEP. The district plans of 42 districts have been formulated and appraised and their implementation has just begun. It is, therefore, important at this juncture to have a clear idea about the effectiveness of implementation strategies. In this endeavour, it is not only desirable for us to benefit from the experiences of other primary education projects in the country but also profit from the world-wide experiences of International Institute for Educational Planning, UNESCO, UNICEF, World Bank, European Community, Overseas Development Administration and other agencies who are providing support and cooperation for achieving the goal of EFA.

Mr. J. Hallak, Director, IIEP, Paris observed that such as major workshop on school improvement organised three and a half years after the Jomtien Heads of State Meeting indicates the long way India has travelled from charters to development and implementation of programmes as well as achievement of targets. The district level plan implementation strategy is a challenging task. Various countries of the world such as Brazil, Chile and other European countries have witnessed different phases of decentralization. Decentralized planning in these countries has, by and large, remained a policy rhetoric. To India, the concept of decentralized planning is not new. It is an opportune moment that the District Primary Education Programme has begun in India with an action framework. The enactment of the Panchayati Raj Bill would given necessary impetus to the implementation of the DPEP. The National Policy on Education, 1986 and the nation's involvement in the efforts for primary education and eradication of illiteracy through a continuous emphasis on decentralized plans has created a new environment in the districts. The combination of ambition and caution through decentralization would go a long way in realizing the goals of UEE in the fullest sense of the term. However, district plans should proceed in steps and expand in stages.

From a methodological point of view, the strategic approaches to planning environment, strategies, structures and processes address two major concerns: (a) sustainability; and (b) generalization—i.e., how to generalize from experiences gained at different levels. The workshop is a part of the strategic approach—the approach to action which demonstrates the eagerness of the Indian Government to learn from international environment, share its experiences and enter into partnership with international agencies.

Mr. Hallak observed that IIEP is extremely proud of its association with NIEPA and its long standing association with India which started about 30 years ago. The study conducted by IIEP and NIEPA on 'Quality of Basic Education' in Madhya Pradesh has helped in understanding various issues related to quality of education. The on-going projects in South Asia also are an indication of the strong bonds between NIEPA and IIEP. The topic of the workshop is promising and the work involved is enormous. In order to proceed systematically, the country should reflect on: (a) the concept of "effective planning"; (b) the concept of district planning and school based management; and (c) whether school based management is possible. Effective district plan ought to become outdated before it is implemented. One must have a crystal clear concept of district planning and school based management before venturing into various implementation strategies.

Mr. S.V. Giri, Secretary, Ministry of Human Resource Development, (Department of Education), in his welcome address gave an overview of District Primary Education Programme (DPEP) in the country. He pointed out that two years ago in August, 1992, the country started working on the basics of the project. The district planning exercise initiated in Madhya Pradesh at that point of time was part of the Dhumkuria Project. Since then, the nation has come a long way. We have already successfully completed the planning exercise in 42 districts and we are now moving from the planning phase to the implementation phase. A distinguishing feature of the district plans has been the participatory effort which by all reckoning is highly innovative and path breaking. Initial efforts to implement the programme meant putting the system in place which involved a number of preparatory exercises to be completed. The country has, as a now, taken care to see that the administrative expenditure is kept to the minimum, limiting it to six per cent and additional building expenditure not to exceed 24 per cent of the total expenditure. This would imply the availability of at least 70 per cent of the funds for utilization in programmes for improving teaching and learning activity through various participatory processes involving teachers and the community at the local level and also through capacity building at all levels. The DPEP is a national exercise within the parameters laid down by the CABE (Central Advisory Board of Education) in acceptance of external aid. This effort of the nation in evolving the DPEP as a national exercise is indeed commendable since, in this programme, effort of all concerned participants is involved. This is an immensely challenging task in which the country needs all the support at the implementation stage.

Hon'ble Minister for Human Resource Development, *Shri Arjun Singh* delivered the inaugural address. The Minister departed from the text of speech which was circulated in the Workshop. The Hon'ble Minister, while considering the uniqueness of this workshop, stressed on two important areas of concern: (i) the progress and failure of India during the post-independence era; and (ii) the challenges that lie ahead. According to him, in 1997 India would cross half a century mark of a nation which has been independent of colonial control. This 50 years of independence is not a very long period in the history of a nation, yet it is long enough for the people of India to take stock of what India has achieved and what it could have achieved during this period. This process of self-evaluation perhaps would help us determine what needs to be done during the coming years. As we enter the 21st century, the challenges and opportunities that lie ahead and the manner in which India faces these challenges and takes advantage of the opportunities will determine whether in the 21st century India would deserve the right position in the comity of nations, he further pointed out.

India does not harbour any feeling of acquisition against any nation, but simultaneously, we can not allow India to be a second class nation, he said. However, to achieve this there are certain parameters to be achieved first. The first parameter, according to him, which needs to be achieved is total literacy and universalisation of primary education in the country. If we fail to achieve this, as we have failed to do that in the last 45 years, the nation as a whole cannot go ahead. Because, in the absence of total literacy and UEE, a particular section of Indians may become advanced and the country may become rich, but the people of India as whole would not be empowered. Therefore, this is the first parameter and, this workshop assumes certain crucial importance for it aims at operationalising the implementation strategies of the DPEP which has UEE as one of its objectives.

The commitment to achieve the goal of UEE has now become very high in India, not only at the official and political level but also at the state and community level, he said. According to him, the political commitment is further reflected in the Prime Minister's commitment of six per cent of GDP for education which had declared in Delhi Summit and subsequently in the parliament. How to translate this commitment into concrete action at field level would need to be decided in this workshop, he stressed. He further pointed out that the DPEP concept is an indigenous one and its intellectual lineage can be traced back to the eminent economist, Dr. V.R. Gadgil. The Programme of Action, 1992 and all other programmes thereafter have helped in evolving the concept of the DPEP. To him, since we are going to implement the DPEP in our own backyard, we need to be self-committed and need not expect outside help. We need to evolve our own strategies to achieve this goal, he remarked.

In implementing the DPEP some states are going very quickly. But mere desire to achieve the goal of UEE is not going to help. What is needed is hard work to translate the ideas into implementation and action. However, problems may crop up in the process of implementation of the DPEP, and these problems need to be foreseen and attended to in time.

Besides, he drew the attention of the state level administrators present in the workshop to the failure of many developmental and educational schemes in the past because of lack of public awareness about these schemes. He stressed that every individual is willing to educate his/her children in order to enjoy the opportunities of citizenship. But, a lack of awareness about their own contribution towards development does not permit them to realise their own potential. This leads us to another important aspect of implementation of the DPEP—i.e. peoples' participation, the minister said.

The Minister hoped that the workshop should not merely stress on taking stock of what we have done in the last three years, but what is expected of it is a 'plan of action' which can be implemented and to which all the representatives of the state governments present in the workshop should be personally committed. There is no dearth of resources. But whatever resources India has need to be used optimally, he further stressed. Finally, he expected that the outcome of this workshop should be useful to improve the conditions of the toiling masses of this country are waiting for since independence.

Dr. N.V. Varghese who proposed vote of thanks observed that the theme of the seminar marks the next logical step—from planning of implementation. For almost eighteen months, the country was engaged in preparing district plans and initiating studies. This was a process of mutual learning and developing planning competencies at the state and district levels. The first phase of the DPEP emphasized on the professional input whereas during the second phase, the emphasis needs to be on creation of an environment for effective implementation of district plans where the need for political commitment and administrative support is crucial.

The DPEP was, infact, conceptualized in the sense of urgency in the operationalization of the objective of UEE, Dr. Varghese stressed. NIEPA and IIEP had shared a long history of collaborative effort. The study of Madhya Pradesh was initiated in 1990 and the findings of the study made useful inputs in evolving strategies for UEE in India. The DPEP is one effort which was commonly addressed by the gained from the contributions of various participants-educationists, planners and administrators alike. Dr. Varghese expressed gratitude to the Hon'ble Minister for his presence and continued leadership in this major project and thanked all participants of the workshop for their keen interest in this national endeavour.

Valediction

The deliberations of the workshop came to an end on 20 August at 16.00 hrs. *Dr. (Mrs.) Chitra Naik,* Member, Planning Commission, New Delhi, delivered the valedictory address. At the outset, Dr. Chitra Naik, congratulated the organisers of the Workshop and appreciated the initiative taken by NIEPA for involving administrators, academicians and NGOs to evolve appropriate strategies for the implementation of the District Primary Education Programme.

The DPEP is a unique action research project for achieving EFA. The DPEP is a project for liberation of administration from conventional impediments. Since the administrators are enslaved by the rigid and routine rules, there is an urgent need to change this culture in order to meet the challenges for achieving EFA. Although the DPEP is addressing the school age population, it has to cover all the age groups as primary education is a fundamental right irrespective of age group. The DPEP has to create social habit of learning rather than treating it as part and parcel of culture. The existing culture of non-schooling needs to change to the culture of schooling. For this, the DPEP has to play a crucial role. It is difficult to bring about this change but it is possible as it is proved by some individuals and organisations. However, lack of culture of structured learning is a constraint to initiate any educational change.

Since the DPEP envisages participatory planning and flexible administrative structure, there is ample scope to adopt appropriate strategies for achieving universal primary education. In business and industry, if one wants to get profit, one has to innovate and introduce changes for increasing the production. Similarly, for educational development, innovations and change are essential. The past may have good things but for future one has to break away from the past in a phased and systematic way.

There is a need to shift from quantitative to qualitative aspects in monitoring educational programmes. The quantitative approach conceals the problems associated with person to person interaction. At grass root level the problems need to be analysed from a humane angle. This requires ethnological analysis and deep understanding of the problems at grassroot level. Our administrators at various levels need training to understand the real situation. The statistical information, although essential, may not be sufficient.

In the past, it is the economic order that decided the destiny of the poor and the deprived. But now, education is essential to improve the conditions of the disadvantaged, deprived and the poor. It is not easy either to bring about changes in the management or manage changes in education. Any change in education needs to be a collaborative exercise of the government and people as they are like two wings of a bird. Collaboration with NGOs and other educational organisations is also essential. It is true that it is not easy to have collaboration between the government and NGOs. The problems need to be understood and overcome. The people (Village Education Committees) should be involved to decide the curriculum for the children. Similarly, the pedagogy has to undergo suitable changes in order to meet the needs of both children and adults. It should be rather educational communication than pedagogy.

While appreciating the participatory process of planning and flexibility in approach involved in the DPEP, Dr. Naik emphasized the need to develop qualities indicators to monitor the District Primary Education Programme.

The proceedings of the Workshop came to an end with a vote of thanks by *Dr. Govinda.* While expressing his gratitude to the participants and resource persons of the workshop, Dr. Govinda observed that this Workshop has succeeded in highlighting issues pertaining to schools and their functioning as central to initiating educational changes in the country. The presentations in the workshop clearly indicated that a small beginning at the school level can make a big leap forward in our educational progress. This, in his view, is more significant when one considers improving the quality of education as a serious concern. He hoped that the suggestions emerging from the workshop will be useful to the state and district level functionaries to evolve strategies to implement various activities envisaged under the DPEP.

DPEP: From Planning to Implementation

The DPEP is an exercise in decentralised planning and disaggregated target setting in education. It is a home grown idea drawing the intellectual lineage from the Wardha experiment of the thirties in developing district plans to universalise elementary education. It is firmly rooted in the National Policy on Education, 1986 and Programme of Action, 1986. The goal is universal primary education and the route is not confined to formal schooling.

The DPEP is a centrally sponsored national programme evolved on the basis of varied experience the country possesses and supplemented by the experiences of various international agencies directly involved in funding primary education projects in the developing countries. The Government of India has received funding support for this programme from various sources from abroad. Although the sources of funding vary, the approach to plan and implement the programme is unified. The approach is to develop primary education in an integrated framework taking into account inter-district variations in levels of development and inter-relatedness of various education related programmes. The effort is not to develop uniform plans, but to develop plans which vary in terms of priority and intervention strategies. The strategies are flexible and funding is ensured for activities which justifiably lead to the attainment of objectives of the programme.

The objectives of the DPEP are: (i) universal access to primary education through formal schools or their alternatives; (ii) to reduce overall dropout rate at primary level to less than ten per cent; (iii) to increase the achievement levels by 25 percentage points over and above the measured baseline levels: (iv) to reduce disparities of all types to less than five per cent.

The criteria to identify districts under the programme are: (i) educationaly backward districts with female literacy below the national average, and (ii) districts where Total Literacy Campaigns (TLC) have been successful leading to enhanced demand for primary education.

The planning process under the DPEP is participatory which ensures mobilisation, planning from below and developing planning competencies at all levels. The participation is not confined to any committee approach. It involves consultations and deliberations with Village Education Committees, Local Government Bodies, Teachers' Unions, Parent-Teacher Associations, Women Groups etc. The experience of Total Literacy Campaign (TLC) forms a reliable asset in this regard.

The DPEP envisages convergence of services at grassroot level and hence involvement of departments other than education becomes essential. It involves participation by representatives of people at the local level and direct beneficiaries of the programme. While consultations are broad and varied, the outcome needs to be concrete and specific which can be translated into identifiable targets and intervention strategies. Various district specific studies are also initiated in the DPEP districts. The emprirical evidence generated from the studies forms the basis to evolve realistic strategies. The district plans arc to be internally consistent, well sequenced with clearly defined strategies and monitorable activities.

The programme envisages to provide to each district a maximum amount of Rs. 400 million over a period of six to seven years. These funds are additionalities and are not substitutable. The DPEP funds are over and above the normal developmental expenditure the state and district otherwise would have incurred. This implies that: (i) the DPEP may not fund any of the on-going programmes which the State Government is supposed to fund; and (ii) the State Government is expected to maintain the budgetary provision for primary education atleast at the 1991-92 level in real terms.

The DPEP is an effort to link the in-school processes with broader objectives of overall development of primary education in a district. The DPEP is not ervisaged as an enclave project. Many strategies and interventions may have wider applicability. Such interventions can be extended to other districts. The sustainability and replicability of the strategies become essential elements to successfully implement the programme. Rigorous monitoring and detailed reporting are unavoidable elements to ensure proper implementation of the programme.

Responses by the International Agencies

In the absence of their Ambassador, the representative of the European Community, *Mr. Orus Baguene* read out the message which highlighted the importance of education in social change. The pursuit of the goal of universalisation of elementary education is recognised as a human right and an investment in the future for improving the quality of life of the people at large. Referring to the Indian Prime Minister's plans to raise educational resources to six per cent of the GNP, Mr. Orus Baguene appreciated the Indian Government's steps to achieve UEE and EFA. This, he felt, reflects the country's commitment to the goals of EFA. In the courts of structural adjustments, the social sector programmes are becoming important means of mitigating the adverse impact of new economic policies, he remarked.

The international agencies are watching with great interest the ambitious and innovative approach of the Indian Government in translating its plans into practice. The efforts towards achievement of major objectives of promoting gender equity in primary education in India are commendable. Such efforts serve as inputs not only in educating but also in empowering people. There needs to be a search for new models, which would mobilise all participants and emphasise coordination with all related social sectors for holistic and integrated development. It is in this context that European Commission has pledged a grant of $ 180 million for the implementation of the District Primary Education Programme. The workshop, he hoped, would set the stage for evolving implementation strategies.

The UNICEF Chief, *Mr. John Rhode* emphasized that the idea of EFA was truly reaching every child. Free and compulsory education, though a pious thought, is not always practical. Since the Jomtien conference, a new momentum has been generated the world over in achieving the objectives of EFA. The Indian Prime Minister's declaration of providing six per cent of GNP for education is a political commitment and the Hon'ble Minister for Human Resource Development also emphasized the need for transforming this commitment into reality. The DPEP is an exciting experiment with an in-built concept of flexibility. Referring to local initiative, he pointed out that positive examples are plenty in India. The idea of decentralization with emphasis on smaller units at block level was first reflected in the Community Development Plans in the early fifties. In 1994, this is being addressed through the DPEP where the National Policy, the Central Sector and the State Plans are emphasizing on flexibility and district specificity in terms of needs and strategies. Commending the success of the Bihar Education Project, he also pointed out the importance of having an autonomous management system under the DPEP.

The major challenge that should be taken up is the involvement of the local community in education whereby a true dialogue is possible between the educational functionaries and the community members.

The success of these efforts depend on decentralization not only to the level of district authorities but to the people at large. It is the community "ownership" of educational institutions and programmes that is important. The DPEP with its emphasis on individuality of children, making learning an enjoyable experience, competency building, training of teachers and empowerment of women in general is a commendable effort to achieve the objectives of EFA. Through such continuous efforts, the problems of gender disparity and child labour would, in due course of time, fade away from the country and education would be imparted to all in a true democratic sense of delivering our basis promises, he hoped.

The World Bank representative *Ms. M.E. Lockheed* commended the Indian Government's efforts to achieve EFA. The World Bank is watching with keen interest India's efforts to evolve the DPEP as a participatory process, she said. It was nourished by its firm foundation of district level planning strengthened by technical guidance and support from the national and state governments. It is a wonderful process to watch. The DPEP is a programme without precedence of scale which ultimately aimed at improving the quality of life of the people and this is a model to be emulated throughout the world. She congratulated the Indian Government for organising such an important workshop for exchange of experiences in school improvement and anticipated stimulating three days of discussion. Conveying World Bank's best wishes for the full implementation of DPEP in the coming future, Ms. Lockheed observed that the Bank was pleased to cooperate with other donor agencies in this massive effort and looked forward to the deliberations of the workshop.

The UNESCO representaive *Mr. Victor Ordonez* reflected on the theme of the workshop and emphasized the need for a planned approach to evolve implementation strategies. He congratulated NIEPA and IIEP for choosing this particular time to organise the workshop. Considering India's part experience in this endeavour, there is a need for caution and patience. At present, the focus is on districts. Various districts are at various stages of development and some are ready to move much faster than the others. The DPEP thus can take into account this diversity. It is necessary for the country to strike a balance between : (a) the central and the state government guidance to the districts, (b) emphasis on home grown inputs and those from international agencies; and (c) patience and impatience, he pointed out. Education is a slow and painful process. It is up to the districts to ensure that adequate balance of all inputs is maintained to achieve their targets. In the end, he pledged the support of UNESCO, Paris and Delhi Offices in this endeavour.

3. Project Management : Major Concerns

The DPEP has been conceived as a medium term investment programme, designed to improve learning achievement, reduce dropout rate and increase access to primary education. The programme would also strengthen the capacity of national, state, and district level institutions and organisations to plan, manage and evaluate primary education.

The basic assumption of the DPEP is contextuality. Therefore, the relative emphasis on access, equality, quality and achievement would vary from district to district. This assumption will also be true for the programme in terms of its components and contents, as also for the structures adopted for management and monitoring. The bedrock of the programme is to build national and local level capacities to plan, manage and implement the programme for the development of primary education. In keeping with the objective of the programme, the formulation of the district plans has to ensure a process of capacity building. Taking into consideration, the scarcity of project management skills, the programme envisages particular measures for strengthening state level resource institutions and DIETs, networking of the institutions with NCERT and NIEPA on the one hand, and with state level social science research organisations/IIMs/university departments on the other.

Until now, state level resource institutions were strengthened mainly with reference to teacher training. In future equal emphasis would also be laid on administration and management training of educational functionaries, NGOs, members of the VEGs, district and sub-district project team members etc. One of the very first steps in project formulation would be to identify key functionaries in the state education departments and other state level organisations and train them to train state and district level functionaries. The state level organizations will be engaged in training of state and district level functionaries. As far as possible, the resource persons will have to be drawn from a network of resource institutions, so that one can help develop capabilities to plan and implement the programme on a long term basis.

The setting up of management structures for implementing the DPEP will have to be evolved on imaginative lines. These structures must also define in very specific terms the responsibilities of individuals and groups. These structures must help to generate an information base which can be used at local levels. Specifically, in the context of social sectors there is a need to generate, manage and interpret information with integrity. The pace of the DEPE must never be a forced one, but one that takes into consideration the variations in context.

National Management Agency (NMA)

This national level agency will be governed by a Council and an Executive Committee representing the government of India agencies as well as state education departments and leading educationists. This agency would be responsible for appraisal of new proposals, supervision of on-going projects and management of national technical assistance programme.

National support for implementation of state and district programmes would be managed by NMA and provided through annual budget and work programme with NCERT and NIEPA and through contracts with other research and development organizations.

The guiding principles of organising the National Level Structure (NLS) are: (i) NLS should have adequate financial and administrative powers commensurate with its tasks; (ii) the role of NLS would essentially comprise of facilitation, capacity building, appraisal, coordination and overall direction of the programme; and (iii) NLS will be a lean organization with minimal permanent staff. Most of its work will be carried out through contractual arrangements with institutions and individual consultants.

State Implementation Societies

The group work in the workshop clearly argued for a differentiation between administrative and technical structure at state and district levels. The administrative structure for project implementation at the state level may be the state societies with a wider participation.

The State Governments have established registered societies to receive, disburse, and account for funds and to oversee project implementation. In the implementation scenario, the State Society and Department interface will have to be worked out. The state implementation unit needs to be set up with a core staff of two types: (i) the managerial staff who perform supervisory function; and (ii) the executive staff who are directly involved with the project implementation process. These staff should be appointed as quickly as possible and they should be competent persons who have the potential for undertaking the management tasks required. Until they are in position, the project runs the risk of not achieving the change in management culture that is so urgently needed. The EMIS need to be an essential part of the state structure to monitor the project activities.

The technical structure envisaged at the state level are SCERT and SIEMT. State Council of Educational Research and Training (SCERT) and State Institutes of Education (SIE) with support from national programmes would assist districts to introduce improved classroom practices and in-service teacher training. The SCERT has to be strengthened in all the DPEP states: (i) to enable it to act as a nodal agency to develop training modules; (ii) to train key resource persons; (iii) to develop new approach and methodology of teacher training; and (iv) to provide resource support to all areas. Its role has to be more of a facilitator than direct involvement in training. In addition SCERT has to be strengthened and encouraged to undertake research and evaluation studies in primary education. This in turn will strengthen and improve the quality of training imparted.

A distinction was made, in this context, between educational statistics to be maintained and supplied periodically and other aspects of monitoring which relate to the improvement of the quality of services provided. The latter may be new to this programme. Such information has to be collected at district, block, cluster and village levels to facilitate effective monitoring of various programmes.

One of the weakest links in educational process is the poor competency in managing the implementation of programmes. The educational supervisors and administrators at all levels need orientation in planning and management. The State Institute of Educational Management and Training (SIEMT) is proposed to be set up for developing key persons' skill in planning and management. Development of such a structure may take a long time. Till such time these structures are in place, resource support will have to be arranged from outside. State institutes of administration can be associated with the project in order to build up the capacity in planning and management.

District Implementation Unit

A project implementation check list has to be prepared for each project component for monitoring the overall execution of the project. The district project management unit will be responsible for this task so as to assess whether the key activities have been carried out.

To provide technical support at the district level, the DIETs are to be augmented. The DIET will have to act as the main resource support base at the district level to train functionaries in key areas and to evolve district specific mechanisms in plan formulation and implementation. All training programmes including management training need to be detailed and carefully scheduled to incorporate information on trainees, training needs, expected outcomes, training duration, location, resource persons and evaluation.

A systematic network plan is needed to identify the coverage of various services at state, district, block and village levels. The type of activities each service will perform with objectives, time tables, and the outcome of joint activities; participating voluntary organisations and NGOs will also be included to create a pool of resource persons, community mobilization and interaction. The Block Resource Centre and cluster level teacher meetings may provide technical inputs. However, the programme needs further support at the community level for its implementation. There is an urgent need to form VECs and train the members in community mobilisation to achieve and effectively intervene in the functioning of schools to make them more sensitive to the local realities and to ensure improved enrolment, attendance and retention.

In order to allow for a continuous learning process, a monitoring and evaluation system is needed to review the impact of the project specific objectives. This can be done initially on a quarterly basis. The main management task is to bring about a change in working practice from a 'routine mode' to 'mission mode'. Putting new approaches in place will require sustained efforts. In other words, there is a need for management of change rather than change in the management structure *per se*. This calls for careful analysis of the present and changed roles that are to be performed by persons at all levels starting from the top to bottom including community members and teachers. Once their role and functions are clearly defined, resistance to change may be mimimal.

Mobilization of and participation by community will be essential for improving enrolment, retention, achievement and school effectiveness. The existing mechanisms for mobilization are VECs, teachers' unions, teacher-parent councils, and MS groups. Whether these mechanisms are sustainable in the long run is an important question. For example, the nature and type of mobilization that is necessary for UEE will be different from that of TLC. The existing structures of TLC are no doubt effective. However, they are meant for the short run only. Mechanisms for mobilization under DPEP need to be institutionalized for their sustained contribution to the programme.

The DPEP is not about small sporadic experiments. It attempts to bring about change and transformation on a large scale. The answer here lies in Panchayati Raj bodies being formally vested with primary education responsibilities. In the first instance the Sarpanchas will have to be oriented and attempts would have to be made to get them involved in project activities.

4. School Improvement: Strategies for Intervention

In the ultimate analysis, success of any educational programme depends on facilitating effective, meaningful and efficient functioning of schools. The main objective, therefore, is to implement the district plan in such a way that it improves the actual functioning of schools and teaching-learning process therein. The linking of district plan implementation with improvement in school functioning is a major task is to be accomplished.

Important questions in this regard are how to ensure that district plan implementation processes are sensitive to the varying concerns at grassroot level and result in significant improvement in the quality of functioning of every school? What strategies are to be evolved to ensure that district plan objectives are realised so as to reach village level properly? How to ensure that community and school take the new initiatives to improve the actual functioning of schools? How to change the perceptions of local community so as to enable them to think that schools are their own rather than being that of government only? In other words, how do we guarantee that the district plan implementation will be school and community centred rather than district office centred?

For improving the functioning of schools, wide ranging actions are needed at various levels and many school-based problems ought to be addressed. For example, poor condition of schools, unattractive school environment, isolation of school from the community etc. are various aspects influencing the functioning of schools.

Actions at School Level

For improving the school, it is necessary to act in the school itself. Such initiatives should help: (i) to improve the conditions for teaching-learning process; (ii) to pay attention to classroom teaching and evaluation practices; (iii) to strengthen the school management practices; and (iv) to pay special attention to small schools with low enrolment.

For improving the conditions of teaching-learning process care needs to be taken to provide adequate instructional facilities for teachers and essential learning materials for children. Equally important is to ensure that the teaching-learning materials are optimally used in the classroom interaction process.

Improving the classroom teaching and evaluation practices involve planning for teaching which means chalking out time table for the whole year in advance as well as a monthly calender. Further, the centre of activities is the teacher and he/she is to be oriented well to perform the job effectively within the constraints of minimum available facilities. Improvement is also needed in the school-based learner evaluation practices and in this regard every primary school teacher may have a copy of Minimum Levels of Learning (MLLs) for various subjects in the language that he/she can easily understand. Further there is a need to make innovations in the routine teaching function for improving the classroom teaching. There are successful experiments whereby the classroom teaching practices are improved. The work by the Child Resource Centre (CRC) is a case in point.

The CRC's intervention programme for school age children (formal and non-formal) (6-14 years) advocated the use of activity oriented teaching methods among teachers as a means for faster progress with the school curriculum. It was the experience of the CRC, that short-term interventions on a regular and sustained basis in schools can help maintain the enthusiasm and motivation of the teachers. After a period of time due to such interventions the teachers become positively influenced towards the gains of activity-oriented learning and teaching approaches, and adopt it as an integral part of their teaching methodology.

The key to success of the project is the teacher. The project believes that if the teacher could be made to feel enthusiastic about the implementation of an idea, to become involved in it, own it, the practice could hope to become institutionalised. Other process mechanisms used by the CRC were 'continuity' and 'sustained effort' and 'need-based support'. In rural areas sustained effort is more difficult to maintain. The CRC team is continuing in its efforts to make policy level changes in curriculum, and is now working out this with the District Institutes of Education and Training in collaboration with the UNICEF.

The school management practices are to be strengthened for improving the quality of primary schools. The essential factors of school management to be taken seriously include time devoted for teacher-pupil interaction, annual and monthly programme of work to be prepared and adhered to, all elements of curriculum to be completed in time, teachers to strictly follow a predetermined time table, students' evaluation to be regular, regular feedback to parents etc. Further, the leadership capabilities of school headmasters are to be enhanced for ensuring better in-school management.

About 85 per cent of the rural primary schools run by government or local bodies are engaged in multi-grade teaching and therefore multi-grade teaching should form the focus of special intervention strategy. Since many rural primary schools are small sized having enrolment of 25 to 50 or 60 in five classes the quality improvement programmes in primary schools should involve special component plans to deal with these small rural schools.

Action at the Local Level

The local management environment is to be improved for making the schools function efficiently. An important step for effective implementation for school improvement measures under the district plan is to shift the school management focus from district education office to local level mechanisms nearer to the primary school. There are three main factors to local level management which are community involvement, professional resource support and monitoring of school functioning.

The role of community in school management is quite important and school teachers and headmaster should have positive attitude towards involving community in school management process. The role of Village Education Committees is quite crucial in this regard. In some states VECs are already constituted and functioning. It is yet to be ascertained how far these VECs have been able to contribute towards improving the school management in these states.

As of now, in most states very little or no professional resource support is available at the local level for teachers and the DIETs cannot give this support to all schools of the district. This is perhaps the reason behind the idea of establishing Block Resource Centres (BRCs) and Teacher Resource Centres (TRCs) under the DPEP. But critical questions in this regard are to be sorted out. For example, how to find enough qualified people for it? What kind of training these persons are to be given? And how to develop appropriate training materials? It is desirable to see and evaluate experiences gained under the APPEP in this regard.

The local level monitoring system of school functioning is quite ineffective and there is an immediate need to create local monitoring system which may not be merely concerned with control and adherence to rules but should play a supportive role. Such monitoring system should involve school staff, i.e. head teacher as well as assistant teachers, local community as well as local educational authority, i.e. block level officer.

Actions at District and State Levels

The task of implementation of district plans begin with accepting the new roles of officials as facilitators rather than controllers. Thus, role and responsibilities and attitude of district and state level officials are desired to be changed accordingly. At the district and state level there are three main tasks for improving the school management. These are augmenting institutional facilities, strengthening resource support system and streamlining the distribution system.

For strengthening the resource support system, strengthening of SCERTs and DIETs is necessary. These organisations will have to become more innovative in providing resource support in the implementation of district plans. These institutions will have to pay particular attention to the task of improving teacher performance as the competence of teachers working in primary schools continues to be a matter of concern. Further, equipping the management authorities at the local level, including headteacher as well as personnel working at the district level, with necessary knowledge skills and values is also crucial to the success of district plans. Here also the role of DIETs, SCERTs and SIEMT proposed under the DPEP is important. For undertaking the new job of implementation of district plans, for district and local level people it is desirable to encourage the SCERTs and DIETs to strengthen their educational research activities because effective improvement in school functioning will demand continuous analysis of the process and devising improved methods for achieving the instructional goals.

The 'PROPEL' and the 'AIEP' experiences show how community involvement and micro-level planning can contribute to increased enrolment and improved quality of education in schools and NFE centres. The 'PROPEL', the acronym for the project 'Promoting Primary and Elementary Education' is an action research project in the state of Maharashtra, which is following a strategy based on area-specific and participatory planning, with each village/habitation and Panchayat perceived as units. Coordination of this project was at three levels: (i) Panchayat cluster (5-6 panchayats), or planning sub-area; (ii) Serving about 6000 households (about 35,000 to 45,000 population); and (iii) The total project area (a block).

The first phase of the 'PROPEL' project (1979-1984) focussed on development of a model of education for out-of-school children. The next phase (1985-1988) studied the replication of this model of education in other areas, and the present third phase from 1988 sees a widening of its scope to the creation of an environment for education through attention on the creation of a learning readiness for children of the age group 3-6 years. It is also supplemented by efforts for adult education which focusses on the 15-35 age group. Intervention at formal schools for making learning a joyful experience was also planned alongwith NFE activity.

The achievements of the 'PROPEL' show that out the 137 villages that the project covers, 89 villages have no out-of-school boy or girl upto the age of 14. The VECs in all the villages have taken an interest in micro-planning of education for their children and others. They are taking care of NFE centres, Child Recreation Centres, Women Development Groups, Jan Shikshan Nilayams and Formal Schools.

The success of the 'PROPEL' project lies in its demonstration of the fact that communities can be mobilised and assisted to plan and manage their own education. It is tough task to break the barrier of educational orthodoxy, but, the 'Propel' has shown that it is not impossible if concerted efforts are made.

The 'Area Intensive Education Project' (AIEP) of Tamil Nadu is an 'entire' (integrated) approach to education. The project aims to achieve the goal of UPE in ways relevant to the life of the community. The focus of this project was on the improvement of school facilities, making learning relevant and meaningful as well as mobilising community support to further these ends.

The project is located in Krishnagiri block of Dharmapuri district in Tamil Nadu. The block comprises 76 villages and 14 hamlets, on urban area and a hilly tribal village. Beginning with 10 villages in 1989, it has now expanded to cover the entire block. This project is an exercise in decentralised, community participative and micro-level planning approach encompassing early childhood education, primary, non-formal and adult education. Separate management structures were evolved to facilitate decentralised planning and decision making under this project. The project implementation process clearly shows the practical difficulties such as inter-sectoral coordination, bureaucratic delays, and transfer of the project staff, etc. It showed how difficult is it to introduce changes so far as the existing administrative system continues.

The quality of school functioning considerably depends on ensuring the availability of basic infrastructure and pedagogic resources in the school. To ensure that these reach the schools properly and in time, the state and district levels need to streamline the system for distributing textbooks and school equipment. Such initiatives help in creating a favourable learning atmosphere. It utilization in classroom transaction process depends on the effectiveness of internal management of the school. These micro-level experiences have shown that when the community is active and involved, the functioning of the schools improved. The challenge is to translate these micro-level experiences on a wider scale with active involvement of the teachers, community and educational authorities.

Report of Group 1: Changes in Management Structure and Processes

The DPEP is one of the innovative programmes which aims to achieve EFA by 2000 A.D. For effective implementation, the DPEP proposes to adopt innovative approaches. This itself calls for a review of the existing structures and processes in the DPEP. The group has independently dwelt upon the two important aspects of the topic—i.e. structure and processes.

Structure

The DPEP has three important goals—universal access, retention and achievement. The structure should ultimately help to achieve these objectives of the programme.

The DPEP is one of the centrally sponsored schemes. The funds under the DPEP would be additional to what is being spent on programmes at the present level. The external aid under DPEP would not be more than three per cent of the total central budget. In any given state only a limited number of districts are selected under DPEP. Hence, the question of dismantling the existing structure altogether and creating new structures does not arise. Further, the experience which the existing structure has gained over a period of time cannot be lost sight of.

The two major difficulties with the existing structure are: (i) Procedural delay; and (ii) Rigidity.

The group, therefore, suggests specific interventions in the existing structure to take care of these difficulties. The group has thought of the following two important structures which are essential for better implementation of the DPEP: (i) Administrative structure; and (ii) Technical structure.

Administrative Structure

The group suggests a five-tier administrative structure. The levels in the administrative structure thus specified by the group are (i) National; (ii) State; (iii) District; (iv) Block; and (v) Village.

National Level

At the national level, there should be 'Project Board' to function as the apex body. It should have proper representation of the States. It should evolve the networking with national resource institutes. There should be a forum, in this body, for inter-state interaction.

State Level

The group suggests the formation of a 'Society' as state level apex body. The main features of this society, as suggested by the group, are as follows: (i) The 'Society' will have autonomous status; (ii) It will have its own rules and regulations; (iii) It will have representation of politicians, academicians, social workers, teachers and NGOs; and (iv) It should have all powers for project implementation and to carry out all its functions.

The group also suggests that the society should have a cadre of managerial staff which would be of supervisory nature. It should have other executive officers. These separate structures may be necessary to facilitate quick decisions, flow of funds in time and monitor programme by incorporating necessary modifications. Needless to add that a reliable EMIS is an essential step to monitor the programme.

District Level

There should be a 'Society' at the district level too. These societies formed at district level should act as units of the state level society. The composition of these societies will be similar to that of the state level society. It will have full powers delegated to it to carry out its functions. It will have proper management structure more or less on same pattern as that of the state level society. The existing district head will act as the chief of the society.

Block Level

At the block level, there should also be a 'society' which should have proper representation of the local people and organisations. The existing Block Education Officer should act as the incharge of this body.

Village Level

The Village Education Committee is the nodal body at the village level. It can have the sub-committees of the existing panchayats wherever they are functional. All financial transactions should be managed by the VEC.

Linkages

The groups considers that it is very important to have proper linkages of this new set up with the existing setup as both have to function in a coordinated way. At the state level, departmental secretaries of Finance, Planning, Rural Developments etc. should be members of the society. The State Education Secretary should be incharge of executive committee of the society with all executive powers. The linkages with existing Directorates of Education are important. All Directors should be members of the society.

The panchayat bodies should be strongly represented in the society. The Chairman of Zilla Parishad or Local Boards should be the Chairman of the society. The district head, collector or chief executive officer of Z.P. as the case may be in the state has to be the chief executive assisted by District Education Officers so that all other departments like health, ICDS etc. can be involved.

Technical Structure

Capacity building is one of the important objectives of the DPEP and hence proper technical structure is to be evolved. The group proposes a five-tier technical structure with the following bodies: (i) SCERT at the state level; (ii) State Institute of Educational Planning and Administration (SIEPA) or SIEMT at the state level; (iii) DIET at the district level; (iv) Resource Centres at the block level; and (v) Cluster Resource Centres at the cluster level.

The SCERT should act as a nodal agency for imparting training to all important functionaries like teachers, NFE volunteers, ECE workers, etc. It would train the key resource personnel only. It would work with new approach and methodology in imparting training. It would be the resource support institute in areas like MLL, NFE, women's empowerment cell etc. At the State level training of educational functionaries in the areas of planning and management should be the responsibility of SIEPA or SIEMT. The SIEPA/SIEMT would train administrators in planning and management of education. It would also take up research activities related to its area of operation.

The DIET will have to act as the main resource support institute at district level. It should impart training to functionaries in key areas and evolve district specific mechanisms in plan formulation and implementation. The BRC (Block Resource Centre) should provide training to block level functionaries especially teachers. The CRC (Cluster Resource Centre) will concentrate on around 10-12 schools in the periphery of five to eight kms. It should have supervision and academic units. It would evolve local specific methods—i.e. teaching-learning aids; teaching strategies; model lessons, etc. This should provide a forum for the teachers to have close interaction to share their experiences and difficulties.

The suggested technical management structure will have local modifications depending on the existing situation.

Processes

The group is of the view that, in the context of DPEP, there is a need for introducing some changes in the management processes that are associated with the change of management structure. In short there is a need for management of change rather than change in the management. This calls for careful analysis of the present and changed roles that are to be played by persons at all levels starting from the highest point down to the level of teachers and community members. Once these roles are clear to different functionaries, the resistance for the changes in the process will be minimised. It is further felt that the new structure should not be manned by fresh recruits. They should rather be, as far as possible, drawn from the existing cadres so that at the end of the project they may come back to the parent department.

Keeping in view the major objectives of the DPEP, the group made the following suggestions (a) training of the members of the VEC more through discussions than through written communications; (b) making enrolment drives through innovative ways; (c) organising welcome functions for the new entrants (children) at the begining of the school session; (d) demonstrating play-way and role-play method of teaching in public in the presence of the parents and other members of the community; and (e) change of school timings to suit the requirements of particular class of children.

While it is felt that the above measures will considerably reduce the difference in enrolment, dropout and learning achievements among gender and social groups, it is also necessary to attend to the following aspects; (a) gender discrimination must be avoided in text books and other activities in schools; (b) social awareness and mobilisation through VECs to be ensured to change the outlook towards education in general and gender in particular; and (c) language and other specific issues of the tirbals should be taken into account in the preparation of textbooks. In case production of group specific textbooks is not possible, teachers' guides and handbooks may be prepared in a suitable manner to address these specific issues.

Reduction of dropout rate will fall considerably from the steps suggested earlier. In addition, the following steps should also be taken for facilitating retention of children in schools; (a) making the surroundings of the school building more attractive with the help of students, teachers and the community; (b) making classroom transactions more participative and joyful through appropriate and frequent teachers' orientation and motivation programmes; and (c) arranging frequent visits of the parents to the school either to see their children at work or their progress or use the school building for some community work beyond the school hours.

Learning achievement will, in addition to what has already been said earlier, increase if there is a sense of joy and pleasure in the whole teaching-learning process in the schools by proper orientation of the teachers and making provisions for activity based materials and work books for students as envisaged in MLL.

Thus, there is a need for special attention on school and its activities where the teacher plays a critical ro' :. For playing his/her role successfully the teacher has to be equipped with proper competencies through orientation, supply of teaching-learning materials and proper recognition. It is further felt that efforts must be made to appoint properly qualified teachers, particularly in the remote rural areas and in areas with concentration of particular disadvantaged social groups and minorities. This calls for necessary changes in the policy of recruitment and posting of teachers. In certain cases, the VEC or any other suitable committee may be given the responsibility of recruiting and appointing teachers to avoid exodus of teachers from remote rural areas.

The question of linkage between the existing management structure at different levels of administration and the new structure for the DPEP as has been suggested needs careful consideration. The group feels that educational administrators and others in the existing statutory bodies at different levels, in addition to their role in the present structure, should have proper representation in the changed structure so that there may not be any conflict at any stage. The linkage between these decentralised bodies and the suggested resource structure on the one hand and between state bodies and central bodies on the other need to be established properly to ensure necessary professional and technical support at all levels. Convergence of the activities of different government departments like education, welfare, health, rural development, planning etc. should be made.

Planning Process

All the above processes calls for area-specific planning. This can be ensured by calling upon people of different professions and social groups to express their specific needs. This should be done by holding a number of meetings and discussions starting from the village level to block level and finally to district level.

It is felt that the members of the organisations that have been suggested in the management structures should be properly trained and motivated to facilitate the above stated meetings and discussions and finally to prepare the plan for the district. Such a plan, it is felt, will be readily acceptable to all the people of the district as their own plan and eventually they will extend full cooperation in proper implementation of this plan.

The technical aspect of the preparation of the plan is, however, not lost sight of and it is strongly felt that necessary technical and professional support should be extended to all the districts either in the way of training the district and state planning team or by commissioning some professional institutions or individuals to facilitate preparation of good district and state plans. The group suggested expansion of DPEP acronym as Disaggregated Patience Elicitated for Progress, to take account of the implicit spirit of implementation of the programme.

Members of the Group

Arora, H.G.	Bansal. Kumud
Chahande, Sanjay	Das, Balendra Kumar
Das, A.K.	Grover, D.C.
Karandikar, Suman	Kumar Suresh
Menon, P.	Padhi, D.N.
Ramanujan, V.A.	Sharadamma, P.
Shukla, S.	Sujata, R.S.
Umashankar, P.K.	

Report of Group II : Monitoring Framework

The essential feature of the implementation of the DPEP is to introduce decentralised processes with regard to identification of educational inputs, creation of teaching-learning conditions and situations, and the management of education. For this purpose, the following are sought to be concretised by the group: (i) community involvement; (ii) integration of educational programmes with other developmental programmes at the village level; (iii) coordination among different programmes within education sector; and (iv) bringing education closer to life experiences.

This is fairly a complex task and presents several challenges. From monitoring point of view the following two considerations are relevant; (a) ensuring certain minimum conditions of schooling to be fulfilled and certain standards to be ensured. This essentially leads to centralised way of looking at things; and (b) providing for the initiatives to come up at school level and incorporation of inputs through outside initiatives (NGOs, etc.). This needs very flexible but effective ways of monitoring to avoid inactivity, lack of initiative or even confusion.

The Group made a distinction between educational statistics to be maintained and supplied periodically and other aspects of monitoring which relate to the improvement of quality in education process. While the group considered the former as essential, the main thrust of discussion was to delineate those educational processes to be generated through various inputs, both physical and qualitative. For this purpose, greater sensitivity to professional autonomy of teachers and schools, delicacy and complexity involved in seeking inter-institutional collaboration, and complexities of coordination of activities and initiatives by individuals and institutions, may have to be shown.

For example, some of the physical inputs like finances and school building will ultimately contribute towards improving educational processes. Many other quality inputs like teacher orientation programmes will be difficult in the sense of establishing direct link between input and output. This would necessitate identifying appropriate indicators and mechanisms to monitor them. For example, it is necessary but not sufficient to monitor the number of teacher orientation programmes organised or number of teachers trained, but also the quality of these programmes in terms of learning that takes place and the use of that learning in their classroom transactions.

Information will have to be collected at various levels, viz., school, village, cluster, block, district and state. The nature of such information and the forms in which these are to be collected may have to be specified. Quantum of information to be sent 'up' to the state level may be kept to the minimum. Details regarding what is to be monitored, and the periodicity need to be specified.

With the implementation of the DPEP, inputs like textbooks, teachers and other associated efforts like coordination with other agencies will be sought to be improved. Towards this goal, monitoring efforts will be directed to discern appropriate actions. Also, readymade tools for these may not be available. They may have to be devised afresh in the present context. For example, certain 'inputs' of proven potential developed by NGOs or other agencies. This may have to be done at the state and national levels to develop a resource of professional known persons and agencies and make it available. For these purposes, it would be a good idea to commission teachers, researchers, etc. from different institutions with specific assignments. These awardees should do their assignments through, inter-alia interactive process with teachers and others. Perhaps, they could be located at schools for the period of fellowship.

There should be continuous monitoring at all levels for which project staff be made responsible. Suitable guidelines may have to be evolved with reference to the nature of data, periodicity, development of indicators and their utilization for seeking improvement in the overall implementation of the DPEP. For that, the group suggests that a national committee may be constituted to provide guidelines to the state and district level staff. Also, a committee at the state level should be constituted to translate these guidelines into a concrete monitoring programme suited to the conditions of the state.

At the lower levels, district education committee, block education committee and village education committee should be made responsible for well-defined monitoring tasks. Project staff, head teachers and teachers will also carry out routine monitoring according to pre-determined guidelines with necessary training support.

All information collected for monitoring may be stored in retrievable form on computer system for building up a Management Information System (MIS) for the project. Computerised MIS should be developed at the state level with guidance from the national committee.

Different ways of utilising information collected through monitoring mechanism would mean adoption of different evaluation approaches, namely, (i) Evaluation specific inputs, processes and out-puts; (ii) Organisational effectiveness; and (iii) Programme evaluation.

The specific aspects of the DPEP which need to be looked into from the monitoring point of view are as follows:

i) There is a need for monitoring of inputs, processes and outputs at various levels; school/village; cluster; block; district; and state. These have to be defined in terms of variables/indicators on which information has to be collected, periodicity of data collection, processing and providing feedback to users/ administers/teachers etc.

ii) Statistics to be collected on a regular basis to provide information on access/participation; retention/drop-outs; and quality/achievement. For achievement, periodic surveys of learner achievement will be required.

iii) Monitoring of quality aspects is to be particularly stressed. For example, one can easily find out how many in-service training programmes were conducted, and the number of teachers trained but one has to monitor also the quality of training, effectiveness of transaction, impact of training on class-room teaching etc. This could be done through periodic review of activities, and special studies using observation technique.

iv) Monitoring mechanism has to be thought of for each level, with specific responsibilities assigned to individuals/ institutions for collection and analysis of data at school level, teachers will do some monitoring at their level, e.g., of the progress of students by evaluating them from time to time; at higher levels, data from schools/VECs, will have to be processed and used at cluster, block, district levels. *Computerisation* of all the data for monitoring purposes is essential and for that necessary software should be developed at the state level.

v) Detailed programme and guidelines for monitoring should be developed at the national level. For that, a small committee may be appointed with specific terms of reference. Committees at state and district levels should also be established for implementation and supervision of the monitoring programme.

Members of the Group

Damodaran, E.	Desle, Balachandra
Jalali, Jayshree	Josephine, Y.
Kutty, K. Mohd.	Lalitha, N.
Lakshmanan, P.	Ordonez, Victor
Sharma, Mukesh	Sharma, R.S.
Shukla, Meenaxi	Srivastava, A.B.L.
Yadav, M.S.	

Report of Group III: Capacity Building

Capacity building aims at self-reliance. Building capacity and morale should go hand in hand. To plan, manage and implement the DPEP, capacities have to be built at all levels. These levels may be categorised as: (i) Individuals (e.g., public representatives, planners, managers, administrators, teachers/NFE instructors, headmasters, supervisors, etc.) (ii) Organisations (Central Government, State Government, District Administrator, Block Administrator, NGOs. (iii) Institutions (NCERT, NIEPA, Autonomous Societies, Textbooks Boards, SCERT, DIETs, Schools etc.)

Initial Steps

The process of capacity building should be directly linked to the functions the individuals are supposed to perform. However, a proper orientation to the programme and its logistics is essential at all levels to facilitate better communication between different units and individuals involved with implementation of the programme. Similarly a general orientation in gender sensitization, mobilisation, community participation, management information system etc. becomes necessary to develop a more balanced perspective. At the school level capacities have to be built at all levels in areas such as classroom management, institutional management and multigrade teaching.

Levels	*Target Groups*	*Areas of Capacity Building*	*Institutional Mechanism*	*Networking*
School				
Village				
Cluster				
Block				
District				
State				
National				

The group recognises that capacities to plan, manage and implement small innovative educational projects exist in the system but capacities to plan, manage and implement large projects and programmes are limited. There is, therefore, the need to recognize existing capacities and identify the capacities which need to be built. The group proposes a format to clearly identify the targets and target groups in capacity building.

Capacity building should not be regarded as a one-shot event. It should be continuous and should aim at upgradation of skills and commitments. The group in this context recommends that: (i) there should be training coordination committees at national, state and district levels to evolve training strategies and materials and to monitor and evaluate their effectiveness; (ii) the use of distance learning mode in capacity building (iii) creation of intermediary levels between village and block level to impart training for teachers, NFE instructors etc; (iv) training process should also aim at recognizing good teachers who could be used as trainers; (v) there should be specific and separate training strategies for teachers and community; (vi) there should be orientation of teacher associations regarding the DPEP; (vii) system be evolved to break professional isolation of the teachers and for their professional growth; and (viii) Orientation of parents.

Capacity Building of Trainers

The group recognizes the importance of DIETs and SCERTs in the effective implementation of the DPEP and that majority of DIETs are not fully functional. The DIET faculty members do not have relevant primary school experience and experience in multigrade teaching. The faculty in DIETs perpetuate models of teaching which rely heavily on lecturing, role learning and examinations. The group, therefore, recommends that: (i) there should be attachment of faculty members associated with pre-service and in-service in primary schools with a view to give them first hand experience in multigrade teaching and school management; (ii) the services of NGOs engaged in pre-service and in-service be utilized; (iii) DIETs should control pre-service intake to maintain the quality of training; (iv) orientation of development functionaries in the DPEP districts; and (v) capacity of SCERTs should also be assessed and strengthened wherever needed.

Educational Administration

The group recognizes the lack of facilities for effective functioning of DEOs. There is a need to raise the status of DEOs as a part of capacity building. Redressal of grievances of teachers should be attempted on a priority basis to liberate DEOs and teachers to professionally contribute to successful implementation of the DPEP. Rajasthan is an example in this regard.

The group recognises that capacity building assumes stability of staffing. It is, therefore, recommended that transfers of staff in the DPEP districts should be restricted to the DPEP districts only. It is also necessary that recruitment and promotion procedures for all staff be streamlined and all vacants posts be filled before implementation of the project and before the academic session begins.

There is no system of regular and recurrent training of educational planners and administrators. Each of the DPEP project should, formulate a perspective plan for organising training programmes for educational planners and administrators at different levels. NIEPA can cover only key persons at the state level. However, considering the large number of institutional heads and educational personnel working in districts and blocks, it is necessary that each State Government should identify suitable agencies capable of sharing training responsibilities for educational personnel. These institutions shall carry out the following activities in consultation with the nodal training institute; (i) identification of training needs; (ii) development of training modules; and (iii) conduct of pre-service and in-service training programmes.

State Level Mechanism

While there are many institutions like the State Institutes of Education, State Institutes of Science Education, etc. which impart training and conduct research pertaining to pedagogical aspects, there is hardly any institution for training and research in areas of planning and management of education, more so when education department employs the largest number of personnel at different levels. To orient and train the state, district and block level educational planners and administrators, there is a need to establish a separate state level mechanism for this purpose. Apart from the function of training, such a mechanism could also promote, sponsor, conduct research, including action research in areas related to planning and management of education, provide professional and resource support to the state and district level agencies as well as undertake evaluative studies of various programmes and activities.

Linkages and Networking

The state level mechanism would be an apex body in the field of educational planning and management which would act as a nodal agency and provide professional support in that area.

Since no single state-level institute may be in a position to offer all the facilities required for pre-induction and in-service training programmes, a strategy of networking with other appropriate institutions, like the State Institute of Education, District Institutes of Education and Training and Colleges of Education should be evolved so that appropriate training programmes for new recruits and the service educational personnel working at different levels could be arranged on a regular and systematic basis. The group recommends that special attention be devoted in the DPEP implementation plans to the issues of teacher training, teacher empowerment and in-school professional support.

It is noted that: (i) Evaluation of school effectiveness in developing nations have consistently highlighted the importance of teacher-related competencies in children's academic progress; (ii) the majority of rural primary schools compound resource limitations with the need for multiple class teaching; (iii) primary teachers are pre-service trained by instructors who have no primary teaching nor multigrade teaching experience; (iv) pre-service teacher training perpetuates models of teaching which actually rely heavily on lecturing, rote learning and examination. They do not "practice what we preach"; (v) primary teaching remains a low-status profession with inadequate academic and professional upgradation possibilities; (vi) failure to improve all aspects of the teaching-learning process at Class I will perpetuate low levels of enrolment, poor pupil motivation, poor attendance high drop-out and high repetition and will impede all related DPEP strategies; (vii) innovative programmes consistently highlight the importance primary teachers; and (viii) all block/district/state/national level capacity building will be futile if teaching in classrooms is ineffective, unmotivating and irrelevant.

The group, therefore, suggests that:

i) In each of the DPEP districts, a widely representative Task Force on Primary Teacher Training and Empowerment be elected to develop objectives, strategies, implementation and monitoring plans for improving pre-service, in-service and on-the-job training for primary teachers with special emphasis on Class I and multi-grade teaching;

ii) Special attention be given by each Coordinating Committee to identify outstanding teachers with recognised professional excellence in Class I and multi-grade teaching say, one from every 10-15 schools. These resource/master/clinical teachers should be requested to offer planned, frequent, in-class visits and support using demonstration lessons; team-teaching; life-relevant curriculum themes, teaching aids and strategies; strategies for motivating and monitoring individual children's progress in basic skills; techniques for peer-tutoring, group work and cross-age tutoring; strategies for yearly, term, monthly, weekly and daily planning etc.

iii) "Resource Teacher" support should be particularly targeted to Class I children, especially in those schools with significant disadvantages.

iv) Each district Coordination Committee on Primary Teacher Training and Empowerment be requested to develop creative and concrete proposals for teacher support and training, preferably using short courses, professionally relevant distance education courses, local/national/regional attachment training, workshops, cluster level meetings, school to school visits, resource centres, accredited 'mixed mode' courses etc., to operationalise the links between theory/research and daily classroom practices.

v) Each district level coordination committee force on Primary Teacher Training and Empowerment be mandated to meet regularly, to consult widely at the village and block levels and to communicate transparently on initiatives, activities and issues to all VECs, Resource Centres and Resource Teachers, and to State Level Co-ordinating Committees on Teacher Training and Empowerment.

Members of the Group

Capoor, Indu	Goel, Ved
Ghatak, D.G.	Indiresan, Jaya
Irvine, Jim	Khullar, Mala
Mukhopandhyay, S.	Premi, Kusum
Palaniynadi, R.	Singh. Abhimanyu
Satyanarayan, A.	Taid, T.R.
Thiagarajan, S.	Venugopal, S.

Report of Group IV: Alternatives to Schooling

The group deliberated on the following issues: (i) relevance and need of the concept of alternative schooling; (ii) identification of target groups; (iii) identification of alternatives—structures and strategies; (iv) advocacy and modalities for reaching out; (v) ensuring quality of education and equivalency—cross structure migration; and (vi) cost and financing of alternatives.

Relevance and Need

Reaching out to each and every eligible learner, the letter and spirit of universalization of education, through formal schooling howsoever efficient and large the network be is not possible. This is largely true in the global context. The early establishment of open schools during 1916 to 1922 in Australia, Canada and New Zealand bears this out. Formal schools may not be able to reach education to geographically and socially isolated population. Even if school is provided, the marginalised groups within this section of population may not be able to take advantage of it. Hence alternatives to formal schooling is necessary for ensuring greater universalization of education.

Alternatives by themselves are not the solution. There would be a tendency to believe and treat alternatives as second rate. How can alternatives be effective? This must be a major consideration. Also alternatives must clearly target the well defined clientele groups.

The 'alternative' should not be seen as alternatives to schooling, meaning thereby an alternative structure to communicate an educational programme of the formal system. This would be self-defeating prophesy since formal schooling with all its rigidities and non-relatives is not an adequate and right reference point for comparison. Thus 'alternatives' should not be read as alternatives to schooling. It is not even alternative schooling. Within the spirit of the DPEP the alternative mean alternative education. To that extent, it should not borrow from the formal system.

Identification of Target Groups

In this context, there is a need to identify the target groups for alternative education with reference to social, locational or geographical, economic and vocational, educational, age and sex related categories.

The SC/ST category of learners particularly who reside in remote and interior tribal belts, despersed locations, hilly tracts etc. are one focussed group for the alternative education. Migrating population—the agriculture labour, construction workers banzaras or bohemian communities, the early school drop-outs, handicapped and working children are the other groups. A major focussed and prioritised group is the girls and women cutting across all the social and economic categories.

While formal schooling is level determined and age specific, alternative education would have to be educational level guided but age free. This would not be restricted to the age of 14 years, since there is no social, educational or moral ground to deprive a person, a girl in particular, of an educational facility just because she could not avail it when she was below 14.

While it requires a detailed exercise in quantitative estimation and projection, keeping in mind the population of working children, non-schooled children and youth, early school dropout and neo-literates, the estimated population who can benefit from the alternative education can be above 60 million.

Identification of Alternatives

There are two issues involved in it—alternative context and processes and alternative structures. A rigid, abstract and prescriptive instructional programme that characterises formal schooling would not be attractive and effective. The programme must have built-in relevance, flexibility and freedom to learn. Referring to the practice of National Open School, the group held the view that the programme should be offered in modular form where the learner would have an opportunity to choose from a variety of learning tasks including some occupational areas designed on the overall paradigm. The learning tasks would be spelt out in terms of measurable competencies; and it should be possible to achieve the competencies on a flexible time frame allowing self-paced learning.

The learning tasks would be provided in self-instructional modular format; whether strictly programmed instructional material or semi programmed material would depend upon the subject and levels of education. Special care would be needed to ensure proper designing, layout, illustration and production to make the instructional materials attractive.

There are evidences of successful alternative education with 600 hours of contact classes in a year as much as 100 hours in a year. The group does not recommend any fixed hour of face to face classes; this should be determined by the needs of the learner, availability of the instructors and other considerations of physical facilities. Nevertheless, the group was unanimous in professing and instructional process where face to face classes are used more for problem solving and interaction promotion learning skills and inadependent learning—learning to learn.

There should be careful avoidance of the frightful marriage between education and examination so that the latter does not drive the learners out of alternatives once again. The assessment should be continuous, demonstrative and open to form a part of learning itself.

Regarding alternative structures, the group was of the opinion that the task of universalization is too complicated and massive to choose one or a few strategies. All weapons in the arsenal must be pressed into service so that maximum number of learners can be reached out. In this context, continuation and energising the non-formal education centres was considered important.

There are good number of successful micro-level experiments. Besides, such experiments help in model building and despite the criticism that they are individual centred and non-replicable, such projects also provide educational coverage effectively. Howsoever small be the coverage by one project, a hundred micro-projects need to be reckoned with.

The third strategy identified was tutor-centred delivery. In many villages in the country, the only educated person is the teacher. Wherever school is not feasible or schooling for a particular group of people in the village is not possible, the teacher or educated and qualified person can tutor a group of learners. Experiment with parent tutors in distance education in New Zealand is quite successful. Reference was made to the successful Andhra Pradesh experiment in tribal areas where the poor tribal students are tutored by a local youth as teacher.

Another strategy suggested was the senior school and college students tutoring group of learners on a token payment of fees that could support the education of the school and the college youth more in the form of scholarship in lieu of work.

While the structural alternatives suggested above are intended to take education to the grassroots, these need an umbrella or a cementing framework for delivery and quality management. The alternative contents and processes and distributed delivery mode are the basic features of open schooling system. There are significant experiences of open schooling at the elementary and secondary levels in India through Andhra Pradesh Open School and the National Open School. The latter has appointed a nation wide experiment in delivery of high quality education with enormous flexibility and freedom to learn through a distributed and networked 400 study centres all over the country. Drawing upon the experience, the group believes that open schools are the most relevant structural alternative. An open school should be set up in each state; the non-formal centres, tutor based learning centres, micro projects should be linked up with the open schools. Besides, state open schools should also set up study centres in elementary and secondary schools to derive the advantage of the physical infrastructure and benefit of qualified teachers. The national level institution on open schooling should provide resource support in the form of capability building for curriculum developers, courseware authors, tutors and counsellors and managers, also provide curriculum and instructional materials. The open schools must come in big way to provide a system frame to the alternative education.

Advocacy and Modalities for Reaching Out

That, just creating the alternative is not enough. It needs adequate advocacy support to reach out to the targeted clientele group. The objectives of the advocacy would be, besides environment building and information dissemination, establishing equivalency in public eye and targetting the relevant groups.

One set of strategies comprises use of radio and television through advertising fillers, programmes, etc. for reaching out with information. Second set of strategies comprises; kala jatha, processions, street theatres, folk mode; posters, leaflets and banners, seminars and conventions etc. using school system and personnel, the teacher and headmasters; and Panchayats and other local community leaders including religious leaders.

The third set of strategies is printed advertisements in unusual places, mass consumer items for example on match box, cigarette cases, Bidi wrappers, soap wrappers, fertilizser packs, sweet boxes, toothpaste cartons, back of textbooks and exercise copies, and host of such other places.

Ensuring Quality of Education and Equivalence

Quality of education is ensured at three points; entry behaviour, instructional processes comprising curriculum, reading materials and face to face instructional processes, and exit control—the efficiency of the assessment system. Since the goal of the DPEP is universalization, any restriction in entry would be self-defeating.

For ensuring quality, primary emphasis would have to be on instructional process. The curriculum should be flexible but well defined where competency levels match well above the usual formal system. The instructional materials, with examples of IGNOU and NOS at hand, can be developed in a manner that these are qualitatively superior to the usual textbooks available to a formal system; superior in content and quality, structured presentation as well as in lay out, printing and production. As practised in the open schools, the tutors can be drawn from the existing and retired school teachers to ensure instructional quality. Further they can be trained in pedagogy of alternative open and non-formal education. The evaluation would have to be user-friendly and open but with predefined standards, known both to the learner, the tutor and the assessors.

The equivalency, apart from rigidity and closedness of the parallel system, comes from the maintenance of standard and quality. For example, the qualifications and certificates of National Open School is recognised by as many as 57 universities; whereas IITs and Delhi University kind of reputed institution recognise, another university in an obscure corner refuse to provide equivalence. The cross sector migration is also the function of quality and equivalence.

Alternatives are often constructed as cheap and that sends the signal that it is cheap in quality too. In fact, there is no established relationship. Whereas the salary cost in formal primary education is about 95 per cent, the administrative cost in nonformal open learning is less than 15 per cent.

According to current estimates worked out by NOS with respect to its open basic education project, unit cost of education in the alternative framework would be Rs. 300 per level (from III to VIII are proposed to be covered by a three level graded curriculum) or Rs. 1000 (rounded off from Rs. 900) for entire elementary education. This estimated cost would include instructional materials, about 180 face to face classes, management and supervisory cost. This unit cost is in comparison to approximately Rs. 700 per child per year in formal schools.

There is yet another tendency to ask for social financing in case of alternatives. This is unjust. This variety of education is for those who are comparatively weak, the education is less expensive and contributes significantly to the national goals and concerns. Hence funding and financing policy of formal primary and elementary education should be extended to alternative education. Incentive schemes to formal education should be extended to the students of open schooling. Finally, the group was emphatic that contributions of teachers or educated youth to educate the deprived through alternative education must be paid for an compensated. The whole concept and propagation of voluntarism is veil to undermine mass education. Should volunteer teacher be an effective toll of education, this should be equally practised in formal school, college and professional education. Otherwise, it indicates the silent avoidance of accountability of the system.

Members of the Group

Hallak, J.	Kaul, Vineeta
Mukhopadhyay, M.	Menon, Shyam B.
Pandey, K.A.	Raju, J.S.
Rahman, Syed Makibar	Srivastava, Ranjana
Sujatha, K.	

Summary of Recommendations

The DPEP is a centrally sponsored national programme firmly rooted in the National Policy on Education and Programme of Action, with funding support from external sources. It is an exercise in decentralised planning and management of primary education at the district level. Alternatives to formal schooling becomes necessary to achieve the object of universal primary education. Hence DPEP emphasises on non-formal delivery mechanisms, especially in localities where shool is not viable and among groups where formal system may not be feasible. Participatory planning and capacity building form important components of the programme.

The participants of the workshop deliberated upon various dimensions of DPEP and made the following recommendations for effective implementation of the programme:

1. There is a need to create separate management structure for effective implementation of the programme. The management structure thus created should be sustainable in the long run.
2. The programme management structure may have two separate compoents:

(a) administrative structure to plan and monitor the implementation of the programme; and

(b) technical structure to provide academic resource support.

3. Administrative structure involves creation of bodies/ councils/committees at national, state, district and lower levels to plan and manage the programme. Such societies as envisaged by the MHRD may be constituted with representation from educational functionaries and representatives from the public.

4. Technical structure is essential to provide academic resource support for the programme. There is a need to augment SCERT and DIET. Similarly, there is a need to create Block Resource Centres and cluster level teacher centres to facilitate more frequent in-service training of teachers.

5. Local level capacity in planning and management of education is very weak in India. At present there exists no organisational arrangement at the state or district level to provide training in educational planning and management. Hence there is a need to create new structures like SIEPA or SIEMT. Similarly the DIET staff, especially in the planning and management branch, also need to be trained in these dimensions.

6. The new management structure, so far as possible, may be manned by people drawn from the existing cadres. This may establish a better linkage between the existing structures and new structures on the one hand and ensure sustainability of the programme on the other.

7. There is a need to ensure convergence of services at the grassroot level. At present, different departments/agencies are involved in the delivery of various services related to education. Co-ordination between these departments is the first step in this direction.

8. For purposes of monitoring the implementation process, there is a need to constitute a National Committee to provide periodic guidelines. Such committees need to be created at the state and district levels also.

9. There is a need to develop indicators to monitor the programme. The Committee to be constituted can guide and help the state and district level authorities to develop the necessary indicators.

10. Regular and frequent flow of information is essential to ensure effective implementation of the project. This can be facilitated through computerisation of the information system. There is a need to develop computer based EMIS at the district level.
11. In-service training of teachers and other educational functionaries is a very essential component of the programme. There is a need to develop training plans and review in-service training programmes to ensure their relevance and quality. Since various agencies are involved in different types of in-service training programmes, there is a need to constitute Training Co-ordination Committees at state and district levels.
12. In-school management is very weak especially in the rural areas. Therefore, at the school level, capacities are to be created for institutional planning and management, classroom management and multi-grade teaching.
13. NGOs operate in many localities. Many of them are involved in in-service teacher training activities. Their services may be utilised wherever found appropriate.
14. Teacher trainers, very often, lack direct experience in handling primary classes. Therefore, attachement programmes whereby the trainers are attached to selected primary schools for a brief period may be helpful.
15. The teachers trained under the DPEP programme should not be transferred. Transfer, if unavoidable, should be to other DPEP districts only.
16. There is a need for networking of resource organisations at state and district levels to ensure better academic support for the programme.

Source: Report of the NIEPA-IIEP Workshop on Distrcit Level Plan Implementation Strategy with Particular Reference to School Improvement (August 18-20, 1994). New Delhi: National Institute of Educational Planning and Administration.

5

The Case of the District Primary Education Programme

—*Dr. N.V. Varghese*
NIEPA, New Delhi

India has one of the largest network of primary schools in the world. With around 577 thousand institutions enrolling more than 100 million children and employing around 1.8 million teachers, primary education has become a gigantic public enterprise accounting for considerable amount of public investment in India. Planning and managing such a large and expanding system is a major challenge. Realising this formidable tasks, public policy measures in India in the recent past have been directed towards decentralisation of planning and management of primary education. The District Primary Education Programme (DPEP) is, perhaps the most recent effort in this direction.

The DPEP was initiated in 1993 as a centrally sponsored programme with external funding support from various international agencies. In the pages that follow, I have made an attempt to analyse the process of decentralisation of educational planning initiated under the DPEP.

DPEP in the Indian Context

The DPEP is conceptualised on the basis of the present level of educational development in India and is a reflection of the current concerns to revitalise the primary education scene in India. The DPEP in its conceptualisation takes into account: (i) the educational context; (ii) the resource context, and (iii) the planning context.

The Educational Context

Primary education in India has expanded remarkably in the post-independence period. At present more than 95% of the rural population has a primary school within a walking distance of one kilometre (NCERT: 1995). The number of primary schools increased from 209.7 thousand in 1950-51 to 577 thousand in 1990-91. The gross enrolment ratio (GER) at the primary level increased from 42.6% in 1950-51 to

102.7% in 1991-92. Enrolment in primary classes increased from 19.5 million in 1950-51 to around 101.6 million in 1991-92 (Department of Education:1993). Besides there are around 277 thousand Non-formal education centres enrolling around 6.8 million children.

The decadal growth rates of enrolment show that the fifties was a period of faster expansion of the system followed by continuously declining growth rates in the sixties and seventies. The decade of the eighties witnessed signs of recovery in growth rates in enrolment. This recovery is very marginal and even now the growth rates are less than half of what they used to be in the fifties.

A closer scrutiny of the recovery in growth rates shows that is more a phenomenon of the post-mid-eighties and that too primarily due to the higher growth rate experienced among the deprived groups located in the backward regions of the country. More significantly, according to the recent survey (NCERT: 1995) nearly 80% of the increase in schools, nearly 66% of the additional enrolment of girls are accounted by the educationally backward states of India. Similarly, more than three-fifths of the non-enrolled in the age group 6-11 in the rural areas and more than four-fifths of the non-enrolled in the urban areas are accounted by the lowest 40% of the population. In other words, the problem of non-enrolment is increasingly getting confined to the backward regions and deprived groups.

The optimism on account of the expansion of the system diminishes progressively as we move from enrolment to retention and further to levels of learner achievement at the primary stage. Dropout rates at primary level continue to be as high as 48% in the eighties. Recent studies on primary education have shown that levels of learner achievement are rather low (Dave et.el: 1988; Govinda and Varghese : 1993; Shukla: 1994; Bashir et.al. 1993; Jangira 1994; Varghese: 1994).

What is interesting to notice in the development of primary education in India is that additional investments to improve access benefits only a few but the marginalised groups; investments to improve retention benefits a larger group and investments to improve quality of education benefits almost everybody covered by the primary education system. Consequently, the pressure on public policy is to shift investments from programmes focusing on quality of education. In fact, from the mid-eighties onwards, this is precisely what has happened in India - a shift in emphasis from equity in access to equity in achievement. The measures adopted in this direction can be broadly categorised into four (Varghese: 1995a):

(i) the Operation Blackboard Scheme to ensure minimum facilities in the schools.

(ii) defining the Minimum Levels of Learning (MLL) to be achieved by primary school children;

(iii) establishment of District Institutes of Education and Training (DIET) to improve teacher competency and teaching learning process; and

(iv) decentralisation of educational planning and management. The DPEP takes into account this change in the focus of public policy measures.

The Resource Context

It can be argued that some of the recent trends in the allocation of resources to education has positively contributed to the progress of primary education in India. In my view an increase in investments in adult education and an increase in plan allocation to primary education might have helped in maintaining, if not improving, the growth rates in primary education. First, adult education accounted for nearly 3% of the total resources allocated to education in the First Plan. This share showed a consistent decline in the subsequent plans reaching the lowest level of 0.3% in the third plan. In the eighties, plan allocation to adult education showed marked increase. It accounts for nearly 9% of the total allocation to reduction in the Eighth Five Year Plan. In the late eighties Total Literacy Campaigns were initiated in India. All evaluation studies (NLM : 1994; Varghese : 1995b) have shown that the success in TLCs has contributed to an increased demand for primary education in India.

Second, public expenditure on education as a share of GNP has increased in India from 1.2% in 1950-51 to 3.9% in 1989-90. The share of elementary education during the corresponding period increased from 0.48% to 1.72%. However, plan allocations to education which is a reflection of new initiatives and programmes, have been declining in India (see Tilak :1995 for a detailed discussion). During the first two decades of planned development (1950-1969) allocation of elementary education as a share of total allocation to education declined from 56% to 24%. However in the next two decades there was consistent increase p.a. in the share of resources allocated to primary education from 24% in 1969 to around 37% in the Seventh Plan (1985-90). Allocation to elementary education in the current plan (1992-97) is around to 47%. Although this trend is positive, it is to be noted that we have not yet reached the levels of allocation made in the First Plan.

Another trend worth noting is that the share of plan expenditure on primary education to total educational expenditure has been declining in India. In the eighties, this share has increased from 5.9% in 1980-81 to around 12% in 1991-92. As noted earlier, an increase in plan allocation reflects the resource base for new initiatives in primary education. During this period the Centre's share in plan allocations to elementary education increased from around 5.3% in 1980-81 to 9.7% in 1984-85 and further to around 28% in 1991-92. Therefore, it can be argued that the increase in the share of plan expenditure to total expenditure on primary education is primarily due to the improved share of the Centre. It is quite probable that the share of the Centre in resources is increasing partly due to the introduction of many externally funded projects in India.

The argument is not that the resource base to primary education has reached an all time high in the eighties. In fact, in terms of allocation to education as a share of the total plan allocation, allocation to primary education as a share of total plan allocation to education and the share of plan expenditure on elementary education as a share of total expenditure, the situation in the eighties continues to be worse than that in the fifties. Therefore what is argued is only that there seems to be a policy of according increased priority in public funding to primary education and it has helped arresting the continuously eroding resource base of primary education. The external funding under DPEP may further help to increase the resource base to primary education.

The Planning Context

Primary education in India is predominantly a state funded activity. This public character of primary education necessitates planning and public action to effect the direction of change in the sector. Educational planning in India is an integral part of the overall economic planning. Hence, the efforts towards decentralisation of educational planning is to be seen in the context of changes in the overall planning process.

India has adopted planning within a mixed economy framework as the basic strategy for its economic and social development. Under this framework, planning is seen more as an Instrumental Inference' than as an alternative to market mechanism. The macro goals of the system and principal action directives are derived from the planning process while the micro-analogues are left to be implemented through the markets (Chakravarty : 1987). Basic questions relating to how much to save and where to invest are left to the planning process.

India has a multi-level planning framework which assumes: (i) a vertical division of responsibilities corresponding to the spread effects of activities considered; (ii) a disaggregation of economic activities and plan targets by regions and sub-regions; and (iii) existence of hierarchy of levels of planning with territorial jurisdiction and a system of internal relationship (Prasad : 1988). Under the multi-level framework, planning in India is carried out at the national, state and district levels.

In the initial stages the major focus of planning efforts in education was on expanding the system depending on the sole delivery mechanism of formal primary schools. Planning efforts during this period were mostly confined to the central level. At the national level the education division of the planning commission in consultation with the concerned departments and ministries develop Five Year Plans for education. Normally working groups on specified areas of education are constituted to help developing the Five Year plans in education.

At the state level educational activities are carried out by two agencies: (i) the secretariat which is responsible for policy making and coordination; and (ii) the directorate which is responsible for direction and regulation (Mukherjee : 1970). Many states are having separate directorates for different levels of education and some of the states have separate secretariates for school and higher education each headed by a separate secretary. Most of the states have constituted a planning cell to look after educational planning activities.

There are no such planning machinery or mechanisms existing at the district level. The National Policy on Education 1986 envisaged setting up of District Boards of Education (DBEs) to initiate and coordinate educational planning activities. However, DBEs are yet to be constituted at the district level.

Planning exercise is, perhaps, more rigorous and elaborate at the national level than at other levels. Planning at the state level is mostly an exercise in disaggregation and regionalisation of national plans. This is partly due to the fact that the states feel that the scope for state initiatives are limited. Increasing bureaucratisation of the planning process with the introduction of centrally sponsored schemes indirectly reduces the scope for state initiatives. It is also true that planning competencies are rarely developed at the state level. Even though planning cells are created at the state level, "these units are not effectively manned by technically trained persons" (Mathur : : 1980).

The educational development efforts in India were increasingly targeted towards educationally backward states and state was recognised as the unit for initiating educational planning. Efforts towards decentralising educational planning had only a limited success.

For example in 1969 the Planning Commission made an unsuccessful effort to decentralise planning process to the district level.

In the absence of availability of planning competencies and machinery at the district level, the commission had to reconsider it decision. In the early eighties a Committee was set up to study the possibilities and feasibilities of district planning in India (Planning Commission:1984). The committee in its recommendations clearly indicated the areas of decentralisation in educational and primary education is identified as one of the major areas viable for decentralised planning and decision making.

The empirical evidence on the progress of education in the eighties showed that there are educationally backward districts even in educationally advanced states and there are educationally advanced districts even in educationally backward states. Therefore, it was realised that for purposes of proper planning and targeting, district is more appropriate unit. And hence from the late eighties onwards the efforts are on to strengthen educational planning at the district level. The Eighth Five Year Plan (Planning Commission: 1992a) addresses this issue. In fact the National Development Committee on Literacy (Planning Commission: 1992b) and the Eight Plan made categorisation of districts based on the levels of literacy and enrolment in primary schools in order to prioritise actions and activities to be initiated in different districts.

Despite these efforts, district plans in the present context are meant at best to implement central and state schemes. This is primarily due to the fact that the scope for district planning is very limited in India due to various constraints. The major constraints to initiate planning at the district level are:(i) lack of resources base at the district level;(ii) lack of planning competencies; and (iii) absence of a planning machinery.

First, the resource allocation decisions are taken at the state level. The share of 'untied funds' or 'block grants' is very meagre (Nanjundappa : 1991). Moreover the districts do not have any authority to mobilise resources of their own. Hence districts are left with too little 'resources at' their disposal to initiate any district specific programme. Given the nature of resource allocations, the districts are compelled to make proposals to implement the state level initiatives.

Second, planning competencies are not developed at the district level (Varghese : 1994c). The districts in India are primarily used to the traditional role of revenue administration. A shift from this traditional role to the developmental role at the district level was mostly confined to implementation of various programmes initiated by the central and state governments. Hence no serious planning work in the realistic sense of the term could be taken up at the district level (Prasad : 1988). Perhaps, such a need was never felt too. Therefore, many a district are not adequately equipped to take up rigorous planning exercises in education. What takes place in the name of planning at the district level is nothing but effecting changes in the budget figures, perhaps on an incremental basis. The rigorous exercises of any realistic assessment of the situation, fixing the targets, elaborating any intervention strategies, costing of the plans etc., are relatively non-existent at the district level (Varghese: 1994c). Third, related to the second, is the question of any planning machinery to draw up district plans. In the present set up district level educational officers are responsible for developing educational plans. Given their busy schedule and competency, this is a tall order expectation. Therefore, if district plans are to be drawn up, an organisational arrangement to draw up district plan is also to be envisaged. The District Primary Education Programme (DPEP) tries to overcome these constraints to facilitate a process of decentralised planning in India.

DPEP Versus the Earlier Efforts.

District Primary Education Programme is conceptualised and concretised on the basis of varied experience the country has acquired and expertise gained in the process of planning and implementing educational programmes in India. First, our experience of practicing decentralised planning has shown that in the present setup the scope of local initiatives in district planning is very limited. This is primarily due to the fact that crucial resource allocation decisions are taken at the national or state level. The districts have virtually very little authority to allocate resources to the programme or activities which they consider to be dear to them. DPEP attempts to alter the pattern of resource decisions to encourage local initiatives at the district level. Under this programme the district plans are assessed and resources are allocated directly to the districts.

Second, the experience of centrally sponsored programmes shows that it increases bureaucratisation of planning process and reduces the role of local level units implementation agencies. Normally, these schemes are planned at the central level and executed at the local level. Under the DPEP only guidelines are prepared at the national level. The plans are to be prepared at the local level. Local initiatives and educational innovations are almost impossible in a departmental mode of planning. Therefore, DPEP, unlike other centrally sponsored schemes envisages to go beyond the departmental concerns to plan education through involvement of local bodies and community at large.

Third, planning in India continues to be largely sectoral. Sectoral planning helps to exercise bureaucratic controls and establish vertical linkages. DPEP attempts to provide an area approach to planning emphasising on the horizontal linkages in place of vertical linkages. The ideas of convergences of services, inter-departmental co-ordination and public participation in planning are supposed to promote area approach to planning.

Fourth, the Total Literacy Campaigns (TLCs) are initiated and completed in many, districts in India. TLCs are major effort in successfully mobilising local initiatives to prepare comprehensive plans at the district level. The successful completion of TLC projects (for a review see NLM: 1994; Varghese:1995b) have shown that planning competencies, if needed, can be developed at the local level. The DPEP attempts to build on this experience gained by the districts and the preference given to TLC districts in DPEP funding helps to strengthen this experience further.

However, there is a basic difference in the approach to and process of planning adopted under TLC and DPEP. The Adult Education Departments have played very marginal role in TCLs. It is largely planned and implemented through different committees not necessarily connected directly to the education departments. Primarily education is a continuing programme and is implemented through the existing institutions and control mechanisms. Therefore, unlike TLC, DPEP envisages a stronger role for the education department both in facilitating planning and in implementing programmes. Therefore DPEP is envisaged to be more departmentalised and bureaucratised than TLCs.

Fifth, primary education in India has reached a stage where the focus needs to be shifted from increasing access to improving achievement level. Therefore, emphasis in DPEP planning is increasingly shifted from creation of new institutions to improving effectiveness of the existing institutions. Perhaps, planning and management of existing institutions and the teaching learning process therein forms the focus of DPEP planning exercise.

Sixth, India has some experience in planning and managing externally funded projects. But most of these projects are small scale projects focusing on some of the selected aspects of primary education. Although project planning is a part and parcel of these exercises, comprehensive area specific plans keeping district as the unit was never attempted under the externally funded projects in India.

The DPEP builds on the experiences gained from these project planning exercises. Bihar education Project funded by the UNICEF, Lok Jumbish Project and Shiksha Karmi Project funded by SIDA, Andhra Pradesh Primary Education Project funded by ODA, Mahila

Samakhya project funded by the Dutch and Uttar Pradesh Primary Education. Project funded by the ODA are some of the externally funded projects operating in India, DPEP expands the scope of educational planning from project planning to district planning. In fact DPEP is an exercise in decentralised planning in a project mode.

Lastly, DPEP attempts to professionalise educational planning. As noted earlier, planning competencies are virtually non-existent at the district level. The Indian experience shows that percolation of competencies from national to state level and further to lower levels is difficult, if impossible.

DPEP is an experiment to alter this process of competency building exercise by starting from local level to the state level.

Where do we locate decentralised planning under the DPEP in the context of planning of education in India? Planning under the DPEP lies between project planning sponsored schemes and TLC experiences on the one hand and between project planning exercises under various externally funded primary education projects and our own experiences of practicing district planning in education on the other. It is less bureaucratic and departmentalised than traditional centrally sponsored schemes; but more departmentalised than TLC programmes. It is more broad based project planning but more focused, targeted and closely monitored than traditional district plans.

It is an exercise to locate the limits of de-departmentalising planning without losing control and direction by public authorities.. It is an effort to professionalise educational planning by developing planning competencies outside the boundaries of the department.

The effort is not to make the departments redundant but to redefine the role of the department to facilitate better and improved quality of services from the existing institutions.

The DPEP Initiative

How does DPEP decentralise educational planning? The approach adopted under the DPEP and the parameters indicated in the guidelines help promoting decentralised planning in education. The efforts made under DPEP to effect decentralised planning in education can be broadly categorised into (i) creating the facilitating conditions; (ii) initiating the planning process; and (iii) developing planning competencies.

Creating Facilitating Conditions

DPEP is a centrally sponsored programme of the Ministry of Human Resource Development with funding support from external agencies. The sources of funding under the DPEP are varied. However, approach to planning is uniform across the DPEP districts. The approach is elaborated in the DPEP guidelines, (Department of Education: 1995). The guideline provides only a framework within plans are to be developed. Although the approach to planning is unified, the DPEP does not envisage uniform plans across districts.

The guidelines only ensure that the plans are prepared within the framework of national concerns and priorities. The parameters are flexible to ensure that local variations are reflected in the plans. An analysis of district plans prepared under the DPEP shows that they very vary much across districts in terms of priorities, strategies and programmes.

The DPEP ensures funding support for the district level programmes.

Under this programme each district can get a maximum of Rs 400 millions. It was noted in the earlier section that the present practice of centralised resource allocation decisions reduces the scope for districts to initiate their own programmes. Assurance of resources has improved possibilities of developing district specific plans with local specific intervention strategies.

No external or internal agency are to be depended on to develop district plans. The district plans are to be developed at the district level. each district constituted core groups on district planning and the plans were developed by them through a process of mutual consultation. Very often the plans are not prepared by the district administrators. The formation of core groups helped in broad basing the planning process. The core group consisted of people from other departments, professionals from resource organisations and NGOs and representatives of the public. What is encouraging about the planning process under the DPEP is that each state had its own pattern of forming core groups and preparing plans. Based on the experience in the first round of plan preparation, three patterns can be identified (i) DIETs playing the major role in plan preparation; (ii) state level institutions playing a significant role; and (iii) local consultants playing a major role. The role of education department was more in terms of organising these activities than developing plans per se.

Professional support to the planning process is ensured under the programme. The planning process under the DPEP was elaborate and needed technical inputs which was not available at the district level. Hence there was a demand for developing planning competencies at the district level. This was facilitated through constituting a National Core Team. This national core team had 12 core groups each representing an area of specialisation and headed by a specialist in the area. Frequent interactions between the state, district and national core groups either in the form of meetings, workshops or training programmes helped developing planning competencies at the district level. While the major technical support for drawing up district plans were provided by national institutions, they themselves did not prepare any plans. This helped in professionalising planning process by developing local capacity in planning of education.

Educational plans are to be ultimately tested in the schools and classrooms. Therefore, schools need to be made more active and effective agents in the planning process. In the existing framework schools do not exercise any freedom to initiate any activity. DPEP, attempts to activate the school processes by ensuring each school with a limited amount allocated annually to improve facilities and to meet expenditure on account of consumables. This amount is to be spent in consultation with the Villages Education Committees. This has helped in ensuring that institutional planning process is initiated in schools and planning for facilities has become local specific. This may also strengthen the power and authority of the headmaster of the school and increase the involvement of the local communities in decision making process.

By restricting the share of civil works to 24% and project management to 6%, the DPEP has ensured substantial amount of resources to plan for education specific activities. The DPEP parameters also ensure that the planning exercise will not get confined to civil work activities and it increases the scope for promoting district specific activities directly promoting teaching-learning dimensions of primary education.

The notion of medium term plans, and annual plans under the DPEP helped in making plans more and more realistic. The initial plans are only indicative and the annual plans are more specific and elaborate. This gives a chance to revise the plans as and when required. The plans are also modified with each stage of implementation. This plans are also modified with each stage of implementation. This approach gave the district authorities the scope for experimenting and initiating activities of their own on a regular basis. In other words, this provision in the guidelines helps in making planning a regular feature of educational process at the district level.

Studies as a part of the planning exercise provided a strong empirical foundation for the plans. It also helped in effecting changes in the very attitude towards planning - a shift from experience based to information based planning. As part of the DPEP many studies were initiated in all the districts.

In general the studies pertained to the areas of :

(i) assessing learner achievement and its determinants;

ii) assessing teacher motivation and competencies;

iii) gender issues;

iv) issue specific to the tribals,

v) issues pertaining to production and distribution of textbooks; and

vi) studies on state finances. These studies helped in deriving local specific intervention strategies.

Initiating the Planning Process

The planning process envisaged under DPEP has broadly two dimensions: (i) professional and technical; and (ii) participatory. The effort under the DPEP is to professionalise local level planning in a participatory mode. The professional and technical dimensions pertain to the actual drawing up of plans which involves assessing the present situation, assessing the tasks involved, elaborating the strategies and programmes and costing of the plan. The organizational arrangement to professionalise planning exercise was through (i) support from National Core Groups; (ii) support from state and district level resource organizations; (iii) plan preparation by DPEP Planning Core Groups both at the state and district levels.

In the normal planning process district plans are seen as a process of regionalisation of national and state plans and the effort at the district levels is essentially to work out the implementation implications of the state plans. In this framework first the state plans are prepared and then district plans are formulated. To facilitate decentralised planning, this process has been reversed under the DPEP. Under the DPEP, the district plans, based on the guidelines, are prepared first and the state plans component plan is drawn out only after the district plans are complete. In fact the state plans are nothing more than the intervention strategies to facilitate implementation of district plans (Varghese: 1944b). In fact this strategy has worked very well to shift the location of planning process to the district level and to strengthen the district planning groups to initiate district specific intervention strategies.

Other dimension of the DPEP planning exercises is the emphasis laid on the participatory process of planning. The very fact that the local people are preparing plans ensured better participatory process. Participatory process meant : (i) participation by other departments to ensure convergence of services at the micro-level; (ii) participation by elected representatives of the local bodies like Zilla Parishads and

Panchayats; (iii) participation by academic and resource organizations to provide technical and professional input to the plan preparation process; (iv) participation by educational functionaries at all levels in primary school headmasters and teachers; and (v) participation by general public including parents. As can be seen from the table below there was fair amount of participation that took place in the plan preparation process. As per the information available there were around 1016 meetings held where more than 72000 people participated in the six DPEP states accounting for 23 districts covered under the DPEP. The number of meetings to be organised, the process of organising these meetings etc. are decisions taken at the state and district levels. Hence, there are variations between states and between districts within states in terms of participation in the planning process. Perhaps variations between districts within a state are larger. In fact each district developed its own plan for participatory process.

Participation Meetings

	No. of Meetings			*No. of Participants*		
	State level	*District level*	*Sub district*	*State level level*	*District level*	*Sub district*
Assam	5	26	242	120	379	16815
Haryana	14	13	127	109	160	2480
Karnataka	11	33	60	440	911	4114
Kerala	4	17	59	108	109*	889*
Maharashtra	5	50	245	20	429*	32481*
Tamil Nadu	10	20	73	400	562	2935
Grand Total	49	161	806	1197	11492	59527

*Note : *Information on all districts are not available .*
Source : World Bank (1994)

Developing Planning Competencies

DPEP envisages to build capacity in planning and management of primary education in the country. Capacity building exercise that took place under DPEP can be broadly categorised into five areas: (i) planning; (ii) research; (iii) improvement in pedagogical skills; (iv) programme management; and (v) monitoring. The district planning process itself was an exercise in capacity building. As noted earlier, modes of capacity building were meetings, workshops/training programmes and learning by doing. The national resource organisations played an important but a faciliating role in the initial stages. With the plan preparation process completed in the districts selected in the first phase of the programme, consider able amount of capacity is already created at the local level. The effort needs to be to consolidate the capacity already created by institutionalising it. The efforts to set up institutes or departments like State Institutes Educational Management and training may help institutionalising the process of capacity building in planning.

Improving pedagogical skills and teacher competency is another area of concern directly related to the improvement of levels of learning amount primary school children. Institutional mechanisms like the SCERTs and DIETs may be sufficient to provide pre-service training of teachers. Since the existing institutional arrangements are not sufficient enough to provide in-service training on a regular basis, the DPEP envisages to create new arrangements like Block Resources Centres. The major concern is to improve the frequency and quality of in-service teacher training..

India has a wide network of educational and social science research organisation. However, the extent of search done in the area of primary education is not very large. Therefore, the effort under DPEP is to bring together researchers and to encourage them to undertake research in the area of primary education. The effort is to bring together the existing research capacities which is now located in different individuals and institutions so as to create a critical mass in research in primary education.

Indian plans are criticised for its bad implementation. it is often pointed out that these plans reflect desirability than feasibility. To facilitate faster implementation of the programme a separate society is envisaged under the DPEP. The society ensures local flexibility, quick flow of funds, wider representation and local decision making. It is envisaged that the societies will establish better linkages with the departments so as to transfer efficiency of programme implementation to the primary education scene as a whole.

One of the areas where capacity needs to be created is the area of programme supervision. DPEP envisages to develop domestic capacity to monitor and supervise educational programmes. For this purpose, a plan is developed and one of the national level Institutes has take up the responsibility of organising regular programmes to develop supervisory capacity.

Lessons from the DPEP Experience

DPEP is at varying levels of implementation in various districts. In 42 districts, the plans are apprised and approved and are in the process of implementation. In another 10 districts, the plans are being finalised and in another 12 districts plan preparation is still in the initial stages. Therefore, it is too early to make an overall assessment of the programme. However, our experience in the initial stages give adequate scope for speculating on the process of decentralisation of educational planning process initiated under the DPEP.

The first and foremost difficulty in decentralising planning process is to clearly understand the programme at various decision making levels. Some view DPEP as yet another centrally sponsored scheme whereas other view it as a totally new and different programme. Some see it totally in a project mode while others see it in a planning mode. Therefore establishing communication network to ensure that the programme that is planned is exactly in line with the programme that is visualised is a major task. The mode of communication is either through circulars or meetings. Meetings are found to be more effective mechanisms to understand the programme. However, frequent change of personnel at the state and district level is a major hurdle in facilitating the communication process especially through the mode of meetings.

Planning process involved participation of people outside the education department. However, implementation is visualised as mainly the responsibility of education departments through creation of new structures like State Implementation Societies and district project implementation offices. Very often than not, these societies are headed by people who were not actively involved with the programme at the planning stage. Therefore, there is a need for continuous orientation and interaction with the personnel in the implementation process which is not an easy task. It may be true that the new officers indirectly help increasing the role of central government in decision making process.

What is the role of central and state government in facilitating decentralised planning? DPEP experience has shown that an active involvement of the centre is perhaps unavoidable in the initial stages primarily due to its role in facilitating planning process. Perhaps, there is need for a reduced involvement of the centre in the planning process in the coming years to promote local initiatives and decentralisation. This can be done only through strengthening planning capacities at the state and district levels. Therefore, the major issue is when and how to plain for the withdrawal of agencies external to the districts involved in the decentralised planning process. One of the major difficulties in facilitating decentralised planning is that the local authorities look for a blue print directive and frame work from the centre to prepare plans. Perhaps, people are more used to prepare plans under strict directives than under broad guidelines. This change from a regime of 'directives' to 'guidelines' to prepare plans is a major change which has positive implications to promote local initiatives. It may take a longer time duration to make the planners socialised to this process of planning. The withdrawal of involvement and initiate by the centre becomes a necessary condition but it can be done only in a gradual way.

Preparation of plans, the articipation process and studies are visualised as an integrated process at the national level. However, in the process of implementation these three dimensions remained as three distinct and parallel activities at the state and district levels. Even today, the mechanisms of feedback to integrate the results of the participatory meetings and studies into the plan remain weak. In the absence of such mechanisms, participation was more in the form of sensitisation and studies remained as something that is added on to the programme. Perhaps, there is a fear that the initiative and control by the education department may be reduced if the programme is more research based and participatory. The inbuilt mechanisms in the system do not encourage or promote research and participatory. The in built mechanisms in the system do not encourage or promote research and participatory process. Therefore, to make planning process more realistic needs a sensitisation of the higher level policy makers and competency building at all levels.

Capacity building under DPEP has some obvious limitations. The time limit provided was limiting factor to facilitate capacity building. At national, state and districts levels, availability of persons rather than competency of the persons was the major consideration to be involved with the programme. In many states the members of the group were identified without due consideration regarding the competencies required.

Consequently, there were changes in the core groups when the planning process on. With every change in the personnel, the programme had a slow progress. Even in training programmes which were conceived sequentially to facilitate advance level trainings, many participants were new and hence, the efforts were not very satisfactory. With all these limitations, the decision to prepare plans only at the districts level has contributed to capacity building. The very fact that the states and districts are not relying on national resource organisations to prepare their annual plans is a positive indication of capacity building, that has taken place. Therefore, the argument is not that capacity building has not taken place at the district level.

What is argued on the other hand is that there is considerable scope for improving the process further.

Planning is seen as a 'one-shot' affair at the local level. The immediate purpose in the first phase was to prepare the plans. Once that exercise is over, there are no serious efforts to make it a regular feature by consolidating the efforts made in the first phase. There is a lack of organisational mechanisms to institutionalise the capacity that is created. In many areas especially in the area of research, capacity building was mostly in the form of encouraging researchers to promote research in primary education. In the second phase of the programme efforts are being made to broad base research capacity in different institutions or individuals located in different places. But the limitation of this approach in a country like India is apparent in the absence of institutional mechanisms to bring them together.

The process of implementation has shown up a variety of issues. Till now many believed that financial resource is the major constraint to universalise primary education in India. However, now it is increasingly realised that the system deficiencies are considerable and are a major constraint in achieving the targets. many districts realise that they are not in a position to absorb the amount allocated. Since the expenditure pattern has to be corresponding to the plans and activities envisaged, many districts feel the need for improving plans even after the planning exercise is over. With the restrictions imposed on civil works, utilising the budgets involve a considerable amount of preparatory work at the district level. Very often than not such preparatory work is not adequately done at the state and district levels. In other words, the process under DPEP has shown the areas of decision making which constraints the process of decentralisation. The time lags in implementation of various activities arise partly because of the delay in the decision making process which is a reflection of the inefficiency of the system of general administration. How can DPEP improve efficiency and effectiveness of these delivery mechanisms in primary education continues to be a major question. To put it differently, will it be possible to decentralise any one sector when the structure of planning, decision making and general administration still remain largely centralised. Although creation of societies may provide a temporary solution, it may not solve the problem altogether.

Another concern from a more broader angle is with regard to the effect of DPEP in achieving EFA. A not so positive pattern that is emerging in many DPEP states is that EFA is equated with DPEP and all efforts are getting diverted to the implementation of DPEP. The project districts are limited in number and it does not account for a major part in any DPEP state. Therefore, focused attention to DPEP districts adversely affects the achievement of EFA goals in non-DPEP districts. It is quite probable to conceive of a situation whereby DPEP is successfully implemented but the country still remains far from achieving the goal of UPE. In other words, DPEP is initiated to achieve the target of universal primary education. But it can become a major constraint in achieving UPE unless concerned efforts are continued to promote primary education in non-DPEP district. What is argued is that if DPEP provides professional and technical resource support to primary education, similar efforts are required in the non DPEP districts to ensure that the DPEP efforts do not distort the overall primary education scene in the country. The efforts to extend the programme to new districts may not be an answer to this problem. The solution lies in ensuring that universalising primary education in the DPEP districts will not be at the cost of universalising primary education in other districts.

Source: DPEP Calling, November, 1995.

6

Let Not the Dead Seize the Living: The DPEP Saga

—*Dr. R.V. Vaidyanatha Ayyar*

Dept. of Education, MHRD, Govt. of India, New Delhi

The implementation of District Primary Education Programme (DPEP) began in November 1994. This, therefore, is an opportune moment for introspection: to reflect on how DPEP began, where it has reached and where it is going.

Nobert Wiener put forth the thesis that there are four important elements in the process of technical innovations. Before a new idea can arise in theory or in practice, some persons must have introduced it in their own minds and this change must have come to be preserved in accessible records, thereby causing a change in intellectual climate; the second element is the existence of proper techniques in the absence of which an idea, much like the many precocious visualizations of Leonardo da Vine (e.g., the submarine), remains trapped in the realm of abstraction; the third, an environment which makes it possible, to paraphrase Plato, for philosophers to become artisans and for artisans to be philosophers, and, finally, an economic climate which provides the werewithal to produce and distribute the product in large volume. The genesis of DPEP neatly fits in the Wiener Scheme.

The Main Unit of Planning : A Much Debated Point

The question of what should the main unit of planning has been much debated in India and like much else in public policy the debates is an unending argument. Education has been no exception. In 1977, nine states which accounted for seventy-five percent of out-of-school children were identified as educationally backward and targeted for focussed attention. In practice, this mean priority to the nine states by the Government of India in the National Adult Literacy Programme and in the rather modest Non-Formal Education (NFE), and a sympathetic consideration by the Planning Commission of plan proposals of these states to expand access with their resources. All the same, this prioritisation came to be questioned by states which were left out by the classification as well as by academics, particularly votaries of district and block level planning. In the light of Natinonal Policy on Education (NPE), 1986, the question of prioritisation came to the fore and was considered in 1989 by the Working Group on Early Childhood Education and Elementary Education set up for the Eight Five Year Plan. The group was willing, but not quite to concede the argument for district-based classification. Based on a statistical analysis of literacy and enrolment data by districts, it came to the conclusion that the state-based classification continues to be valid; however, backward districts in other states could be considered for focussed attention without detriment to the hundred most backward districts, all but two of which were in the educationally backward states.

Intellectual Leap to District-Based Projects

The intellectual leap to district-based projects was effected during the period 1990-91. The stimuli were provided by the successful emergence of the district-based Total Literacy Campaign (TLC) model and by the need to translate the vision of the Bihar Education Project (BEP) document into action plans. The Department's Eighth Five Year Plan proposals, first formulated in September 1990, do not mention district planning at all; however, the subsequent proposals of November 1991 have an elaborate exposition of district projects. The 1991 document visualized that by 1993-94 state plans would become a compilation of district plans. The document classified districts into four categories, each with a distinct strategy. These categories were (i) high literacy districts, (ii) total literacy campaign districts, (iii) low literacy districts; and (iv) externally assisted project districts. The strategy in the high literacy districts, aimed at reaching Universalisation of Primary Education (UPE) will mainly be a matter of mopping up the remaining unenrolled children, improving educational management to ensure better coordination, improved supervision and effective monitoring of existing schemes. In Total Literacy Campaign districts, the strategy lay in taking advantage of the community mobilization for activities that can function in the campaign mode. These activities included house-to-house survey of out-of-school children and their enrolment, provision of teacher motivation through block-wise camps and regular meeting at school complex or at cluster levels, organisation of group activities in schools to enhance community-school interaction and enlivening the school atmosphere, provision of NFE programmes for school drop-outs and working children, and holding of regular community-teacher meeting to find community solutions to school/NFE problems and to exercise moral authority over the school. About 250 districts were targetted for coverage in this category. The document's prescription for low literacy districts was measures for access and participation and a focus on participation of rural and tribal girls. The document hoped that the externally assisted districts will be able to plan for Universalisation of Elementary Education (UEE) in a more ambitious manner and to provide the lead and the model for formulation and implementation of district plans.

Soon after the preparation of the Eight Five Year Plan proposals in September 1991, the concept of district planning was field tested in Bihar Education Project (BEP). In Sitamarhi district intense participative planning exercise was undertaken during November 1991-May 1992. The concept of district planning as set out in the Department's 1991 Eight Plan document was incorporated in paragraph 7.4.6 of the Programme of Action (POA), 1992. It is this paragraph that DEPE seeks to operationalize.

District Planning Becomes Official Policy
Programme of Action 1992

"Further efforts would be made to develop district specific projects, with specific activities, clearly defined responsibilities, definite time-schedule and specific targets. Each district project will be prepared within the major strategy framework and will be tailored to the specific needs and possibilities in the district. Apart from effective UEE, the goals of each project will include the reduction of existing disparities in educational access, the provision of alternative system of comparable standards to the disadvantaged groups, a substantial improvement in the quality of schooling facilities, obtaining a genuine community involvement in the running of schools, and building up local level capacity to ensure effective decentralization of educational planning. This is to say, the overall goal of the project would be reconstruction of primary education as a whole in selected districts instead of a piecemeal implementation of schemes. An integrated approach is more likely to achieve synergy's among different programme components."

Comming to the second element of the Wiener Scheme, India, unlike many other developing countries, has the ncessary technical resources for initiating the planning process. National Institute of Educational Planning and Administration (NIEPA) had a tradition of training educational functionaries in various aspects of educational planning. However, in the absence of any scheme for area-based development of education, philosophers remained philosophers and artisans. The NPE 1986, provided an impetus to work in areas like micro-planning, computerized Management Information System for Primary Education (COPE), the National Curricular Framework, Minimum Levels of Learning (MLL) and survey of Learner Achievement. From a technical point of view, the challenge to operationalisation of the idea of district projects essentially lay in logistics, in working against entropy and pooling the resources that lie dispersed among different resource institutions like National Council of Educational Research and Training (NCERT) and its affiliates, NIEPA, universities, management and social science research institutions and Non-Governmental Organisations (NGOs) and in deepening and widening the project management skills, particularly in the states and districts.

In his classic study of the world education system Philip Coombs makes the vital point that while financial resources would not solve all the problems of education, without resources reform would remain an empty rhetoric. The Department's Eighth Five Year Plan document did not propose any sepcific provisions for district projects. In districts not covered by externally aided projects, the district projects were expected to be financed through the ongoing schemes. Given the overall resource constraint and given the need to briskly complete the schemes started after NPE, 1986, it is very likely that, but for the window of opportunity opened by the Social Safety Net Credit in July, 1992 the idea of district projects could not have been tried on a sufficient scale during the Eight Plan. Chance, Louis Pasteur said, favours the prepared mind. The opportunity provided by the Social Safety Net operations would not have been availed of but for the fact that by then there had been considerable churning of the idea of district planning and that the policy frame for availing of external resources for primary education and the broad principles of managing basic education projects were in place. One sometimes comes across the view that the decision to avail of external financing of primary eduation was precipitate; reality is far from it; there was considerable deliberation within the Government on the whole question and the policy evolved over four to five years in response of the offers by different external agencies to finance primary education.

Since 1987, the World Bank was keen to finance primary education. In 1989, Overseas Development Agency (ODA) decided to scale up the pilot project the Andhra Pradesh Primary Education Programme (APPEP), so as to cover all the primary schools in that state with an outlay of 32 million pounds. In 1990, UNICEF expressed its willingness to finance an Education for All(EFA) project in Bihar, in 1991 Swedish Internatinal Development Agency (SIDA) expressed a similar willingness in respect of Rajasthan (Lok Jumbish), and European Community in Madhya Pradesh. The World Bank along with UNICEF, UNDP, UNESCO sponsored the World Conference on EFA held in Jomtien in 1990; it is noteworthy that the Secretary General of the Conference was a World Bank official, Mr. Wadi Hadad. Following the reassuring role played by the Bank in Jomtien, it was decided to pose a test case project for IDA assistance covering ten districts of Uttar Pradesh (UP). The parameters for this assistance were developed in a Seminar organised by NIEPA in November 1990. These parameters were adopted by the Central Board of Advisory Education (CABE) at its 46th meeting held on March 6-8, 1991. The primary concern of these parameters was to avoid a dependency syndrome.

CABE Parameters for External Assistance in Education

The Group takes note of the attempt of the Department of Education, Government of India, to tap external funds in the field of basic education from bilateral sources as well as multilateral agencies. While endorsing this effort, the Group is of the view that external funding should be an additionality to the resources for education, that the projects must be in total conformity with national policies, strategies and programmes, that the project formulation should be a process of capacity building, that the project must be drawn up on innovative lines, emphasizing people' s participation, improvement of quality and equality of education and a substantial upgradation of facilities. The Group notes that in the implementation of the externally aided projects, the State Governements are handicapped by the stipulation requiring the States to first incur expenditure from their own resources and claim reimbursement subsequently. The Group would recommend a specially earmarked ways and means advance to the States for the implementation of the externally aided projects including the World Bank assisted Technician Education Programme. Further, the outlay on externally aided projects should be an additionality to the State Plan in the Education Sector.

The CABE parameters along with the principle of contextuality, taken from the Department's Eight Plan proposals, constitute the basic building blocks of DPEP. They have been guiding the implementation of DPEP in all its aspects, financing, planning, management, implementation and capacity building. DPEP is the first externally financed project to have built in the additionality principle in its guidelines. The salience of the additionality principle lies in that it seeks to ensure that external financing does not replace the resources provided to education by the State Government, as happened with APPEP during the first few years of the project. A "conditionality" of DPEP is that the 1991-92 plan outlay on elementary education should be maintained in real terms.

A Major Lesson Incorporated

Further, by 1992, there was considerable learning experience with project planning and management. Experience with the first generation projects like APPEP, BEP and UP Basic Education Project (UPBEP) provided a broad sense of what could be and needs to be done and, more significantly, of what are the blind alleys and booby traps. A major lesson that was incorporated in the design of DPEP was the necessity to implement the programme through State Societies. The departmental mode of implementation is beset by an acute sclerosis that blocks free flow of finances to the project and insulates the project from other stakeholders in primary education. It was in BEP that the society model was introduced and very soon its potential efficacy was demonstrated; it was later extended to Lok Jumbish and UP Basic Education Project. It took quite a while and a great deal of persuasion to convince the UP Government and the World Bank of the society model. Doubts about the society model lingered on even after IDA credit to UP Project was approved. The reservation mainly centred on the accountability of the states in an arrangement in which IDA funds flow from the Government of India (GOI) to the State Societies. During the appraisal of DPEP, a visit to BEP convinced the Bank functionaries that the society model can be operated without in any way detracting from the accountability of the state government. As a matter of abundant caution it was agreed that states as well as State Societies would be parties to the project agreement.

Separately the society mode came in for criticism from some who rightly assailed the practice of seeking to protect projects from the hostile environment by sequestering project implementation structure from the main Education Ministry.

The criticism though valid went awry when it was dogmatically asserted that projects should be implemented directly by the Education Ministry and any other alternative was the use of the "back door". The problem is more complex and not amenable to an 'either/or' solution. All that the society structure does is to follow the strategy of DPEP, a beach-head to over-haul the system. The basic dilemma is this : the education departments are in such a state of disorder and so engrossed with a plethora of routine tasks that they cannot straightaway perform the new tasks of education; the other extreme of requested project structures creates enclaves which are reclaimed by the wild environment at the end of the project. The society model seems to resolve this dilemma by creating a parastatal organization embedded in the department but functioning autonomously, separated from the department not by a Great Chinese Wall but by a permeable membrane which facilitates osmosis of the good practices and thereby transformation of the department itself. An analogy is the recent practice of 'intrapreneurship' whereby firms set up autonomous units within the organization, let the Enterprise successfully develop and later hive off the 'interprise' as a separate unit or alternatively, integrate it into the corporate structure. The metaphors that come to mind are the lotus in the pond separate but deriving its sustenance from the pond and at the same time cleansing the water in the pond, or more surrealistically "an island engulfing the surrounding ocean". Another question that cropped up during the consideration of the society model is the post project scenario: Would the society merge with the department or retain its entity. Pragmatism prevalied; with intrapreneurship it makes sense to cross the bridge when one reaches it. All that the society structure does is to follow the strategy of DPEP being a beach-head to over-haul the system. However, it cannot be emphasized enough that the societies-department interface is complex and subtle. Unless the dialectical interplay between the society and the department is delicately managed the society structure may tend to function in isolation initially as in BEP or be reduced to an appendage of the department without an identity as initially in UPBEP and later in DPEP, Haryana. Either way the objectives underlying the programme strategy and structure would be defeated.

Learning Experience of the First General Projects

To come back to the learning experience of the first general projects, adult education originally envisaged to be a programme component of BEP and UPBEP. A year's experience with BEP had established the merit of organizing adult education exclusively through structures and funding mechanisms, instituted by the National Literacy Mission Authority, and of fostering linkages between TLCs so organised in BEP. This experience was built in LJ, UPBEP and DPEP. Experience with BEP also established the need to moderate expectations arising from the anticipated flow of substantial financial resources, to temper enthusiasm by systematic planning and rigorous procedure, and to balance process orientation with concern for outcomes through devices such as baseline studies, developing and monitoring performance indicators and institutional mechanisms for non-impressionistic and independent evaluation. The move away from the conventional rigid schematic pattern of the centrally sponsored scheme began with BEP; the ceiling of 24 per cent on civil construction and 6 per cent on administrative overheads was laid down in BEP. However, during the course of implementation, it was found necessary to develop a set of financial parameters which balanced flexibility, parsimony and cost-effectiveness.

BEP had also demonstrated the need to insulate the day-to-day management of the project from external agencies; it is significant that Lok Jumbish docsnot have SIDA representation. APPEP as well as BEP demonstrated the criticality of systematically planning for capacity building. All in all, when on July 3, 1992 the Departmetn of Education received the surprise offer of Social Safety Net Adjustment Credit the moment in time had arrived for district project descent from the realm of ideas to the world of praxis.

"What science can there be a matter in which, as in all practical matters, nothing can be defined and everything depends on innumerable conditions the significance of which is determined at a particular moment which arises no one knows when?"

—Tolstoy, *'War and Peace' Book IX, Chapter XI*

"Seen from six thousand feet above her, the tiny ship seemed to gain a little on almost every track and slowly pass one marked reef or buoyed mud flat after another. But from the deck it was not easty to discern the progress, every time the ship came about there seemed to be hesitation and contradiction, so that she would hang in the wind with sails flapping before she came around and filled on the new track. It looked from close quarters as though the captain and the crew were thoroughly confused about the whole affair".

—Philip Mason, *The Men Who Ruled India.*

The first meeting with State Education Secretaries held on January 19, 1993 initiated the planning process in the First Six States of Assam, Haryana, Karnataka, Kerala, Maharashtra and Tamil Nadu. The period from July 3, 1992 to January 19, 1993 was devoted to developing and negotiating with IDA the parameters for SSN credit. Within ten days of screndipitous offer of SSN credit, the department was ready with a package to develop an improved version of the Sitamarhi plans in low literacy of the Sitamarhi plans in low literacy and successful TLC districts. Right at the very beginning of the dialogue, the World Bank reiterated its willingness to work with the CABE parameters, akcnowledged that the NPE, 1986 provided a robut and comprehensive policy frame, and accepted the strategy of district planning. There was ready acceptance of the low female literacy criterion; the second criterion called for some persuasion. The acceptance of the second criterion enabled coverage of states like Kerala where quality and achievement were the main challenges to the Universalisation of Elementary Education and which had a grievance that national policies and programmes penalized states which invested in education and which were successful in achieving near-universal participation.

The Sitamarhi experience also influenced the decision to concentrate on the primary stage (classes I-V). The other considerations underlying this choice were a desire for realistic prioritization, the keenness to reinforce the additionality principle and give a go by to the, much-reviled but hardy perennial, 'brick and mortar' approach to education. This approach has been so well described by the Vice-President Mr. K. R. Narayanan in a 1992 symposium:

"Something that Nehru said about the village school still rings in my ears very clearly. He attacked the entire system adopted for spreading primary education. He said that we have a 'brick and mortar' approach to primary education. When we give funds, the first thing the State Governments do is to ask the Public Works Department to build schools. Why not have a little shed where to put instruments or to provide shelter, and teach under the mango tree? Then we pay the teachers who fashion the future generations to become 'chaprasis'. Like Nehru, we are crying in a wilderness in a louder way today because the building is more important than the people who study, learn and work there. That approach continues in our system."

The DPEP process is as much as process of learning as of unlearning, a painful process of catharsis, of exercising deeply held fixations about education and externally financed projects. It takes quite a while and a great deal of trauma to register that DPEP is not like other IDA projects in fields as diverse as power and sanitation, that the ceiling on investment of Rs. 40 crore is not an entitlement, that there is more to education than opening of schools and appointment of staff and that planning of DPEP is not drawing of wish lists to match the putative allocation of 40 crore rupees per district. The essence of DPEP is holism, of simultaneously addressing issues of non-enrolment drop out, quality and learner achievement. MLLs having been laid down only for the primary stage and MLL based pedagogic interventions having been initiated on a pilot scale only in 1991, DPEP could not have addressed the upper primary stage except through the conventional way. Better that the scarce resources be targetted on the primary stage leaving it to the states to address the access issue at the upper primary stage in the true spirit of additionality.

However, the DPEP guidelines do provide for the quality and achievement issues of upper primary stage to be addressed at an appropriate time.

To everyone connected with DPEP, the embryonic DPEP Bureau and the states and districts, the defining characteristics of the turbulent period from January 1993 to March 1994 (when the appraisal process was completed in the First Six) were discovery, learning, excitement, tension and trauma. To develop a complex process intensive project like DPEP in one state, with no more than rudimentary concepts to fall back, was difficult enough but to simultaneously attempt to develop district projects in six states, soon to increase to seven with the heavy addition of Madhya Pradesh, was foolhardy and dare devilry. One can understand the scepticism of quite a few at the ability of the DPEP Bureau to deliver what it brashly promised to develop in time - a new genre of project that passed muster along with all the studies necessary to provide the analytical underpinning and that too in a prickly self-reliant mode.

The odds that states faced were very heavy. I have already outlined the trauma associated with the unlearning process. The capacity for project formulation was very limited and that for a process project like DPEP, with its simultaneous and equal emphasis on participation and professional rigour, much more limited. The schedules were exacting and so were the expectations from the process. Amorphous concepts like participation had to be given meaning and coherence, and their mutual inconsistencies reconciled. The field functionaries were beset with many dilemmas. One such dilemma was posed by the participative process; consultative process, if not to be a more tokenism, necessitates close association of the communities in the planning process. Balanced exercise of power and responsibility is a time consuming learning process, the only way to learn is through involvement; in the initial stages of the learning process consultations with communities may yield wish lists or arouse unrealizable expectations. To identify local needs and work out cost-effective, sustainable and replicable solutions was difficult enough but to evolve them through a participative process in the limited time available taxed the ingenuity and daunted the spirit of the field functionaries. In her article published in the July issue of DPEP Calling, Amita Sharma tries to explain how in Madhya Pradesh they attempted to cope with this basic dilemma.

The Search for Alternatives

While it was easy to decry the brick and mortar orientation the search for alternatives was painful and taxing. The hastily assembled National Core Group provided invaluable support in individual functional areas but what the field functionaries were looking for was a blue print which could be replicated. Such a blue print, apart from being just non-existent, was incongruent with the idea of a contextual process project which expected the district plans to reflect the variations among districts and to be home grown. To many field functionaries the DPEP Bureau appeared to be issuing diktats of what is verboten, detailing what not to do but not what to do. To argue in reply for models that "Bengalis should develop Bengali solutions to Bengali problems" is sparkling wit but poor solace and plain insouciance. It was not a surprise to come across a few learned critics who scoffed at the banality of the planning process in the field. Given the poor capacity and given the initial stages of internalizing the DPEP, they were not wholly off the mark but where they were amiss was their failure in recognizing that the administrative system is resilient enough to cope with a crisis, that there can be no learning except by doing and that was being witnessed was the initial stages of a learning process. No child learns to walk without faltering and stumbling.

And then there was the very vexatious task of coping with the inevitable dilemmas of a process project to be financed by a Bank. By its very nature, a process project entails a process of exploration which excludes *ab initio* definitive detailing, but yet without sufficient detailing it is not possible to secure an investment approval. And to cap it all in the eyes of the field functionaries, the rules of the game appeared to be different and, worse, all the time changing. DPEP is not like a typical Bank project, not merely in programme design but in its organization. The states are accustomed to GOI being a conduit for external finances, to GOI line departments being friendly facilitators helping the states to access external finances and to soften and cope with the tough demands of the Missions of external agencies. But they were in for a shock with the new role of a GOI line department, a role necessitated by the CABE parameters to depart from the conventional "donor" driven projects. What was put forth was national programmes with multiple sources of financing and a single credible and effective national mechanism for technical support, supervision, monitoring and evaluation. It is only this strategy that ensures autonomy of policy and programmes, ownership and capacity building that are central to the new development cooperation paradigm. It is to this end that the DPEP Bureau had to assume the role of a financing-cum-technical intermediary and take on functions hitherto performed by external agencies and their "Missions". But all the same the new role had the appearance of excessive centralization underlying DPEP. Wits were not wanting who called DPEP centralized decentralization.

Aggravating the tensions generated by the new role of the DPEP Bureau was the process of transforming the rudimentary concepts of DPEP into praxis. The financial and design parameters began to acquire concreteness and coherence only as the planning proceeded. The *DPEP Guidelines* were issued on April 16, 1993 and the financial parameters on April 27, 1994. However, the iterative development of the parameters imposed an element of uncertainty on an even otherwise arduous planning process. Field functionaries were baffled by what they perceived to be varying versions of, what grossly but perhaps accurately called, "what is permitted and what is not." While the DPEP Bureau had to do what it had to do, the angst and frustration of the field functionaries were genuine and understandable. The right perception of any matter and a misunderstanding of the same matter, as Kafka pointed out, do not wholly exclude each other.

Quantity beyond a point, according to Marx, becomes quality. The saying is an apt description of the transformation that took place after the addition of the 19 districts of Madhya Pradesh to the 23 of the First Six. It was on May 6, 1991, well before the whole idea of district projects was articulated in the Department's Eighth Plan document, that European Community (EC) evinced interest, in general terms, to fund a primary education project in Madhya Pradesh. Even as what seemed to be a never-ending dialogue with EC proceeded, attempts were afoot to cobble together a credible proposal covering 14 districts and bearing the picturesque name *Roopantar*. With UNESCO offering to locate additional external financing, similar work began in five districts for another project bearing an equally pictureque name of *Dhumkuria*. It turned out that UNESCO had only EC in mind and that EC procedures for approval of a project-specific grant were very exacting and time consuming. An unanticipated breakthrough happened, in October 1992 when EC decided to support primary education by way of programme assistance back-to-back with SSN Credit. Agreement was reached on the financing arrangements on July19, 1993; the intervening period of nine months was a period of exploration and probing, of understanding each others positions. The far-reaching financing agreement legalized the role of DPEP Bureau had to take on the legitimate task of coordinating with different agencies financing the programme and of devising a single mechanism for supervision, monitoring and evaluation. As per of the approval process of the financing agreement DPEP was labelled, in December 1993, as a Centrally Sponsored Scheme with the salience that unlike such schemes DPEP adopted a programmatic approach and did not lay down rigid schematic norms and that the entire central share was to be mobilized during the Eighth Plan from external sources. The EC financing agreement was programme support and as such legitimized the role of the DPEP Bureau in appraising the plans prepared by districts and states. The financing agreement specifically acknowledged that national capabilities existed in considerable measure. The financing agreement is also innovative in that it harmonized fast disbursal of foreign exchange, so necessary at that time, with the slow absorption of resources that characterizes the initial phases of a procéss project. An important lesson that emerged as the planning process proceeded in the First Six was that while the medium term Seven Year Plan provided perspectives, the actual operational tool would be the annual work plan in synch with the processes, ou0tcomes of the previous work plans and emerging tasks and needs. It was also decided that the first year of implementation would concentrate on placing the systems in place and setting the processes in motion. This strategy, a natural strategy for process projects, has implication for the "tradition of financing" which tends to equate progress with expenditure and disbursals. Be that as it may be, contrary to the wild fears of ideologues, there was no excess money in the field "carrying the risk of soaking the new Panchayat Raj, to its roots in corruption". But then you cannot argue with prejudice and believing is seeing.

Transitions are not smooth, more so if a policy regime changes. Madhya Pradesh is no exception; the planning process was consequently more turbulent than in the First Six. And then there was the problem of scale; given that it was only the nature of EC support that had changed the coverage of the programme could not be curtailed. But this meant the planning was not on a clean state, that one had to cope with the hangover of a mind-set associated with a state "top-down" project planning and of a perception that very little was left there to be done. It also meant that the logistical challenge was more intense. The situation was tense; even as the perceptions in the state had to be altered one had to cope with the criticism that an unduly large number of districts were chosen.

Here, again, the DPEP Bureau did what it had to do. Much of public policy and management is negotiations; a good negotiator should not crave to be liked "Waiting", counsels the Chinese Book of Prophecy," is the essential principle. All things are accomplished through waiting. Time is the vehicle. If we perseveringly maintain a correct attitude, the force of inner truth is able to work on the whole situation". The Indian system of goverance does indeed respond to a crisis; it is a tribute to the Madhya Pradesh system that it could put its act together and come out credibly. So much so, a new theory to explain the performance in M.P. is floating round: the DPEP should operate on a sufficient scale to elicit the proper response from the state Government.

A Historic Decision

One should ever expect the unexpected. It was expected that implementation would commence in July 1994 as soon as the planning process in the First Six for the Medium Term Plan was completed; however, implementation in 42 districts of the seven states could commence only in November 1994. The processing of innovative internal financing arrangements required time. Traditioally, with the exception of family planning, the terms on which external financing is passed on to the states depend on the source and terms of external financing. While grant money is passed on as grant, only 30 per cent of IDA loan is passed on as grant and the remaining 70 per cent as loan, repayable in 20 years with a moratorium of five years on 50 per cent of the loan and carrying an annual interest of 13 per cent. Even the IDA assistance for the rehabilitaticn of earthquake victims in Maharashtra was no exception. Being a centrally sponsored programme DPEP could not have differential terms for financing the activities in states and districts. Ultimately the government decided to equate primary education with family welfare and pass on all external finances including IDA loans as grant. This is a historic decision which was mentioned in the Finance Minister's Budget Speech in February, 1995. The belated start up, however, necessitated carry forward of the activities of 1994-95 into 1995-96.

People, observed Dostoevsky, only like to count their sorrows; they don't count their happiness. The nation as a whole and more particularly all those connected with the DPEP, in the government, in the resource institutions, in the DPEP Bureau, states and districts, can take pride in what has been accomplished against heavy odds. It is not anyone's case that the planning process is perfect; far from it; yet the idea of district planning has been shown, some hands-on experience with planning gained and an enabling frame with adequate resource base created to facilitate universalisation of primary education in all its dimensions.

A Multi-Financed National Programme

Rather than fatalistically bemoan *dependencia*, relations were established fully consistent with CABE parameters, which "acknowledged India's special capability" and which proceeded from "self-confidence, dignity and professional excellence". For the first time in the world a mechanism for joint supervision with equal partnership of the host country and the financing agencies has been set up. This does awaywith the practice of each agency having its own Missions, pre-appraisals and appraisals and its own monitoring and evaluation mechanisms. While the first Joint Supervison Mission in February, 1995 was led by the World Bank, the second in September, 1995 by EC, the third would be led by GOI. The DPEP has come to be recognized as a multi-financed rational programme; ODA had decided to support DPEP in five districts each of Andhra Pradesh and West Bengal taking note of the fact that Government of India has radically altered the planning of primary education projects and acknowledging that the DPEP guidelines provide a satisfactory basis. UNICEF in its bridge programme for 1996-98 has formally decided to mesh its educational programmes with DPEP. The planning process in 12 districts of Orissa, Himachal Pradesh and Gujarat has begun and is scheduled to begin in 40-50 districts of the seven states where the programme is under implementation. These are expected to be financed by a second IDA credit. It is likely that DPEP in Gujarat would be financed by the Dutch.

It is a matter of gratification that the entire planning process and conduct of studies were done with national expertiese; the wealth of information generated by the baseline assessment has been described as a national treasure. New methods of analyzing school effective factors such as HLM analysis have been utilized by NCERT and NIEPA and there is a better and more empirical understanding of school effectiveness. NCERT and NIEPA has played a stellar role in supporting the states; their experience had established the need for networking, for bringing together state, national and district resource institutions in the field of education, social sciences and management to build capacities for primary education reform. The institutional infrastructure for planning, action research and training is being expanded with the creation of institutions like the state counterparts of NIEPA, Block Resoure Centres and Cluster Centres. It looks as though in a few years school complexes as visualized by Kothari Commission would fall in place. The linkages envisaged with institutes of management and administrative training is slowly transforming the perception of education planning and management; it is increasingly being perceived as a part of the large public system, a perception which parallels the much sought-after convergence between education, school health, nutrition and child care. NIEPA is playing a lead role in this transformation. The transformation of Regional Colleges of Education into Regional Institutions and the new focus on primary education, together with increasing demand for pedagogic support has led to a resurgence of effort in the NCERT family in the areas of peadagogy and training.

Slowly, but surely, institutional structures are falling in place. The National Elementary Education Mission (NEEM) has been set up with DPEP as it core, the minuscule DPEP Bureau is a little more visible in terms of numbers; a youthful and vibrant technical support group has come to be and is being expanded up; the professional excellence of the national organization is already in evidence in the manner in which the planning process is being organised in the new states and linkages established with national experts and resource institutions in different areas such as research, evaluation, pedagogy, teacher training and educational planning and management. There is greater role clarity of the support group as a catalytic facilitator rather than provider. The MIS system is falling in place and being debugged, work of the evaluation frame has begun and there are reasons to believe that it would emerge as a world class model. In all the seven states, excepting Haryana, structures have come into being at the state level and in the districts; relationships have been established with all the key institutions and actors; financial and administration arrangements have been firmed up; there is great insight into the labyrinthine procurment procedures. What is particularly noteworthy is the increasing reliance on Village Education Committees and Mother/Parent Teacher Councils. Construction of classrooms is being organised through communities in Kerala, Assam, Madhya Pradesh; other states are also veering towards that mode of construction. Activities have been initiated in all states to improve instructional material and thinking has begun on reforming the content and process of education. Lastly, but not unimportantly, expenditure is looking up.

"Now this is not the end. It is not even the beginning of the end. But it is perhaps, the end of the beginning".

—Sir Winston Churchill

"Most companies, particularly in hightechnology, tend to rest on laurels and are passed by. We have got talented people; we just need to keep coming together to push the limits. I don't see any signs that we are not doing that, but I can come in very day to make sure that we do."

—William H. Gates III of Microsoft.

"We must learn to perceive what we don't know before we understand what we do".

—Discovering

What has been accomplished is a marvellous *tour de force* but history is replete with many examples where a battle has been won but the ward has been lost. Let there be no illusion that we have touched anything but the fringes of the complex that DPEP is set to solve. True enough the expectations of the second Joint Supervision Mission have been pitched high but what it has to say about the context and process is of great relevance and significance. Soft is hard and hard is soft, so goes the managment maxim. There is the perennial danger that at the end of the day nothing but the brick and mortar approach would prevail. There is need to collectively work, evolve and practice and praxis of improving the content and process of education. We have largely to rely on the inner strengths of our country, build on the past thinking, trials and innovations leavened by selective infusion of relevant comparative experience. In areas of identified need such as multi-grade teaching one should not hesitate to act on the sagacious observation of Rabindra Nath Tagore at the foundation of Viswabharti:

"Our problem is that we wish to remain isolated from the world in the prison of our own scholarship. It is not easy to free India from this spirit of isolation. We must build up a relationship with the world, to serve and be served, to give and to receive. We want to be one with the world's learning."

Programmes no less than individuals and nations cannot inhabit too long in their rarefied air of idealism. Marx came into conflict more than once with those whom he called the alchemists of revolution who felt that pure Will would surface as motive power and that the advent of revolution can be hastened by undertaking direct revolutionary actions. Rather than counting on heroes and heroic efforts a long and arduous process like DPEP calls for institutions building and institution rejuvenation. Heroes, though great personalities, are mortal individuals. The managment structures at all levels, national, state and district are still inadequate; strategic planning on the future of the national structure should commence. In the Ninth Plan more domestic resources are expected to be provided for elementary education as a result of the Prime Minsiter's announcement on the six per cent GDP norm; it is legitimate to expect that considerable domestic resources would flow into DPEP and over 300 districts, including all the low female literacy districts, would be covered. What are its implications for the national structure? Should it be hived off as an educational trust or bank? What would be the long term arrangements for technical support of the program? These need to be worked out and necessary approvals obtained. Rather than emerge as a leviathan it should emerge as a lean and effective organisations working with other organisations in a matrix network, promoting a variety of approaches and cross fertilization of ideas and experiences in a country which is the microcosm of the developing world. Similar exercise need to be carried out in states and districts.

While a beginning has been made to work with local communities, we are still far away from the task of grappling with the tasks of training and orienting the communities. Then there is the huge inert land mass of educational administration; it needs to be stirred up. The training strategies to improve the functionality of educational administration need to be worked out and implemented.

The first generation projects and DPEP have conclusively established in that there can be no academic renewal unless SCERTs are rejuvenated and DIETs operationalised. The essence of DPEP is holism, pooling all resources and implementing the extant central and state schemes and DPEP interventions together in a coordinated manner. It would be ironic if the quality of implementation is related to the sources of funding; in many states DIETs are not fully and properly supported, the faclities have not been established as envisaged and there are no plans for staff development. It appears as though the brick and mortar approach is engulfing the institutional innovation of DIET. Openness should be the cardinal principle of institutional reform. Instead of being inward-bound and inward-looking institutions should work in co-operation with other institutions and NGOs. Networking is still in the relam of ideas, concrete plans have to be drawn for networking. One should not minimize the organizational complexities or the intricacies of coalition or alliance building.

While thinking on academic aspects has begun, the enormity of the tasks cannot be minimized. We have not yet touched earnestly, except perhaps in Madhya Pradesh, alternatives to schooling; the nitty-gritty of gender and tribal education has to be detailed; the special needs of physically handicapped needs to be addressed. Now that NCERT has revised the MLLs, the pedagogic and teacher training tasks need to be addressed with dispatch and resolve.

The praxis of planning continues to be weak, while the impact of the learning experience on the planning in the three new states gives us hope, the need to document the learning experience and be in a position to advise the states what to do rather than what not to do is crucial. There should be greater rigour in the preparation of the annual work plans.

While much has been accomplished in the conduct and analysis of baseline achievement surveys, the methodologies, conduct of surveys and analysis need to be honed. The quality of the data so far collected is such that inter-state comparison cannot be robust. More importantly, there is need to develop a macro-analytic frame linking these surveys with classroom observations and equally important by extract and disseminatethe findings that have a bearing on quality and achievement to practioners. The connection between research and action is weak. While qualification is important, qualitative indicatiors and assessment are equally important.

The management of external finances is a sensitive area; bargains tend to obsolesce. Apart from vigilance, reversal of the knowledge asymmetry is paramount. To their country operations agencies bring in their rich experience in operating in different countries fortified by close interaction with other agencies. More often than not, for conducting the operations they have more qualified, dedicated staff than the receipient of finances. Countries which wish to ensure that resources are fungible, need to match the knowledge of the agencies. Apart from deep knowledge of the sector, we should continue to acquire a deep understanding of the operations, operational styles and mind-set of providers of finance, and the analytical capacity to weigh options and to make intelligent choices. Only then can we effectively continue to coordinate the activities of agencies.

To paraphrase the UNESCO Constitution, it is in the minds of men that failure begins and it is in the minds of men that safeguards against failure should be built. DPEP is as much psychological struggle with uncogenial mind sets of which the brick and mortar approach is only one.

One has to combat cynism in all its manifestations. There is the low brow cynicism exemplified by the witticism that teacher can be transferred but not transformed. One has to disregard wordly-wise men, the "voice of reason".

More pernicious is the high-brow cynicism which masquerades as idealism, which posits that nothing can change unless the total system changes. Totalism is often an elegant alibi for inaction, or worse the royal road to totalitarianism. There is some merit in attempting a change for the better in one's limited domian.

Inaction also springs from the lure of buzz words which abound in educational planning and management. Myron Weiner is not off the mark when he observed that "I was often struck by the fact that people in India often say the right things but little seems to get implemented.

The relationship between rhetoric and behaviour in India seems so different from in the West. Speaking of mantras, in the West we have the impression that Indians see mantras as potent, that if they say the right words often enough, they will change the world."

The meaning of buzz-words needs to be explored in specific contexts and translated into actionable plans. While doing so one has to remember that rationality is bounded, that perfectionism calls for "powers of pre-science and capacities resembling those which we usually attribute to God."

Basic to the praxis of process projects like DPEP is the belief in the virtues of incremental action as opposed to the comprehensive and definitive, but elusive choice. Incremental action in turn presupposes abandoning the deeprooted oral tradition and instead documenting the processes, willingness to evaluate action with an open-mind and without possessiveness and to institutionalise change, breaking with the deep-rooted generalist tradition of "before me the chaos and after me the deluge."

The praxis of DPEP calls for shunning the attitude of business as usual, of having done it all and of being ever right. Evolution is the law of nature. Even "God changes". "Today's achievement is only tomorrow's confusion" and "possessiveness cheapens the thing that was precious". The critical power of reflection, introspection, objective evaluation, tends to make an intellectual situation of which the creative power can profitably avail of... to make the best ideas prevail". Reform is change, creative destruction. To impede natural selection is to cohabit with death. "If the dead shall live, the living die." The dead, as the French say, seize the living (Le Mort Saist Le Vif), we should not let that happen.

Source: DPEP Calling, December 1995.

7

DPEP : The Logic and the Logistics

Dr. N.V. Varghese
Fellow, NIEPA, New Delhi

The PREMISE

From UEE to EFA

Universal Elementary Education (UEE) continues to be a Constitutional provision and national commitment in India. In the initial stages, the strategy was to achieve this goal by relying entirely on the formal system of education. Hence, the focus was to expand the formal schooling facilities and facilities within the schools.

From the seventies onwards, India moved towards a more realistic approach of diversifying the channels of delivery and alternatives to formal schooling were initiated. To start with, this marked the beginnings of nonformal education in India. In the late seventies, the government launched the Notional Adult Education Programme. By the eighties, an integrated approach to universalise education emerged which later got incorporated in the broader objective of Education For All (EFA). At present, EFA in India includes formal primary schools, alternatives to primary schools, pre-primary education and adult education. This change in perspective from UEE to EFA is in line with the changes taking place in the international scene. The Jomtien and Delhi declarations reiterate our commitment to EFA.

From Access to Achievement

India has made tremendous progress in expanding schooling facilities and in improving enrollments in the primary classes. However, the retention rates and achievement level of students continue to be stagnant at very low levels. Therefore, the attention is increasingly shifted from enrolment drives to strategies designed to improve retention and learner achievement.

The National Policy on Education and the Programme of action have underlined these very dimensions of educational development in India. Therefore, the focus seems to be shifting from equity in access to equity in achievement. This, in fact, takes into account the contextuality of educational development in India. There are many states and districts which have already achieved almost universal primary enrollment, and they need to focus on programmes to improve the retention rates and levels of learner achievement.

The idea of having uniform priorities universally applicable to all the situations need to be replaced by policies and programmes which are area specific. A more flexible approach to incorporate these dimensions is essential in this context.

Shift in Targetting

India started with the overall objective of expanding the primary education system. With the emergence of disparities in the process of development, the effort was to target the efforts. In the subsequent periods, our efforts were focussed on the backward regions, disadvantaged groups and girls in general. At the present level of development, it is realised that what is to be achieved is more difficult than what is already achieved.

Even in terms of access, the groups and regions left out at present are the most deprived. The traditional strategies may not succeed in bringing them to schools or to its alternatives. Identifying such groups and localities is in itself a difficult but unavoidable task. This necessitates disaggregated target setting and detailed micro-planning exercises. At present, district forms the lowest viable spatial unit for initiating and implementing decentralised planning in India.

Educational efforts at the district level are channelled through different agencies and departments. Although such differentiation may be an administrative convenience, it creates hurdles for the beneficiaries as well as difficulties in implementing the programmes and in assessing the achievements made.

Therefore, what is advocated is an integrated approach to develop education in any given district. It envisages a total coverage of the geographical area for any intervention strategies. In the given circumstances, the notion of targetting is concretised in terms of analysing and understanding the inter-district disparities as well as those within a district. One may visualise any district plan as a set of inter-related micro-planning exercise.

Experience from Externally Funded Projects

India has already implemented many externally funded projects at the primary level of education. Many of these projects have, however, focussed on a limited number of related dimensions than on any sector as a whole. We have gained rich experience in planning and managing such externally funded projects. The Bihar Education Project funded by UNICEF, Lok Jumbish project by SIDA, Andhra Pradesh Primary

Education Project by ODA, Shiksha Karmi project by SIDA and the Mahila Samakhya project by the Netherlands, are examples of such externally funded projects. The Uttar Pradesh Primary Education Project funded by the IDA, perhaps, takes into account many of the essential processes and dimensions of a district based educational plan.

The experiences drawn from planning and managing many of these projects have been very helpful in drawing district specific plans in India. The positive external funding possibilities provided yet another opportunity to experiment with district planning in education. Needless to add, the funding agencies with their rich experience in planning educational projects in other countries helped in developing similar programmes in India.

TLC Experience

The Total Literacy campaigns initiated by the end of the eighties and beginning of the nineties was one of the few exercises undertaken in India with total participation of the community in planning and managing an educational programme. The success of ILCs gives one hope and confidence about initiating such people-centered programmes in future. The experience drawn from planning and managing TLCs have become a valuable input in the process of conceptualising and preparing plans at the district level.

DPEP : *The Perspective*

The Objectives

The District Education Programme (DPEP) is a programme conceptualised and evolved on the basis of varied experiences the country possesses, and supplemented by the experiences of various international agencies directly involved in the funding of primary education projects in the developing countries. Over a period of time, the sources of funding got diversified and the approach to planning primary education and the DPEP became more specific, concerete and unified. However, the DPEP is not an effort to develop uniform plans. In fact, this goes against the very premise of the programme.

The DPEP considers that what is to be done at the district level needs to be decided at the district level itself. It is envisaged as a centrally sponsored scheme with flexible parameters (Department of Education, 1994). These parameters are meant to ensure that the plan is with the framework of national concerns and priorities.

The objectives of the programme are: (i) to provide all children access to primary education through formal primary schools or its equivalent through alternatives; (ii) to reduce overall drop out rate at the primary level to less than 10 percent; (iii) to increase achievement levels by 25 percentage points over and above the measured baseline levels; (iv) to reduce disparities of all types to less than 5 per cent. (Department of Education, 1993).

The focus of each plan may vary, depending upon the level of development of primary education in the selected district. In some districts, the priority may be more for access; in certain cases the focus may be on retention; and in still other cases, on achievement. Only a close scrutiny of the districts in a more disaggregated fashion can provide us a clue regarding the areas of emphasis.

The criteria to identify districts under the programme are : (i) educationally backward districts with female literacy below the national average: and (ii) districts where TLCs have been successful leading to enhanced demand for primary education (Department of Education, 1993). It is quite possible that these two categories of districts can be from the same state. The priorities and planning concerns may be different in these two category of the districts.

Planning from Below

The problematic of multi-level planning in general and district planning in particular lies in the satellite imagery view, i.e. looking at the people and their problems from above (Misra, 1991). The common practice of decentralised planning in India conforms to this pattern. The usual practice is of preparing plans for the district at the state level. The district plans are generally seen as a process of regionalisation of national and state plans. And the effort invariably is to work out the implementation implications of the state plan.

The DPEP is an attempt to initiate a process of planning from below. The framework of the programme envisages to initiate and complete the process of planning first at the district level. The state level intervention strategies and plans are meant to facilitate the successful implementation of the district plans.

It can be seen that looking at linkages between state and district plans in this framework changes the relative roles to be played by agencies at different levels. This process of planning ensures that state plans are not prepared unless and until the district plans are complete. And the state level plans are nothing but efforts to achieve district level targets.

Planning Competencies

One of the reasons for the failure of decentralised efforts to develop operational plans at the district level in India is the lack of planning competencies at the district level. The DPEP envisages that the planning responsibility be undertaken entirely by the people at the district level. This necessitates developing planning competencies at the district level.

The best way to develop competencies is to initiate planning exercise in realistic fashion. The planning methodologies are simplified and easily understandable by the people at the district level.

The national and state resource organisations help in developing planning competencies. This help is of two kinds: (i) in developing basic framework for planning education at the district level; and (ii) organising programmes to train the local level people. In the context of DPEP, the NIEPA developed a document detailing the methodology of district planning (Varghese, 1993) and organised as well as participated in several workshops. But it does not directly and actively intervene in the planning exercise. The experience in the last one year has shown that such competencies can be developed at the local level itself.

While the broad parameters are decided through a consultative process, the districts have the full freedom to fix targets, evolve strategies and schedule activities. In short the planning exercise takes into account local requirements and prioritises them, and thus it becomes an exercise in developing local level competencies in planning. Moreover, financial outlays are ensured to achieve the thus set targets.

The district plans under the DPEP envisage first to achieve the horizontal integration of the district level programmes and then to vertically integrate them with the state level and national level initiatives. This helps in ensuring local autonomy, competency and administrative capability. The process of capacity building is a part and parcel of the planning exercise.

The district plans are drawn for a period of 6 to 7 years with detailed schedules and activities for each year. The allocations are made each year based on the performance in the previous year and evaluation of the proposals for the coming year.

Participatory Process of Planning

The district level plans are developed by people who are the direct beneficiaries of the programme. This necessitates a consultative process to arrive at areas of convergence in order to set priorities. The consultative process under the DPEP is not confined to any committee approach. On the other hand, the emphasis is on consulting the public. The local level bodies like the Panchayats, parent teacher associations, teacher unions, Village Education Committees, and educational functionaries at the local level are to be consulted in order to evolve a plan that can be owned by the local people.

Participation in the planning process takes place at different levels. First, participation by the different departments involved with the delivery of educational and related services in a district. Second, participation by the people who have to own and operationalise the programme. This has taken place in a very successful fashion in many of the districts. The consultative process has indeed raised the expectation of people from the programme and created an urgency in implementing the programme.

The major thrust of the plans is not only to develop education but also to create conditions for initiating development efforts at the local level. The DPEP, in this sense, is an exercise in expanding the capabilities of people to enable them to take responsibilities of their own development within the broad contours drawn by the national and state priorities.

The necessary shift is from the sophisticated process of model building to a simple and down to earth expression of felt needs in a systematic way. This liberates the plans and planning process from the bureaucratic controls and technocratic approach. The TLC experience about the participatory process may be an asset to redefine the roles of different actors in the process.

The Logistics

Studies as the Basis to Evolve Strategies

Each district is expected to undertake and complete studies specific to the means which are to be emphasised in the plans. Such district studies help evolve strategies which are applicable in the specific context of the district. The problems of the district may vary. Some of them can be resolved at the district level while others require interventions at the state level.

Studies conducted by the district form the basis for evolving such intervention strategies. In the previous year all the DPEP districts have initiated several studies in the areas of learner achievement, teacher motivations, problems specific to deprived groups, textbooks and curriculum issues, gender issues and state finances. These studies have come out with number of intervention strategies to improve the efficiency of the system. The district plans are expected to incorporate these findings while detailing out the annual plans.

Planning and Classroom Practices

The DPEP envisages to link district plans with school processes and classroom practices. It is an effort to bring together the pedagogical necessities and broader educational concerns. The ultimate objective is to improve the school processes and outcomes.

To many a planner, the operational efficiency of the units (schools) is an assumption, and hence the action lies outside the classrooms. The conventional educational planner never enters the classrooms and the typical pedagogue never gets out of the classrooms. While the vision of the former is too wide and broad to be understood and appreciated by the pedagogue, the vision of the pedagogue is too narrow and myopic to be considered seriously by the planner. Resultantly, the planner is isolated from the action and the actions are isolated from the plans. To build bridge between them is difficult, if not impossible. The DPEP makes a serious effort to link these two sets of actors.

Improving classroom practices and school management, no doubt, is a condition *sine qua non* for the success of educational programmes. The programme envisages creation of local-specific favourable conditions to improve teacher competencies through frequent in service training programmes, and improvement in school management through training of educational functionaries in planning and management.

The efforts to strengthen state level resource organisations like SCERT and district level institutions like DIET, and to create new structures at block and cluster levels and management training institutions like SIEMT, create the favourable conditions.

External Funding : An Additionality

The success of planning and implementing the plans at the district level depends on the freedom to allocate and reallocate funds by the district level authorities. In India, very often, the funding decisions are made at higher levels and hence planning at the local level becomes an exercise in dovetailing the priorities set at the state level. The idea of untied funds is seldom effected in practice. The DPEP envisages to provide a lump sum amount at the disposal of the district to allocate as per the requirements detailed out in its plans. A maximum of Rs. 40 crores is envisaged for each district. The amount is to be seen as indicative, and the actual allocation depends on the type of programmes to be carried out in the district plans.

It is to be noted that the planning exercise is not oriented to draw an expenditure plan for the amount indicated. An indication of the extent of allocation provides an opportunity to the planners to draw the plan more realistically as well as encouragement and confidence that the amount will be available if plans are drawn logically and consistently.

One of the features of the DPEP is its funding source. substantial share of the funds are drawn from the external sources. And the funding sources are getting diversified over a period of time. It is a centrally sponsored scheme and hence the source of funding is less important for the districts. The more crucial points is a guarantee from the Union Government that the funds will be made available as and when needed as per the requirements projected in the district plans.

These funds are to be seen as additionalities and are not as substitutes for the existing programmes. In other words, it means that the DPEP funds are over and above the normal developmental expenditure the state and district would otherwise incur (Department of Education, 1994). This, in more concrete terms, means that:

(i) the DPEP may not fund any of the ongoing regular programmes which the state governments are supposed to fund in order to maintain the existing levels of efficiency of the system and

(ii) the state government is expected to maintain the budgetary provision for primary education at least at the 1991-92 level, in real terms.

This has considerable implications for planning. While the district plans are drawn to achieve the goals of universal primary education, the funds under the DPEP may not be sufficient to meet all the requirements. At the same time, the districts are supposed to achieve the plan targets. The gap between what is actually required and what is actually allocated by the programme is to be funded by the state. In this sense, the DPEP funding needs to be seen more as a mechanism to reduce the financial pressure on the district and state than as sufficient allocation to achieve the targets.

Other financial considerations clearly indicate the priorities within the primary education sector. The civil works cost is to be restricted to a maximum ceiling of 24 per cent and the management cost to a maximum limit of around per cent. Therefore, the districts are left with 70 per cent of the DPEP allocations to be devoted to their programmes of improving the educational system.

Management Structure

The DPEP envisages district management structures to facilitate better implementation of the programme, closely monitor the activities and facilitate a faster flow of funds. These structures are envisaged at the national, state and district levels (For details, see Department of Education, 1994). The focus of all these new structures is to facilitate implementation of district plans. In other words, the new structures are supportive to the district plans.

Developing a Management Information System (MIS) to collect information needed to monitor DPEP activities is an essential element in the programme. Similarly, the structure at the national level envisages to set up a programme evaluation and research unit to facilitate studies in the area of primary education. All these structures are supposed to get merged with the existing organisational arrangements by the end of the project period.

Externalities

In the first phase of the programme, it is to be implemented only in selected districts and that too in some of the states. Even in the selected states, all the districts are not covered under this programme. At present the programme covers 42 districts 19 districts of Madhya Pradesh, 5 of Maharashtra, 4 of Assam, Haryana and Karnataka each, and 3 districts of Kerala and Tamil Nadu each. The planning process is complete in these districts. The programme has been extended to 5 districts of West Bengal and Andhra Pradesh where the planning process has been initiated. It is expected that 110 districts will be covered under this programme by the end of the Eighth Five Year Plan.

Many of the components of the programme are equally applicable to other districts which are now not covered under this programme. Moreover, the lessons learned from planning and implementing this programme can be extended to other districts. The effort is to improve the system level of efficiency to manage the educational initiatives. Mobilisation, participation and school effectiveness are cardinal elements of the programme. It envisages to revive the initiatives within the school to make it more effective. All activities are oriented to promote this initiative of the schools.

Finally, the DPEP is not an exercise in finding unique solutions. The effort, on the other hand, is to experiment ideas and innovations which may have wider applicability. Its success and sustainability depend on how realistic we are in designing the programmes and how careful we are in implementing them.

The focus is essential on the process dimension. Funds provide only a necessary condition for the success. The sufficient condition is provided by our own capacity to plan and implement programmes. Even though plans are prepared at the district level, in the final analysis they are to be implemented in the schools and classrooms. How effectively this linkage is established, will determine the success of the programme.

Source: DPEP Calling, September 1995

8

DPEP : An Exciting Field Reality

DPEP has successfully translated itself from an exciting concept to an exciting field reality. The experience and learning would be of value not only to Primary Education but to the entire field of development management. At core of its success is the building of national capacity to effectively implement and manage a programme of such a wide scope. Another factor is the professional support and back up available to the programme, which is well into its second year of operation.

The DPEP implementation necessitated an open and more direct approach to programme planning and execution. The objectives and more importantly the processes of DPEP demanded a system different from the existing administration yet at the same time working in close partnership with it. With its focus on contextuality and equity, the programme emphasis is on decentralization and participatory planning. The structures and systems as they have emerged are open, transparent, flexible and accessible. Consequently, the programme is sensitive and has attuned itself to the demands and needs of the member states and districts. What is distinct is a sense of ownership and an intensive involvement in the programme, cutting across all levels from national to village.

Key Roles

Within the overall programme design, the key roles that have emerged for DPEP are:

Managerial - Efficient management and coordination is at the core .of a programme as wide in scope and scale as DPEP. The programme has succeeded in putting in place effective management structures.

Leadership - The programme has identified certain priority areas which need closer attention and greater professional inputs. DPEP is providing leadership in these by exploring new insights and enabling creative experience sharing. These are Planning Management, Improving Learner Achievement and Special Groups.

New areas- DPEP has undertaken some pioneering initiative in areas hitherto left untouched or dealt with sketchily in the realm of primary education. In the absence of any reference material and precedents, these areas have been continually evolved and strengthened. These are Research, MIS and Appraisal.

Management Functions

The innovative nature of DPEP requires a management structure with good policy access, substantial authority, high degree of flexibility in appointing staff and consultants and access to information on programme activities, accomplishments and problems.

Management Structures

National Elementary Education Mission (NEEM) has been set up with DPEP at its core. The two organs of NEEM are ther General Council (GC) and Project Board (PB).

General Council

GC provides policy direction to the DPEP and facilitates centre - state coordination. Chaired by the Minister of Human Resource Development and comprising 35 members, the Council would meet annually. The Resolution for the constitution of the Council has been issued.

Project Board

The GC is assisted by DPEP Project Board (PB). Headed by the Education Secretary, it is an empowered body with full financial and administrative powers to implement the programme. The broad functions of the Board include recommending policies, considering annual Work Plans and Budgets (WPBs) of the state and national sub-projects, approving changes in norms for new programme components and activities, promoting convergence of services, reviewing DPEP progress and providing guidance to the DPEP Bureau.

Technical Support Group

To enhance access to professional support and competencies the Bureau has an arrangement with Ed.CIL for consultancy services to provide technical assistance to the DPEP programme. A Technical .Support Group (TSG) has been placed within Ed.CIL. The role of TSG lies in harnessing available expertise and bringing it together to contribute to DPEP.

TSG provides support in the following areas:

- Planning and Management.
- Pedagogy and Evaluation

- Civil Works
- Supervision
- Appraisal

The TSC comprises consultants selected on the basis of their experience and expertise in relation to the needs of the programme. Young professionals have also been recruited and assigned individual state responsibilities for supervision.

In the states well into project implementation under DPEP - I, autonomous societies have been registered and all the systems and structures have fallen into place. GOI is represented in the GC & .EC of the Society. All the societies have adopted the financial service and administrative regulations. Regular EC & GC meeting are being held to review progress and implementation.

At the district level the operational units are District DPEP Committee, headed by the Collector, and District Task Force — the executive body at the district level. At the village level, Village Educational Committees have been formed, VECs are entrusted with monitoring of education services and seeking involvement of the community in strengthening primary education.

> ***DPEP Bureau***
>
> *The total responsibility for the implementation of the programme rests on the Bureau. Headed by a Joint Secretary, it is responsible to the Project Board and General Council for the implementation of the programme within DPEP Guidelines and in consonance with external financing agreement. The DPEP Bureau has the responsibility and authority to apprise, supervise and evaluate district, state and national sub-projects and to provide for technical assistance to the implementing states.*

Networking

A key issue while developing the new management structure under DPEP was to harness the experiences of different States and the technical expertise spread out in a wide network of institutions. The programme has a built-in component of linkages with institutions and NGOs at the national and state level.

NIEPA is a partner institution extending support for capacity building in ares of educational planning and management through organisation of training of trainers workshops, developing module for planning and management, networking of libraries, research on strategies for tribal education, developing information systems and documentation.

LBSNAA is a partner institution for capacity building in appraisal and supervision of the programme by developing and conducting training programmes with the district teams. Several workshops have been held in this respect. The teams are accompanied by resource persons from the states. The training modules have been developed in collaboration with NIEPA.

NCERT has a network of Regional Institutes of Education and through its links with SCERTs and DIETs extends support to DPEP for curriculum development and teachers' training.

The states have linked up with resource institutions including NGOs, for specific tasks such as preparing training modules for .headmasters, VEC members, text book preparation.

DPEP is negotiating with Management Institutes of national status to enhance their in-house capacities in Educational Management and develop them as nodal or regional centres. Proposals along these lines are being finalised with institutes such as the IIMs.

The programme provides for establishing SIEMTs to extend technical assistance and training in education planning, management, research and monitoring to state and district education staff. Based on the successful experiences gained from establishing similar institutes in Rajasthan and Uttar Pradesh, other states have started the process of setting up SIEMT either as an independent institution or within SCERT.

A continuous dialogue is maintained between GOI and State Project Offices (SPOs). State Education Secretaries write a Demi Official letter to the JS, DPEP, detailing progress and highlighting problems. The other modalities include quarterly MIS reports, EC Meetings held every quarter and the annual GC Meetings.

In the EC Meetings held over last year the decisions taken have been of critical importance to the implementation of the programme. GOI has played a significant role in facilitating quick decision making, monitoring progress and rising resource support.

A two-way information flow has equipped all the participants with common understanding and vision of the programme. The communication is further strengthened through interaction of the SPDs with the Bureau, various missions including Planning Assistance Missions and visits of the young professionals.

"DPEP Calling" - a monthly newsletter and a publication of the Bureau is another effective tool of information sharing. It carries articles and analysis of various issues and helps build a common perspective. Many of the states have launched their own DPEP newsletter.

Civil Works

Strengthening physical infrastructure for primary education is an important component of DPEP. The programme finances Civil Works which include new schools, major repairs and rehabilitation of schools, construction of toilets, residential schools and SIEMT. The state and district civil works proposals are appraised by the civil works unit at TSG.

Good practices in construction and low cost designs are being compiled for dissemination to the states by the unit.

Financial Management

The fund flow channels have been established from the centre to the state societies and from the state societies to other institutions and districts. In turn districts have established systems for passing on the funds for programme implementation to various agencies.

Procurement and Disbursements

The Procurement procedures as spelt out by IDA are being followed. Establishing procurement processes within DPEP was a major managerial challenge. Since the guidelines were very different, it required an orientation and clear understanding by the Bureau to be able to guide the states.

A unit at national level was set up to act as nodal reference point for all queries regrading procurement.

The procurement processes have filtered down and clarity has emerged. The states and districts are striving to achieve the procurement and expenditure targets.

Now that processes have been put into operation in the field and tested, useful feedback is being received from the states, indicating that the procedures to an extent have been internalized.

The procurement procedures need to be reviewed in view of the practical field problems and also the basic ethos of decentralisation of DPEP.

Leadership Functions

The focus of the programme is on decentralised participatory planning and qualitative improvements and pedagogic investments to achieve Universal Elementary Education. Consequently, Educational Planning and Management, Improving Learners Achievement and coverage of disadvantaged groups are the key areas of the programme that merit special attention. Though these core issues .have been on the agenda of the planners and implementors, DPEP has placed them centre stage and provided leadership and guidance in addressing them. As a result new interesting initiatives and processes have been set in motion.

Planning and Management

Recognizing the contextuality of UEE, an integral and innovative feature of DPEP is decentralized planning and management of the programme. There are lot of hopes from the new management strategies as they are to have a catalytic affect on the entire existing system and transform it. The task for DPEP thus goes beyond educational administration to encompass management of a larger public system.

District represents a viable unit for planning. In the absence of planning competencies at the district level, the plans are not very realistic. There is also a tendency to be driven by the resource allocations available under various programmes and schemes of the state.

The emphasis on planning and management within DPEP is thus geared towards building capacities at the village, district and state level. The entire process of the plan preparation is an exercise in itself in developing competencies. Community participation is another factor which is important to ensure that the plans deliver. DPEP envisages that the primary responsibility of VEC would be to undertake micro planning. A sense of ownership within the target audience would make the programme more effective and strengthen local supervision and monitoring. Thus the entire process is focused on preparation of realistic plans at all levels, involving community and participating institutions.

VECs have been constituted and have undergone orientation training given by the state. A series of workshops with project/planning teams of DPEP-I is being planned.

TSG works closely with NIEPA for capacity building and training for planning and management in DPEP. The Unit offers its technical and academic support to the Central and the state level for project prepa-mration and planning and also for preparation of Annual Work Plans.

The focus of training workshops has been on internalising core concepts that are central to the planning process within DPEP. These are community participation, micro planning, gender and tribal planning and decentralized planning. In addition to providing support to DPEP-I states, the focus has been extended to cover new states. The experiences gained during DPEP-I have been shared with new states through workshops conducted at the national level and have proved to be valuable inputs for the planning process of DPEP-II states.

Planning assistance missions have been mounted to work closely with the states on plan preparation. The national training activities and the planning missions are sequenced to ensure follow up on trainings. Regular information update is received through the visits of the Bureau officials and the Consultants, TSG.

A close collaboration with other units of the TSG is maintained by the Unit for providing inputs for capacity building, conduct of studies, documentation and networking.

Improving Learner Achievement

DPEP is designed to improve quality of teaching and learning, increase retention and expand access to disadvantaged groups. The areas of support are:

(a) pedagogic issues such as curriculum development, definition of minimum levels of learning, text book development, and

(b) teachers training with an emphasis on multigrade teaching, revamping in-service training and institutional building at various levels.

The pedagogy and teacher's training unit at TSG ensures integration of appropriate academic interventions for renewal of teaching-learning materials and in teacher training modules. The unit also compiles and disseminates information on innovative practices and learning materials to states and districts.

The apex institution for providing technical support in this areas is NCERT within which a National Training Resource Group has been set up.

The Pedagogy and Teacher Training Unit of TSG has initiated a process of renewal of teaching-learning material. A series of workshops was held at the national and regional levels to identify processes that would led to the development of interesting, rich and relevant materials and to identify resource persons who could contribute to such processes. The platform was also used to develop a clear and common understanding of key concepts of Pedagogic improvements such as child centered, activity based, joyful teaching and learning.

Consequent to the workshops, all DPEP-I states have held state level follow-up workshops with writers, authors, illustrators and the core staff of DPEP States offices, SCERTs and DIETs. The Unit works closely with the states and renders technical assistance. The process of renewal of textbook materials is therefore well under way in each of the DPEP-I states.

A national sharing workshop on Teacher's Training was held in Delhi from November 21-23, 1995. Resource persons were also drawn from NCERT. NGOs, agencies and experts from the area of Teacher's Training were invited. The participants included State Project Directors, Teacher Training experts from DPEP offices and faculty of SCERTs and DIETs. The workshop showed that the states have done substantial work in re-designing Teacher Training and have garnered the support of NGOs in this process. There has been a significant improvement in the staffing of DIETs, to an extent due to the persistent follow-up by DPEP.

States at this stage, require more sustained resource support specially in the area of multigrade teaching. There is a need to disseminate definition of teacher competencies and also the good practices in Teacher Training.

New Areas

To substantiate qualitative inputs and the processes, DPEP has continually evolved and strengthened areas which have hitherto remained unaddressed.

Special Groups

Universal Education demands focused attention for enlisting participation of girls and tribal children.

GENDER *- A focus on Gender is inculcated in the state and the chosen districts right from the beginning when they become partners in DPEP. Only those districts are selected for the programme where the female literacy rate is lower than the national average and where TLC campaigns have successfully generated a demand for elementary education. The findings of the baseline studies and surveys showed the gender disparity. Though an integral and central focus of the programme, gender sensitisation, leading to realistic gender planning and interventions, requires more concerted efforts.*

At the national workshop organised in Delhi, the states consulted on evolving appropriate strategies for addressing gender issues and reviewed their respective plans to strengthen gender strategies and interventions. Resource persons worked with the state teams and dissected the work plans from a gender perspective. The workshop also defined specific activities/programmes that should be taken up.

TRIBAL *- A workshop at national level was held to help the state project teams to identify appropriate feasible strategies for tribal children and review that plans accordingly. The textbook renewal also pays attention to developing material which is sensitive and in consonance with local environment and needs of tribal children.*

Research and Evaluation

DPEP has developed a strong research base that feeds into all aspects of programme planning. The studies undertaken are action research and field oriented and have contributed significantly towards validating experimentation.

An important study undertaken by the National Evaluation Cell, TSG is on evaluation of Managerial Structures and Processes under DPEP. Considering that DPEP is not a blue print project and is an evolving process, it is judicious to study the management structures in the initial stage. This would ensure that structures and processes are streamlined and suitably adjusted to DPEP requirements. Also it is necessary to see whether the structures are fulfilling the roles envisaged for them. The study methodology and instruments were finalised in consultation with the states and leading resource institutions at a National Workshop.

A review of baseline study design is underway. The tests in language and Mathematics are being reviewed and revised. A working group with NCERT, NIEPA & NEC members has been set up and national workshops on the subject were held on October 1995.

Evaluation Study on Classroom Processes and School Functioning has been launched. Studies on Institutional Development processes with focus on SCERTs and DIETs and Teacher Training are punned for the next year.

Apart from evaluation studies, the unit has developed guidelines for research support grant under DPEP.

Documentation of baseline database of various districts provides useful and interesting information mirroring the diversity cross and even within districts on educational processes and system. The Unit is in the process of documenting different databases. It also proposes to develop prototype material for dissemination of baseline data amongst DPEP mangers at all levels.

The National Evaluation Cell has conducted a series of discussions with the states to assist in national evaluations. The Unit plans to undertake field visits to assess the research component and needs in various states and assist them in developing it further.

Management Information System

Work on developing a responsive MIS started simultaneously with the launch of DPEP in 1994. Keeping in view the requirements of the programme, two softwares have been developed. PMIS - Project Management Information System which provides information on the interventions approved and the progress against each and EMIS - Education Management Information System which provides information on educational indicators.

PMIS essentially serves as Annual Work Plan finalisation tool as well as progress monitoring tool. The software is integrated and modular in nature.

EMIS developed by NIEPA, is designed to overcome limitations of lone time delays in the availability of data and consists of school statistics, performance indicators, aggregation of database at the district/state level.

An interface between PMIS & EMIS is being developed. Most of the states have either procured hardware or have rented/borrowed it.

Appraisal

Preparation of Project Plans and Annual Work Plans is another unique feature of DPEP. It is decentralized process with sufficient scope for professional inputting and participatory planning.

The Annual Work Plans of districts, based on activity and budget oriented cycles, are received by the states and forwarded to GOI along with state level proposals. The plans are scrutinized by the Bureau and the TSG and revision and modifications if any, are incorporated after detailed discussions with the states. Ample scope for mid term corrections is available.

The process of decentralized and participatory planning initiated at the time of project formulation has consolidated itself, as was evident in the plans for 1995-96 in the districts and states. Developed in continuum to the previous year's objective and overall design and strategies, the plans reflect sharper understanding of the outcomes of project preparation studies, especially gender, tribal, teacher motivation and text book production — thus leading to better planning and prioritisation. Further training on Capacity Building for decentralised planning is envisaged for DPEP-I and in a different context for DPEP-II states.

A mid term review of workplans was conducted in December 1995 to review achievements under 94-95 and 95-96, for realistic release of funds to DPEP-I states. This would also provide basis for pragmatic planning for 1996-97.

Appraisal of new districts and state plans was undertaken by DPEP .Bureau and TSG. Meticulous planning was done to equip the missions with clear terms of reference, checklists, formats for reporting and background material. The entire exercise was conducted on schedule. It has led to greater clarity about DPEP within states and process of capacity building has been initiated. There is a greater understanding within states of their weak areas and the necessary inputs required. Consequently the states have initiated a process of realistic and participative planning.

Source : DPEP Calling January 1996.

9

DPEP : Reaching the Unreached

Education development has been deemed central to strengthening human resources for which primary education is the necessary foundation. Low educational achievement among certain population sections, particularly among the poor, Scheduled Tribes, Scheduled Castes and women, is a major constraint to their social and economic development. Scheduled Castes and Tribes have remained socially, educationally and economically disadvantaged and have, in fact, been subjected to exploitation despite various .Constitutional provisions, legislations, policies and programmes intended to assure them social justice. This situation can be partially attributed to their social and geographic isolation from the majority population and also to the apathetic attitude towards them. Women in India experience a similar situation.

> ***Education for Women's Equality***
>
> *The National Policy on Education, 1986, perceives education as an agent that could bring about basic changes in the status of women. It states: "In order to neutralize the accumulated distortions of the past, there will be a well-conceived edge in favour of women. The National Education System will play a positive, interventionist role in the empowerment of women. It will foster the development of new values through redesigned curricula, textbooks, the training and orientation of teachers, decision-makers and administrators, and the active involvement of educational institutions.....*
>
> *The removal of women's illiteracy and obstacles inhibiting their access to, and retention in, elementary education will receive overriding priority through provision of special support services, setting of time targets, and effective monitoring."*[1]

In their case, however, their social status and attitudes of others towards them are largely responsible for the discrimination and social injustice they face.

Thus, the general improvement in the standards of primary education depends largely on the augmented participation of those social strata/groups which had been difficult to reach or had eluded reach for some reason.

It would be appropriate to state the policy perspectives in this context.

The National Policy on Education, 1986 (as modified in 1992), .makes particular mention of education for equality. It emphasizes the removal of disparities and equalization of educational opportunity by attending to the specific needs of those who have been denied equality so far.

The NPE details the policy approach to women, Scheduled Castes, Scheduled Tribes other educationally backward sections and areas, minorities and the handicapped. It also spells out the approach to Adult Education, Early Childhood Care and education and Non Formal Education as necessary support for attaining the larger objectives of UEE.

The Education of Scheduled Castes

The NPE states that the "central focus in the SCs educational development is their equalization with the non - SC population at all stages and levels of education, in all areas and in all the four dimensions— rural male, rural female, urban male and urban female."[2] It is contemplated that measures such as provision of incentives, pre-matric scholarship, facilities for students from .this social group in hostels, constant micro - planning and verification to ensure that the enrolment, retention and successful completion, of courses by SC students do not fall at any stage, recruitment of teachers from SCs, convergence with other development programmes, judicious location of school buildings to improve the access situation and innovations would contribute towards attainment of policy goals.

The Education of Scheduled Tribes

Measures, such as the following are envisaged to bring STs at par with others:

- opening primary schools in tribal areas
- development of curricula and devising instructional materials in tribal languages at the initial stages, with arrangements for switching over to the regional language
- encouraging educated and promising ST youth to take up teaching in tribal areas after due training

- providing large scale establishment of residential schools, including Ashram Schools
- introduction of incentives/scholarships among STs
- opening Anganwadis, Non-Formal and Adult Education Centres on a priority basis in areas predominantly inhabited by STs
- designing curriculum at all stages of education to create an awareness of the rich cultural identity of the tribal people as .also of their enormous creative talent.

Other Educationally Backward Sections and Areas

The NPE proposes to provide suitable incentives to all educationally backward sections of society, particularly in the rural areas. Provision of adequate institutional infrastructure is envisaged for the hill and desert districts, remote and inaccessible areas and islands.

Minorities

Greater attention will be paid to the educationally deprived sections of minority population in the interest of equality and social justice. Constitutional guarantees given to them to establish and administer their own educational institutions and protection to their languages and culture will continue. Simultaneously, objectivity will be reflected in the preparation of textbooks and in all school activities and all possible measures will be taken to promote an integration based on appreciation of common national goals and ideals, in conformity with the core curriculum.

For successfully taking the policy statements to the field and imparting quality education, development of a child-centred and activity based process of learning at the primary stage has been envisaged. Further, there is scope for first generation learners to set their own pace and be provided supplementary remedial instruction. As the child grows, the component of cognitive learning is proposed to be increased and skills organised through practice. The policy of non-detention at the primary level will be retained, making evaluation as disaggregated as feasible. Corporal punishment will be firmly excluded from the educational system and school timings as well as vacations adjusted to the convenience of children.[3]

All population segments, including first generation learners, receive due attention in the Policy, which goes into details of measures that can adequately address their specific situations. Reducing the disparities in dropout, learning and access for girls, SC and ST students, thus, has high policy priority.

Basis and Spirit of the District Primary Education Programme

The Constitutional provision ensuring free and compulsory education to all children upto the age of 14 years and the policy orientation combine to provide the right impetus to primary education in the country. Backed by such well defined and supportive Constitutional and policy guidelines, the District Primary Education Programme was evolved and seeks to achieve the goal of Universalisation of Primary Education (UEE). It imbibes the spirit of the Policy provisions and in trying to approach the present situation holistically, has the essential ingredients required to reduce the disparities in access, dropout and learning among every group that comprises SFGs.

> **_Special Focus Groups_**
>
> *Often, attention is focussed on and energies spent on those children who are visible, while the disadvantaged sections go unnoticed. An approach such as this, needs to be rectified so that each State takes into account all categories of children coming within the ambit of DPEP, during planning and implementation. And, this calls for identification of the groups requiring special treatment followed by evolving group specific/need based strategies for every such group identified. In a nutshell, the relevance of addressing the concerns of Special Focus Groups has always occupied centre stage in the scheme of affairs in DPEP.*

The programme also builds upon the nation's earlier experience in the area of primary education and the experiences gained in implementing the Bihar Education Programme (UNICEF supported), the Lok Jumbish Project (SIDA supported), the Andhra Pradesh Primary Education Project (ODA supported), Shiksha Karmi Project (with SIDA support), the Mahila Samakhya (with Dutch assistance), Operation Black Board (OB) and also the planning experience of the Basic Education Project in Uttar Pradesh (with IDA assistance).

Learnings from these experiences pointed out various needs for realizing the desired educational improvement of the nation's children. In attempting to effectuate the functioning of systems in place, it is of utmost importance that earlier approaches and efforts be reinforced by a holistic planning and management approach. In the context of the SFGs the programme provides the scope for integrating the gender perspective and the concerns of the identified social groups in all aspects of planning and implementation. It emphasizes on gender ad SFG oriented planning and implementation processes sensitive to the specific needs of girls and other groups comprising the SFGs. Its decentralized approach encourages the involvement of representatives of all local communities, particularly women, in all decision making processes. The DPEP also stresses on adopting an area-specific approach which is contextual and sensitive to local conditions.

Thus, the programme's success critically hinges on all eligible children being in school for at least the stipulated four/five years in the primary level, which necessarily implies working towards universal enrolment, enhanced retention and improved standards of learning/achievement. In this context, it has been increasingly felt that all children must be reached and taken care of.

Consequently, the programme takes into account the demand and supply side issues concerning access, retention and achievement through the multipronged approach adopted by it.

This initiative, further, aims at achieving the goal of UEE in replicable, cost-effective and sustainable manner. The programme nurtures the larger interest of overhauling the primary education system by establishing a responsive, sensitive and effective system that understands the importance of primary education for all children regardless of social context or gender, as also the traits of children, and works towards providing the necessary environment. Apart from revitalizing the present system by integrating practices and approaches amenable to needs and priorities, DPEP also strives to enhance capabilities and motivate the entire machinery to address the issue of primary education in all its dimensions as well as address the specificities of micro situations.

In effect, the DPEP is committed to reduce/eliminate gender and social disparities in regard to enrolment, retention and achievement/performance of all children in the primary school level. This forms the basis for its emphasis on innovative approaches, decentralized planning, reaching all categories of children, capacity building, institutional strengthening, mobilisation of community support and, most importantly, empowering the mainstream education machinery to sustain its efforts.

More specifically, the DPEP supports, in selected districts, the development and implementation of programmes to:

- reduce differences in enrolment, dropout and learning achievement between gender and social groups to less than five per cent
- reduce overall primary dropout rates for all students to less

than ten per cent

- raise average achievement levels by at least 25 per cent over measured baseline levels by ensuring achievement of basic literacy and numeracy competencies and a minimum of 40 per cent achievement levels in other competencies by all primary school children
- provide access for all children to primary schooling or its equivalent non formal education
- strengthen the capacity of national, state, and district institutions and organisations for the planning, management and evaluation of primary education.

From Research to Plan : the DPEP I Experience

The shift from the stage of pious postulates to a more experiential and informed understanding of specific interventions within defined time spectrum has been made possible by a series of research activities in the case of the DPEP I States. Accordingly, six project preparation studies were completed in the project states and districts of the DPEP I States. Three primary education beneficiary assessments conducted were:

- baseline assessments of learning achievement
- studies of factors affecting enrolment and dropout for girl students
- studies of the educational context and needs of ST students

The two latter studies are of relevance in the context of the Spatial Focus Groups. As these studies sought to bring out the ares of disparity and discrimination among girls and boys and social groups, they were envisaged to provide input into the formulation of plans and strategies for augmenting the levels of participation and performance of girls and tribal children in primary education.

The gender studies had two parts, viz,:

- a review of existing state and district policies and interventions for girls education, including a review of curricula and textbooks for gender bias
- a largely qualitative field study conducted through semi-structured interviews and group discussions with district and block officials, teachers and community leaders, parents, girl students, girl dropouts and girls who had never enrolled in schools.

The field study focussed on perceptions of causes of girls continuing in school, of nonenrolment, of dropout and of gender equality in communities. The study reports indicated strategies and action plans based on research findings.

The tribal studies conducted also had two parts, viz,:

- a status report that summarises secondary information on the demographics of tribal peoples, the tribal development plan programmes and available educational schemes and programmes
- field study carried out in blocks with highest ST population in two of the baseline achievement study sample districts in four states and one baseline district in Maharashtra, for a total of five districts. Eight questionnaires were administered by trained investigators to students, parents, community leaders, teachers and non-formal instructors. Group discussions were also conducted in each community and the results recorded in investigators diaries.

Apart from the initiatives taken by the states to commence the planning (AWPB) process by dissemination and discussion of study results across the project districts, national workshops were organized to facilitate exchange of ideas among the states and also interactions with experts. This approach has clearly brought out some ways of mainstreaming the SFGs in the planning process. The outcomes of discussions and interactions together with research findings have proved useful in the fine tuning the strategies and interventions in the DPEP I States.

The AWPBs were drafted by the states and broad gender strategies were presented along with the prevailing situation in the State at the National Workshop on Addressing Gender Disparities in DPEP. This workshop brought together all the SPDs from the 7 DPEP states and also the gender coordinators and district representatives. The objectives of the workshop were to:

i) evolve appropriate strategies for addressing gender issues in DPEP

ii) review and refine State/District action plans to strengthen gender strategies and interventions.

It afforded an opportunity to the participants to undertake a focussed and rigorous planning exercise, supplemented with inputs from resource persons. The AWPBs were reviewed in the process. Screening and sieving of information generated, prioritising the group specific / area specific needs / gaps, was meticulously done before any strategy envisaged to address the concerns of SFGs was incorporated in the AWPB.

Some of the interventions planned are:

- ECCE linkages with primary schools
- Provision for alternative schooling
- Flexible school timings to suit the needs of girls
- Residential schools
- Gender - sensitive curricula and text books
- Recruitment of women teachers
- Improved school buildings and the provision of toilets for girls
- Educational incentives
- Gender sensitization of teachers, supervisors and project managers

To ensure that these interventions achieve the programme objective of reducing gender disparities, the role of community in creating an atmosphere supportive of education for girls and other disadvantaged groups, is critical. While programmatic enrichment is possible with well designed plans and strategies, the sustainability and ultimate outcome of the programme depends largely on community attitude and support. This implies the need of seriously working towards community mobilisation and involving the community with various activities related to DPEP. This alone will bring them closer to the programme, dilute / eliminate skeptical views held earlier and result in ownership of the programme.

Towards this, efforts are on to involve the village community to support the education of children from these groups. Steps have been taken to mobilise women's groups in the village, which already exist in some of the DPEP I States, to actively support education of the girl child. As a sustained input for bringing a gender sensitive vision among the village community and local school management it is envisaged that women's groups would exert the right pressure for girls education. The women's groups would also be empowered to hold the local educational system accountable. Some of the specific strategies devised to mobilise women are:

- empowerment of the VECs, MTCs, PTAs to take on the responsibility of promoting education in the area
- mobilisation of informed and active participation to the local level to build and sustain and environment supportive of girls education
- involvement of community and women's organisations in

mobilisation, school management, monitoring, enrolment, retention, levels of achievement and classroom practices, with the specific agenda of highlighting the importance of girls education

- formation of women's collectives at the village level and local activists trained to catalyse collective action around educational issues
- intensive capacity building of community and women's groups to focus on issues of education for girls.

A National Workshop on Primary Education and the Tribal Child for the DPEP states and districts of Assam, Karnataka, Kerala, Maharashtra and Tamil Nadu was held in Delhi during June 1995. It was attended by the SPDs and officers responsible for the tribal children in their respective states. The states came prepared with their states and district plans to address the concerns of tribal children. Participation in this workshop enabled the state representatives to interact, understand each others situations and learn from their experiences, adapt and apply in their own contexts what was discussed or shared in the workshop by programme personnel or resource persons. This deliberation contributed in sharpening the focus of the AWPBs (1995-96) vis-a-vis tribal children.

On March 19 & 20, 1996, a two days workshop on National Strategies for Tribal Education under DPEP was held in Delhi. The workshop provided a platform to the DPEP States to:

- highlight the problems of tribal education in the DPEP States/ Districts which could not be effectively identified and attended to by the State/District strategies
- develop national strategies to support and supplement the State/District strategies in the identified gap and priority areas in tribal education.

State / district overviews of the situation pertaining to tribals were presented by the participating DPEP States, along with the interventions and innovations initiated and the problems faced. The group work resulted in the following list of ares for which some national strategies could be useful for the states:

- guidelines in policy framing and planning
- capacity building
- pedagogic intervention
- monitoring and evaluation
- networking and research

- advisory and clearing house role.

Another National Workshop on tribal strategies was organised in Delhi in July 1996, which aimed at orienting DPEP II States project officials in planning and implementation of tribal strategies. All the DPEP II States (Andhra Pradesh, Gujarat, West Bengal and Orissa) except Himachal Pradesh were represented at the workshop. The Assam and Madhya Pradesh (DPEP I States) teams were invited to share their experiences in addressing the issues concerning tribals in planning as well as in the field.

Sharing of expert opinions by resource persons in key areas such as micro planning, school mapping in tribal areas, long drawn language and pedagogic issues and intense group work in each thematic area helped in evolving alternative / workable strategies for tribal education in DPEP.

Broad strategies developed by the states for bettering the educational situation of girls and the tribal children, include:

- women's empowerment and education, training in gender sensitivity, elimination of gender bias in learning materiels, enhanced role of women in Village Education Committees and organisation of awareness campaigns
- community mobilisation, addressing the issue of home language vs medium of instruction at school, improving the access situation by providing new schools for the tribal children.

Strategies were also evolved for other categories of children, such as, minority children/girls (Assam, Kerala, Madhya Pradesh), children of prostitutes (Madhya Pradesh) etc.

Experiences with the DPEP I States have provided leanings that are important for the future as they can.be effectively employed in similar ventures. Some of the learnings have been that:

- Research has the potential to bring out a number of issues pertaining to access, retention and achievement and identify social groups that need special inputs— both being closely linked with strategy development and planning. The recommendations offered by the studies for countering some of the prevalent situations to eventually improve the educational status of the nation's children, also suggest the relatedness of research and planning for a programme like DPEP.
- Apart from identifying the SFGs, research throws up further research needs that can be woven into the plans.

- Research provides a good basis / support for the conceptualization and concretisation of the action plans. Research was useful through the entire planning process in the DPEP I States.
- Simplified participative methods such as school mapping can contribute towards programme enrichment by generating information useful for area specific planning and also inviting the participation of local communities.
- Cross exchange of ideas and experiences between the states at various workshops helped strengthen the plan components that have a bearing on the education of girls and tribal children.
- There is a large pool of resources available within the country that have been harnessed at different times for the programme in the DPEP I States.
- Experiences of earlier generation educational projects, such as BEP, Lok Jumbish, APPEP, UP Basic Education Programme, etc, have provided valuable insights into ground realities, successful and .unsuccessful programmatic details, processes, innovations, implementing methods, etc.

Notes

1. Chapter 4, National Policy on Education, 1986 (with modifications undertaken in 1992).
2. Chapter 4, NPE, 1986 (with modifications undertaken in 1992).
3. Excerpts from Chapters 4 & 5, National Policy on Education, 1986 (with modifications undertaken in 1992).

Source: DPEP Calling, November 1996.

10

Social Assessment Studies

Though the Gender and Tribal studies conducted in the DPEP I States were meant to assist planners formulate adequate measures for handling the emergent priorities of these sections of society, some gaps were evidenced. It was seen that States had, for various reasons, not been able to pay due attention to the needs of the groups requiring tailor made inputs. One, their efforts had not shown the desired results vis-a-vis the interventions attempted, though some progress has been made in terms of planning, and two, some unserved sections of children continued to be unserved because enough is not yet known about them.

Thus, with an intent of making focused and meaningful interventions in regard to all the otherwise unreached or marginally covered groups or those that are educationally lagging behind, the Social Assessment Studies (SAS) were conceived of and conducted as a precursor to the planning process of the DPEP II States, viz, Gujarat, Himachal Pradesh and Orissa.

The TORs of the agencies/institutions commissioned for these researches were more or less in line with what formed the guidelines for the six studies for the DPEP I States. A conscious decision was taken to allow the SAS to be somewhat exploratory/diagnostic in nature and not confine themselves to the concerns of tribal and girl children alone. It was envisaged that this would facilitate identification of different disadvantaged groups and unravelling the unknown about them, based on which need based planning could be attempted.

It has been learnt from experiences in the DPEP I States that there may be other groups such as minorities, nomadic tribes or migratory population that are equally disadvantaged as girl children and SC/ST children. Accordingly the objectives of the SAS and the study methodology provided ample scope to identify and examine the predicament of other unserved groups. Statewise and districtwise variations in the groups that have emerged is only expected as their identification has been in the context of the State/District.

All the 12 project districts in the DPEP II States have been covered by the SAS. The identified research institutes were governed by a common TOR which spelt out the study objectives, specific steps, scope, methodology and report. The study objectives were:

- To analyse the specific problems of girls and tribal children with respect to their enrolment, retention and achievement in the state and with special reference to DPEP districts. If any state considers it desirable to analyse the problems of children belonging to other significant socially disadvantaged groups, it may include that in the study.
- To assess the available evidence on the effectiveness of various schemes that are in operation for these groups of children. The assessment would be based mainly on published and unpublished information available in the public domain supported by some primary information.
- To assess the views and perceptions of the community on the constraints in ensuring effective participation of these children and possible strategies for overcoming these constraints.

The specific steps involved were as follows:

- To review all available literature/research on the problems of education of girls, tribals and children of other identified children group, if any
- To analyse statistics on enrolment and retention of girls, tribal children and other identified groups from 1985 to 1995
- To review the schemes in operation for the girl child and children belonging to the major tribal population in each of the project districts that emerge
- To elicit community responses on social attitudes to education of girls and children belonging to tribal population and other identified groups and gain an insight into the specific factors that affect access, retention and learner achievement. The role of cultural factors including the medium of instruction being mother tongue in learning would also be examined.

The scope of the SAS were limited to the following:

- Review of published/unpublished secondary material as outlined in the methodology
- Analysis of the results of the Focus Group Discussions
- Analysis of the responses to the semi structured questionnaire.

The study methodology included:

I

An analytical review of literature

The review of literature included all material in the public domain from 1985 till date, for which the following were sourced:

- annual reports of the Education Department
- annual plans and five year plans
- academic dissertations and exercises
- books
- journals, reports of Tribal Department/Social Welfare Department, Reports and Studies of Tribal Research Institutes
- studies by SCERT as well as other institutions/individuals evaluating and reviewing the schemes in operation for the tribal child and girl child
- district level educational statistics and general statistics regarding women and tribal population
- any other unpublished material in the public domain.

II

Focus group discussion

Community responses were to be elicited through (FGDs). The FGDs were envisaged to provide some understanding of the perceptions and opinions of parents and villagers regarding the following:

- constraints and problems they face in continuation of schooling girls, tribal children and children of other identified groups, if any
- their expectation from the school system
- the ongoing schemes in operation.

Though the methodology for FGDs had been suggested, there was room for making alterations if duly documented and justified. At least 10 FGDs in each of at least two selected project districts were to be held. The number of districts could be increased, if required, to cover major tribal population of the identified project districts. The FGDs with tribal communities were to be conducted in a district with substantial tribal population and the FGDs on girls were to be conducted in the other district. Similarly, it was possible that FGDs be held for other identified socially disadvantaged groups. The principal investigator conducted and moderated the FGDs.

The villages for FGDs were selected on the basis of the following criteria:

- villages where enrolment/retention rates are low for tribal children/girls/children of other identified groups
- villages where enrolment/retention rates are high for tribal children/girls/children of other identified groups.

An equal number of FGDs were ideally to be conducted for both the above mentioned criteria.

The following were to be taken into consideration during group formation:

- For FGDs on girls education, the groups may include representatives of parents, community leaders, teachers and other important persons of the area like health worker or an elected member. Special attention needs to be paid to include those belonging to low socio-economic status
- For FGDs in tribal populations, the group should comprise members of the tribal community
- For FGDs on other identified sections, the groups should comprise members of that section
- Women must have a representation in the groups
- The size of the groups should be between 6 to 10.

The investigator was empowered to modify the above, subject to documentation and justification.

The following leading questions on which the views of the participants were to be sought by the investigators moderating the FGDs, were provided:

- Do they feel education as imparted by schools to be important for their children? If yes, why? If no, why?
- Why are the girls being taken out of school more quickly than boys?
- Why are tribal children being taken out of school more quickly than others?
- What are the specific problems the children of identified socially disadvantaged groups face in terms of schooling?
- What are the problems girls/tribal children/children of other groups face in school in terms of teachers attitude and peer group attitude?
- What are the problems faced in the understanding of the

course (medium of instruction, contents of textbooks, etc.)

- What are the problems they face in terms of physical facilities (distance from home, toilets, etc.)
- What do the participants feel about different schemes that are in operation in these areas (Are they aware? Level of awareness, their responses to functioning, etc.)
- What are their expectations from the school system?
- What are the ways to overcome the constraints they experience?
- In what ways the community can participate in overcoming the constraints?

III

Semi-structured questionnaire

If FGDs are considered insufficient, semi-structured questionnaires may be developed to elicit information and views of the community. The questionnaires can be developed by the state agency/institute conducting the study, with special reference to DPEP districts and target groups.

IV

Report

One interim and main report was expected.

1. The main report contained the following from the bibliographic surveys, FGDs and review of schemes and statistics:

- Analysis of the situation of the tribal child and the girl child in line with the statistics
- Overview and analysis of the main findings
- Highlight gaps
- Discuss the strategies
- An annotated bibliography with the following details:
  - Name of author, title, publication details
  - State the objectives, scope and coverage, design, methodology, tools and instruments, results
  - Must contain the reviewer's assessment of the study
- An annotated statement of the schemes, their coverage, any evaluative study done on their operation and effectiveness

Methodology for Focus Group Discussions, a statement on the main observations and an annexure of the list of places where the FGDs were conducted

- An annexure of the data sources and the places where the data search was carried out.

Research Findings and Pointers

Prior to going into the details of the SAS outcomes, this section starts with a brief look at facts pertaining to the research agencies involved, geographic coverage of the studies, their status, the FGDs conducted and the respondents.

Table I shows the Statewise coverage, agency/institution entrusted with the responsibility of conducting the research and the present status of the SAS conducted.

Most of the districts covered by the SAS are either tribal dominated or have a fairly large representation of tribals. In Orissa, e.g., out of the 11 villages covered, only two villages were SC dominated. The statewise number of FGDs organised and the participants are given in Table 2.

The number of participants for each FGD ranged between 3-20. The group composition also varied— some of the FGDs were held with single category participants, as in Orissa, while others had a mixed group of participants. It is seen that the categories of respondents included in the FGDs are directly related to the SFGs.

Governed by a common TOR, the SAS reports have given the findings and recommendations differently— the emphasis varying from study to study. Apparently, such variations are based on what is deemed to be high in the order of priorities vis-a-vis the district/ state. There is, therefore, no uniformity either in the SAS findings and recommendations or in the way they are presented. The studies have also gone into the details, in varying degrees, of the literature available, the status of educational strategies and inputs for SFGs and the status of schemes/programmes operational in the State for the SFGs.

Table 3 provides an overview of the subjects covered by the SAS conducted in the 12 project districts in Gujarat, Himachal Pradesh and Orissa. The statewise variations in emphasis are clearly reflected in the table.

The findings and recommendations of the SAS can be best understood when classified in terms of the three main objectives of the studies as specified in the TOR. It is attempted to present the same as statewise findings and recommendations in the light of the study objectives.

The study findings clearly point towards various actionable areas with reference to 'demand and 'supply issues at the micro and macro level. They have brought out the status of girls education and also that of the tribal children. The factors contributing to their low educational status have been amply stated. Further, the SAS have identified some migratory groups whose children's access to education is a matter of concern.

The perceptions of parents and the children themselves reveal new insights and may form the basis for planning and strategy development in the DPEP II states.

The findings that have emerged can broadly be stated as:

- Insufficient numbers of schools. Long distances have often to be walked by children to school; sometimes across jungles and difficult terrain.
- Negative parental attitude towards girls education.
- Financial circumstances, primarily economic, adversely affectgirls access to school.
- Domestic work confines girls to their houses.
- Tradition and social customs that perpetuate/reinforce negative attitudes towards girls education, e.g. early marriage or marriage is the ultimate end in girls life.
- Caste based bias and consequent attitude formed among peers and teachers.
- Teachers involvement with business/other activities.
- Apathetic attitude of teachers.
- Students subjected to corporal punishment at school.
- Teaching aids not available.
- Migratory nature of work compels parents to remove children from schools.
- Problems with medium of instruction, particularly in the tribal areas.
- Non-local teachers face language barriers as well as problems in commuting to work.
- Knowledge about tribal life and culture not known by teachers.
- Absence of child care support services keeps girls out of schools.
- Text books do not include much of tribal stories, culture, etc.

The recommendations made by the SAS are in tune with their findings. The major intervention areas pointed out are:

- Motivation of teachers.
- Creation of a supportive environment in the schools.
- Sensitisation of teachers regarding the situation and needs of tribal and girl children and children of other disadvantaged groups.
- Development of appropriate materials for fulfilling the task of proper orientation and sensitisation on SFGs including gender concerns, among DPEP functionaries, education functionaries, teachers, VEC members, etc.
- Development of appropriate material for awareness generation among community.
- Provision of alternative schooling for children in nonsupportive situations that compel them to be out of school.

The emergent recommendations suggest the importance of innovations and experiments in the context of SFGs. Are/group specificities can be concretised by adopting such an approach. It will show the way of making effective and sustainable interventions.

TABLE 1: Statewise Research institute and Coverage of SAS

State	*Institute*	*Districts Covered*
Gujarat	Sardar Patel Institute of Economics and Social Research	Dangs, Panchmahal, Banaskantha
Himachal Pradesh	Institute of Tribal Studies, Himachal Pradesh University	Kullu, Chamba, Sirmour, Lahaul & Spiti
Orissa	Nabakrishna Choudhury Centre for Development Studies	Bolangir, Dhenkenal, Gajapati, Kalahandi, Rayagada

TABLE 2: Statewise Number of FGDs and the Participants Covered

State	*Number of FGDs*	*Participants*
Orissa	56	Teachers (10), Mothers (1), Fathers (1), Community Leaders (11), Parents (11), Girls (11), Boys (11)
Himachal Pradesh	11	Up-Pradhans, Panchayat members, Parents of children studying in school or who have dropped out or are non starters, teachers of schools, anganwadis, balwadis, members of Mahila Mandals, representatives of target groups, village functionaries like VEOs, grameen sevaks/sevikas, panchayat secretaries, forest guards, etc.
Gujarat	32	5 villages in Dangs: Mothers, Parents, Teachers (11) 4 villages in Panchmahal: Mothers, Parents, Social Workers, Teachers (11) 7 villages Banaskantha : Parents, Social Workers, Teachers (10)

TABLE 3: Statewise Overview of the SAS Coverage of Subjects

Subject	*Gujarat*	*Himachal Pradesh*	*Orissa*
Review of literature	D	P	D
Assessment : schemes for SFG	D	P	D
Problems of girls	M	M	M
Problems of tribal children	D	D	D
Problems of other groups	D	D	P
Existing education facilities	D	P	M
NGO involvement	D	P	M
Community perception	M	M	D
Suggested interventions	M	M	M
Methodology of FGDs	D	D	D

***Legend** : D = Detailed M = Moderate P = Partial*
Source : DPEP Calling, November 1996.

11

National Social Assessment Studies Sharing Workshop

A two days National SAS sharing workshop was organised in Delhi on September 24 & 25, 1996. The workshop brought together teams from the DPEP II states, Gujarat, Himachal Pradesh and Orissa and also from Andhra Pradesh and West Bengal. Statewise representatives from the research agencies/institutions that had executed the SAS were also present. The workshop aimed to provide a platform for sharing the principal findings of SAS with planners, administrators and implementors. The process would help to weave the action-points emerging from the studies in the design of:

- tribal child specific strategies
- girl child specific strategies
- integrated strategies and interventions to ensure the inclusion of an equity perspective, particularly in the context of
  - Staffing patterns/management
  - Pedagogical improvements
  - Community mobilisation
  - Civil Works
  - Capacity building

In this way, the workshop envisaged to assist the states in:

- refining their plans
- ensuring that the principal recommendations of the studies are integrated in the AWPB of the states and districts.

To strengthen the state and district plans, resource persons were invited and were attached to each of the participating DPEP II state teams for the group work. The resource persons were expected to help the teams evolve:

- a better understanding of how to ensure that research findings are integrated into the strategy design.

- an understanding of the risks and uncertainties that could affect the success of planned strategies and interventions.
- strategies and an action plan for enhancing girls, tribal children and other disadvantaged groups participation in the educational process.

Expected Outcome

- Better understanding of how it is possible for research findings to be integrated into strategy design and action plan.
- Evolve statewise strategies and action plan for enhancing the education of girls, tribal children and children from other disadvantaged groups.
- Integrate research findings into AWPBs of 1996-97/1997-98 and in long term planning.

Workshop Methodology

Participants at the workshop played the key role in the sharing and planning exercise. The organisers and resource persons merely facilitated the process and tried to enrich the outcome with relevant inputs. The researcher and programme implementor combined well in sharpening the focus of the state and district AWPBs on SFGs.

Proceedings

The proceedings started with introductory remarks about the workshop, its objectives and expected outcomes. Shri R.S. Pandey, Joint Secretary, DPEP Bureau, MHRD, chaired the session on State Presentations of the Social Assessment Studies and exhorted the states to learn from each other, the DPEP I experience as well as to successfully incorporate SAS findings and outcomes of other research studies and surveys into the annual planning exercise in each district and state. He also emphasised the need to address the special needs of the social groups and communities in each district so that meaningful strategies could be crafted and implemented with peoples participation. The presentations were made in the following order:

Orissa

Himachal Pradesh

Gujarat

Besides presenting the essential findings and recommendations of the studies, the state research teams shared some of the qualitative aspects of the studies which brought out the area specific/group specific details about the people and their lives. The migratory and shifting population of Gujarat and Himachal Pradesh came in for lengthy discussions particularly with reference to the access related problems of children of such families.

Majority of these families in Gujarat are compelled to migrate to the sugarcane growing areas in Bharuch and Surat, during October and November, where they get employment. As the employment is offered in 'pairs, often both parents have to move out of their villages or one parent alongwith an older child goes. In the first situation parents take their children alongwith them and there is a break in their schooling, if they were going to school. In the second situation also, the child automatically drops out of school. As this is a seasonal phenomenon occurring every year in Dangs district, children in sizeable numbers drop out of school temporarily with many of them leaving school for good. This was expressed as a major concern area.

In Chamba district of Himachal Pradesh, there are people who shift from the upper reaches to the valleys alongwith their cattle during winters. The practice is for the whole family to move. These social groups maintain two houses, as it were. There are other groups which keep moving frequently from place to place. These are situations arising out of people's livelihood question which severely impact upon childrens education.

Lahaul and Spiti is under snow for the better part of the year during which time children experience great difficulties in going to school. The long distances to school further aggravate the situation. The long distances to school further aggravate the situation. The population density of this district being extremely low has many unserved habitations. And children have to traverse long distances to school and back.

In the context of the above, the Himachal Pradesh team shared the State's experience with the existing residential schools (Ashram Shalas). Such schools are currently being run by the State Social Welfare Department and there is a great demand for the same. The process of admission is looked after by the District Magistrate. The present demand for these schools suggest the need for increasing the spread of such facilities, so that more children have access to primary education.

The language issue emerged as a major constraint in the teaching learning process in the tribal pockets of Orissa and Dangs district of Gujarat. There are tribals who do not communicate in Oriya, at all. They are familiar only with their own language-Koshali, Kul, Seva, etc. A similar situation was encountered in Dangs where the local people communicate in Dangi. Teachers serving in primary schools among such people are often not familiar with these languages, which limits/restricts the learning achievement among the children.

Caste based discrimination is evident in parts of the project districts in Orissa. The caste factor assumes so much importance for the teachers in the primary schools that they are not able to rise above their personal bias in this regard and fail to operate with an equity perspective.

Early marriage, household responsibilities, sibling care, parental attitude towards girls education are the main reasons for girls being out of school. The group specific detailed factors that have surfaced in this regard are definite pointers to the actionable ares and issues. Commenting on the presentations made by the three DPEP II states, the Chair acknowledged that it would seem as if DPEP seeks to perform a task that is difficult, but where improvement can be registered if the primary education system is reformed. We may have to work on its strengths and also see to it that the supply side is functional in terms of teachers attendance, availability of free textbooks and scholarships in time, wherever such provisions are committed. For improving upon the plans, the research outcomes can be used alongwith DPEP I experiences/interventions in regard to addressing gender and tribal concerns. Visits to some DPEP I states my also assist in the process of planning.

Access to schools is a major issue causing concern. Similar problems pertaining to access, as pointed out by the SAS are encountered in the hills of Uttar Pradesh for which way has been found. We need to look at this in the light of our contexts.

It was suggested that the plans may provide for ways of involving the community in supervision activities and formation of State and District Resource Groups.

After this session the two other DPEP II states Andhra Pradesh and West Bengal shared their experiences, though no SAS was conducted in either of these states. The Andhra Pradesh presentation focused on the 'Social Project' and the 'Problems faced in Tribal Areas' based on experiences in the Andhra Pradesh Primary Education Programme (APPEP).

The objective of the Social Project was to increase enrolment and retention, particularly of girls and SC/ST children through community participation. Specific activities undertaken in the project have been:

- Conduct of workshops and training programmes
- Awareness building activities to motivate parents (community mobilisation)
- Organisation of VEC/Vidya Sangham

- Visits to homes to meet parents
- Establishment of pre-schools, anganwadis/balwadis/creches
- Appointment of ayahs
- Formation of pre-school ply groups
- Supply of supplementary reading materials
- Adoption of APPEP pedagogy
- Construction of Kutcha school buildings

The characteristics of the case study method as a research technique were explained in terms of the process that it is, its characteristic features, its tools and its outcome. Research ethics demand absolute confidentiality and mutual trust between research and the research subject. As the research method is highly qualitative in nature, some vital points that facilitate researchers entry into villages were also discussed.

Problems faced in tribal areas were presented as 'access', 'enrolment', 'retention and 'quality'. Many of the problems pointed out were similar to those reflected upon by the earlier speakers from Gujarat, Himachal Pradesh and Orissa. In the context of 'access' the inadequate coverage of schools, lack of motivation among tribal parents, teachers unwillingness to serve in tribal habitations, lack of community participation and non involvement of voluntary organisations are the main deterrents.
Enrolment is affected by:

- Non maintenance of census register
- Lack of door to door survey to enrol children
- Lack of enrolment campaigns
- Parents are not convinced of the importance of their children's education
- Teacher absenteeism
- Poor teaching
- Seasonal work participation of pupils
- Tribal eradication
- Migration
- The factors that have a bearing on retention in the tribal areas include:
- Female child labour
- Female work participation and sibling care

- Early marriages
- Agriculture labour
- Grazing cattle
- Lack of ancillary facilities
- Poor teaching
- No teaching
- Incomplete schools
- Lack of ECCE facilities
- Unattractive classrooms
- Unserviceable curriculum
- Lack of community control over school
- Lack of Parent-Teacher Associations
- Note making education joyful activity.

On the quality front, under qualified teachers, their professional deficiency, language problem, lack of knowledge of MLLs, lack of training in child-centred activity oriented instruction, pupil absenteeism, non-suitability of working hours, lack of guidance, lack of supervision, lack of monitoring of the work of teachers and lack of encouragement from the community to the teachers to work are the principal restricting factors.

Continuing with the presentation on Andhra Pradesh, an overview of programmes planned for 1996-97 in five districts was provided alongwith details of programmes implemented in Adilabad tribal area. Programmes planned for 1996-97 are:

- ECCE centres
- New classrooms
- Supply of materials
- Special grants to teachers @ Rs. 500/-
- District Resource Centres
- Teachers Centres
- Improvement in environment, drinking water and toilet
- Community participation campaigns
- Workshops/seminars

Programmes implemented in Adilabad district have been as follows:

Access

- Rationalisation of the teachers posts
- Opening of community schools/Blwadi Programmes in school-less habitations
- Encouraging voluntary organisations to open schools.

Enrolment

- Village census register
- Door-to-door survey to enrol children
- Incentives to school committees which achieve cent per cent enrolment and attendance.
- Construction of school sheds with two rooms— one for teachers residence and other for running school by supplying tiles free of cost.
- Teacher doctor programme to infuse confidence in villagers.

Retention

- Activity based instruction
- Mid-day meal programme
- Supply of minimum educational materials as package of incentive
- Residence of the teacher in school
- Contracts with parents about the progress of the child.

Quality

- Improving the competence of teachers
- Training in minimum levels of learning
- Training in activity approach
- Preparation and supply of instructional modules
- Supply of instructional kit
- Filling up of vacant posts
- Strengthening supervision through Project Educational Counsellors
- Payments of teachers salaries through bank
- Monthly review of academic work done
- Teaching through bilingual method

- Daily schedule of academic work
- Frequent orientation in activity method
- Adoption of APPEP principles
- Incentives to those who do good work

After a rather detailed presentation by Andhra Pradesh, it was West Bengal's turn to share their experiences with SFGs. Pressed for time, West Bengal began by speaking about the SFGs that have been identified. The Baseline Assessment Studies (BAS) conducted by the Indian Statistical Institute have helped identify some disadvantaged social groups and have provided an insight into the situation of their children.

The groups thus identified include:

- the minority population of Murshidbad district, particularly their girls, who are educationally deficient
- children from economically backward groups from the Sundarban area, of 24 South Parganas engage in collection of prawn seeds (eggs). Each egg fetches Rs. 10/- in the market. Despite the risk involved and the fact that these children have to spend so much time in water, the remunerative nature of the work assumes greater relevance in their life situation and children stay out of school.
- first generation learners have been considered as yet another segment of children who call for special attention and treatment.

No SAS has yet been carried out in West Bengal. The state presentation spelt out its expectations from any SAS that may be conducted in the state in the future.

Following this presentation, resource persons briefly spoke on planning, gender, tribal education, research supported planning, etc. Comments by the Resource Persons further helped in providing conceptual clarity among the participants. By the end of this session, the state teams were more or less in a state of preparedness to embark upon their plan refinement exercise.

After lunch, the participants split into statewise groups. The lone representative from Andhra Pradesh joined the Gujarat team while the three member team from West Bengal joined the Himachal Pradesh and Orissa teams. Professor V B Shastri, retired professor of Anthropology in Behrampur University was attached to the Orissa team, Dr. Ila Patel, IIRMA to the Gujarat team and Dr. Deep Das joined the team from Himachal Pradesh. TSG Consultants moved between teams to assist the group activities and also see to it that the group work was progressing in the desired direction. TSG Planning, Research and Pedagogy unit members also attended the workshop and helped facilitate and integrated approach.

The starting point of the group work was an assessment of the existing WPBs 1996-97 and 1997-98 in the light of the discussions so far and the objectives of the workshop. This helped identify the gaps in the plans and ways of addressing such gaps were discussed at length.

The existing plans have tried to cover the concerns of girls and tribal children. A few initiatives, such as mobile and residential schools, have been planned for the migratory population in Gujarat and Himachal Pradesh. The plans propose interventions to ameliorate the language issue, integrate the tribal and gender perspective in textbooks and teacher training programmes. To assist in these activities State and District Resource Groups have been envisaged in the plans. Apart from the direct interventions planned, there is ample scope to build in the SFG perspective in many of the other proposed activities, though this has not been indicated in the plans. It is imperative that such possibilities be known to the programme implementing teams otherwise it is likely to result in lost opportunities.

The teams were provided with inputs on how the desired perspective can be built into the plans, the scope to innovate, the ingredients of holistic planning, how plan needs to take into account every aspect of the proposed activity, etc. It was explained to the teams how the plan documents should be self explanatory and the underlying strategy possible to understand from them.

In the course of the group work the teams pointed out that as they were well into the WPB 1996-97 it may not be feasible to incorporate many changes. However, with the delay in official launch of the project there is likelihood of large scale spill overs to the next financial year. The consensus was, therefore, to concentrate on improving upon the AWPB 1997-98 and the long term plan of the states and districts.

Before closing the session on group work at the end of the first day, the state teams undertook to work on plan refinement in order to sharpen their focus on the SFGs, using the SAS inputs and discussions at the workshop. Team members distributed responsibilities amongst themselves prior to dispersing for the day.

The teams continued with group work during the pre-lunch session on the second day of the workshop. They took off from where they left the previous evening. The group members efforts to improve the plans proved to be very useful and saved a lot of time. Each member shred his/her thinking while others reacted to it by way of strengthening the proposed interventions. After a couple of hours discussions of this nature, the state teams were in a position to finalise their plan presentations.

Post lunch, the teams presented the proposed plans which seemed to be more specific and clear after the planning exercise.

After each state presentation there were questions raised and points made by the participants. This, further contributed in clarifying the plan intent and sharpening its focus. The significant features of the suggested modifications are:

- There has been a marked increase in the number of interventions planned for the SFGs
- Every aspect of the proposed activity has been accounted for the detail as separately costed sub-activities
- More options have been considered by the teams while working on plan refinement
- SAS inputs have been drawn upon, alongwith past experiences from DPEP I states, other education projects and inputs from the workshop
- The plans now propose innovations
- The plans have been made realistic and are closer to ground realities
- The AWPB interventions proposed for the SFGs during 1997-98 form part of a larger strategy design which has been evolved for the entire project period

The modifications summed up above, reflect attitudinal changes, sharpening of perspectives, introduction of new strategies/ interventions and agencies involved in the implementing process.

In the context of Gujarat, the focus of the SAS has been essentially on the tribal population, which may be legitimised by the fact that the project districts have very high tribal representation. Though gender concerns got marginalised to some extent in the SAS, it was possible to balance out this gap at the workshop as a result of the gender specialist attached to the team for the group work. Her knowledge and experience of working in Gujarat furthered the team members understanding and approach.

Internalisation of the gender perspective was evident from the state teams ability to see the link that exists between certain state policy and programmes and achievement of the goals of UEE, e.g., the impact of the ongoing drinking water scheme on enrolment, retention and achievement. A new found ability to recognise the importance of state government interventions in matters linked with enrolment, retention and learner performance, e.g., timely distribution of text books, modification of school timings, etc., is also noticed. These alongwith incorporation of health check ups in the AWPB are pointers toward efforts at convergence.

The team members perceived with clarity the ways in which the interests of girls, tribal children and children from other SFGs can be made a part of the general awareness building activities. Their ability to look beyond what has been the practice in their state, is apparent from the proposed attachment of para teachers in single teacher schools and Shiksha Karmis in tent schools meant for the migratory tribes. It has been suggested that care be taken to incorporate the gender and tribal perspective in text books and this is proposed to be ensured through revision of textbooks and preparation of textbooks accordingly. Workshops have been envisaged for preparing training methods, developing teaching materials, audio/video material, posters and folders which adequately address the concerns of SFGs and are free of any bias. Some of the research ares identified also pertain to revision of textbooks for elimination of gender bias, dropout and tribal education, etc.

The modifications suggested by Himachal Pradesh have been made specifically with reference to gender concerns and tribals. Their suggestions clearly bring out the change of perceptions following their participation in the workshop. There is marked clarity in regard to the essential details that go with any intervention. For each activity the step by step breakup of sub activities have been indicted for incorporation in the plan. e.g., in the context of formation of resource groups the team spelt out the process of their empowerment vis-a-vis the role envisaged, for conducting the awareness campaigns for women they have gone into the details of material development, the mode to be adopted as well as those who will be involved in the process.

In view of the large scale involvement of women in the PRIs, special awareness campaigns have been planned for them, and in this case also the step by step details have been indicated. Workshops have been planned for developing gender sensitisation modules and materials with the help of TSG and DPEP I States. Identification of NGOs to help in gender issues finds special mention. Towards strengthening efforts at gender sensitisation, there is a proposal to document real life success stories or stories of womens struggles for compilation and distribution. It is proposed to start ECE/ECE centres in areas uncovered by the ICDs, even in ICDS blocks and the intent to invite community involvement has been detailed as sub activities.

Himachal Pradesh even makes room for the innovative science programme for girls, which would try to develop scientific temperament among girls. Clubbed with this are issues such s eco-education and family life education which are considered vital to the lives of girls in the hills.

The state has suggested more focussed interventions for the tribal population. But there is a shift from the conventional to experiment with some successful interventions such as the Shiksha Karmi. The language problem was known but no strategy to counter it was evolved. At the workshop they were exposed to experiments being carried out in this regard in some of the DPEP I States and they have thought of incorporating the development of a bridge language inventory in their plan. To strengthen the approach towards tribals in programme implementation, orientation of all concerned functionaries has been built into the plan.

The striking feature of the suggested modifications made by Himachal Pradesh is the emphasis on follow up and development of feedback formats to facilitate follow up.

In its earlier plans Orissa had emphasised on placement of personnel in charge of gender and tribal concerns, both at the state and district level. There were few direct interventions reflected in the plans which pertained mainly to the language issue, NFE, ECE and to some extent to teaching - learning material, awareness campaigns, etc.

At the workshop, there was expressed intent to consolidate on the existing plan vis-a-vis the SFGs. Towards this, the team from Orissa suggested experimenting with Shiksha Karmis in the tribal areas. It has been proposed that textbooks and materials be reviewed from the gender and tribal perspective to ensure an equity perspective. Visit to MP has been suggested to understand their experience with the bridge language inventory which they propose to introduce in Orissa. In regard to teacher appointment, there will be explicit stress on appointment of female teachers. The teachers training programmes will include gender and tribal centred issues. The team also suggested provision of residential facilities to teachers in tribal areas to ensure their presence at site.

There are clear indications of improved perceptions as also inclusion of specific interventions to improve the situation of SFGs in the state.

Shri D. Jhingran, Deputy Secretary, DPEP Bureau, MHRD, was present during the states presentation of plans. Before summing up the workshop he made some observations about the plans proposed by the states. On the whole he expressed satisfaction at the way the plans sought to address the concerns of the SFGs. He pointed out that having taken this major step forward, a lot now depends on the why the plans are translated into action. With these remarks he thanked the participants, resource persons and organisers for their time and efforts in consolidating the plans.

Workshop Outcome

On the whole, the workshop can be said to have served the purpose for which it was organised. It was useful as it:

- provided forum for sharing and exchanging research findings, ides and experiences alongwith the opportunity to improve upon action plans
- provided a learning experience which will go a long way in fine tuning the basis for interventions under DPEP
- facilitate the participants in acquiring conceptual clarity and understanding of issues
- enhanced planning capabilities among the participants
- established that this is part of replicable method of plan refinement

However, with specific reference to the plans, two follow up issues emerged in the course of the workshop:

- The modified plans will need to be incorporated in future planning in the states
- For incorporation of the planning exercise undertaken in the workshop the SPOs and DPOs should be guided by the planners who attended the workshop.

The participants did not see any major constraint in this, as they were nominees of SPOs and DPOs but being new states just bout to launch their DPEP project, the apprehension was understandable.

Participants Feedback

A Feedback From was circulated among the participants to record their impressions about various aspects of the workshop.

The presentations on the SAS findings for revising the state/district plans were found to be useful by most participants and very useful by a few. They were in general agreement that sharing of the SAS findings of other states and the methodology used helped in refining one's understanding of the issues identified in one's district.

According to the participants the group work and assistance provided by the resource persons were also found useful.

Research, Planning, Community Mobilisation, Pedagogy and Monitoring are all areas in which more inputs are required. In this context assistance from the national component has been sought by way of experts for workshops at the state level and issue of directions to the states to involve researchers in the planning process.

It was heartening to note that the participants found the workshop useful.

Research Support for Future Planning

Strengthening Efforts

The SAS were envisaged to provide insights into specificities pertaining to sections of population which have existed in isolation and have been removed from mainstream development efforts, so that their concerns can be duly addressed in the plans. The SAS conducted have revealed valuable information about SFGs based on which some interventions have been planned by the DPEP II states.

The realisation of experiences in DPEP so far has been that researches are of proven worth in working out action plans. Information must be available for evolving meaningful plans. And a good plan provides the basis for systematic and meaningful implementation which in turn optimises the result output in the field. Conversion of effort and resources can thereby be maximised. Relevant information helps in prioritisation of issues and assists in development of plans that are, in a way, responses to existing realities.

Follow up

The following have been mentioned as follow up activities that can be taken up at state/district/sub-district level:

A. Planning

- hold workshop on actual activity and intervention necessary at the state/district and sub-district level.
- setting up residential schools gender issues
- dissemination of information of DPEP

  developing a dialogue between NGOs and state/district functionaries involved with DPEP
- conduct annual survey on the progress made using comprehensive survey forms for VEC, Block sub-division, district levels. The results can be used for addressing the emergent weaknesses in the plan of action and initiate modifications
- seek district level inputs for addressing issues raised by the SAS

The post workshop follow-up measures could be:

- Follow-up with the states towards incorporating the strategies and interventions evolved in the National SAS Sharing Workshop, for SFG in future Action Plans

- Fine tuning the Action Plans in collaboration with State/ District level DPEP project management in the light of the National SAS Sharing Workshop outcomes
- Develop their state and district AWPB 1997-98 with focussed interventions for SFGs
- Ensure that the SFGs perspective is integrated in the plan and the idea is internalised by project management
- Develop research in areas identified by the National SAS Sharing Workshop
- Ensure that the researcher and planner work together in finalising the state and district AWPB 1997-98.

B. Research

Research needs spelt out are in the areas of:

- Santhali language and commonly used vocabulary
- Nature of migrating tribes and education of their children
- Socio-cultural and economic aspects of tribal communities and the other communities, from a gender perspective
- Monitoring
- Isolation of teachers
- How to motivate teachers to become accountable to the local bodies and VECs
- Case studies of Sevasrams/residential Sevasrams
- Awareness of SIs and teachers about DPEP
- Identification of tribal components of a particular area

Thus the research process needs to be streamlined in a manner that it yields useful information presented in a systematic fashion. Efforts in this direction will obviously have to begin at the pre-research stage and run through execution of the studies. There is also need to provide inputs in the post research stage when research inputs will be used in designing strategies and plans.

Measures to render the 'research to planning exercise fruitful:

- Organisation of orientation programmes for research agencies at various stages of the research process, viz., pre-study to orient them about DPEP, the study objectives and how the study results are proposed to help/be used in developing need based and focussed plans oriented towards SFGs post data collection and analysis prior to report writing to ensure that the information generated is presented in an organised fashion so that maximum benefits can be drawn by planners from these studies. This exercise will also ensure that all the qualitative details find a place in the report and information is not lost.

- Involvement of persons with some basic understanding of the programme through the entire research and planning process is very crucial.
- The TOR for the studies should focus on issues that have a bearing on planning. It may be desirable to separate the empirical studies from generating status reports about ongoing schemes, review of literature and research, etc.
- The timing of the studies should be such that all information is available to the planners well before they embark upon the planning exercise for the states and districts.
- Proper identification and selection of research agencies.

Courtary: DPEP Calling, November 1996

12

National Sharing Workshop

Held in response to a long felt need among the States, the National Sharing Workshop on Teacher Training was meant to enable DPEP States to share information on current activities in teacher training, the processes adopted, achievements, difficulties and new solution/ methods identified. As the workshop schedule indicates, the first two days (and a little of the third) were devoted to presentations by the States and feedback/comments by participants and resource persons. Participants also had the benefit of presentations by Lok Jumbish, Shikshak Samakhya, and the U.P. Basic Education Project. The latter part of the third day focussed on identifying some of the major issues/ areas where support is needed by the States, possible follow up actions from the workshop and hints towards the role of the national component in this regard. Time had also been allocated at the end of every session to enable resource persons to comment, highlight issues and share information that might be of value.

As the first 'sharing' workshop in DPEP, there was, initially, a little hesitation among the participants. This soon gave way to vigorous discussion and exchange of information, experiences and anxieties. What emerged was the desire to define the issues and problems and find workable solutions for them. Whether it was the desire to avoid dilution leading to 're-invented' cascades or the lack of resource persons giving rise to generation of resource groups at district and State level or the belief that the teacher training process needs to be dramatically improved, resulting in introspection and even overhauling the training programme, it was evident that in every State there is serious concern for quality while struggling with the numbers of teachers who need to be trained.

Keen interest was also displayed in the presentations by U.P. Education Programme, Lok Jumbish and Shikshak Samakhya, with DPEP States looking for different ways of addressing problems and concrete ways of realising abstract goals.

In a number of instances — as in addressing gender issues, teacher motivation, development of training capacity, community involvement, etc. the experience of these projects offered many lessons. The discussion was also enriched by the presence of resource persons — whose comments were often incisive and thought-provoking — as well as resource institutions in National Council of Educational Research and Training (NCERT) and Indira Gandhi National Open University (IGNOU) whose contribution towards the content and reach of teacher training will benefit DPEP States greatly.

Finally, the workshop resulted in identification of common concerns and specific needs. An agreed-upon plan of action for the next few months was also drawn up to address these concerns.

I

Where we are

Emphases in training programmes

By and large, training programmes evolved in DPEP States lay emphasis on the MLLs, activity based and child-centred teaching methods, content areas, and creation and use of teaching learning materials. The amount of time allocated to each naturally varies from State to State. Content areas are centred around the new MLL-based textbooks as well as up gradation of teachers knowledge and skills in content areas. Diagnostic tests conducted in Assam reveal particularly low levels in content areas and this is being addressed in the State's training programme. Haryana has opted for emphasizing language learning in the early years of the programme, with mathematics and other aspects being brought in as teachers develop greater confidence. Madhya Pradesh found it expedient to hold two separate programmes— one for the 'approach' aspects and the other for 'content' areas.

Karnataka is addressing the attitudinal and HRD aspects of teacher training with the help of an NGO specialising in this area. Maharashtra too has explored possibilities of aspects such as personality development, yoga and HRD in training to address attitudinal development.

Often, the nature of the training programme and its objectives has been evolved through a consultative process, with an attempt being made to assess the needs of teachers as well. A general consensus seems to be that overloading training programmes with information is detrimental to its objectives and that it would be better to break the envisaged curriculum into parts and conduct separate training programmes for the parts over a year or two. Some of the States have made an effort to distinguish the present training from earlier training programmes included in Special Orientation Programme for Primary

School Teachers, MLLs etc. Others, who are functioning in an environment where there has been little or no training before, are evolving modules suited to present requirements.

Discussion on what needs to be emphasized in training programmes yielded two areas that need to be addressed:

- identification of teacher competencies
- multi-grade multi-level education.

While many of the States have separate gender sensitisation programmes, the nature of this aspect and the way in which it can be incorporated in our training programmes was discussed in response to the Lok Jumbish presentation. Apart from Karnataka no other State has emphasized the needs of disabled children, and discussion is still needed on addressing tribal issues in training programmes.

Methods

A range of methods is being explored using background papers, demonstration lessons, field trips, activities, making and using teaching-learning material, group discussions. A common concern however, is that despite the best intentions training sessions tend to lapse into lectures. This is partly due to dilution as the training programme passes down the cascade s well as to the lack of exposure of trainers to a range of training methods.

There was considerable discussion on this problem: should all the trainers have primary school background, how can DIET staff and BRCCs best be oriented, can training material help trainers go beyond lecturing. Some of the States have responded by trying to minimise lecturing (Assam has tried to ban it at the CRCCs training ! Karnataka is relying on use of activities and AV material, and Maharashtra has tried to allocate a minimum 40% of the training time for activities). Participatory and experiential methods used by Lok Jumbish and the U.P. Education Programme were appreciated by the participants.

An understanding is emerging that different methods are required for different objectives. That skills are not developed in the same manner in which concepts, information or attitudes are acquired. Kerala felt that it needs to offer teachers more 'practice' time during training programmes. The methodology utilised by Madhya Pradesh in its 'approach-based' training will be different from that adopted in the 'content' training.

However, it is quite clear that there is need for greater exposure to various training methods, particularly in aspects such as attitudinal development and sensitisation and capacity to cater to the needs of special focus groups.

Training materials

The number of 'modules' varies from State to State, as does nature of the material. Often the material has been prepared in a collaborative effort between experts and teachers. In Maharashtra, there has been considerable development of material for teachers at the district level, including guides on MLL-based teaching, use of low cost teaching aids and even a dictionary between the tribal language of the district and Marathi. In Assam, a range of materials helpful to teachers has been evolved (including material in a tribal language — Bodo — and a book helping teachers learn how to draw and use drawing for teaching purposes). By and large though, there is need for material that teachers leave training with, and use later on. Madhya Pradesh acknowledges this as a weak area where more work is required. Kerala expressed a desire to generate material such as an 'activity bank' which the teachers can use for classroom purposes. The nature of such material, however needs more discussion.

Cascade and resource support

Virtually every State is struggling with the huge numbers of teachers that need to be trained. To that extent the cascade model seems inevitable. At the same time, being aware of the negative impact on quality as the training programme flows down the cascade, a number of efforts are being made to counter this. Assam has 're-invented' the cascade and tried to make more resource support available at the sub-district level; Karnataka and Haryana have reduced the number of items to two, while Madhya Pradesh has attempted to bring together practitioners and experts at every level by organising resource groups at district and State level.

As resource groups emerge at block level and are trained, the problem of dilution is likely to be a little less. However, it cannot really be mitigated until training is seen as a recurrent process. There is consensus on the recurrent nature of training. In Haryana, different emphases are laid on every aspect of the training programme (language at first, maths later on). Tamil Nadu envisages training as being repeated every 2-3 years. Karnataka, too envisages later refresher and content-oriented training programmes.

However, the issue is by no means closed. The conflict between having to orient large numbers of teachers in a short duration and an emphasis on quality, tends to remain. An option being actively explored is the capacity building of the sub-district structures in the form of BRCs and CRCs. As their roles and requirements of them become clearer, capacity building strategies for these structures need to be evolved and implemented. At the same time, these structures need to be empowered to respond to teachers needs as and how they arise.

In the meanwhile, States have involved institutions and NGOs for resource support to the programme. Karnataka, Maharashtra, Madhya Pradesh and Assam have involved NGOs in the conceptualisation and conduct of training programmes. And Karnataka in particular has been able to obtain the support of a number of institutions for various kinds of training programmes.

Ongoing teacher support

As in the case of the recurrent nature of training, there is consensus that teachers need ongoing support through sub-district structures. All States have activated the BRCs, while CRCs are yet to be set up in Karnataka and Tamil Nadu. Madhya Pradesh and Assam have evolved detailed specifications for the roles to be played by the CRCs, including monthly meetings, school visits for on-site support to teachers and obtaining feedback to respond to teachers needs. Kerala and Assam intend to use CRCs to make coordinated inputs, discussion papers and other support material (including newsletters and even a radio programme) to cater to teachers needs as they arise. *The role of these sub-district structures is still under discussion and a distinction is required between the inputs to be made by and into CRCs, BRCs and DIETs.*

Monitoring and Evaluation

This is being looked upon as the key to ensuring quality. Very often, a training package is being trialled before being implemented on a large scale. It was as a result of this that Haryana decided to overhaul its programme. Karnataka, too trialled its package with 52 teachers before scaling it. The State has also decided to review the training programme after every 10 programmes are conducted. Tamil Nadu too intends to have a mechanism whereby feedback can be woven in into future training programmes.

However, in many ways this has also emerged as a weak area in the programme. Many of the States (and Madhya Pradesh in particular) have requested for help in evolving ways and means of evaluating training programmes.

II

Profiles

Assam

Assam has a huge backlog of untrained teachers, coupled with an inadequately staffed SCERT and DIETs that are not yet fully functional. BRCs have been set up a few months ago and CRCs have just been established. The training programme lays emphasis on joyful learning, MLLs and content based modules along with teacher motivation. Training methods have been chosen with a view to being participatory, experiential and activity based. A range of training material on various aspects has been evolved.

An initial training programme of 5 days will be followed by a 2 day programme repeated every 2-3 months. There is considerable emphasis on supporting teachers through school visits, newsletters and other materials. A re-invented cascade model is being attempted to minimise dilution. The key issue facing DPEP Assam is: how to generate and sustain resource report for teacher training.

Haryana

Teacher training was emphasized from the very beginning of the programme and the SCERT, in collaboration with NCERT and RIE, organised a workshop to evolve a training package. The experimental edition of this was to be used for the training of resource persons, but at first the floods and later on the lack of response by key persons prevented the effort from being successful.

The SCERT then tried this package with teachers and realised that there was an overload of information and more emphasis was required on activity. This led to a mid-course correction in the plan. The training package is now being overhauled, with greater emphasis laid on language learning in the first year. The training will be more cyclical in nature. To minimise dilution, most of the trainees will be trained directly by the SCERT and will then train teachers directly.

Conflict ... and an Option : Capacity Building

The conflict between having to orient large numbers of teachers in a short duration and an emphasis on quality, tends to remain. An option being actively explored is the capacity building of the sub-district structures in the form of BRCs and CRCs. As their roles and requirements of them become clearer, capacity building strategies for these structures need to be evolved and implemented. At the same time, these structures need to the empowered to respond to teachers needs as and how they arise. In the meanwhile, States have involved institutions and NGOs for resource support to the programme. Karnataka, Maharashtra, Madhya Pradesh and Assam have involved NGOs in the conceptualisation and conduct of training programmes. And Karnataka in particular has been able to obtain the support of a number of institutions for various kinds of training programmes.

Monitoring and Evaluation : The Key to Quality

Monitoring and evaluation is being looked upon as the key to ensuring quality. Very often, a training package is being trialled before being implemented on a large scale. It was as a result of this that Haryana decided to overhaul its programme. Karnataka, too trialled its package with 52 teachers before scaling it. The State has also decided to review the training programme after every 10 programmes are conducted. Tamil Nadu too intends to have a mechanism whereby feedback can be woven in into future training programmes. However, in many ways this has also emerged as a weak area in the programme. Many of the States (and Madhya Pradesh in particular) have requested for help in evolving ways and means of evaluating training programmes.

Kerala

In Kerala, DPEP is being introduced in a phased manner as follows:

(a) 20 schools in each block: grades I and II during 1995-96, grades III and IV in 1996-97;

(b) the remaining schools during 1997-98.

DIETs and sub-district structures have been in place for quite some time, training programmes for trainers and teachers have been held. These programmes focussed on MLLs, learning strategies, skill development and arranging demonstration lessons. Training modules were prepared in a workshop conducted by the SCERT. The State team felt that during the training programmes need insufficient time was kept for skill development and that other material and modules need to be developed.

Teachers have been involved in development of teaching-learning materials and are interested in adopting new teaching practices. The delivery mechanism is fairly strong but resource support is required in terms of exposure to alternative teaching-learning practices and material. It is in view of this that the State team has evolved a strategy for providing exposure to their trainers, particularly through a training of trainers, setting up of a resource centre, using teacher support material, etc. An effort has also been made to identify teacher competencies to be developed.

Karnataka

The baseline study revealed that over 90% teachers need in-service training, while facilities for this are restricted to the district headquarters. The present training packages laid emphasis on subject matter, often at the cost of aspects such as multi-grade teaching, preparation and use of teaching aids; etc. DIETs are in the process of being set up and the State has made an effort to acquire resource support by involving institutions and setting up a core group. Development of:

(i) modules followed preliminary meetings and needs assignment, leading to a conceptualisation in two parts: content & methodologies orientation, and

(ii) an HRD programme.

The package evolved was reviewed by experts as well as trialled with 52 teachers and modified then in the light of feedback from this experience. The distinguishing features of this package are its emphasis on gender aspects, needs of disabled children and evaluation in addition to MLLs and other aspects of teacher training. There is ample scope for trainees to perform activities themselves, undertake field trips and use audiovisual material. A two-tier cascade model has been evolved whereby the experts who prepare the training package impart training to resource persons, who then train teachers. Close monitoring of the programme is woven in to ensure quality.

Madhya Pradesh

The distinguishing feature of the work in pedagogical aspects in Madhya Pradesh is the collaborative efforts by SCERT, RIE and an NGO, Eklavya. At the State level, a technical resource group has been set up, along with district resource groups at the district level. However, since teachers and block level people are present both in the State level group and vice-versa, this is different from the usual cascade.

While some of the DIETs are in the process of being established, BRCs and CRCs are in the place. The training programme evolved, is being implemented in two parts. The first part focusses on the approach and methodology of primary education while the second part focusses on the content and textbooks. The approach-based part of the training has already been conducted, and the content based part will follow later. Some background material has been prepared for the approach-based training while the content-based training will be centred around textbooks that are being developed through a process of training by the SCERT in four blocks, and Eklavya in one block.

Maharashtra

Maharashtra has a number of strong institutions at various levels — SCERT, Textbook Bureau and Maharashtra Institute of Educational Planning and Administration. DIETs are being made functional in all DPEP districts while BRCs and CRCs are in place.

A great many programme such as Bal Melas, Gath Sammelan, etc., have been held at the grassroots level. A number of workshops at the State level — on training methodologies and issues in transforming the teaching-learning process—have led to evolution of the training package.

A residential in-service training workshop for primary teachers emphasized MLLs, teaching-learning material, learning methods and processes. A range of methods and materials is used: background papers, assignments, group work, lesson preparation, exercise's demonstrations etc.

Teacher motivation and involvement is a major aspect. Efforts towards this are made through teachers conventions, a bimonthly newletter for teachers, booklets and materials produced at district level and "bonus" training programmes.

Tamil Nadu

In Tamil Nadu, it is quality rather than access that is the main issue. There is a greater need for contemporary teaching methods and renewal as well as development of training programmes that are geared towards this emphasis on quality.

The Directorate of Teacher Education Research and Training, DIETs and BRCs are involved in teacher training. The State has not yet set up CRCs, as BRCs are easily accessible. Teachers and HMs are trained in all aspects of teaching to make education joyous and meaningful. Supervisory staff is also trained to ensure a high quality of teaching-learning process. Current training programmes build upon earlier one's such as SOPT/MLLs and emphasise upon the use of new textbooks, development of low cost teaching aids, etc. Training modules were developed involving teachers, authors, educationists and others. It is envisaged that training will be repeated every 3-4 years. Feedback from training programmes will be used to modify modules.

Lok Jumbish Parishad

This presentation, made by Dr. Lalit Kishore, highlighted the process aspects of this project. Starting from an analysis of the reasons for Rajasthan's educational backwardness, strategies were evolved that were people oriented, de-centralised and participatory, but also focussing on quality.

At the beginning of the programme, while the situation in teacher training was poor, there was also available a rich NGO resource and the experience of the Shiksha Karmi project. The strategy that was evolved harnessed this resource while also emphasising the development of State Institute of Educational Research & training and DIETs. The teacher training evolved aims at developing the teacher as a person, ensuring linkage with curriculum and textbook reform, development of skills and enhancing teacher motivation. At the same time, the other key objectives of the programme, especially the focus on gender aspects, are not lost sight of. The methods adopted are experiential, participative and activity based. The whole programme seeks to replace the culture of teacher condemnation with one of teacher support.

To facilitate teacher training, an interactive cascade was evolved, where each link in the cascade has a dynamic relationship with the one above and below it. A recurrent training, it is also voluntary in that teachers are free not to attend it — which seems to help ensure their presence. A careful selection of trainers, backed by training and exposure, as well as regular planning and evaluation, enable master trainers to play their role effectively.

Notes from discussion on presentation by LOK JUMBISH

1. Lessons from Lok Jumbish:

- Don't sacrifice the process for the sake of speed. Experiment, try out.
- Go slow on key issues.
- Involve everyone at all levels, only then will decentralisation be there.
- a holistic approach, with things woven into each other rather than, say, a special session on gender.

2. Ideas on curriculum:

Lok Jumbish has modified the MLLs. An example was given from the EVS component.

Regarding competencies in EVS the State resource unit faced a lot of problems. At the primary level a child is unable to relate to expectations such as becoming a good citizen, etc. On the other hand a child is curious about the local environment. Therefore EVS needs to focus on natural and social environment of the local area/district, local history. Local objects and environment are more important to a child than national heroes.

For example, some aspects included in geography: direction, local climate, wind, movement of the trees leaves, sky, symbols, map making, class map, school map, village map.

The principles adopted:

- knowledge is not given as an end product to the child
- the process of finding out is more important, discovering and generating knowledge for oneself rather than receiving it from the teacher.

The project took the strengths of many projects, especially the series of books for children entitled Khushi-khushi, brought out by the Prathmik Shikska Karyakram of Eklavya.

3. Gender aspects

To facilitate attendance of women teachers in training programmes, creches/day care centres were arranged for their children during the training.

Gender sensitisation includes-

- pictures of girls doing things, but more importantly gender sensitisation is woven into every session.
- role plays (where males play female roles) has been found useful, as has the production of 'play-lets' by women.

Because of all these steps, women teachers feel a part of everything. Finally, listening skills are emphasized, where discussions are not for or against something and agitate the mind.

Shikshak Samakhya

Shikshak Samakhya, as Dr. David Harding informed the participants, is a mass scale programme supported by UNICEF in many states. A teacher motivation programme, it seeks to achieve among teachers a renewed commitment to their professional responsibilities and a change in the way they interact with their students in the classroom.

Moving away from the cascade approach, the programme adopts a teacher-teach-teacher approach and draws its resources from district, block and cluster levels. The material for the highly participative sessions of the training too are prepared by teachers. Emphasising 'joyful' learning, there is an effort to achieve an immediate and visible change in the classroom, especially through the use of different teaching practices and the use of the simple and colourful and classroom aids at low cost. The community and the administration are involved in this support to the teacher as well as change in the classroom.

Notes on presentation by SHIKSHAK SAMAKHYA

- A major success of this programme is that it has succeeded in achieving a collegeality among teachers whereby they share and work out their problems, try out new ideas and methods between themselves and the children, there and then. Whether it is in the physical sprucing up of the classroom and the painting of a blackboard at children's height on the walls, or the use of learning aids and interactive teaching practices, the fairly immediate change tends to sustain motivation and further community participation.
- In terms of teacher training there is a need to have well-defined teacher competencies. Greater attention needs to be given to the established principles in the initial phase of training.
- A major pedagogical question raised was: Do we really need new textbooks? Perhaps we don't need to change textbooks but teacher training. It is possible to improvise, using old textbooks; in other words, old books used with new methods? This might be achieved if a thematic approach were applied, with sequencing not being rigid and the teacher having the flexibility to introduce other material.
- Shikshak Samakhya looks upon its training programme as one that could be coordinated with, or seen in convergence with, DPEP.

U.P Basic Education Project

A major problem confronting this project, Shri Madhukar Gune informed the participants, was that of the enormous numbers of teachers to be trained. Using the cascade mode and activity-based methods, a first cycle of training was completed, focussing on effective teaching, teacher motivation and language and maths competencies for classes 1 and 2. In the second cycle, the primary focus is on language competencies for classes 1-5. The methodology here is more MLL-based, and also addresses aspects such as effective classroom interaction, multi-grade situations and gender bias.

Training manuals evolved at the State level were revised on the basis of feedback from initial rounds of BRC level teachers training. Training modules contain worksheets and each participant is required to maintain a learning journal. While training kits are available at the BRC level, each teacher is also given a carry-home kit at conclusion of training.

Development of instructional material has centred around the development of supplementary readers, which has involved teachers, writers and illustrators. The series, entitled *Indradhanush* will be trialled in 60 schools for two months and then revised on the basis of this evaluation. Thus, the teachers training in cycle 3 will be based on reinforcing language competencies through use of these supplementary readers.

Finally, a pre-induction programme has also been evolved for newly appointed teachers.

Notes from presentation by the U.P

EDUCATION PROJECT

Some distinctive aspects of the project:

- There is a 6-week school readiness programme in the beginning of class one.
- Classroom practices are monitored closely through continuous comprehensive evaluation.
- For multi-grade teaching, teachers take help of peer leaders, self-teaching, etc. For such class-work, the maths kit evolved by the programme is very helpful. An effort is also made to practice cooperative teaching: exchanging roles by two or more teachers according to proficiency.
- By and large, kits given to teachers gather dust because there has been no participation by teachers. Therefore the contents should be devised by the teachers themselves, which will generate a sense of ownership.... And this is what has been done.
- The training manual was prepared in a series of programmes; however there is no fixed manual but a constantly evolving one.
- There is also a support system for teachers by their seniors.
- Every BRC has a school nearby, which facilitates practice teaching during training programmes.
- The project is using school libraries as community-based learning centres.

National Council of Educational Research and Training

Presenting the suggestive training design evolved by the NCERT, Prof. G.L. Arora informed the participants that in addition to primary school teachers, it is also meant for headmasters, CRC Coordinators and resource persons at block and district level. Providing for universal coverage, this is a recurrent programme, designed to be flexibly used. The main components of this package include awareness, content upgradation and pedagogy. Additional components for head teachers and CRCCs and resource persons have also been detailed. A distinguishing aspect of this package is that it facilitates involvement of participants in the planning, implementation and evaluation of their learning experience. Training methodologies include self study and discussion, learner centred approach, demonstration, observation, immediate feedback and practice.

Notes on discussion on NCERT's presentation

NCERT's focus has been on:

Quantum of Content, and

Duration of training

The most crucial issue is the identification of resource persons and master trainers. Should it be on the basis of seniority or some other basis? Sometimes senior people have lost touch with active teaching, though they might have expertise. One possible solution lies in the DIETs. But there are many problems there e.g. resource persons get transferred. States need to build a strong cadre of Resource Persons.

Teacher motivation : Teachers do not like to participate in-service programmes, especially during vacations. There is a hostile group of teachers. How do you ensure willing participation in training? We have to break this culture of hopelessness. Motivate them to participate in training programmes as well s teaching in school.

There is a lack of coordination between the curriculum/materials group and the teacher training group, resulting in difficulties.

What are the competencies we are seeking to develop among teachers? A lot of material is available, and more is being developed.

Teachers and RPs require additional reading material. Some mechanism has to be developed for this. And this material will be in addition to in-service training material prepared.

NRG's work: The National Resource Group set up by the NCERT has undertaken the following tasks, among others:

1. Documentation of in-service teacher training practices in the country; compiling and disseminating these to the State;
2. Preparation of a suggestive training design.

The NCERT would also be undertaking an exercise for assessment and peer group support for teacher training.

Indira Gandhi National Open University

Briefing the participants on the possibilities in the use of the distance mode for in-service training of primary education personnel, Prof.

Mohan Menon of IGNOU began by highlighting the needs and context that underline this effort. The diversity of needs, the large number of teachers to be trained and the need to cut down on transmission loss, indicate that a range of solutions is required. The varied aspects of the problem require solutions that integrate different models, make use of all available techniques and media, and use all resources available. In this context, the distance mode can supplement or reinforce other training experiences and help in reduction of transmission loss. At the same time, it can accommodate contextual and individual variations.

At present a fair degree of infrastructure and expertise is available in the form of radio and TV channels, as well as expertise in material development. Emphasizing the contextualised nature of input, Dr. Menon pointed out that the formulation of distance training strategy and identification of programmes would be based on identification of the needs of specific States and even specific districts. To support this effort, national, State and district level institutions would be involved. It would even be possible to offer credit for short modules, if desired. One important aspect of this approach would be that it would be integrated with the existing programmes rather than trying to substitute them. In fact, even existing training material could be used if needed, with required adaptations. Following this Prof. Menon used a diagram to explain the technical aspects of the tele-conferencing programme of the School of Education, IGNOU, to bring forth the various dimensions and possibilities for distance mode in teacher training.

In the discussion that followed, it emerged that there is a readiness to try out the possibilities of such inputs. For instance, Karnataka had tried this out in the case of women Panchayat members and would welcome this idea, though in an integrated fashion with the DPEP training programme.

Madhya Pradesh reported that when the distance mode was tried out for training of VEC members, they experienced difficulties in transporting TV sets and availability of electricity. They suggested that if the relay took place during the CRC training or meeting, it would help. Assam pointed out that instead of the district level, the programme should be thought of at the block level. Programmes would have to be made at State level because of local language. This would also require expertise to be available at State level for whatever interactive component that is included.

III

Concerns, Questions, Issues

Teacher motivation and teachers needs

Teacher motivation is an issue that generates concern all around. Yet, exactly how is this best likely to be achieved?

There is a tendency to see teachers as functionaries whose main shortcoming is that they fail to perform their tasks properly. There is instead a need to realise that the teacher may be as much a victim as a villain. That is/he has a difficult situation to handle (multi-grade, multi-level and often multi-lingual classrooms) for which is/he is ill prepared (training is often lacking or when imparted does not seem to help the teacher work in the situation) and hardly supported (there is no on-site counselling). In such a context the nature of the administrative machinery (and the school inspector was mentioned as the face of this machinery) does not really add to the motivation of the teachers.

What is required is to identify teachers needs and use them as a basis for determining the emphases our training programmes should have. It would also help generate 'ownership' of a training programme by teachers if something as simple as the following were done asking teachers their expectations at the beginning of a programme and actually attempting to cater to them as far as reasonably possible.

What kind of training needs assessment is required? Should it be based entirely on teachers perceptions of their needs? A suggestion was made that initially a training design could be made that would expose teachers to a number of new aspects, but over the years a situation could be arrived at where a more 'bottom-up' approach for identifying teachers needs could be evolved. This would naturally need to reflect in the design and sequencing of training programmes, which would not be rigid but flexible enough to respond to teachers needs as they emerge.

Among the problems identified as being faced by teachers were the following:

a. coping with different paces at which children learn.

b. handling multi-grade, multi-level situations, and

c. understanding the MLLs.

There was also some debate on whether it is acceptable to talk of teacher 'competencies' as the word tends to leave out aspects such as attitude towards learning. And, it was asserted, a person who does not have the urge to learn cannot really teach and will also be difficult to train.

The Teacher : As Much a Victim as a Villain

There is a tendency to see teachers as functionaries whose main shortcoming is that they fail to perform their tasks properly. There is instead a need to realise that the teacher may be as much a victim as a villain. That s/he has a difficult situation to handle (multi-grade, multi-level and often multi-lingual classrooms) for which s/he is ill prepared (training is often lacking or when imparted does not seem to help the teacher work in the situation) and hardly supported (there is no on-site counselling). In such a context the nature of the administrative machinery (and the school inspector was mentioned as the face of this machinery) does not really add to the motivation of the teachers.

What is required is to identify teachers needs and use them as a basis for determining the emphases our training programmes should have. It would also help generate 'ownership' of a training programme by teachers if something as simple as the following were done asking teachers their expectations at the beginning of a programme and actually attempting to cater to them as far as reasonably possible.

What kind of training needs assessment is required? Should it be based entirely on teachers perceptions of their needs? A suggestion was made that initially a training design could be made that would expose teachers to a number of new aspects, but over the years a situation could be arrived at where a more 'bottom-up' approach for identifying teachers needs could be evolved. This would naturally need to reflect in the design and sequencing of training programmes, which would not be rigid but flexible enough to respond to teachers needs as they emerge.

Among the problems identified as being faced by teachers were the following:

a. *coping with different paces at which children learn.*

b. *handling multi-grade, multi-level situations, and*

c. *understanding the MLLs.*

Content and Quantum

In what way should the issue of content of training programmes be looked at? There was general agreement that no single in-service training programme can be regarded as complete in itself and that a certain degree of phasing is required. This could be in the form of variations of the following:

a. focussing on all the subjects for classes 1-2 in the first year, and 3-4 in the next.

b. focussing on a single theme, such as language leaning, for classes 1-5 in the first year, and another theme the following year...It was suggested that in this approach it might be possible to first address issues that teachers are more comfortable with (such as language), and then move on to aspects (such as mathematics) which teachers find difficult. In fact, Haryana stated that it might opt for this approach.

While the 'standard topics' are covered by most training programmes, it was asked whether there is an effort to explore issues such as the following:

1. In discussions, there is usually an anti-behaviorist tie-up with the romantic in that 'joyful' learning is predominant. However, it is also recognised that learning can be a painful process too, and often is. How can this be taken into account?

2. Classroom contexts: What is the impact of classroom organisation on the learning process? The common arrangement is one where the teacher sits on one side and all children in rows on the other side. Are there ways in which the teacher can capitalise on the kinds of classroom organisations or structures available to him/her?

   Or, can an analysis of the classroom dialogue be used as a resource for learning?

   Should a teacher correct errors? There is often an insistence that teachers should not 'correct' errors, for this would not exactly be child-centred. At the same time a teacher is in a difficult situation, with little time available, and has a mandate to 'deal' with errors? How should this issue be handled in a training programme?

3. Is the multi-lingual nature of the classroom a problem or an asset? And what should one do with it?

4. MLLs have recently been revised. What bearing does this have on training, material, and the issue of diversity across the districts?

There was also considerable discussion on the duration of a training programme. Exactly how much can be covered in a few days? Some of the States shred their experiences. While Karnataka found it difficult to complete the modules they had included, Tamil Nadu felt that it was in a position to cover them. From the discussions, particularly those on the U.P. education Project and the Lok Jumbish project, it emerged that it is not really a question of the number of modules, but the nature of interaction and the kind of processes that a training programmes tries to trigger off. Thus rather than a fixed number of modules to be covered a more flexible approach might be more fruitful.

A related issue was that of the training of each level in the cascade. Usually, the CRCCs and the BRCCs seem to get more or less the same kind and amount of training as teachers do, with an additional day or two. A suggestion was made that, compared to the present quantum, each level requires a much greater degree of training than the lower level.

Methods

In a situation where training programmes tend to rely heavily on lectures, what are the kind of methods that can be incorporated into current efforts? A few participatory and experiential methods were reported in the presentation of the U.P. Education Project, Lok Jumbish and Shikshak Samakhya. However, a number of aspects emerged for more detailed discussions later on at the State level.

Classroom Context : Some Important Questions

What is the impact of classroom organisation on the learning process? The common arrangement is one where the teacher sits on one side and all children in rows on the other side. Are there ways in which the teacher can capitalise on the kinds of classroom organisations or structures available to him/her?

Or, can an analysis of the classroom dialogue be used as a resource for learning?

Should a teacher correct errors? There is often an insistence that teachers should not 'correct' errors, for this would not exactly be child-centred. At the same time a teacher is in a difficult situation, with little time available, and has a man date to 'deal' with errors? How should this issue be handled in training programme? Is the multi-lingual nature of the classroom a problem or an asset? And what should one do with it?

Training Programmes : A More Flexible Approach

There was also considerable discussion on the duration of a training programme. Exactly how much can be covered in a few days? Some of the States shared their experiences. While Karnataka found it difficult to complete the modules they had included, Tamil Nadu felt that it was in a position to cover them.

From the discussions, particularly those on the U.P. Education Project and the Lok Jumbish project, it emerged that it is not really a question of the number of modules, but the nature of interaction and the kid of processes that a training programmes tries to trigger off. Thus rather than a fixed number of modules to be covered a more flexible approach might be more fruitful.

1. What kind of methods will facilitate the communication of concepts such as 'activity', joyful learning, etc.? A number of trainers have not experienced activity based learning for themselves either in schools or in training. Thus methods used in training programmes tend to contradict the very concept of activity based learning which sees the learner as an active participant rather than a passive recipient. There is a need to explore the possibilities of trainees actually doing activities among themselves and analysing them as step of developing the ability to convert them into classroom practices.
2. In the shift towards emphasis on skills and child-centredness rather than teacher-centredness, there is a tendency to reduce the concept of activity based learning to 'song and dance'. This naturally leads to an outcome that is often criticised for being merely 'active without learning'. There is a need to counter this by emphasizing the analysis and reflection aspects of activities, as well as helping teachers perceive how activities are not ends in themselves but means to promoting learning.
3. A related question is: can 'activity-based time' be seen separately in a training programme and if so, what should be its proportion in the training programme? Many of the States pointed out that they had allocated time for activities, implying that there would be non-activity time (which might end up by being based on standard lectures delivered with a view to impart information). Instead of this, perhaps what is needed is a conceptualisation of training which looks upon the training

process as one where it is not as if information is imparted to passive trainees, but one where the trainees construct this information through a variety of processes, are active and participate in their own learning process. From this point of view, it becomes difficult to separate the time when the participants are active and when they are not.

4. While the notion of flexibility in a training programme is considered generally desirable, there is little understanding of how complicated it is to run a programme which, while having a general direction can also be altered to cater to emerging needs. To what extent then should a training programme be detailed in advance? Should there be a meta-content or should this changing evolving programme come from teachers?

Materials

There was considerable discussion on materials that can be used during teacher training or by teachers later on. This aspect seems to present a common difficulty in that there is usually an 'information overload', coupled with a presentation that is not really designed to motivate the reader. Also lacking in such material is an understanding of the teacher's situation or an effort to see things from his/her point of view.

Such research as exists indicates that materials for teachers, especially teachers guides are hardly read by them. This leads to serious drawbacks in the classroom processes as no training programme can expose teachers to every required aspect. A number of resource persons pointed out the lack of reading habit among teachers, which only makes the chances of teacher education material being read, even less.

What is required is material that reflects the philosophy of the programme, which does not attempt to thrust complete answers and information upon learners (pouring knowledge, that is, into empty vessels), but is more open ended and leaves its readers with something to reflect upon or stimulate them in one way or another.

A few examples of useful materials for teachers were mentioned but they are obviously too few. This also brought to the fore the realisation that specific capacity building is required in this area and that many training programmes have suffered from being unable to prepare quality teacher education material in time.

In this context, the possibility of using discussion papers for monthly meetings at CRCs, a newsletter for teachers (carrying lucid and comprehensible articles on academic issues, activities for teachers, pull-out materials that can be used in classroom, etc.) and even radio programmes was discussed.

Cascade and recurrence

This is obviously a major concern and the various efforts to minimise the dilution that 'reduces the cascade into a trickle' were shared by the States. What this brought forth also was that there is a great scarcity of good resource persons at all levels. At present such resource persons as exist are greatly stretched in a effort to ensure quality. Strengthening of resource support to training is therefore very important and capacity building strategies would be required to address the need. While the institutional base for this (involving allied institutions, NGOs and strengthening existing institutions such as DIETs) is fairly clear, what needs to be worked out is the nature of this strengthening.

While no State sees training as a one-time input, there is considerable variation on the nature of recurrence. A common pattern is that of repeating a 6-7 day programme after an interval. One variation is that of Assam where, because of logistical difficulties, a 5-day programme is followed by 4 programmes of 2 days duration each. All States see potential in the monthly meeting at the cluster level and the school visits by the CRCC to continuously reinforce training. However, it is not yet quite clear what kind of inputs would be required during this recurrent interaction and how the nature of the required input would be arrived at.

Resource development

Development of academic and technical resource for teacher training is a major requirement in most States, especially in Assam. Three aspects of this issue were explored.

a. Institutional tie-ups, with institutions such as the RIEs, university departments (such as a Department of Linguistics), etc. One major aspect in this effort is to be able to define the roles of these institutions very clearly and obtain from them appropriate inputs (the possibility of conflicting roles or duplication were mentioned). Karnataka is a good example of utilising resource capacity of institutions.

b. Involving NGOs. Once again, while role definition is considered important, it was emphasized that this option is not to be seen as a magic mantra, but one that should eventually lead to improvement in the existing structures.

c. Upgrading institutions such as the SCERTs and the district and sub-district structures. A major issue here is that of understanding the nature of upgradation and staff development required and then working out the ways in which this might be achieved. An overall strategy for institutional development in each State is required.

What is needed eventually in States is a resource group looking specifically at teacher training. Further discussion is required on how this might come about and the nature of the task to be performed by such a group.

District and sub-district structures

A major problem confronting the States is that of DIETs not being fully functional and in a position to support the programme as required. At the same time, the emerging role of DIETs was also discussed. With the BRCs and the CRCs taking over the training function, the role of the DIET would be more in terms of coordination, academic support and quality control.

A major challenge to have emerged is that of sustaining the BRC and CRC motivation levels and a strategy needs to be evolved for the purpose.

At the cluster level, in addition to the nature of tasks identified there is a greater need to enable teachers to introspect and think over the problems they have in school. This would determine the kind of teacher help and support that the CRC could provide, and the kind of activities to be undertaken at the cluster level. With this in mind, an issue discussed was what should be the background and nature of recruitment of the CRC coordinator? To what extent should seniority be the basis of selection? In this context the Assam model of selection was appreciated.

Another possibility to emerge was that of a small district group which helps the team address questions that trouble teachers — ranging from problems such as most children being undernourished or how to handle say four unresponsive children in a class of 50. A sustained effort would be necessary to generate such a group.

Evaluation

While quality control is a major issue, ways and means is which training programmes can be evaluated are not clear at all. This is especially true if training is process-oriented rather than information-based. A number of States have identified this as an aspect in which they need help.

(It was pointed out that, among other factors, logistics too tend to affect quality greatly. The nature of arrangements that need to be made and the kind that are ultimately made, can reduce the quality greatly.)

Apart from the desire to look at training programmes objectively or attempting to 'measure' outcomes, it is also necessary to undertake evaluating in order to abandon what does not work (though obviously not changing for change's sake). Thus the drive for quality does not stop at evaluation; it also needs the conviction to change what does not work.

Processes

Change process

It needs to be understood that what is being attempted is a process of change, of transformation in the school and teacher training itself. This naturally takes time; it is a whole process and needs to be seen as such. Therefore, the training design too needs to be different from what it is now.

At the same time, there is conflict in terms of the (long) time required for such change to occur and the fact that there is very little of it available. What are the implications of this for the kind of strategies required?

A linked aspect is that DPEP is attempting to work within the system rather than setting up a parallel structure. This naturally tends to reduce the kind of autonomy that might otherwise be possible; at the same time this is more likely to lead to change within the structure itself. What are the implications of this?

In the process a large number of difficulties have already manifested themselves and more are likely to emerge. while not wishing away these difficulties, a common principle could be to avoid cynicism, to be realistic yet not believing that change is impossible.

As a matter of long term vision, it should be realised that there are a number of areas where there is a need to further our understanding. For instance, the meaning of concepts such as child-centred learning, activity based learning, etc., needs to be explored and converted into concrete actions. If these can be given some coherence over the next year, it would help greatly.

What is being advocated therefore is an approach that does not suffer from being either too idealistic or cynical. At the same time, it is one that does not let things happen without check and evaluation.

Community involvement

Though the question arose, no real understanding could be developed on this aspect. Is it true to say that if training is not linked to local community needs, change is not really being implemented? (Some innovative practices in the world where this is being achieved, were hinted at.)

A related question is that of the community mobilisation aspect in teacher training. How can this be included effectively so that teachers are able to work better with the community? More understanding on this needs to be built.

The Process of Change

It needs to be understood that what is being attempted is a process of change, of transformation in the school and teacher training itself. This naturally takes time; it is a whole process and needs to be seen as such. Therefore, the training design too needs to be different from what it is now.

At the same time, there is conflict in terms of the (long) time required for such change to occur and the fact that there is very little of it available. What are the implications of this for the kind of strategies required?

A linked aspect is that DPEP is attempting to work within the system rather than setting up a parallel structure. This naturally tends to reduce the kind of autonomy that might otherwise be possible; at the same time this is more likely to led to change within the structure itself. What are the implications of this?

In the process a large number of difficulties have already manifested themselves and more are likely to emerge. While not wishing way these difficulties, common principle could be to avoid cynicism, to be realistic yet not believing that change is impossible.

As a matter of long term vision, it should be realised that there are a number of areas where there is a need to further our understanding. For instance, the meaning of concepts such as child-centred learning, activity based learning, etc., needs to be explored and converted into concrete actions. If these can be given some coherence over the next year, it would help greatly.

What is being advocated therefore is an approach that does not suffer from being either too idealistic or cynical. At the same time, it is one that does not let things happen without check and evaluation.

Terminological problems

Some of the resource persons felt that cliches prevent people from enhancing their understanding, particularly because there is a tendency to believe that once a term has been enunciated, all that it implies has been captured or apprehended. Yet it is clear that issues have not been problematised sufficiently. This indicates that there is a need to move away from the abbreviations and terms to a more focussed awareness of the problems being addressed.

Yet another manifestation of this was pointed out in the repeated use of the terms 'package' and 'covering' training contents. There is a danger that having completed the package might give the feeling that the task is completed; in fact it is just the beginning. Secondly the rage of inputs is much beyond the package itself. Thirdly, a package is restrictive in that rather than just a structured programme what is required is a multiplicity of delivery mechanisms that include more innovative strategies for reaching a large number of people and on an ongoing basis.

Similarly, it is dangerous to believe that having 'covered' an aspect in a training programme ensures that it has been internalised and will manifest itself in classroom practice.

Finally, all this indicates that the pace of the programme must not get in the way of the kind of introspection that is constantly required to enable DPEP to become a process rather than a superficial exercise.

IV

Looking Ahead

Hints for Strategies and Action

In the long term

For any qualitative improvement to take place, the District Primary Education Programme envisages a situation where:

- teachers have contemporary and internalised pedagogical understanding, which they are able to implement effectively and independently in consonance with their school environment.
- teachers have academic support within reach from a structure that is able to assess and respond to their needs as they arise and
- the system is able to renew itself by obtaining feedback from the field as well as by keeping in touch with contemporary pedagogical developments, which it is then able to disseminate and help teachers put into practice.
- institutions at State and district level are strengthened and have the vision to support teacher education objectives.

A series of steps would be required to move towards the above goals of the teacher training aspect of DPEP. Some of these could be as follows:

A. Developing an understanding

There is a need to understand in more concrete terms what we want to see happening in schools. While terms such as 'activity-based learning' have been around for quite some time, their classroom manifestation has been very limited. Naturally, this concrete understanding has to be evolved in manner specific to various States (even seemingly unrelated issues have bearing on this; e.g. the fact that schools in Assam and Kerala have classrooms filled with furniture, as against say Madhya Pradesh schools, places certain restrictions on the interpretation of activity-based learning). The various possibilities that exist in our schools to promote child-centred education need to be explored before our trainers can communicate these concepts convincingly in our training programmes. There is therefore a great need to undertake research or innovative projects in schools that would help us elaborate these concepts in manner appropriate to specific States and may be even districts.

B. Evolving the training programme

There is evidently a need to move away from the existing pattern of training, where number of resource persons (who might not even have had contact with each other earlier) conduct a large number of sessions over a few days. What is the nature of training programmes that seem to be worthwhile? The following might help the process of evolving various aspects of such a programme.

- An effort is required to locate required to locate required teacher competencies as well s assessing teachers needs.
- An examination of various models and practices available to us is required in order to conceptualise the kind of training programmes useful for us and the areas of focus that are desirable.
- Models that have successfully facilitated teacher motivation to come about or involve teachers in decision-making and implementation processes of the training itself need to be explored.
- Grassroots events (such as Shikshak Melas or VEC involvement in support of teachers involvement of teachers association) that add to teacher motivation, are some of the other possibilities available.
- A close link between the textbook development process and

the conceptualisation of teacher training would facilitate the internalisation of new understanding greatly.

At present

What seems to be emerging is a need for more organic model of teacher training. Some of its characteristics could be:

- attempting to locate the training programme in the local context, rather than conceptualising it in a decontextualised manner
- a more flexible sequencing of contents and duration of focus on each area
- an intermeshing of sessions to ensure a more integrated programme rather than one made of combination of discrete inputs
- using a diverse range of methods appropriate to the development of skills and attitudes as well as an understanding of content
- creating an experience for the teacher, approximating the kind of experience s/he might then generate for learners (in other words, making learning enjoyable and activity-based for the teacher in the training programme)
- providing enough opportunity for the teacher to actually practice some of the skills s/he is required to utilise in the classroom
- focussing on internalisation of principles, communicating processes rather than quick fixes, leaving open-ended questions for teachers to build upon rather than providing all the answers
- ensuring a mutually respectful interaction between the resource person and the teacher during the training, thus approximating the interaction desired between the teacher and the child in the classroom
- monitoring the programme through regular feedback to tailor it to the needs of teachers as they emerge.

Handling the 'cascade'

The kind of training programme emerging from the above exercise is hardly likely to be easy in the standard cascade system. Apart from working out alternative modes of the cascade, there is clear need to build capacity at all levels. What is required is not centralised training programme going down the line but one that is re-examined at each level, taken apart and reconstructed by that level. It is only such an exercise that will lead both to 'ownership' s well as the kind of capacity building required to successfully conduct the training exercise. It is thus not merely a matter of identifying resource persons and creating resource groups, but of defining their roles, especially their role in adapting and reconstructing the training process.

An Organic Model of Teacher Training

- *What seems to be emerging is a need for a more organic model of teacher training. Some of its characteristics could be:*
- *attempting to locate the training programme in the local context, rather than conceptualising it in a de-contextualised manner*
- *a more flexible sequencing of contents and duration of focus on each are*
- *an intermeshing of sessions to ensure a more integrated programme rather than one made of a combination of discrete inputs*
- *using a diverse range of methods appropriate to the development of skills and attitudes as well as an understanding of content*
- *creating an experience for the teacher, approximating the kind of experience s/he might then generate for learners (in other words, making learning enjoyable and activity-based for the teacher in the training programme)*
- *providing enough opportunity for the teacher to actually practice some of the skills s/he is required to utilise in the classroom*
- *focussing on internalisation of principles, communicating processes rather than quick fixes, leaving open-questions for teachers to build upon rather than providing all the answers*
- *ensuring a mutually respectful interaction between the resource person and the teacher during the training, thus approximating the interaction desired between the teacher and the child in the classroom*
- *monitoring the programme through regular feedback to tailor it to the needs of teachers as they emerge.*

A second aspect is that of sustaining the positive effects of teacher training. This can be achieved best through contact programmes in the form of:

a. monthly meetings at the CRC, school visits by the CRCCs, and other inputs through the BRC;
b. Teacher support material such as activity banks, newsletters, discussion papers, radio programmes. (This would naturally require teams at the State or district level who can produce such material).

Main Tasks Ahead

Among the tasks to be addressed in the coming years are the following:

1. *Multi-grade, multi-level classrooms: while the States will explore the issue, hold workshops, evolve teacher's guides on this aspect, the national component would try to collect such documentation as has been done of successful practices in this area, study a few projects to prepare case studies on them and organise a national workshop to discuss the various issues to have emerged.*
2. *Teacher support material: States would go ahead with the plan to develop newsletters, discussion papers etc. The national component would put together a range of interesting material and hold a few National Exposition Programmes to provide exposure to State and district teams.*
3. *DIET operationalisation: while the States would provide information on the current status of the DIETs, the Bureau would put together the final Report. The national component would also initiate a discussion on possible strategies for the professional staff development of DIETs.*
4. *Documentation of teacher training practices: This would be undertaken by the NCERT and made available to the States shortly.*
5. *Assessment of teacher training programmes: the NCERT would organise this assessment through workshops and field visits.*
6. *Defining teacher competencies: The NCERT would take this up and disseminate information on this aspect*

Eventually, it should be possible to create a community that has the resources to work on its own and is not dependent on outside resources.

Indications for action

It was broadly agreed among the participants of the Workshop that the following areas would be emphasized in the near future:

- multi-grade teaching: evolving the concept, exploring the various organisational strategies available, the pedagogical principles involved, and resource materials available.
- institutional development, especially of district and sub-district level structures.
- locating indicative teacher competencies.

Some of the guiding principles agreed upon were:

- initiatives would be taken by the States individually; no 'spoonfeeding' by the national component.
- issues and strategies identified would be State specific rather than general.
- as they are scarce at present an attempt would be made to pool resources; thus major workshops at State level might include personnel from neighbouring States in order to maximise the benefit.

Among the tasks to be addressed in the coming year are the following:

1. Multi-grade, multi-level classrooms: while the States will explore the issue, hold workshops, evolve teacher's guides on this aspect, the national component would try to collect such documentation as has been done of successful practices in this area, study a few projects to prepare case studies on them and organise a national workshop to discuss the various issues to have emerged.
2. Teacher support material: States would go ahead with the plan to develop newsletters, discussion papers etc. The national component would put together a range of interesting material and hold a few. National Exposition Programmes to provide exposure to State and district teams.
3. DIET operationalisation: while the States would provide information on the current status of the DIETs, the Bureau would put together the final Report. The national component would also initiate a discussion on possible strategies for the professional staff development of DIETs.

4. Documentation of teacher training practices: This would be undertaken by the NCERT and made available to the States shortly.
5. Assessment of teacher training programmes: The NCERT would organise this assessment through workshops and field visits.
6. Defining teacher competencies: The NCERT would take this up and disseminate information on this aspect.

Other Tasks Ahead

Other task ahead would include:

Development of textbooks based on MLLs so that teacher training methodologies can develop round these.

Reviewing how teacher support at grassroots level is functioning at cluster levels.

Workshop for resource development.

Examining whether there is good reading material for teachers available in all the major languages of the State; whether supplementary material is required and identifying it.

District and State level newsletters for teachers.

Other tasks

These would include:

- Development of textbooks based on MLLs so that teacher training methodologies can develop around these.
- Reviewing how teacher support at grassroots level is functioning at cluster levels.
- Workshop for resource development.
- Examining whether there is good reading material for teachers available in all the major languages of the State; whether supplementary material is required and identifying it.
- District and State level newsletters for teachers.

Source: DPEP Calling, March 1996.

13

Empowering the Girl Child through Education

Viewing education as the basic agent of change in the status of women, the National Policy on Education calls for the national education system to play a positive interventionist role in the empowerment of women.

In its effort to create a closer link between education and the life of people, the NPE had envisaged a two-pronged strategy:

First, the removal of disparities in access and the second the equalisation of opportunities through affirmative action programmes. These programmes would be specifically tailored to address the specific needs of those denied equality to date.

India is already home to the largest number of illiterates in the world. Of the 263 million illiterate Indians, 197 million are women. The literacy rate differential is also reflected in all other human development indicators. Women's access to health care, adequate nutrition, sanitation facilities, clean drinking water is significantly less than men's access.

Reflective of the low status of women is the most sensitive indicator of human development, the infant mortality rate. India has a skewed sex ratio, with 829 women to 1000 men in some parts of the country. During the field surveys for the gender studies, researchers found in some blocks of Haryana, sex ratios of 500 girls to 1000 boys in the age group 0-6 years.

Development thinkers across the ideological spectrum agree that education is one of the most significant factors in changing the status of women. The skewed sex ratio and the high infant mortality rate are as much a cause as an effect of the disparity in educational opportunities between boys and girls. According to the 1991 census, the female literacy rate at 39.42 per cent is bout two-thirds the literacy rate of men at 63.86 per cent.

It is recognised that in rural India, of every 100 girls who enrolled in Class I only 1 entered Class XII. In urban areas, the situation is slightly better with 14 girls of every 100 making it to Class XII. A majority of the girls in rural areas drop out in primary school. Of the 100 who enroll in Class I, only 40 join Class V, an attrition rate of 60 per cent.

Among disadvantaged groups, the Scheduled Castes, the Scheduled Tribes, linguistic and religious minorities and families living in difficult-to-reach areas, the drop-out rate is much higher.

The District Primary education Programme (DPEP) which aims to restructure primary education, so as to enhance enrollment, retention, achievement and school effectiveness, was created to reach out to the goals set out in the NPE and implement the strategy of decentralised planning, disaggregated target-setting of the Programme of Action 1992.

Now operational in 42 districts spread over seven states, the programme is being implemented in districts where the female literacy rate is below the national average or where the total literacy campaign has successfully generated a demand for elementary education.

The initiative is aimed at achieving the goal of UEE in a replicable, cost-effective and sustainable manner. Building on the experience of similar initiatives launched earlier, the programme emphasises an area-specific approach, which is contextual and sensitive to local conditions.

Integrating a gender perspective in all aspects of planning and implementation, the decentralised approach within DPEP actively encourages the involvement of local communities, particularly women, in all decision-making processes. The DPEP is committed to reducing gender disparities in enrolment, retention and levels of student achievement. It has marked gender focus with all planning and implementation processes sensitised to meet the special needs of girls' education and women's empowerment.

Providing Educational Opportunities to all Girls

One of the objectives of DPEP is the reduction of gender disparities in enrolment, retention and learner achievements. Providing all girls with access to educational opportunities is the primary goal of the programme. To achieve this, efforts are on to:

- Make the educational system more supportive to the needs of girls and women.
- Create an environment which enables women to demand education for themselves and their daughters.

In the seven states where DPEP is now operational, strategies to improve girls access to educational opportunities and women's empowerment are significant highlight of the overall planning and implementation process.

Some of the interventions are:

- Provision for alternative schooling
- Flexible school timings to suit the needs of girls
- Residential schools
- Gender-sensitive curricula and text-books
- Recruitment of women teachers
- Improved school buildings and the provision of toilets for girls
- Gender sensitisation of teachers, supervisors and project managers.

To ensure that these interventions achieve the programme objective of reducing gender disparities, an atmosphere supportive of education for girls and women needs to be evolved within the community. Towards this efforts are on to involve the village community in the day-to-day functioning of the school and to mobilise the local community to support the education of girls.

As part of this strategy efforts are on to mobilise women's groups in the village to actively support education for themselves and for the girl child. As a sustained input for bringing a gender sensitive vision to the village community and local school management, it is envisaged that women's groups would expert the right pressure for girls and women's education. In addition, the women's groups would be empowered to hold the local educational system accountable.

Some of the specific strategies devised to mobilise women are:

- The VECs, MTCs, PTAs be empowered to take on the responsibility of promoting education in their ares.
- The mobilisation of informed and active participation at the local level to build and sustain an environment supportive of girls' education.
- Community and women's organisations be involved in mobilisation; school management; monitoring; enrolment; retention; levels of achievement and classroom practices. Their mandate: to highlight the importance of girls education.
- Women's collectives be formed in villages and local activists trained to catalyse collective action around educational issues.
- Intensive capacity building of community and women's groups to focus on issues of education for girls.

Research Activities Provide Sharper Focus

DPEP strategies for girls' education and women's empowerment are sharper and more focussed. The shift from the stage of pious postulates to a more experiential and informed understanding of specific interventions within a defined time spectrum has been made possible by a series of research activities.

The activities include baseline diagnostic studies at the sub-district level for assessment of learner achievement levels and gender studies to clearly bring out the areas of disparity and discrimination among boys and girls.

The second major input has been to draw on the existing experience of innovative programmes within the country and to draw from them strategies for girls education and women's empowerment.

The strategies so identified are gender sensitive and based on the specific needs of girls and women. DPEP is also drawing on their unique implementation methods. This is evident in the integration of the Mahila Samakhya experience, use of alternative schooling methods and in the generation of innovative teaching-learning materials.

The third has been to elicit and integrate pool of expertise from amongst women educationists, activists, academics, development workers and non governmental agencies who have experience in the education of girls and women, into the DPEP management and advisory structures.

Baseline Studies on Learner Achievement

Baseline studies were conducted in 42 districts to achievement; baseline studies were conducted in all seven states. The findings are based on data collected from 850 schools, interviews with 2712 teachers, 14,341 students studying in the last year of primary school, 13,021 students in Class II and 1,099 drop-outs. Students in the last year of primary school were tested for reading comprehension and maths using standardised achievement tests reflecting curriculum objectives. The basic literacy and numeracy skills of children in class II were tested. Among drop-outs, the study attempted to learn the level of retention.

It was found that the average achievement levels in both reading comprehension and maths among both boys and girls was well below 50 per cent of the maximum score in many districts. Differential in achievement levels between boys and girls is insignificant though overall boys outscored girls. The status report was remarkably similar in all six states. However, in three districts of Haryana and in Karnataka, girls outscored boys on all tests.

The achievement differential between children from socially disadvantaged groups and the rest was also minimal. SC girls outscored all girls in one district of Kerala, Tamil Nadu and Karnataka and in two districts of Maharashtra.

The poor learner achievements in Class II are an area of principal concern in DPEP. Studies have found that the highest percentage of drop-outs occur in the first two years of primary schooling.

The studies on girls education and women's empowerment, conducted in 21 districts spread over six states, attempted to understand prevalent attitudes towards the empowerment of girls and women through education. The studies mapped the levels of gender disparities in access, enrolment and retention; provided information on the causes of non-enrolment and the high incidence of drop-outs among girls and the status of girls education in these six states.

Conducted in eight villages of each block in every project district, the gender studies included a mix of structured interviews with key respondents and group discussions. In all 15,000 parents and neighbours, 650 teachers, 1,100 students, 600 drop-outs and never enrolled children and 500 officials participated in the exercise. In each block, researchers interviewed between 30-40 teachers, 50-60 girl students, 20-30 drop-outs / never enrolled children and between 20-25 school administrators and community leaders.

The studies also found large interdistrict variations in enrolment and retention rates. In some states, like Assam, there were also significant diversity at the sub-district level. Across the country, girls appear to be dropping out or never entering a school as they are expected to work at home or in the fields. Household chores and the care of siblings were highlighted as factors keeping girls out of school. In addition, parents reported the high incidence of teacher absenteeism and their lack of motivation as another cause of keeping girls out of school.

In tandem, the gender and baseline studies have provided sub-district data which helps in formulating area-specific plans. They have helped identify retention of girls as a primary goal of the programme. The studies have shown, enrolment rates are rising and many districts are close to achieving universalisation of enrolment. However, even in areas where enrolment rates are near universal the drop-out rates particularly amongst girls, remain extremely high.

An Effective Synergy of Goals

Addressing the needs of girls has been a major concern in all educational programmes and schemes. The 1991 census found that the decennial growth rate of female literacy in the country was 9.54 per cent. The literacy rate among men grew at a slower rate of 7.76

per cent. The demand for education by women received a fillip through the TLC. The mobilisation of women through the **Total Literacy Campaign**, part of the larger National Literacy Mission, has been one of the most significant achievements of the programme. Women made up over 60 per cent of the learners in many of the districts. The Total Literacy Campaign experience has shown a rise in women's enrolment. Today TLCs are in operation in 336 districts. Following up on TLCs, post-literacy campaigns have been launched in 130 districts, nation-wide.

Other programmes have also been emphasising the participation of women in educational planning and implementation. As part of **Operation Blackboard** 50 per cent of all future recruitment of primary school teachers will be women.

Under the **Non-Formal Education Scheme,** NFE centres run exclusively for girls get 90 per cent assistance. Now 40 per cent of all NFE centres set up will be exclusively for girls.

These integrated nation-wide schemes which have a strong gender focus are implemented in tandem with smaller innovative programmes. One of the largest is **Mahila Samakhya,** or Programme for women's equality through education. The programme does not aim at service delivery. It views education "as an on-going process of empowerment, which transcends mere literacy".

This vision of the Mahila Samakhya experience is being dovetailed with DPEP. It has established the validity of gender-sensitive approach to women's education based on the priorities and felt needs of rural women as articulated by them.

Launched in 1988, Mahila Samakhya is operational in 15 districts spread over four states. First started in Karnataka, Uttar Pradesh and Gujarat, the programme was extended to Andhra Pradesh in 1992. In all the 2075 villages, spread over 15 districts, where women's sanghas or collectives have been formed, there has been a perceptible difference in the attitude of women towards education and to their own place in society. Here 'learning and change go hand in hand'.

Since 1991, the Mahila Samakhya approach has been adopted by the Bihar Education Project. The programme is operational in 1500 villages spread over seven districts.

In Madhya Pradesh, the programme is being launched in one block of three DPEP districts. In Karnataka, the Mahila Samakhya Programme in Raichur district pre-dates the launch of DPEP.

Assam is interested in the Mahila Samakhya design and is planning to launch initiation activities in 1995-96. Maharashtra is also considering the Mahila Samakhya approach in the Mahila Prabodhan Programme of DPEP.

The Samakhya strategy is particularly relevant for DPEP. The goals of the two programmes can be synergised quite effectively. Strategies can be evolved for environment building, awareness generation amongst women especially. Strategies for the actual management of educational initiatives so as to make schooling more effective and accountable to the local community can also be evolved.

Some of the salient aspects of the Mahila Samakhya approach which can be easily replicated in DPEP are:

- Interventions be based on women's needs.
- Strategies emerge from priorities set by village women.
- Mobilise and build an informed body of opinion among women for education.
- Ownership of the programme by the women of every Sangha or village women's collective.
- Evolve an informed gender-sensitive agenda and pressure group for education within the community.
- Actively participate in educational management and monitoring of village-based pre-school and non-formal education centres, monitor teacher attendance and girls enrolment.
- Create a forum for convergence of services, to support sibling care, health and economically productive activities, to address the needs of girls and women holistically.
- Establish local accountability of educational projects to community, parents, particularly mothers.
- Creation of project management structures that are gender-sensitive at all levels and play a facilitative role for grassroots-based activities.

DPEP has also observed the experiences of the Shiksha Karmi project in Rajashthan. Shiksha Karmis are para-teachers, women and men motivated to educate children but without the formal qualifications to become primary school teachers.

Some Shiksha Karmis have only completed upper primary school. Yet their desire to learn and teach and willingness to put the needs of children, particularly girls first has made a perceptible difference to the attitude of communities, parents and children towards education. The learning centres, where they teach have flexible timings, decided by the teacher in partnership with the community. This allows girls and boys to study at their own pace and to a convenient time.

With the objective of facilitating girls access to school, the project addresses the problem of teacher absenteeism, particularly in remote, difficult-to-reach village.

Functional in 1066 villages spread over 25 districts, the programme has placed 2514 para-teachers in 67 blocks. These teachers reach out to 1,02,454 children in the 6-11 age group.

The programme is particularly interesting as the management structure has been designed to allow NGOs and the state machinery to work as partners. The NGOs are involved in training of trainers, they supervise the training of the Shiksha Karmis and also monitor the work of the para-teachers in villages.

The Shiksha Karmis are usually from the local area, in many cases from the same village. There is a strong sense of ownership and also accountability to the community. Though not as qualified as regular teachers, the Shiksha Karmis have proved to be more motivated and willing to experiment with innovative classroom practices and teaching-learning methods.

Their presence and the people's confidence has led to significantly higher enrolment and retention rates of girls in these villages.

The experience of the **Lok Jumbish** or People's Movement for basic education in Rajasthan has also been incorporated in the overall DPEP vision. Lok Jumbish has evolved an innovative education management structure in which the planning process begins in the VEC. Thus decentralisation and delegation of authority is in built into the programme structure. In its attempt to ensure the village owns the programme, Lok Jumbish has built partnerships with local communities and NGOs to mobilise the community and involve them in micro-planning exercises at the village level. Lok Jumbish has also set up an experimental non-formal education programme which has shown positive results in increasing enrolment of girls. The project has adopted the Mahila Samakhya approach and has organised 294 women's groups by the end of Phase-I.

The experience of the Bihar Education Project has been particularly relevant for DPEP. The decentralised planning model was first fully laid out in the formulation of the BEP. In terms of people's mobilisation, the focus on redressal of gender disparities and location-specific planning, DPEP has been a successor to the BEP.

The other most significant experience has been the adoption of the Mahila Samakhya approach as a key component of BEP. Working with women's group, the BEP-MS programme found the demand for information and knowledge led quite early to a demand for education, particularly for children.

Jag Jagi, an educational innovation of MS in Bihar, means becoming aware and coping with the world. Thus empowerment through education is viewed as women taking control of their lives and dealing in the public space on their own terms. Today over 4160 girls and 2932 women make the Jag Jagi centres a forum for sharing and learning. As part of Jag Jagi, women are involved in creating a supportive environment for girls education. The 'school readiness programme' includes ma-beti melas, (mother daughter fairs), girl child fairs and sports and cultural meetings for girls.

The rise in demand for quality education led to the establishment of Bal Jag Jagi or children's creative centres. While freeing girls from the care of younger siblings, these centres also introduce a desire for learning to a young age in all children.

Realising that ensuring girls remain in school and attend classes regularly is of primary importance, Samooh women (women's collectives) informally patrol the village. Girls found outside school are promptly sent back and the mothers fined. This social monitoring has led to a sharp rise in retention rates in these villages. The sense of ownership has transformed the functioning of many schools in the 20 districts in Bihar.

Through their participation in the VEC and through informal monitoring, the Samooh women are able to curb teacher absenteeism; ensure teachers are in school on time and that the school functions in manner supportive of children's needs. A format for regular monitoring of the school has been prepared and Samooh members complete this task effectively.

Large Scale Resource Mobilisation Effort Launched

In the DPEP plans, initially the approach to address gender concerns had been compartmental and fragmented. However, with a more holistic understanding of gender perspective and the exercise with innovative projects, efforts to mainstream gender in every aspect of planning and implementation is gathering pace. There are concerted efforts to address the overt problems of girls' access to and participation in the education system.

For this, a large-scale resource mobilisation effort has been launched. **State-level advisory teams on gender have been constituted.** Invited experts from range of fields: academia, women's groups, children's rights activists and educationists act as a sounding board for ideas. The group is also an unofficial monitor of the pace and direction of the programme in reducing gender disparities.

These resource groups have been meeting regularly and have introduced fresh thinking and helped the state teams view all DPEP plans and interventions through a gender lens. Mainstreaming gender in DPEP processes involves:

- Ensuring that the plans, all strategies and the interventions which emerge operate to reduce gender disparities.
- Consciously integrating a pro- girl child slant into all strategies and interventions.
- Prioritising the gender-specific components targeted to benefit girls and women.
- Identifying groups with special needs:
- SC/ST girls
- Disabled girls
- Gifted girls

To help state project teams operationalise this commitment to mainstreaming gender, DPEP has actively involved a large body of informed opinion on gender at the national, state, district and subdistrict levels in formulating plans, chalking out strategies, designing implementation procedures. Through local workshops, seminars and meetings, women's development workers activists and non-governmental agencies and academics have been brought together to interact, advise and develop the DPEP strategy and interventions to reduce gender disparities; empower women; mobilise local communities to make a positive intervention in favour of girls' education. Also there are efforts to involve informed opinion builders in the monitoring of the programme to each stage and on every level. At present a national resource group on gender is being constituted, which will support the efforts of state and district resource teams.

These resource groups help project teams access the necessary information and local knowledge to translate plan objectives into implementable strategies. For the project teams the inputs at every stage of plan preparation, implementation, monitoring and evaluation will help ensure quality service delivery at the village level. Convergence with other departments such as health, women and child development, water, sanitation, forests and social welfare can also be streamlined. This will aid the participation of the local community in the programme and create a sense of ownership of the primary school to begin with and later the programme.

'Hidden' Gender Sensitive Components

The strategies identified to reduce gender disparities in education are two pronged : the design and implementation of interventions specifically tailored to help girls access education, and interventions which will make the system more responsive to the needs of girls. In addition, several strategies adopted in DPEP also indirectly benefit girls: improved teacher competence, classroom environment benefits, improved educational management and better teaching-learning and textual material. These strategies too have gender-sensitive components, which are 'hidden', but which provide the necessary slant to the interventions to meet the special needs of girl children.

To operationalise the plan to mainstream gender, project teams have examined budget allocations to learn what percentage of each rupee spent reaches the girl child directly or indirectly. In addition, the effort to set up state resource teams is being replicated at the district, block and indeed the village level. The local talent can be drawn upon for micro-planning exercises using a girl child-centered approach.

The thrust areas are:

Catalysing an Enabling Environment

The evolution of supportive community is the foundation for a process of empowerment of the girl child.

For this, multi-media campaigns to raise awareness of the need for education are planned with the girl child as the focus. In addition, environment building activities such as orientation of the VECs, women's groups by using gender-sensitive materials is envisaged.

Support services like ECCE, primary health care need to be strengthened. In Assam, the gender study found that a significant proportion of girls drop out because of ill health.

Providing Necessary and appropriate Infrastructure

Availability of school near their home is a basic requirement for girls. The provision of separate toilets is being taken up as part of DPEP. To reduce over-crowding, more classrooms are being constructed. In addition, more women are being recruited as primary school teachers. To ensure girls feel secure, Haryana plans to construct compound walls around schools. In Tamil Nadu, a system of local escorts to take girls to and from school is being experimented with.

Flexible school timings to suit girls and availability of alternative schooling facilities are also being experimented with. Educational incentives for schools with high enrolment of girls are also being considered. These incentives would be in addition to the already existing state-level schemes for enhancing enrolment and retention of girls.

Pedagogical Improvements

In all seven DPEP states, the curricula is being revised, text books are being rewritten and designed to eliminate gender bias. There are now efforts to go a step further and introduce positive and progressive role models for girls through texts all illustrations. Special gender sensitisation programmes are planned for text-book writers and designers. Karnataka is experimenting with definition of minimum levels of learning in an equity context.

Training with a Gender Perspective

Through training, the gender stereotypes and role biases are sought to be removed. This is viewed as an on-going exercise which involves all levels of managers, administrators, supervisors, teachers, VEC members and members of PTAs and Mahila Mandals.

In addition, all training programmes are seeking to integrate gender in every component so as to spotlight the importance of the gender perspective in all aspects of work. Capacities at all levels are to be built up particularly at training institutions to handle a regular and recurrent input on gender sensitisation.

Education Management and Monitoring

Critical to the efforts to integrate gender in DPEP is monitoring and management of the programme delivery system. For this, the management information system has to integrate a gender perspective. Data collection and analysis must include disaggregated information related to the girl child.

The MIS for the project is to include gender sensitive monitoring indicators. This will allow progress and responsiveness of the project and the system as a whole to issues of gender to be measured.

Qualitative indicators to measure development of community organisations and women's mobilisation and support for education are to be evolved.

Recruitment and placement policies need to go beyond encouraging women to become primary school teachers and appointing women as coordinators of girls education and women's empowerment. Rationalisation of transfer and placement decisions are issues of concern in all DPEP states. They are to be addressed in manner where the impact of women in decision making, as role models and active determinants of classroom transactions can be enhanced.

Women need to be more visible in decision-making positions and in positions of authority. State societies are increasingly conscious of this and recruitment profiles are showing that more women are being inducted to management positions.

Evaluation of Strategies and Interventions

For project teams at all levels, self appraisal of efforts to mainstream gender will be the first and most crucial step in the monitoring process. This will be particularly helpful in supervision of individual efforts. The gender monitoring cell being set up in states like Karnataka and

Assam will guide school inspectors, headmasters, and other levels of educational mangers in identifying areas of achievement and lacunae in service delivery. Supervision procedures incorporating girl child-sensitive indicators are to be developed. The availability of gender-sensitive monitoring guidelines, self-appraisal methods and supervision indicators make it easier to evaluate systemic responses to address disparities. The introduction of gender issues in the evaluation framework for every level is being operationalised.

Need for Large-Scale Community Involvement

The in-depth analysis of the status of primary education also led to the recognition of the need for community involvement on a massive scale to achieve the goal of education for all by the turn of the century. As the NPE acknowledges, "neither liner expansion nor the existing pace and nature of improvement can meet the needs of the situation".

The formation of village education committees who will be the first owners of the primary school and to whom the educational system will be accountable is progressing. **The VEC is the most critical actor in the DPEP programme.** With responsibility for day-to-day management of the school, the performance of the VEC members will largely decide the effectiveness of the programme.

In many states, like Haryana and Karnataka, half the seats in the VEC are reserved for women. While all members of the VEC will be provided training on gender concerns, there are efforts on to involve the women members in closely monitoring classroom practices and teacher attitudes to pinpoint and address gender bias. They will also be asked to ensure girls attendance and participation in school. The performance of girls in achieving MLL competencies will also be monitored by the VEC, particularly the women members.

The setting up of Panchayati Raj institutions under the 73rd and 74th Amendment to the Constitution ensures decentralisation of authority right down to the village level. The VEC being a part of the wider Panchayati Raj framework will be able to hold the education system accountable. The involvement of women as decision makers in the Panchayati Raj institutions will also provide wider range of role models for girls and facilitate the process of empowering girls through education. The process of involving gender-sensitive resource persons and the local community is being conducted at multiple stages.

State-level and District-level Strategies

In **Kerala,** study sharing workshops have been conducted in all three DPEP districts and at the state level. The suggestions made by participants have been the foundation of the planning process. The district advisory committees which include a cross-section of civil society studied the suggestions which came from the study-sharing workshops and proposed specific interventions tailored to the special needs of girls.

In addition, the DPEP is using the traditional meeting place of women in a village, the Grihasadas. With much of the attention already focussed on children's needs, it was easier to introduce the idea of equal access to education. Also called the Mathru Sangamam, the mother's meeting place idea is now being extended in all project districts in Kerala. In the study-sharing workshops, participants suggested the provision in transport to take girls to and from school. The opening of ashram schools for tribal girls was also mooted.

The Kerala project expects to involve child psychologists in school management, to better understand the needs of children, particularly girls. The efforts to improve the school environment are being supplemented by the supply of revised handbooks and workbooks. These provide a wider range of gender roles and also provide teachers with ideas on gender-sensitive classroom practices.

In **Maharashtra,** a new programme called the Mahila Prabodhan Programme (MPP), has been set up. Working to create a positive attitude towards girls, the MPP works through village level women's groups. Attempting to highlight the chain linking health, economic activities and education in the lives of women, the sahayogini or cluster community mobiliser works to rise awareness of the necessity for girls' education for an improved quality of life.

The *sahayoginis'* work is monitored by the *sanchalika* in every district. They are encouraged to innovate and try out new community mobilisation strategies. The work of the *sanchalikas* and the *sahayoginis* in the field is backed by the availability of source books in Marathi on women's empowerment and on gender sensitisation.

In the long term, the state Project office hopes to launch the mahila Samakhya programme in the Marathwada region, where all five DPEP districts are located.

Maharashtra has also set up a state-level gender resource group which will work with the project office to achieve DPEP objective of reducing gender disparities in enrolment, retention and learner achievement.

In **Tamil Nadu,** the state government has a broad-based programme of incentives for girl children. Aimed at changing the perception of parents towards girls, many of the incentives aim to encourage parents to enroll and keep girls in school.

The DPEP project in the state thus concentrates on complementing these programmes by interventions that will help identify never enrolled girls and girls who have dropped out and help them join an educational programme.

Through school mapping exercises, efforts are on to identify ares with extremely low female enrollment and retention.

Compulsory registration of all school-age children is being taken up in one Panchayat union of each DPEP district. This innovation will be supported by the provision of local escorts for girls in every village. Strengthening of the mother-teacher councils is expected to create the necessary environment to keep girls in school. In addition, a state-level resource group has been set up to help the project team plan and implement strategies to facilitate girls participation in the educational system.

In neighbouring **Karnataka,** the Mahila Samakhya programme has been successfully operating in 5 districts of which Raichur district is also covered by DPEP.

The lessons learnt from the Mahila Samakhya experience have proved useful in planning both state-level and district-level strategies and interventions. Based on the Appraisal Mission's recommendations and the results of the baseline and gender studies, the state project office has been working to improve retention rates and the achievement levels of girls, particularly those from socially and economically disadvantaged families.

The strategy-building exercise began with a study-sharing exercise in Mandya district. The suggestions made by experts and resource persons have been incorporated in the district and state plan. state-level gender resource teem has been formed. In its first meeting, the group suggested incorporation of gender perspective in all training programmes rather than isolate the gender component.

In addition a gender monitoring cell has been set up which will meet every quarter. This cell will examine all DPEP interventions through a gender lens to learn if they have helped girls participate in education.

With thc SCERT, Minimum Levels of Learning with gender equity are being developed. Also, supplementary learning material is being written and illustrated. This will remove gender bias and will also provide positive, progressive and diverse role models for both girls and boys.

In Karnataka, every DPEP district has come up with distinct ideas to eliminate special problems. Thus in Beigaum and Kolar, survey of the needs of disabled girls is on. In Raichur, the survey of disabled girls needs will be accompanied by a campaign to raise awareness of the need for education. The DIET in Mandya is creating a resource group on monitoring all interventions from gender perspective. In Kolar, lady inspectors are being appointed to supervise the progress of DPEP especially in reducing disparities in access to educational opportunities between girls and boys. In Belgaum, district resource centre will also provide karate training to interested girls, as a means of developing feeling of self-worth.

In Raichur district where the Mahila Samakhya programme is operational, the Sakhis and Sahayoginis are also being involved as resource persons on training and community mobilisation.

Assam in the north-east of India faces a unique set of problems. While overt discrimination against girls is unknown, the retention rates of girls in school are extremely low. In addition, the TLCs are still being conducted in the state and their impact on enhanced demand for elementary education is still to be noticed.

The strategy to improve girls' participation in education is thus quite different in Assam. Other than the baseline and gender studies, the census data has been used to identify problem villages and blocks. The analysis of the census data by the state project office found wide variations within a district. The attempt is thus to ensure that intra-district and intra-block disparities are addressed and eliminated in phased manner.

The special problem areas like tea gardens, riverine areas and minority community enclaves are also being considered separately in the planning exercise. In these areas, where cultural or environmental factors are keeping girls out of school, special efforts are being made. The local moktas, or madarasa is being used in primary schooling centre.

In 12 villages of Baganbani block in Dhubri district which has a large shifting population, the concept of Shiksha Sevikas is being experimented with.

The Mahila Samakhya programme is being launched in one block in each of three DPEP districts as part of the effort to empower women and girls through education. Based on the Jag Jagi experience in Bihar, girl child festivals are being planned at the sub-district level.

All these ideas have been taken up after the study-sharing workshops which have been conducted in three districts. To keep the link between research, training and field experiences and to assess the progress of DPEP in improving the status of girls through education, between 20-30 per cent of the research allocation will be specifically tailored to projects on the needs of the girl child.

A state-level resource group has been set up to work with the project team on strategies to reduce gender disparities through DPEP.

Another venture to link women's empowerment with girl's education is being tried in the north Indian state of **Haryana**. To get mothers more involved in children's education, particularly the education of their girls, it is proposed to ensure the presence of mothers in all future parent-teacher association meetings. In addition, mother-daughter fairs are being planned where films on girls education will be shown, children's literature with new role models will be displayed and there will be an opportunity for mothers and daughters to interact with other women and girls.

The effort to mainstream gender in every aspect of planning and implementation begins in the village. At least 50 per cent of the members of the Village Education Committee must be women in the state. Through the efforts of the VEC, the schools, particularly the lead school in every cluster is being viewed as a community centre for gender sensitisation of the community.

Gender Focus in DPEP
Specific Interventions for Girls

The District Primary Education (DPEP) has been taken up in 42 districts of 7 States, all of which are educationally backward, with low levels of female literacy. The decentralised implementation plans include specific interventions for girls.

DPEP is a major initiative aimed at achieving the goals of UEE in a replicable, cost-effective and sustainable manner. The programme builds on the need to effectively reconstruct primary education, as a whole, instead of a piecemeal implementation of schemes. The major strengths of this programme are its sensitivity to local conditions rather than a rigid framework, the approach is contextual and is tailored to meet local situations and needs. Planning and management are decentralised and the emphasis is on involving local communities. ***A gender perspective has been incorporated in all aspects of planning and implementation, and is an integral part of the programme.***

Programme goals include a specific focus on reduction of gender disparities in education, as reflected in lower enrolment, retention and achievement of girls, particularly those from socially and economically disadvantaged groups. The programme seeks to integrate all the measures needed to achieve UEE in the specific context of a district. The effort is to:

- *Manage the process of bringing about change in the educational system.*

- *To make the educational system more sensitive and responsive to the needs of girls and women.*
- *To enable women to demand education for themselves and their daughters.*

Interventions for girl's education initiated under the programme include:

- *Alternative schooling.*
- *Flexible school timings to accommodate girls' needs.*
- *Residential schools.*
- *Gender-sensitive curricula and textbooks.*
- *Recruitment of women teachers.*
- *Improved school buildings with toilets for girls.*
- *Educational incentives.*
- *Gender sensitisation for teachers and project mangers.*

Apart from these specific strategies designed to enhance girl's access, enrolment and retention in the school system, the programme recognises the crucial importance of enabling local communities, particularly women, to play an active role in every aspect of the programme:

- *Formation of village-level women's collectives and training of local women activists to catalyse collective actions around educational issues.*
- *Empowerment of local bodies such as Village Education Committees, Mother-Teacher Associations and women's groups, to enable them to take the responsibility for promoting education in their areas.*
- *Intensive capacity building for community and women's groups to focus on issues of education for girls.*
- *Involvement of the community and women's organisations in mobilisation and school management, and in monitoring enrolment, retention, levels of achievement and classroom transactions, with emphasis on girls.*
- *Mobilising informed and active participation at the local level to build and sustain an environment supportive to girls' education.*

A special training module has been designed to sensitise project mangers, supervisors and education administrators on the importance of girls education and women's empowerment.

With 19 districts, **Madhya Pradesh** has the largest DPEP project in the country. Four major workshops have been conducted in the state in the last year to share relevant and specific strategies for girls education and women's empowerment. Beginning with an overview of the status of girls' education, the series of workshops focussed on the Mahila Samakhya experience; integration of ECCE with primary education. The last workshop in the series examined methods to integrate a gender sensitive approach in all training programmes.

These workshops also provided a pool of resource persons who could be called on to help the state or district-level project offices. A state-level gender core team has been constituted which meets six times a year. Monitoring progress of girl's education and providing support to the various project units is their primary task. Similar teams have also been set up in every district. These teams work closely with the state and district project officers in charge of girls education. The groups include educationists, NGOs, teachers, academics and members of the project team.

Mobilising women to advocate education as a pre-requisite for empowerment is a major concern in the state. The Mahila Samakhya programme has been launched in three DPEP districts. In every district, one block with low female literacy has been chosen.

One of the more interesting aspects of the Madhya Pradesh experience has been the concerted attempt at convergence of services. The health, women and child development, rural development, forests and water departments have all been tapped to address the difficulties which keep girls out of school.

The convergence of services at the community level is strengthened through the involvement of villagers. Community involvement is expected to create a sense of ownership for the programme and the internalisation of the strategies for girls education and women's empowerment. Women's conventions are organised in every district, block and village. The conventions provide the preliminary awareness of the need for girls' education. This is followed-up with back-to-school and enrolment drives.

The enrolment drives are supported by a series of initiatives to keep girls in school. The Shishu Shikshan Kendras serve a dual purpose. By caring for siblings in the 0-3 age group, they free girls from a major chore. At the same time, children are exposed to a learning environment at a very early age.

To cater to children with special needs, particularly girls - from migrant families, drop-outs, never-enrolled, a system of alternative schooling has been developed.

The model developed in Madhya Pradesh is more flexible than the centrally-sponsored NFE programme. Here districts have the flexibility to choose their own teaching-learning material from the prescribed lists. The districts have the right to augment, supplement teaching-learning material to address local needs. School timings can be changed to suit the convenience of students. Vacation timing and schedule are also flexible. Some of the alternative schooling centres can also be exclusively for girls depending on local demand. These efforts are being supported by initiatives to strengthen the state and district level resource institutions.

Review of Interventions

The annual work plans which incorporate these strategies and interventions were reviewed at a National Workshop held in New Delhi on June 1 and 2, 1995. The two-day meeting allowed state project teams to interact with select resource persons, identify and address lacunae in planning and refine strategies to improve girls participation in the educational system.

What emerged was a confirmation that DPEP is a programme which has a clearly defined gender focus and seeks to reach out to out-of-school girls, especially those from socially and economically disadvantaged families DPEP seeks to create an environment that is supportive of and accommodates the needs and priorities of the girl child. This vision of DPEP has also enabled ownership of the programme to vest with the local community. The communities can help evolve area-specific, contextual strategies and interventions to reduce gender disparities in enrolment, retention and learner achievement. At the same time the local communities can enforce public accountability of educational facilities at the local level.

The restructuring of primary education in the country through DPEP thus seeks to catalyse a significant improvement in human development indices and secure the future for every girl child. *

Source: DPEP Calling, August 1995.

14

DPEP : Mahila Samakhya Interface

Backdrop for the interface

Integrating gender perspective has been a focal point for interventions across the educational system in India. Several basic education projects in the country from 1990 onwards have focused on alleviating the distortions of the past and providing an edge to the education and empowerment of girls and women. Empowerment-oriented strategies for women with a clear focus on education were piloted first through programmes like Mahila Samakhya.

The Mahila Samakhya approach and strategies have to a large extent already been accepted by the first generation education projects such as the Bihar Education Project, Lok Jumbish in Rajasthan and the Uttar Pradesh Basic Education Project. The District Primary Education Programme, the latest entrant in the field of basic education, has also tapped the experience of MS.

Both MS and DPEP are run by the Education Department at the national and state levels.

Mahila Samakhya

Launched in 1988, Mahila Samakhya is one of the most successful efforts within the government sector to link women's empowerment with education. Mahila Samakhya views education as an on-going process of empowerment, which transcends mere literacy. The programme is operational in 17 districts, spread over four states: Andhra Pradesh, Gujarat, Karnataka and Uttar Pradesh.

The Samakhya Approach

The Samakhya approach begins with the understanding that women must identify their problems and solutions at their own pace. This vision of the Mahila Samakhya (MS) experience, it is believed, holds lessons for DPEP. MS has been able to establish the validity of a gender-sensitive approach to women's education based on the priorities and felt needs of rural women as articulated by them.

Rationale for the Interface

MS assistance and expertise has had a powerful impact on DPEP gender policies and strategies during the past two years. MS insights and support have strengthened the gender focus within DPEP. MS resource personnel from the States/districts and the National Resource Group have interacted and influenced DPEP plan formulation and strategies.

Both programmes share similar objectives. DPEP and MS are already geographically overlapping in 12 districts. With the DPEP expansion expected to cover nearly all existing MS districts, are convergence is a very important factor for both programmes.

20 months into implementation of DPEP, it seemed appropriate for both programmes to take stock of what had been their experience and for spelling out the possibilities of interaction.

For this a one-day dialogue between State Project Directors was planned. The interface on July 11, 1996 examined the possibilities of a relationship between the two engendered education programmes: The District Primary Education Programme and Mahila Samakhya.

Gender Focus Within DPEP

The programme is being implemented in districts where female literacy rate is below the national average and the Total Literacy Campaigns have successfully generated a demand for elementary education.

DPEP has a marked gender focus with all planning and implementation processes sensitized to meet the special needs of girls education and women's empowerment.

DPEP also seeks to:

- *Encourage the involvement of local communities, particularly women, in all decision-making processes.*
- *Make the educational system more sensitive and responsive to the needs of girls and women.*
- *Enable women to demand education for themselves and their daughters.*
- *Manage the process of bringing about change in the educational systems.*

Participants

State-level decision-makers from both programmes participated in this day-long programme. The dialogue moved from policy to practice and back. The project directors of Mahila Samakhya societies in Andhra Pradesh, Uttar Pradesh, Gujarat, Madhya Pradesh and Bihar participated. DPEP was represented by Madhya Pradesh; Maharashtra; Kerala; Haryana; Assam and Tamil Nadu. The State Project Director of the Bihar Education Project also participated. The interaction was facilitated by the national office of MS and the TSG gender unit.

The Interface

Mr. R.S. Pandey, Joint Secretary, DPEP, highlighted the linkages which geography and common programme ideals have created between the two programmes and hoped they would be strengthened further. For while MS has a much broader focus, both programmes seek to prioritize the catalyzing grassroot level processes. He asked that the group identify the safeguards MS requires to maintain its autonomy while at the same time understand why such safeguards are sought. He also wanted MS to examine the factors inhibiting its expansion and how they could be addressed.

The Samakhya philosophy is rooted in the strength women derive from being active members of groups. Village women's collectives, the sanghas, are the propeller of the programme. The Sahayogini, who facilitates 10 sanghas, plays the role of catalyst. While the programme in all six states has had a different trajectory, in each case education was demanded by the women.

The MS approach needs both time and space especially in the initial years to bring women together in sanghas.

MS strategies for mobilization of women and their active participation in community activities, and local decision-making including educational for were also brought out in the presentation. Women's efforts to establish local accountability of the schools, to play an active role in the management of ECCE and NFE centres and schools, support teachers and participate in panchayat/VEC for were highlighted as areas where MS expertise could benefit larger education programmes.

The Emerging Relationship

The discussion on areas of concern and the identification of issues on which the two programmes can learn from each other, set the stage for a free wheeling dialogue on how to strengthen the relationship.

The first are those States where Samakhya was operational and DPEP was lunched later such as Karnataka and now Gujarat.

In Karnataka, the two programmes overlapped in Raichur. However with the expansion of both DPEP to another 6 districts and MS to another three, there will be total geographical convergence. In Gujarat so far both programmes have been launched in Banaskantha district. In Andhra Pradesh, even though no districts have overlapped, Karimnagar, where DPEP is now starting, will be included in the next phase of expansion.

In these states and districts the larger basic education programmes have benefited a great deal from the already existing MS programme.

The second set is of States which have opted to lunch Samakhya through DPEP: Madhya Pradesh and Assam.

In Assam and MP, conscious support from the DPEP state office and the state government concerned has helped in ensuring a clear articulation of the reason for initiating MS as well as enabled and guaranteed its autonomous structure.

Samakhya personnel at district and sub-district levels have helped in mobilising communities. This process has worked to the mutual benefit of both organisations. The TLC and later the DPEP environment building campaigns, set the stage for the entry of MS. Setting up Sanghas and getting women to analyse and articulate their concerns became that much easier.

Since the agendas are often the same as are the strategies, DPEP will have to ensure that MS is not overloaded.

Finally, there are DPEP states which have opted to take on board the Samakhya experience and evolve a variant of MS, such as Maharashtra. DPEP Maharashtra has adopted many of the Mahila Samakhya approaches in the Mahila Prabodhan Programme (MPP) launched as part of DPEP. MPP is operational in all 5 districts.

A variation to this is the earlier experience of the Bihar Education Project. Since 1991, the Mahila Samakhya approach has been adopted by BEP.

The BEP experience has shown that a basic education project can help start MS by creating enough space within the larger programme. This has enhanced BEP's understanding of gender concerns and helped strengthen both girl child specific and integrated strategies.

The BEP-MS relationship has now reached a crucial stage. The MS programme has developed a distinct identity, which has generated specific requirements in terms of responsive management and decentralised decision making. There is currently an active dialogue within MS-BEP on what shape and structure the future relationship should take.

Differences in Approach

The discussion which followed highlighted that despite common aims and similarities, there are many who believe that in certain ways, DPEP and MS are entirely different programmes. There is of course a difference in target groups. While DPEP reaches out to children, especially girls, seeking to ensure they come into and stay in schools, MS involves women in its activities, views literacy as one of the skills which will help women empower themselves.

Concerns

- *The basic definition of education means different things for DPEP and Mahila Samakhya. Whereas in DPEP it means getting children into primary school, keeping them there, and ensuring they learn the three Rs, in Mahila Samakhya education means an on going process of empowerment which is more than mere literacy.*
- *In DPEP there is an overall EFA framework and goals to be achieved in terms of enrolment, retention and achievement levels for the children of primary school going age. DPEP in a way is a strategy for achieving these goals.*
- *Mahila Samakhya while it also lays stress on local planning, responds as a programme to the set of priorities and pace set by the village women themselves. The education emerges on their agenda, rather than gets superimposed from outside. This process cannot be rushed, is respected by the programme facilitators and is one of the significant non-negotiables of Mahila Samakhya project management.*
- *DPEP takes a holistic view of educational development while Mahila Samakhya is more overtly women centred and works with women's groups on their issues and strategies.*
- *Mahila Samakhya management is gender sensitive and nearly all decision making positions are with women. While committed to gender sensitive administration, the number of women in decision making positions in DPEP is not the only yardstick.*
- *Project management in Mahila Samakhya has necessarily established deep and lasting linkages with the voluntary sector. While DPEP also enjoys this flexibility, it has remained even now more dependent on government structures and systems.*
- *A principal concern now emerging is that expansion of MS cannot be on par with DPEP given the very different processes and time frames.*

Working Together

- *There are equal if not more pros to the MS-DPEP relationship. With both programmes tracing their mandate and vision from the National Policy of Education '86 and its Programme of Action '92, the programmes are high priority in the Department of Education, Ministry of HRD, Government of India. Both programmes are run through committed Government of India funds and are coordinated in the DPEP Bureau which deals with externally aided programmes.*
- *Both Ms and DPEP share a common vision of Education for All by the turn of the century and each in its own way is contributing to the enormous task of achieving UEE.*
- *MS and DPEP give primacy to participatory planning and implementation and prefer to work closely with village communities, parents/guardians and other stakeholders so that there is local ownership and decentralized management. Thus both programmes recognise that process is as important as reaching quantified targets and that local partnerships must be nurtured.*
- *With DPEP progress is measured in quantifiable terms against previously set targets rather than the seemingly non-target driven, more qualitative assessment of empowering processes in Samakhya. Every sangha generates its own targets and their nature depends on the milieu. This sangha-centred approach is akin to what DPEP aims for, in the long term.*
- *The two programmes are committed to ensure that the educational system responds to the special needs of girls and women both through supply side interventions and also by demand creation in local groups.*
- *Project management strategies at state level are similar in DPEP and MS state programmes where they have registered autonomous societies with decision making bodies like the executive committees and General Council.*
- *MS management practices and structures which are gender sensitive and facilitative rather than directorial, have some important lessons for DPEP structures.*

MS tends to look to the women's movement for ideas and support and portrays itself as a women's empowerment or education programme. DPEP because of its very different scale and time schedule remains skeptical of this effort, where results are difficult to quantify.

Mahila Samakhya project directors pointed out that education has become the priority and is the agenda as set by Sanghas. In Samakhya, education is more than the ability to read and write, it is the inculcation of the ability to think about a situation and realize ones own potential to change it for the better. For this the ability to read and write is a pre-requisite and treated as such.

In MS, the concern is with seeing the system through women's eyes and catalyzing changes, at a pace decided by the women themselves as manifested through the sanghas.

This approach, while not unique, is still to be fully accepted within programmes like DPEP, which work as part of the regular educational system. DPEP has found that while integration of gender in all aspects of programme design and implementation is the aim, they have had to work out women-specific strategies. They have looked to Samakhya to lead the way.

Establishing MS

The afternoon session concentrated on demystifying the procedures of establishing the Mahila Samakhya programme. Sr. Sujitha, Ms. J. Kameshwari and Ms. Nishi Mehrotra shared the experiences of establishing Samakhya societies.

Modalities of procurement and reimbursement through DPEP and MS were clarified. As part of the Memorandum of Understanding signed between the two societies, the autonomy and the safeguards required for MS processes are ensured. The annual action plan of Mahila Samakhya and the budget are passed by the EC of MS and funds are made available once in six months from the NGO grant scheme of DPEP. However, MS societies are not covered by the regular supervision mechanism of DPEP.

Outcomes and Recommendations

The day-long meeting brought to the fore both the concerns and the potentials of an emerging DPEP-MS relationship.

As a result of this interface, Kerala expressed interest in launching a Mahila Samakhya programme. DPEP Maharashtra which is implementing the Mahila Prabodhan Programme, in all five districts now plans to launch MS in one of the expansion districts perhaps through NGO involvement. The State Project Director of Tamil Nadu and another participant for DPEP, Tamil Nadu also attended, to learn more about Mahila Samakhya with a view to implementing similar strategies.

Some of the salient issue for convergence and cooperation emerged.

How DPEP can benefit

- It was suggested that DPEP could learn from the MS training processes. MS, over the years has evolved a cadre of trainers who are capable of providing the recurrent, systematised gender sensitisation trainings required at all levels of the DPEP programme.
- MS has evolved tried and tested effective strategies for mobilisation of women and their active participation in community affairs, including educational issues. DPEP can seek to adopt these strategies for community mobilisation, specially for setting up women's groups. DPEP could rather converge with existing MS programmes for the purpose.
- DPEP could learn from MS methodologies on how to evolve local educational interventions based on women's needs and priorities in a holistic manner. Effective convergence in meeting local requirements for non-formal and alternative systems of education, early childhood care, girls participation in schools and teacher/school management can be made to include the active participation of local women.
- MS strategies to mobilise and build an informed body of opinion amongst women for education can help develop a pressure group for more gender sensitive agendas in the village community. As DPEP too is in the process of setting up VECs, with a defined role and mandate, learning from the experience of Sanghas can be useful. The Sangha-VEC linkage would strengthen the agenda and interactions of both.
- In other states, where mother— teacher councils or PTAs are functional, women sangha members can also be made part of these councils/associations.
- In areas where geographical convergence with DPEP exists or can be created, Sangha women can actively participate in educational management, monitoring and running of pre-schools and non-formal education centres.
- MS trainings to build capacities in project personnel, especially field based workers like Sakhis and Sahayoginis, can prove useful for DPEP. Personnel like the Sanchalikas in MPP of Maharashtra, preraks/teachers motivators, even community

workers for NGOs working with DPEP etc. could be provided training using MS methodologies.

- MS networks with grassroots NGOs and other support organisations is effective and has greatly benefited the content and outreach of the programme. DPEP could benefit from these linkages for both capacity building and wider resource support for girls and women's education.

MS could also gain from other basic education programmes in several ways

The MS programme can benefit a great deal from the pedagogical renewal processes initiated and being consolidated under DPEP.

- DPEP should actively consider supporting Mahila Shikshan Kendras which are a unique educational institution evolved in the MS programme.
- Cluster Resource Centres set up in DPEP can be an arena for MS-DPEP training and joint meetings and for better field level coordination and facilitation of village centred and processes.
- MS can play its role as catalyst and create a wider outreach in .tandem with DPEP, provided its processes are fully safeguarded by an undertaking with the DPEP programme.
- At state level there will need to be effective coordination between both programmes. DPEP must clearly articulate its support for MS and its processes.
- It emerged that DPEP and MS need to work out mutually supportive relationship with a clear understanding of possible convergence areas, to reduce any scope of overloading or unreal expectations from each other.

The dialogue helped crystallise issues at the project management level and created the necessary opening for decentralised dialogue.

Source: DPEP Calling, November 1996.

15

Focus on Pedagogical Renewal Process

In April, gender coordinators from the DPEP I states: Assam, Haryana, Kerala, Madhya Pradesh, Maharashtra and Tamil Nadu had met in Bangalore with a two-part agenda: first to define their role within DPEP and the second to chalk out an agenda for the rest of the year.

This workshop was also the first quarterly meeting of gender coordinators. It provided an opportunity for participants to compare notes and learn from each other. This gathering defined the agenda for the August '96 workshop.

The second quarterly meeting of gender coordinators was held in Bhopal, on August 30.

Based on the issues identified by participants during the April meeting, it was decided to focus the Bhopal workshop on pedagogical renewal processes. The objectives of the meeting were to come up with:

- Ideas on how to integrate positive values, images and roles in texts and training material.
- Identify effective methods to use existing material in a gender-sensitive manner.
- Schedule gender reviews at state level.

Pedagogical renewal processes within DPEP are still being worked out particularly as it involves a range of areas. Training designs for all levels of educational administrators, teachers, headmasters need to be overhauled. New material is being developed for the ECE and alternative schooling programmes. This is all in addition to the efforts to develop child-friendly text books which then need to be made available to all schools and students on time.

This pedagogical improvement exercise is a move to overhaul the entire primary education delivery apparatus. The gender coordinators role in this exercise has been limited, the limits having been set both by organisational factors and technical constraints.

While all states are overhauling their in-service training design, some have begun work on re-doing the text books and developing other materials. Gender has been identified as a critical input into both areas. To understand why and to evolve methods to ensure there is integration of gender concerns in future exercises, the Bhopal meeting focused on two seemingly parallel, but in reality complementary, concerns. The first how to conduct a gender review of text-books and integrate gender concerns in training design. The second how to use existing gender-neutral or gender-insensitive material in a girl child friendly manner. The final part of the exercise would examine how to link the process of text book improvement to teacher training design and classroom practices.

Frame for Reference

Textbooks and other learning materials are developed centrally in each state. Efforts are being made to rewrite text books from a gender perspective. Until recently the idea and ideal of femininity as defined in content and illustrations is of women and girls as relative creatures who are inferior and subordinate to men. The female gender is identified with domesticity. The ideal of femininity is of the perfect daughter, sister, wife and mother.

Some states have brought out textbooks and workbooks which are not only gender bias free but also portray boys and girls in shared roles and women excelling in different walks of life, says one study, titled 'From Girl Child to Person.' However, until all text books are reviewed and the changes incorporated, teachers have to use existing materials which continue to present women and girls very feebly, in stereotyped roles and with negative attributes. As the study points out, the text books are likely to have the following flaws:

- Predominance of male characters and male authors.
- Men in lead roles and few women shown in service roles that consist of either menial work or assisting roles.
- Women are seen as passive, timid, disorganised, weak, silly. The qualities attributed to men are courage, bravery, initiative and resourcefulness.
- Visuals show a majority of males in action, as teachers, as leaders, doctors, farmers, women appear as housewives, mothers, maids, seldom as factory workers, pilots or officers.

The Workshop

Representatives from Assam, Haryana and Karnataka joined gender coordinators from Maharashtra and Madhya Pradesh, in Bhopal. Tamil

Nadu and Kerala were not represented. There were three resource persons invited to share their experience. Dr Gayatri Devi Dutt, Deputy Director, DSERT, Bangalore shared the issues raised and the solutions evolved in Karnataka. Dr. Ila Pathak is involved with the Ahmedabad-based women's group, AWAG. The group has done two gender reviews of the primary school text books of Gujarat. Ms. Rashmi Paliwal is working with the Hoshangabad programme of the NGO, Eklavya.

The day-long programme involved taking participants through a four part exercise: The first a review of states experience with texts and teacher training; second comparing this to and learning from the experience of a non-governmental groups which took up gender reviews on a voluntary basis; the third part of the exercise, learning how to make gender-aware material. The final session of the day reviewed ways to measure progress made to date in DPEPI states. For this a series of formats were shared.

Impact of Gender Insensitive Material

- *Boys consider themseleves superior*
- *Girls feel inferior*
- *Girls photo should not be shown*
- *Role indetification: No scope*
- *Girls develop wrong attitudes*
- *Does not empower girls*
- *Teachers internalise this bias*

The Experience of Karnataka

The meeting began with a presentation of the outcomes of last meeting. This set the stage for the first presentation. Karnataka, one of the DPEP I states, has made integration of gender in pedagogical renewal processes a priority. They have examined Classes 1-3 textbooks from a gender perspective. Dr. Dutt shared the experience of the last two years. The gender review identified many blatant and some subtle negative values being promoted through texts and visuals. Thus head count of visuals showed that there were 12 pictures of girls against 88 pictures of boys.

Trying to redress the balance highlighted many unforeseen problems, like the inability of artists to give character to a girls face. With boys, the figures and indeed the facial expressions proved to be no problem for illustrators.

There were the biases of text-book writers and others on committees. Thus, when it was suggested that both girls and boys could be sent to buy oranges and grapes in a maths problem, writers turned round and accused the proposer of promoting consumerism among young children.

Other problems had to be dealt with and compromises made. Thus though there was a desire to make the books entirely gender-aware, in the interests of preserving the language, a gender neutral approach had to be adopted in many sections.

As the process picked up pace, the team learnt new approaches to deal with concerns. One of the first was to ensure there is a gender specialist in every committee. This ensures that there are a number of check points and correctives can be slotted. It was one such committee member who pointed out that though the names of children had been changed in one chapter to include girls, all the pronouns remain male. This was corrected.

Then with most writers and illustrators coming from urban areas, the content and sketches also reflect this bias. A strategic alliance was forged between the two issues. Correcting the urban bias has been much easier and is often used with gender to persuade teams to agree to changes.

Finding gender-aware illustrators however remains difficult and while it is now easier to get gender-aware material into text, changing illustrations is a concern. Thus in a story about a girl who helps a king, the illustration has the king, in the forefront with a white charger and his attendants and in one corner stands the girl. It was suggested that as the story is about the girl who helps the king, the should be given more prominence. While the team reluctantly agreed, when the chapter was finalised, the original picture was retained.

Getting people to understand the importance of each sentence and picture is critical, as is ensuring that there is a gender specialist participating actively at every stage of the text-books renewal process from content to production.

Relating this experience to the efforts to integrate a gender perspective in the training design, Dr. Dutt said that in the teachers guide, there is a separate section which introduces the idea of gender and includes suggestions on how to ensure classrooms are gender-aware. This includes tips on attitude and behaviour. Thus teachers are actively discouraged from asking girls to sweep the classroom.

In addition there is a sensitisation programme for all teachers. This three to five day programme, introduces them to both the concepts and practices of gender in all aspects of daily life.

Evaluating her experience, Dr. Dutt suggested that there is need for more material in regional languages. Karnataka is planning to document its experience with pedagogical improvement practices during the past 20 months. She however felt that despite the training, teachers have not internalised gender concerns. There is a plan to have an advanced gender sensitisation programme for all teachers, particularly as the present training does not help them deal with new situations. This is also a problem with trainers. While they grasp and can translate the ideas for teachers at different levels, if participants question them or present specific classroom situations they are unable to deal with it.

In the discussion which followed, Dr. Ila Pathak, who has completed a series of gender reviews of Gujarati text-books for primary and secondary classes suggested that perhaps there is a need to differentiate training programmes. The first set could be divided into two parts: for women and men separately, while the advanced training could be for mixed groups.

Learnings from the Gender Review of Gujarati Text Books

Ms Pathak detailed the experience of a women's group AWAG. This group included some from the university, others from the newspapers and NGOs. They began reviewing text-books out of concern and a research interest. This exercise received support from the authorities for some time but later the support dried up.

The principles on the basis of which Gujarati text books were assessed are:

- Women should be treated as human beings
- The approach to women and men must be similar
- Text books should present equality of women with men.

In their review, the group of seven women, of whom four were teachers found that women are usually not named in the texts. They are known as women Ramu's mother the farmer's wife, the girl from the next village.

In other cases, the stories advocated values which the group found unsuitable. One of the controversial stories they asked to be removed was of Rani Karmavati, who began the widely practised custom of Rakhi: a festival which celebrates the bond between brother and sister. Karmavati, the story goes, appealed to Emperor Humayun to save the kingdom, under threat from Nadir Shah's troops. By the time Humayun gets there, Karmavati has committed johar, a form of suicide, widely practised by Rajput women when enemy troops are entering a city. Objecting to the story on the grounds that it celebrates *johar*, the team asked for and got the story replaced with a local tale of a warrior queen of Saurashtra.

Similarly, the team also objected to the inclusion of the story of Hadi Rani, another warrior queen, who cut off her own head, to send a reluctant husband into battle. The issues raised in both cases, was that its not enough to show brave women, its also important to promote progressive values.

The attitude of the authors/editors could be summarily stated by pointing out how a boy and girl are treated in the Gujarati language textbook for Std. I.

There is a description of how a boy spends his morning. In the same textbook a girl describes her day.

It was morning.
I got up early.
I started getting ready.
I brushed my teeth and washed my face.
I combed my hair after taking bath.
Mother gave me snacks.
I started for school.
I met my friend on the way
We went to school together.

•

My name is Sarita
This is my mother
My mothers name is Savitabahen.
My father's name is Manubhai.
In that cradle there is my younger brother.
His name is Vijay.
He is sleeping.
I get up early every morning.
I take bath and get ready.
Then I sit down to study.
I play with Vijay (Meaning thereby: I look after Vijay).
I help my mother in housework.

The difference in the routine of a son and a daughter is quite obvious in the example. A daughter shared household chores and baby care with the mother. A son does not.

That is what the makers of the textbooks appear to think to be right thing. They have not expressed any vision of equality for girls. An illustration in the books shows: A Boy flies the kite, while the sister is seen holding the thread.

Much of these efforts Ms. Pathak pointed out require the intervention of at least two people, committed to the task on hand. She cited the example of Dr. Dutt who had found that while she was in the room with artists and writers, the gender issue remained on the agenda. When she was unable to attend, gender-blind or blatantly sexist texts and illustrations would pass through. Similarly, while the individual at the helm was interested in gender concerns, it received priority in Gujarati text-books and later the issue was no longer on the agenda.

Teaching Social Science: Subtle Intergration of Gender Concerns

The discussion on the Gujarati textbook review and the search for supporters at the level of policy makers naturally led to the Eklavya experience with text-book production. It was specifically decided to ask the team working on social science text books to talk with the group as they would be able to show how skills development and concept clarity go hand in hand. In primary schools, participants pointed out, there is more emphasis on skill development rather than on getting children to discover new methods or approaches.

Ms Rashmi Paliwal, who works in Hoshangabad with the non-governmental agency, Eklavya, pointed out that the first step in their text-book production exercise is learning that a text-book is not the sole source of information for children. They have and also need other materials, to provide variety and to grasp the issue. While supplementary materials can be prepared, existing textual and non-textual materials can also be used.

She outlined the main steps which need to be taken, the first being to ensure the legitimacy of proposed change is established. This needs to go in tandem with the requisite policy direction. There is however need to understand that even with support from the policy-makers, resistance will be encountered. For though curriculum can change through directive, text-books remain the same. Teachers are often asked to teach a new curriculum with the new text-books. Involving teachers, both as trainers and as reviewers of text-books is one part of the exercise. The second is to encourage teachers to ask questions. For a teacher who asks questions will usually encourage students to raise queries.

The third is to ensure that while preparing text-books, the emphasis would be on reality-orientation and on discovery based approaches. Thus examples used in the texts and in pictures are of different realities, most close to the reality of the children themselves. This of course means that examples need to be concretised and there should be a conscious attempt to avoid generalisations.

Finally to help children understand social realities: the text and illustrations must make reality meaningful, relevant, involving and relate it to the children's world. In curriculum terms, this has meant that while discussing industrialisation, the children are told not just about the Bhakra Dam and the first steel plant, but also about home-based work and informal sector industries and organisations.

Conclusion

In the discussion that followed, participated talked about the need for more research in the area of gender-aware pedagogical renewal. From Madhya Pradesh, participants suggested that there was need to examine the MLLs from a gender perspective. Also while there is an urgency to implement new strategies, the same emphasis on concurrent monitoring is absent.

Madhya Pradesh has the largest programme, with 19 of the 45 districts coming within the ambit of DPEP. The state has gender coordinators in place in all districts and has also established a gender core group in each district. To benefit from the coordinators in place in all districts and has also established a gender core group in each district. To benefit from the coordinators meeting, the state team asked that all participants visit a neighbouring district and provide ideas on how to catalyse field activities. The day after the meeting, field visit to three villages of district Raisen was arranged. Raisen is one of the 3 districts in Madhya Pradesh where the Mahila Samakhya Programme has been launched.

In Maharashtra also, while there have been efforts to integrate a gender perspective, it has been limited to changes in illustrations and some content changes. What is required is some method to judge progress in implementation and also at the level of understanding and gender sensitiveness among textbook writers and illustrators.

During the free-wheeling discussion it emerged that the women's voice within the system of pedagogical renewal was limited by the same structural factors which served male interests in the wider world.

The position of women was restricted not on the basis of their worth as employees but upon what was perceived as women's role. One of the ways of combating this to make more visible the gender components of each activity.

Ways to monitor progress from a gender perspective were discussed. Training alone cannot change gender relations and ensure that women and girls get a better deal. What it can do is enable both women and men and trainees to question existing classroom practices and help them evolve new teaching-learning methods which are gender-aware.

Follow-Up

At State Level

- Initiate gender review of text-book renewal and teacher training processes.
- Work out frequent monitoring mechanisms to learn the impact on gender relations within the classroom.
- Chalk out plans to include gender resource group in pedagogical improvement process.

At National Level

- Initiate process to evolve monitoring indictors
- Assist state efforts to conduct gender reviews.

16

Building a Gender Perspective in DPEP

As DPEP is being implemented in educationally backward districts which have a female literacy rate below the national average, a twin track approach is being followed. While all planning, implementation, monitoring and evaluation processes have an inbuilt gender focus, the district-specific interventions for girls. To build a gender focus in the task of annual planning and budgeting, the first national workshop on gender strategies was held in New Delhi in June, 1995. Based on the recommendations of this workshop and the expressed need to reiterate strategies to build a gender perspective in DPEP, the second national workshop was organised in New Delhi in December, 1995.

A perspective building exercise was seen as necessary to knit the demands of educational planning with the perceived needs of girl children for schooling. At the same time the programme would help participants understand that gender needs and gender interests have broader implications for planning, implementation, monitoring and evaluation.

As this workshop was a good opportunity at the national level to share experiences and build a common agenda, participants from all 12 DPEP States and the U.P. Basic Education Programme were invited. Each State was represented by the DPEP State Project Director, State level Gender Coordinator and a district level functionary, responsible for evolving girl child education strategies.

Planning with a gender perspective requires a fresh conceptual understanding and new skills to address gender-related concerns. Efforts have been made by different sectors and at various levels for planning with a gender perspective. These have rarely been institutionalised.

The Workshop Design

The workshop design evolved from the cumulative experience of the Gender Planning Training Project (GPTP) which was launched in 1993. The GPTP aimed to raise awareness of how gender plays a key role in the way women and men participate in social and economic activities and promote gender equality within social change.

Adapted to DPEP requirements, the workshop was designed to cater to the needs of planners, researchers, implementors and trainers. The workshop sessions broadly covered three areas:

- Perspectives on Gender Issues in Development
- The Gender Relations Framework (GRF)
- Analysis of diverse situations using the GRF

Discussion on the social construction of gender roles helped participants realise the over-arching importance of socialisation on the lives of girls and boys - particularly that processes are so interlinked that it determines their motivation, expectations, perceptions and attitudes. Participants were having to go through a process of unlearning and almost simultaneously learning 'new' methods of analysis. They began to accept that learning about gender is not just learning about women and their concerns but also involves learning about men.

The understanding that gender is a social construct initiated the discussion on the institutions within which gender relations need to be examined. The GRF looks at the household, the community, the market and the State as institutions in which gender bias is rooted. The strategies for change in the educational system and the wider community will need to address all of these institutions individually and also as a collective. Institutions (The household, community, market and the State) are the formal and informal rules which shape social relations and limit choices. The GRF begins from the understanding that the problem is not women but the skewed gender relations and the inequitable development process. Aiming to transform social relations, the approach views integration as a necessary but not sufficient condition for transformation of gender relations and of broader social structures.

The acceptance of institutions as formal and informal rules which influence organisational structures, employee profiles, resource allocations and in-house practices is the basis of institutional analysis through the GRF. Their impact in different institutional setting is analysed (*See p.* 253).

Relating this institutional analysis to DPEP, four critical areas were examined by the State teams:

- Text Books
- Teacher Training
- Community Support

Institutions / Aspects		Houshold	Community	Market	State
RULES	Men	*Breadwinners*	*Must support*	• *Need qualifications for jobs*	*Head of household/own assets*
	Women	*Caretakers*	*To Care for the home*	• *Clear hours of work*	*Extension of men with no independent identity*
PRACTICES	Men	*Must earn*	*Pressure to work/ earn well*	*Get hired*	*Access to credit against collateral*
	Women	*Must do housework*	*If wants to work, must also handle home*	*Work part-time/get retrenched*	*Not eligible*
PEOPLE	Men	*Do 'outside' jobs*	*Must be independent*	*Higher positions*	*Own/possess assets*
	Women	*Do 'inside' jobs*	*Shoudl be dependent/ potected*	*In 'soft' positions*	*Do not own assets*
RESOURCES	Men	*Access to education/ technology/ information*	*Access to technical qualifications*	*Qualified therefore decision makers*	*Get into business*
	Women	*Illiterate/ home science*	*'Soft' professions e.g., teaching/nursing*	*Follow instructions*	*Home-based industry*
POWER	Men	*Decision makers members*	*Leaders/committee*	*Bosses*	*Work gets accounted*
	Women	*Restricted mobility/ listeners & followers*	*Followers/ supporters*	*Subordinates*	*Work supplement and not recognised*

- Educational Administration

Examining on-going AWP preparations using the gender relations framework began in the afternoon of Day II. The process begins from an understanding of the inherent biases in the institutional framework and how these are reproduced. Identifying how these biases are reflected and integrated in programming strategies and interventions assists in the plan review.

Participants identified the need for gender-aware planning in DPEP as crucial particularly as the programme gathers momentum. The planning process, it was discussed, had to address both the practical gender needs of women and girls, in the context of DPEP and their strategic gender interests.

Gender-aware planning processes necessitate taking a cross-sectional approach. As participants found during group work, every problem, strategy and intervention has a gender dimension, which often gives the issues a higher degree of complexity. From the discussion it is possible to evolve a check-list of factors to be considered at every stage of a gender-aware planning process:

- Articulate the assumptions and stereotypes of women and men involved in the programme.
- Specify the practical gender needs to be addressed and the strategic interests sought to be addressed.
- Ensure there is an understanding of the need for and the importance of gender in planning. This is likely to require a shift in orientation and perspective.

Four Key Elements

A gender-aware planning process will thus have four key elements:

Accountability: Linking the success of the planning process to achievement of greater gender equity ensures that plans are made in consultation with a generally excluded group. Their participation in the process of making the plan and in implementation raises their stake in its successful completion. The ownership of the plan and the sense of responsibility it brings along begins the slow process of empowerment and transformation of gender relations.

> *Through a process of gender-aware planning, implementation, monitoring and evaluation, the attempt is to facilitate empowerment of women to challenge the status quo in gender relations and the development process.*

Transparency: This allows policy advocates and activists to monitor the process by which policies are translated into action plans, plans implemented and evaluated. This ensures that the commitment to advance gender equity is integrated in the plan and a series of specific strategies and interventions outlined and implemented to facilitate women's empowerment.

Flexibility: Gender-aware planning is a new field and there is a dearth of successful experiments, worldwide. A flexible approach allows for field learning to be incorporated and at the same time facilitates accountability.

Consultation: Building-in consultative procedures which regularly feed into the plan implementation process, assist in the reformulation and refining of the plan process based on field-level experiences and the feedback received from beneficiaries and implementors.

Follow-up

- There were suggestions that similar albeit more practical exercises be conducted at the State level or preferably in districts where a larger number of practitioners could benefit.
- Some participants also suggested that if the workshop could be conducted in the regional languages the message would be better received.
- The need to develop monitoring and evaluation mechanisms to check on the impact of different interventions on girls and women's participation in education was underlined.

Many of these suggestions will be concretized during the planned workshop on defining the role of a gender coordinator at State and district levels.

Source: DPEP Calling, April 1996.

17

Strategies for Tribal Education

The two-day workshop on National Strategies for Tribal Education under DPEP was meant to provide a platform to DPEP States as well as to resource persons to share the State tribal strategies that had been adopted and implemented in the DPEP districts, reviewing and identifying the gaps and priorities for strategies on tribal education both at State and district level and finally evolving national strategies to support and supplement the State strategies in the gap areas for providing quality primary education to tribal children. The main objective of the national sharing workshop was to:

- highlight the problems of the tribal education in the DPEP States/districts which could not be effectively identified and attended to by the State/district strategies.
- developing national strategies to support and supplement the State/district strategies in the identified gap and priority areas in tribal education.

Dr. K. Sujatha's background paper on "National Component for Tribal Education : Interventions under DPEP" provided the desired theme under which the discussions revolved.

The first day of the workshop was devoted to reviewing the problems identified and strategies adopted in DPEP-I States/districts with regard to tribal education as well as the experiences of planning and implementation in districts or States by the State nodal persons. Almost all the presentations by the State nodal persons were concluded by a short presentation on their respective expectation from the national component for necessary interventions.

Key Areas

In the morning session of the second day of the workshop, the participants were divided into three groups to discuss each of the key areas like:

- Access to education by the tribal school age children
- Retention and achievement and

- Capacity building

The outcomes of these groups were discussed and debated in an open forum. This part of the discussion appeared at the beginning to have a risk of compromising the diversities, but subsequently addressed the multiplicities of problems and helped in reconceptualising as well as refocussing the national component of tribal education under DPEP, providing adequate space for diversities too.

The session that followed had its own importance: it benefited from resource persons like Dr. K. Sujatha, Prof. Sachchidananda, Prof. K.L. Sharma, Dr. Francis Ekka, Mr. Subir Shukla, Dr. Neeti Mohanty, Dr. Kumar and Dr. R. Indira who provided valuable research findings on different aspects of tribal education. The paper presented by Dr. K. Sujatha on "National Component for Tribal Education under DPEP" provided well defined outlines or framework within which the discussions took shape and created the right environment for suggesting plan policy for the national component. The culminating session, using a participatory method, focused on identifying some of the major issues/areas in tribal education where national strategies can be formulated to support and supplement the State component of tribal education.

The welcome address by the Joint Secretary, Mr. R.S. Pandey, his comprehensive speech on aims and objectives of the workshop, short presentation by Dr. A.K. Singh on the guidelines, the chairpersonship of Dr. K. Sujatha, and Prof. Sachchidananda and the concluding remarks by the Deputy Secretary, Mr. Ravi Capoor helped in circumscribing the discussions on such a diversified issue around a few key areas, such as access to education, problems of retention, contextualising the pedagogy and capacity building.

States Presentation

Except Maharashtra, the nodal persons from all other five DPEP-I States having tribal population made their presentation. The State nodal persons from some DPEP-II State like Gujarat, Andhra Pradesh and Himachal Pradesh also participated in the discussions. However these teams did not make any presentation. The presentation by the State teams focused mainly on the State component of tribal studies, the problems faced by the State nodal persons in implementing these strategies, the issues raised which are neither addressed at all or are inadequately addressed by the state/district strategies and the expectation of the States from National Component of Tribal Education. The State-wise presentations are given below.

Madhya Pradesh

- The State strategies for tribal education under DPEP in Madhya Pradesh include identification of factors responsible for low educational status of tribal children, improving management, access, quality of education, developing BLI, assessing training needs of teachers, contextualising as well as enriching the content of reading material, strengthening SCERT, DIET, monitoring, evaluation and research and last but not the least, mobilising community participation.

The factors responsible for low educational status of tribal children in Madhya Pradesh are small and scattered habitations, geographical isolation, poor economic conditions, illiteracy of parents, lack of proper educational monitoring, education not related to needs of life, drab and uninteresting classroom experiences, engagement of children in collection of forest produce, unsuitable school hours, linguistic and cultural barriers, etc.

The State strategies attempted at avoiding various managerial bottlenecks by creating adequate coordination between Tribal and School Education Departments, forming a Tribal Core Group at SPO level which would include representatives of TWD, SED, SCERT, DPI and TRI and by re-orienting the district officials about the tribal cultural specific problems, etc. Opening Alternative Schools, SSKs, NFE centres and Ashram schools giving priority to tribal habitations under DPEP would increase the accessibility of education to tribal children.

Even though the State/district strategies claimed to have been assessing the learning needs of the tribal community, developing tribal sensitive pedagogic units by involving experts from TRI and SCERT and developing Bridge Language Inventory (BLI), subsequent discussion revealed that a little has been achieved in this regard and the pace of development is slow. In the first case the national component can contribute enormously by reviewing the existing State infrastructure to support these activities and providing the expertise wherever it is needed.

Development of R.O.T.C as Resource Centre for Tribal Education for taking up local specific studies, research and evaluation work will in the long run support these diverse interventions in the area of tribal education. However the national component which supports the research work on tribal education can also share its information with R.O.T.C. Besides, with the help of information from R.O.T.C., researches supported by the national component can become need based.

Assessments of training needs of teachers, VECs, MTAs and

empowering these bodies, mobilising community participation by using local tribal cultural strategies such as folk stories and dance were other attempts taken up by the State strategies.

Dr. Sujatha, the chairperson of the session added that in Madhya Pradesh, the tribal education component is separate from the general District and State components of DPEP since it's inception. In other words, the State component for tribal education evolved separately and independently having it's own unique policy, structure and management system. A cell in SCERT on tribal education has been set up to look after training aspects and research. However, linking Tribal Welfare and Education Departments is and should be one of the major intervention strategies in Madhya Pradesh.

Strategies Suggested for National Intervention by Madhya Pradesh Team

- Regarding development of BLI, the Madhya Pradesh team suggested that national intervention is required in finalising and standardising BLI, and also in imparting training to concerned teachers in the effective use of BLI.
- National component need to take the responsibility of training the State resource persons for developing separate modules for training as well as orienting the teachers in tribal areas, and also provide manpower to supervise these training programmes in the beginning.
- National component should assist the State strategies in developing modules for orienting the tribal education officers.
- National component should give directives in regard to moulding education as a community programme, as well as making the education more participative. The teaching-learning process among the tribes can provide some guidelines as to how to make education participative.
- National intervention is required in monitoring attainment levels of the tribal children. It was suggested that MLI milestoning may be done by graded monitoring. Moreover, the national component should re-examine the validity of MLL measures for tribal children and should initiate efforts to contextualise the MLL measures.
- The responsibility of developing orientation programme or of module to educate and empower VECs/MTAs/ PTAs should also partly rest with the national component.

Kerala

The State nodal persons presented the list of problems and recommendations of the study sharing workshops conducted at Malapuram, Wayanad and Kasaragod which led to planning intervention and budgeting the same. The survey report revealed many pertinent problems and issues related to the primary education of tribal children in the State. The problem areas identified are inaccessibility of schools in geographically difficult areas, absence of NFE centres and ashram schools, lack of awareness among parents, absence of tribal language linker, lack of adequate teaching-learning materials, unaddressed problems of tribal girl child, inadequate incentives, absence of VECs/ PTAs etc. However, according to Kerala team, the State/district strategies have begun intervening in these problem areas.

Besides opening new primary as well as pre-primary schools, providing more buildings, rooms and other facilities like textbooks, dresses, and shoes have been the major interventions. A few other sensitive areas were identified to support and sustain the educational activities going on in tribal areas.

One of the areas of intervention programme under State/ district strategies is mobilization/ awareness. House to house campaign and special campaign to promote girls education are viewed as helpful to tribal education. The State strategies to improve management and capacity development include setting up of BECs. However no mention was made with regard to educating and re-orienting VEC members to make this body effective. Re-orienting parents and strengthening PTAs re considered as major strategies for reducing drop-outs.

The State strategies for learning improvements include preparation of handbook for tribal language, targeted interventions for girls and tribal students, free distribution of textbooks, opening of new pre-primary schools providing in-service training to Anganwadi/ Balwadi teachers, etc. The programme to improve access includes opening of new schools and NFE centres in tribal remote areas.

Strategies Suggested for National Intervention by Kerala Team

- National help is needed in preparation of textbooks for tribal children - specially with regard to which and in what form the tribal folklore and tribal history could be included in textbooks.
- Details regarding how to standardize the curriculum developed in tribal dialect may be remarked at national level.

- National directives to be given on smooth convergence of government functionaries (TWD, Education Department, Panchayat etc.) to avoid administrative bottlenecks and spread UPE among tribes.
- Preparation of modules at national level to provide adequate information and special orientation to State/ district level officers in handling tribal education programme.
- Direct access to the information as well as guidance from the national component by the research organisations at the State level with regard to tribal education.

Karnataka

Poverty, lack of awareness, child labour, ill health, migration problem, unsuitable school calendar, irrelevant curriculum, unattractive and inadequate educational facilities, lack of interest among parents and teachers, language problem and gender discrimination were found to be major hurdles in enhancing educability of tribal children in Karnataka.

The State/district strategies aim at intervening in these problem areas. However, the salient features of tribal strategy at State/district level include preservation of culture, language and development of the community of different tribes. Thus, separate educational plan is envisaged and designed for different tribes like Beds, Jenu Kurubs and Limbaris. Formulation of separate school calender and time table suiting the life cycle and, daily activities of the tribal students and communities are being attempted. Moreover, the Karnataka State nodal persons were found to have actually moved tribal group wise in recommending the medium of instruction and the instructional materials. The textbooks re proposed to be taught in regional language in the classes/ schools having heterogenous tribal groups; whereas tribal dialect could be used in the schools where homogenous groups of tribals study. However, phasing of instruction should be done in such a way that the tribal dialect is used as the mother tongue in the first two years of schooling and in higher classes a mix of tribal dialect and regional language is used for instruction until the latter replaces the former completely by standard V. As a result the child is gradually mainstreamed into instruction in the regional language. The teacher factors such as including provision of residential facilities to the teachers in tribal areas, project allowance and incentives for primary school teachers in tribal areas, are well comprehended by the State component. Monitoring and evaluation could take place on a mid-term and annual basis.

Strategies Suggested for National Intervention by Karnataka Team

- At the State level no office or department is created exclusively to handle tribal education. The National Component can take notice of this and suggest a review of the State policy in the light of this.
- Providing expertise and developing capacity at State/ district levels to develop modules for training and orienting teachers in tribal culture and tribal dialect.
- National intervention is sought for development of TLM.
- The National component can provide expert help from NCERT or other language institutes for developing books and curriculum at State level with n objective of providing "joyful learning" to the tribal children.

Tamil Nadu

Slow growth of education among tribals in Tamil Nadu was due to small and scattered habitations over vast hilly terrain, inadequate cooperation among different departments like TWD, Forest Department, Panchayat, etc., involvement of tribal children in agriculture and household work, lack of parental motivation in enrolling children in schools, etc.

The State/district strategies aimed at increasing intervention in the area of improving access, environment building, capacity building and empowering VLC/MTC, etc. Alternative model of schooling has been adopted in all the tribal blocks under DPEP in order to improve access to schools. Construction of school buildings with toilet facilities for girls are suggested by State/ district strategy to increase tribal girls enrolment. Motivating tribal parents through social awareness camping with the help of tribal NCC students of schools and colleges are also planned to reach out to the more difficult school age tribal children.

Conducting a survey on migratory pattern of parents and starting of residential schools to retain the children whose parents seasonally migrate/or issuing certificates which are valid for continuing classes in new schools are suggested to help in bringing these otherwise difficult to reach school age tribal children back in to the mainstream of education.

It has increasingly been realised by the State/district strategies that empowering the teacher to buy teaching-learning materials worth Rs. 500/-. orienting teachers to motivate tribal children towards formal education, monitoring effectively the existing welfare schemes and strengthening community participation will help in improving retention and learning achievements among tribal children. Intervention programmes have begun in this direction.

Capacity building in the form of educating and empowering the MTC/VLC and ECC workers, establishment of one BRC in each of the three districts are also emphasised in State component.

With regard to the problem of medium of instruction the Tamil Nadu team maintained that preparing tribal language linker is not necessary for the reason that almost all the tribals can speak and understand the regional language i.e. Tamil. However, the resource persons were not in agreement. Besides, the State team was also silent about changes in the curriculum in the direction mentioned by other State teams.

Mr. Ravi Capoor, however, added a few more points such as providing escort services with the help of MTCs as an innovation of DPEP, appointment and provision of special coaching for the tribal teachers recruited from the local areas, etc. Developing textbooks with crucial emphasis on socio-cultural milieu of the tribals and providing tribal culture specific in-service training to teachers and orientation programme to administrators etc. are the other interventions planned in the State. Dr. Sujatha, Dr. Francis, Dr. Haredia and Prof. Indira Deva pointed out various lacunas in the presentation of State nodal persons of Tamil Nadu and expressed concern that the inter-tribal and intra-tribal disparities are not sufficiently reflected in the State component of tribal education.

Strategies Suggested for National Intervention by Tamil Nadu Team

- National policies should assist the State component in re-orienting the community participation modules to make it more effective.
- The Gender component of tribal education is not adequately addressed. National strategy should address this issue immediately.
- The State requires help from the national strategies for formulating training cells to motivate and improve the calibre of tribal teachers. National component also needs to provide expert services in developing training/ orientation module for the members of VLC/MTC and ECC.
- The national component needs to remind the State component regarding the objective of utmost decentralising of the planning

processes and addressing the inter and intra-tribal and gender disparities at all stages of plan processes.

Assam

The presentation by Assam team was more articulate and comprehensive. Tribal scenario in Assam seemed to have some unique features which need to be adequately addressed by the State as well as the national component of tribal education while planning for primary education. Negative parental attitude to education, lack of interest and motivation among teachers to problems of tribal children, lack of community participation, and language incomprehensibility are the major hurdles in spreading education among tribal children.

The strategies for tribal education under DPEP include interventions in areas like increasing access to education, retaining tribal children in the school upto class V and in capacity building.

Conducting Kalajatra to increase the awareness by using Bodo, Sodri and Tiwa songs, skits, slogans, films and printed material developed mainly in Bodo, using existing structures like tribal bazaars and fairs for conducting intensive outreach campaigns to motivate tribals towards education, involving education in tribal pockets, adopting soft strategies to enter the tribal dominated tea estates and giving priorities to tribal areas have already been undertaken for increasing accessibility of education to tribal children.

The textbooks developed in Bodo language are in the final stages. The State strategies also plan to prepare teacher-training material in Bodo language on priority basis.

State strategy places equal emphasis on capacity building. Inclusion of tribes in VECs, preparing VEC handbook in Bodo language, conducting surveys on problems of tribal students in primary schools and providing feedback to the teachers as well as the administrators of tribal areas are various measures that are undertaken by the State strategy.

Strategies Suggested for National Intervention by Assam Team

- National component should address the language issue more carefully. Expert help and monitoring is needed with regard to deciding about the teaching medium, developing teaching materials as well as training modulus.
- National component should assist the State / district resource persons in developing modules for training teachers in multi-grade teaching often required in bi-lingual schools.

Discussion of Strategies

During the morning session of the second day of the workshop, the participants were divided into 3 groups to discuss strategies under the following:

- Access
- Retention and Achievement and
- Capacity Building.

Under access, alternatives to formal schooling like NFE and Ashram schools were suggested. A good amount of hope was placed on the outcomes of interventions like effective awareness campaigns, and community outreach programmes. Under retention and achievement, the workshop suggested a review of relevance of national curriculum, MLL measure used in tribal schools, development of textbooks in tribal dialect incorporating tribal history and culture, setting up of residential schools for migratory tribes. Under capacity building, the need was expressed for a national level group that would oversee coordination and convergence of services at all levels. Besides forming VECs/PTAs in tribal villages, reorienting and empowering these bodies, construction of more ashram schools were also suggested as a vital part of capacity building.

The outcome of each group was presented and discussed by all the participants in an open forum. On the findings of this exercise brief observations and comments were made by different resource persons. The issues raised by these resource persons were also debated. The importance of socio-cultural aspects of tribal education was emphasised by Prof. K.L. Sharma. According to him, the educational calendar must take into account the working cycle of tribal children and their festivals. Generally it was observed that the schools are open during the season when they are busy and are closed when they are free. Development of a curriculum which is not isolated from the life of the tribals and which is relevant to their environment and life was pleaded for by Mr. Subir Shukla. This step might play a crucial role in retaining the tribal children in schools as well as improving their learning achievements.

Reviewing the vital role that the incentives play in retaining the tribal children in school, Prof. Yathiraj Kumar and Prof. Schchidananda suggested that DPEP should also have intervention programme with regard to incentives. They also emphasised the role of incentives in motivating the teachers in tribal schools. Prof. Schchidananda felt that only those teachers who have positive attitude towards tribals and who volunteer to work in tribal areas should be selected. Besides, a special orientation training should also be given to the beginning of their service. He also suggested that the national component should formulate some guidelines with regard to their selection process and prepare training modules for teachers in tribal areas.

Dr. Francis Ekka threw light on the "Linguistic Aspects of Tribal Education". According to him the child can be taught in his mother tongue in critical stages with provision for gradual transfer in the regional school languages. The science subject can be taught in their mother tongue while subjects like humanities can be taught in regional languages. Prof. V.N.V.K. Shastri focused on the economic aspects of the tribal education and pleaded for providing compensation to tribal parents who have to loose the labour if their children go to school.

He also spoke on the absence of relevance of present school education for tribal children which makes them aliens in their own community. Thus there is an urgent need to contextualise the primary education. The increasing role of NGOs in creating a demand for education among tribals so that it becomes need based and is not thrust upon tribles was emphasised by Dr. Neeti Mahanti. According to her the national strategy under DPEP can use NGOs as an entry-point to help make inroads into the more difficult tribal groups so that their children come for education. Besides, the NGOs can assist in providing local based training, environment building, help in giving feed-back about teaching-learning that can be developing material using local knowledge and local language.

Empowering the community by entrusting the key role of sustaining and monitoring to bodies like VECs was found essential by Dr. Rudolt C. Haredia, However, he maintained that monitoring of the project including accountability and transparency must be systematized.

According to Mr. V.C. Veerabadrudu, National Component should provide full expert support in developing material in different languages, provide help in finalizing bridge languages dictionaries and also conduct impact studies. The research findings as well as the success and failure stories must be documented and disseminated under material strategies for circulation.

According to Dr. Sujatha, during pre-appraisal of district and State proposals under DPEP, it was realized that there are common broad issues and inadequate capacities at district and State level for effective intervention to tackle those issues. This necessitated national support and intervention for tribal education.

Evolving National Component for Tribal Eduction

The national component for tribal education was discussed in two parts. The first part comprised the broad issues and constraints of tribal education and identified the gap areas which require national support to improve the education of tribals. The second part covered the action plan for the identified areas along with work plan for coming years.

The issues which were raised by the State teams as well as the Resource Parsons are basically in the area of access, pedagogy, capacity building and policy framing and planning. Access can also be a planning process. Establishment of schools within 1.5 kms radius to tribal habitations is not the only option. Moreover, this is also not a viable option for the geographically difficult terrain. Other alternatives to formal schooling like NFE and outreach schools should be tried. In order to make education sustainable, involvement of the community (VEC/VLCs/PTAs etc.), government and NGO sectors is also needed. Relaxing the norms of school mapping, managing incentives, revising the curriculum and re-writing them in tribal language etc. are other major issues which need to be tackled by both State and national components in order to make education accessible and contextual to the tribal children. Besides, a large number of issues related to capacity building at State/district/ block/ cluster level had been raised by the State teams as well as the Resource Parsons where there is a need for the national component to develop it's own strategies to guide and counsel the State strategies.

The gap area as identified in the workshop by the State nodal persons and the Resource Persons which are to be addressed keeping in mind the emerging role of national component are listed as follows:

Caps Identified

Planning and Management

The district education officers are found to be lacking training in disaggregated areas and group specific micro-level planning, which is the back-bone of DPEP strategy for tribal education. These administrators also lack orientation as well as knowledge about tribal specific culture. The disparities between the literacy rates of tribal males and tribal females is alarmingly high, much higher than the disparity level between generally category males and females. However, the State strategies for tribal education under DPEP lack gender dimension.

Even though most of the existing incentives and special measures are developed to tackle the economic problems of tribals and a significant amount of money has been diverted to meet these programme needs, the planning and management mechanism of these incentives remained weak at all levels leading to delay in supply, poor quality and doubtful relevance. Even though the number of beneficiaries increased over the years, no corresponding change was found in resource allocation in planning and management.

Improving Access

Even though it was increasingly realised that in tribal pockets, more number of NFE and outreach schools need to be tried, the states/districts are facing problems in school mapping in the tribal areas, basically because there is almost no expertise available in the State in school mapping especially in relation to tribal areas. Programmes like community mobilisation, strengthening VECs/PTAs/MTAs and involving NGOs to reach out of school tribal children would need to be re-visualised in a more tribal specific context. Keeping in mind the poor socio-economic background of tribal children, a re-assessment is required on how free the primary education is for the tribal child and what further measures are required to be taken to make their education totally free.

Capacity Building at All Levels

As was expressed by the State teams, there is a need for training and orientation to administrators, resource persons, teacher-trainers on different aspects of tribal education. However it would be wrong to say that there is a dearth of experts at State/district level. Rather, what is required at present is that the State resource persons should be identified and trained by the national core group in developing separate training modules for administrators, teacher-trainers and teachers. It was recognised that the teachers working in tribal areas required special pedagogical training to tackle the special needs and problems of tribal children, especially as the present pre-service and the in-service training modules are found to be devoid of any special component of tribal education.

Even though it was realised that a more powerful and demanding VECs/PTAs/MTs would exercise indirect control over school functioning (e.g. regulating effectively the incentive schemes etc.), the State nodal persons were lacking any directives regarding how to make these bodies more powerful. All the State strategies have included community awareness campaign. But the community awareness modules developed by the State or district components were not found effective. A fundamental error was pointed out in conceptualising the awareness campaign. It was assumed that the tribal parents are not aware of the free primary education being provided by the Government. But as revealed by the State nodal persons, the tribal parents are aware of it but they are not convinced of the relevance of this education for their children. Thus, emphasis should be placed on convincing these parents about the relevance of primary education for their children. However, pedagogical revolution, backed by adequate compensation of the tribal parents for their labour loss, and a suitable academic calender would convince the parents of the utility of primary education for their children. Although it was long back decided to have adequate representation of tribal parents in VECs as well as PTAs, not much has been achieved in this regard. Besides, many of the tribal villages do not have either VECs or PTAs.

Relevance of Pedagogy

The tribal cultural and tribal life styles are not considered while either setting the academic calendar or in deciding the relevance of education. The tribal children are lovers of free nature and independence. The rigid and discipline oriented schooling process is found to create conflict and resistance among the children leading to lack of interest, high dropout and poor performance. The group oriented tribal child finds the present education system more individualistic in nature and thus irrelevant.

Not much has been achieved with regard to incorporating the relevant curriculum containing the tribal experiences and introducing the tribal dialects and bi-lingual primers in the first two grades. However, all the DPEP States teams revealed that they cannot proceed much in this context without getting any expert help from National Component.

Karnataka and Assam teams seemed to have proceeded a step or two ahead of other States in having included tribal groups specific plans in developing relevant pedagogy. The capabilities at State and district levels are not developed for responding effectively to flexible group specific pedagogic needs.

Suggested Action Plan under National Component

An action plan of national intervention for supporting the State strategies for tribal education in the gap areas identified in this seminar is suggested.

The action plan can broadly be divided into:

- Guidance in Policy Framing and Planning.
- Capacity Building.
- Pedagogic Intervention.
- Monitoring and Evaluation.
- Networking and Research.
- Advisory and
- Clearing-house role.

Guidance in Policy Framing and Planning

Since there is a need for flexible, desegregated area and group specific micro-level planning for tribal education any attempt at imposing uniform pattern of planning by State strategies should be discouraged by the national component. A gender component is missing from the State as well as national component for tribal education.

Keeping in mind the wide gap between the literacy levels of tribal males and tribal females, the plan strategies for tribal education have to be further decentralized on the lines of gender both at State as well as district level. The national component along with evolving its own strategies should also guide the State strategies in this regard.

Capacity Building

What the workshop made evident is that enormous help is needed to be extended to the State/district components of tribal education in capacity building. The national component should create orientation of capacity building at every level and impart training to the concerned persons to develop capacity at State / district / block level.

The capacity building is the first step that should precede intervention programme so that the efforts are sustained and monitored in the right direction. The feasible approaches that could be part of national component for developing capacity at National/ State/District/Block/Culture level are listed below.

Identification and Training of Resource Group/Persons

Identification of resource group/persons and organising regular workshops with them at national and regional levels, in a constant effort to develop an understanding of the commonalities as well as the diversities of the problems of tribal education and chalking out more effective programmes to further the process would be the first activity that the national component should take up to build up capacity at State/district/block levels.

The national component should have a national level core group exclusively for tribal education which will not only guide the State component in constituting the State core group for tribal education, but will also provide expert services to the State core group on different aspects of tribal education.

Similar groups can be formed at district and block levels and the State component can provide training and guidance to district and block level core groups.

The target group for training with central assistance is identified as consisting of:

i) Members of State/District/Block/Cluster level Core Group for Tribal Education.

ii) State and district level administrators from Education as well as Welfare Department.

iii) Teacher Trainers i.e. persons from State and district level training and resource centres.

iv) VEC/MTA/PTA members.

The national component would assist the State in designing the training content (tribal culture specific information, items also on re-orientation), as well as developing modules for importing training to various target groups.

The modules for teacher trainer, teacher and administrative officers should be different depending on the areas where these respective groups need to be trained or oriented.

Designing Teacher Training Modulus

The national core group should assist the State core group in developing the training modules for teacher trainers as well as the teachers. The training modules should lay emphasis on the MLLs, activity based and child-centered teaching methods, and creation and use of tribal context specific teaching-learning materials. Besides, section of the training module for teacher trainers/teachers should also contain information on the following:

i) Tribal specific culture.

ii) Items on re-orienting the teachers towards tribals as a social group - placing emphasis on understanding tribal psychology.

iii) Providing facts on grossly incorrect popular beliefs about tribal children such as misconceptions about their low IQ.

iv) Tribal ways of learning - i.e. use of more participatory and oral method in classroom teaching.

Module on Multi-Grade Teaching

Either a separate module can be developed with central assistance or a section on this can be included in the general module for training of teachers.

However, it was realised that an overloaded training programme with an array of information might be detrimental to its objectives and thus there is a need to break the envisaged curriculum into parts and conduct separate training programmes over a year or two. However the training programme should begin with special orientation programmes in tribal areas.

The details of teacher training programme have already been chalked out from a National Sharing Workshop on "Teacher-Training" held in

November, 1995 in New Delhi under the national strategies. The findings of this workshop can be re-designed taking into consideration the special needs of tribal children as well as tribal teachers.

Community Awareness Modules

National component should help the State component in developing community participation modules for VEC/PT/MTA members. These modules should not only contain information on need and relevance of tribal and girl education but also on aspects like planning, administrative, and evaluation processes and the accountability of the school education even to bodies like VEC/PTAs.

Once these bodies are empowered, they will be more demanding which will have an indirect supervisory control on the effective functioning of schools. As a result a real kind of participatory management process will emerge at the grass root level which will help in sustaining these educational efforts.

Role of NGOs

The role of NGOs and allied groups such as traditional tribal systems like Gokulas in Madhya Pradesh, local tribal youth training groups, VECs etc. can be multiple; they can help create a demand for education so that it becomes need based and is not thrust upon the tribals.

These non-government and local bodies/groups can be used as an entry point to make inroads into the more difficult tribal groups so that their children come for education. They can assist in local based training, environment building, help in giving feedback about the teaching-learning material so that it becomes local knowledge based and local language based. Good projects sometimes fail because of lack of community acceptance. These groups can also help in identifying the actual issues with regards to educability of tribal children.

In the area of retention, the NGO can help monitor attendance by putting one youth responsible for 10 children and checking drop-outs by checking quarterly and half-yearly charts. They can encourage the girl child by providing a room for younger siblings who are in their care and can help in developing quality performance infrastructure for teachers and students.

Hence the national component can emphasise the role of NGOs and give the management of DPEP in cluster, to specific NGOs on an experimental basis - may be to one or two NGOs per State. The NGOs should be asked to create alternatives.

The national component can also have a national level NGO forum for preparing tribal areas specific training modules.

Pedagogic Intervention

The tribal children were found to have difficulty in following the classroom teaching in the regional language in the initial school years. The problem was found to be more acute among the tribes who live in the geographically difficult areas and as a result have little or no exposure to regional language and the dominant culture outside their tribe.

Therefore, there is a need to prepare primers in tribal dialect on a priority basis to help such children at the initial stages of primary education. The national component was expected to help the States to develop mechanism to identify such tribal groups and to develop bilingual primers, supplementary reading material in tribal dialect, teacher's guide, etc.

The national component should formulate a pedagogy unit specially for rendering expert service or training to the State / district level resource persons in developing these bi-lingual primers and supplementary reading material in tribal dialect.

Besides, the non-contextuality of the course curriculum has long been debated by educationists. The national component should provide the training to the district resource persons in identifying the course content which are incomprehensible and irrelevant for the tribal children and bring in changes by picking up examples from tribal cultures so that the desired concepts can be attained by the tribal children.

The national component should also include training of teacher trainers and other resource persons in tribal dialect and languages. The national component can create an expert committee of linguists to help meet the specific needs of State / district strategies.

Moreover, there is a need to evolve a clearer understanding of the specific needs of tribal children as well of concepts like activity-based child centered teaching-learning materials, textbooks having scope for local specificity, thereby promoting joyful learning among tribal children at all levels.

The desirable approaches that could be part of the national strategy are listed below:

Identification and Training of Resource Persons

Identification of resource persons which might include linguists, teachers, tribal experts, etc. as well as institutions such as TRIs, RIEs and SCERT for capacity building and organizing regular workshops with them at national and regional levels to identify the issues in developing textbooks for tribal children (such as inclusion of tribal specific content, making the textbooks child-centred and activity-based, promoting joyful learning, etc) and the need for adopting multiple methods in different combination (as per the requirements) for furthering the process.

An assessment has to be made with regard to the training requirement of the resource persons or institutions at State levels who would be responsible for training and guiding the actual persons involved in developing the textbooks and supplementary teaching-learning material in tribal dialect.

Broad basing Resource Network

The national component can facilitate networking between DPEP efforts, and the efforts made by institutions (such as TRIs, RIEs, University Departments), NGOs and individuals to further the efforts made in development of relevant pedagogy for tribal children.

National seminars can offer a platform to share and integrate the disjointed efforts made by different resource groups / institutions and individuals on issues like:-

- Development of bias-free local languages specific books.
- Inclusion of tribal specific content.
- Making these books competency-based.
- Involving psycho-linguists, teachers, artists, NGOs, tribal experts etc. in textbook development.
- Intensive orientation and sensitization of textbook writing teams, etc. and trailling and finalizing the textbooks.

Technical Workshops and Regional Expositions

The national resource group for tribal education would organize technical workshops on issues such as productions, specialists editing of textbooks, criterion for assessment of textbook contents, trialling of textbooks developed for tribal children, etc. Local melas can be organized to extract the tribal culture specific content that could be included in the textbooks.

Monitoring and Evaluation

The national component on monitoring and supervision of the implementation of DPEP should treat tribal education as a special component. The experts associated with monitoring should be oriented to special aspects related to tribal education.

Besides general monitoring, regular feedback from the State should be sought by the national component for monitoring the progress of special programmes of tribal education. The tools and strategies for evaluation of these special programmes would be developed taking into account the common and diverse education problems of tribal children.

The national component should seek periodical reports and review meetings from the State with regard to tribal education. Besides, the national component should train the concerned State/district/block level officials in monitoring and evaluating tribal education.

Networking and Research

It might be possible for the national component to facilitate networking through inventories of institutions, NGOs and individuals who can help. An effort to link DPEP efforts with universities and research institutions might also be undertaken. Networking national/state/district/block level efforts is necessary as tribal education needs different types of researches as a feed-back to plan programmes and policies to suit local needs and help in mid-term corrections of programmes.

The research findings would be exchanged and shared among different States in order to gain from each other experiences. This requires coordination at the national level so that dissemination of information among the different States can take place; for example, different activities that are taking place in Assam can be disseminated to Kerala.

> *There is a need to evolve a clearer understanding of the specific needs of tribal children as well of concepts like activity-based child centered teaching-learning materials, textbooks having scope for local specificity, thereby promoting joyful learning among tribal children at all levels.*

Advisor Role

Another supporting strategy under national component on tribal education would be advisory role of providing guidance and assistance for planning, implementation, monitoring and training related to tribal education programmes.

The State can look up to national core group for advice on any aspect of tribal education either in planning and implementation or curriculum development or on any such related work.

Clearing House

The role of clearing house at national level will be documentation, collection and dissemination of research findings, innovations and information on other aspects of tribal education from different district/State, national and international agencies. The national component should provide a platform for cross-fertilization of ideas through organization of seminars and workshop. Workshops can be organized on themes which need to be immediately addressed by both national and state component in order to speed up the spread of UPE among tribals in DPEP States.

Conclusion

The National Strategies for tribal education under DPEP are an outcome of various exercises. The workshop held on 19-20 March 1996 is one among them. The significance of the present exercise lies in the fact that the national strategy was evolved from the respective States expectations on the problems they faced in tribal education while implementing the programme. Besides, these kinds of exercises might help the national component to address more systematically the emerging needs of new DPEP districts/States. Moreover, this workshop has hopefully benefited the State/district strategies by making the national component more transparent and clearly spelled out.

Source : DPEP Calling, April 1996

18

Strategies of Tribal Education for Intervention

—*Dr. Mahendra Kumar Mishra*
State Project Co-ordinator
OPEPA, Orissa

The District Primary Education Programme envisages improvement of tribal education and girls education in backward regions of India to reduce social disparities. Orissa is a state with acute problems to be addressed in the field of tribal education. On the basis of field experience in the tribal areas, I have witnessed the following seven major issues and problem in the field of tribal education. They are:

- The physical location of the village and the attitude of tribal parents.
- Teacher related problems.
- Problems of the tribal students.
- Teaching learning materials and the primers.
- The irregularities in the educational institutions.
- Lack of inspection/supervision.
- Social and Cultural problems.

The above problems are discussed in detail below.

The Physical Location of the Village

1. The tribals inhabit the forests in a scattered manner. Most tribal villages have a population below 100. So, it becomes impossible to open up separate schools in each village where the required students strength is not available. On other land, tribal habitations remain segregated from each other by some physical barriers like rivers, nalas and forests. So these physical barriers create a hinderance for the children of a tribal village to attend the school in a neighbouring village. To give an instance, in Kalahandi District, there are about 714 villages where there is

no primary school within 1 km. radius. But in 522 villages the population is estimated to be below 100. In such a case the tribal children are deprived of schooling facilities.

A STATISTICAL PROFILE

The Scheduled tribes constitute the most backward group among the weaker sections in Orissa. There are 62 tribes in Orissa with a population of 70,32,214 which constitutes 22.21% of the total population of the State. These figures of 1991 census provide valuable information on the demographic structure of the population.

The tribals constitute 47% in Gajapati District, 56% in Rayagada, 21% in Kalahandi, 21% in Bolangir and 12% in Dhenkanal District of Orissa. The high concentration of Saora tribe in Gajapati and Kandh tribe in Rayagada with their typical ethno-linguistic formation added with inaccessible hilly tract are the major causes of their cultural retention.

The literacy rate of the scheduled tribes population in the State is 18.10% of which 27.93% are male and 8.29% are female. The lowest rate of female literacy rate in Orissa is in Koraput (1.93%) and Kalahandi (4%). Southern Orissa constitutes the highest tribal population in the state with a very low percentage of literate people. The literacy rate for the ST population in Orissa according to 1991 census is 22.31% as against the state literacy rate of 49.09%. The ST female literacy rate of the state is 10.21% which is lower than the ST male literacy rate of 34.44%.

The tribal people of Orissa earn their livelihood through marginal agriculture, slash and burn (podu), depending on forest land products and wage labour. Most of the tribal people have a low economic profile and lend a miserable life.

2. Economic Condition : The tribals depend on forests for 8 months and on agriculture for 4 months. The children of 4 to 6 age group are found to be helping their parents in collection of forest products. In this situation, parents do not desire to spare their children or their labour power and allow them to attend schools.

3. Attitude of the parents: Tribal parents are basically illiterate.

Their illiteracy does not permit them to understand the long term values of education. As education does not yield them any immediate economic return, they prefer to engage their children in remunerative employment which supplements the family income and strengthens the family economy. Further a few parents who have become aware of the values of education, fail to accord education to their children as they cannot afford finances for it.

4. Village Education Committee: In Orissa, VECs have been constituted to preserve and monitor the functioning of the schools. Till now people are not aware of the role of the VECs. Neither the villagers nor the members of the VECs take any active interest to enhance enrolment and attendance of children in primary school.

Teacher Related Problems

1. The relationship between teachers, schools and the villagers is quite thin. In tribal villages, villagers have virtually no relationship with the teachers. Teachers do not get any accommodation facility in the village, which makes them irregular which hampers the normal routine of a school. Further, the apathetic attitude of the villagers, and their simplicity provide ample scope to the teachers to act according to their sweet will.
2. The appointment of untrained teachers in tribal areas diminishes the values of education. However, recently the Government has started posting trained teachers in tribal schools which is a welcome step.
3. The lack of special incentives for the teachers in tribal areas serve as a demotivating factors for the teachers and degrades their efficiency. Teachers feel that their own children would be illiterate in tribal areas.
4. Teachers have a preconception that tribal children are average students. also they don't take special care in promoting tribal education.
5. The pre-conceived notions of the teachers that the tribal children cannot grasp anything beyond nature, forest and agriculture create barriers in expanding primary education among the tribal areas.
6. The non-tribal teachers adopt an attitude of indifference to tribal languages, traditions, cultures and life-styles. They fail to

perceive the human values ingrained in these folk cultures. When they try to impart an education which neglects these human values and culture, they fail to make it interesting for the tribal children.

7. The ideas of the non tribal teachers about tribal environment and culture is narrow and hollow. For this they fail to cite examples from the surroundings and make the concepts complicated for the tribal students. The in built creativity of tribal children remains unknown to the teachers.
8. Teachers face wide gulf between the language used in the books and the native uses while teaching the tribal students. They simply opine that the content of the text books is beyond the comprehension of the students, so teaching becomes futile.
9. No special training on tribal languages, cultures or current problems is being imparted to the teachers serving in tribal areas.
10. Children's engagement in household works agriculture coupled with parent's indifference towards their children's studies deprive the teachers to render their services in the classroom.
11. No effort is made on the part of the higher authorities and the tribal masses to curb the frequent absenteeism among the teachers. The lack of a frequent and recurrent inspection mechanism no doubt aggravates the situation.

Tribal Students

The survey conducted in Koraput and Kalahandi districts shows that only 12% to 30% tribal children attend the school. The reasons for this mass non-attendance are as follows:-

1. Helping parents at home.
2 Discharging sibling care responsibilities.
3. No positive environment or inspiration for students at home.
4. School environment is uncomfortable and horrifying.
5. Teachers inflict heavy punishment and do not help in studies.
6. No regular supply of study materials.
7. Parents have migrated from the village to earn their livelihood because of drought or other natural calamities.
8. Teachers do not bother whether the child comprehends the teaching or not.
9. The content and language of the primers are beyond the

comprehensive ability of the tribal children. They don't find any example or experience of their environment in the books.

10. No health care facilities for the children suffering from malaria, skin diseases and anaemia.
11. Children contribute their physical power to supplement the family income.
12. The school timings hamper the routine household work of the tribal children.

Teaching Learning Materials

Even if cultural differences are marked on regional basis in the state of Orissa, the Government has prescribed uniform primers at primary school stage. Among the 62 tribes found in the state, 25 tribes have their own language and for them Oriya language appears to be an alien language.

Even though the National Education Policy has insisted on teaching the children in their mother tongues at the primary level, this has not been implemented for the tribals. The educationists have thoroughly neglected the tribal language and culture and have ignored the problems of tribal children while framing books for them.

So far as study materials are concerned, the following problems came to light:

1. The language used in the books are beyond the understanding of the tribal children.
2. Sometimes the local teachers also get swayed way by the bookish language and don't try to communicate in the tribal languages. As a result teaching seems to be artificial for the tribal children.
3. The contents of the primary school books are less practice oriented and are more factual and abstract.
4. Teaching at primary schools ignore the local nature, culture and environment.
5. There is dearth of study materials and kits in the class rooms.
6. The kits that have been provided to the schools under the Operation Black Board Scheme are not properly utilised by the teachers.
7. Books are not supplied to the schools at the session beginning by the Tribal Welfare Department and the Text Book Press. This irregularity found in the supply of books creates problems both for the teachers and students. Further, stipends are not given in

due time.

8. Further school fails to work out the idea of utilising the services of the local architects, painters and artists at a low cost to prepare some of the educational kits for the children.
9. If given scope the children can build up their own museum.

Condition of Primary Schools

1. The school buildings are in broken condition and hence not attractive.
2. Lack of care and repair makes it difficult to sit in the collapsing class rooms.
3. Children of 2/3 classes are accomodated in a single class room.
4. Neither the villagers nor the VEC take any active interest to preserve and protect the school building. They preserve the impression that it is the Government outlook and not theirs.
5. No accomodation arrangement is being made for teachers either in the school or in the village.
6. The tribal habitations remain in scattered forms. So, they don't fulfill the needs of the required amount of child population to open a school within 1 km. radius. So, in the tribal areas schools remain far away from the habitations.
7. The number of Ashram schools is scanty. Ashram schools are best fitted for the tribal children.
8. In the primary schools, no effort is made to provide incentives and scope to music, dance, games, paintings, etc. which remain as latent potentialities with a child.
9. In a school, a tribal child undergoes mental stress and strain. A fear free environment is required for their proper development.
10. Physical barriers and communication difficulties also keep the tribal children away from the schools.

Lack of Inspection

1. School inspectors (at the block and district level) are not active in solving problems associated with the primary schools in the tribal areas.
2. The surveys bring to notice that the block level inspectors have not inspected all the schools in their areas.

3. Inspectors do not provide equal importance to the schools of hill areas as they give to the schools of plain areas.
4. The tribal teachers remain indifferent to tribal education. They are also marked with some mental stress.
5. The non-tribal teachers adopt an apathetic attitude towards tribal school management.

Social and Cultural Problems

The community life, the economy, the life style, the traditions of the tribals and their outlook of the world is totally unique. All these have got their humanitarian values and cultural significance. But they have not found recognition in the ideas of local inspectors, teachers, parents and policy planners. The root cause of this can be attributed to the stratification system and the tribal and non-tribal attitude. Thus, a strong consciousness and pro-tribal attitude have not been built up among the people. The NGOs have no doubt taken some steps in this area. But how far the efforts of the NGOs will be successful in changing the institutionalised practices of society is still doubtful. The greatest problem is, the tribals have come to recognize the modernization and the demands of time. But they are not coming forward to bring reforms in the educational status and economic standards. Now a strong campaign is needed for this. The voluntary agencies should try to launch this campaign on a long term basis with constructive ideas.

STRATEGIES FOR INTERVENTION

Physical Location of the Villages

1. A realistic survey should be made in the tribal areas as regards how many children are not coming to schools and about the actual number of schools required.
2. To open up NFE centres in those villages, where there is no school at all.
3. To open up more number of Ashram schools.
4. School buildings having atleast 2/3 rooms should be opened up.
5. To open up pre-school centres.
6. To install tube wells near the schools.
7. To make provisions for toilets.
8. To provide accomodation facilities for the teachers.
9. The school timings in the tribal areas should be fixed keeping

in harmony with their MFP collection and agricultural seasons, school timings should be changed at the block level. The holiday patterns should be changed accordingly keeping in view the cultivation period/MFP collection seasons.

To Increase the Potentialities of the Teachers

1. The teachers should be associated with the day-to-day life-style of the villagers.
2. To provide residential accomodation for the teachers.
3. To enhance the relationship between teachers and students.
4. To appoint trained young teachers in tribal areas.

> ***PARENTAL INVOLVEMENT IN SCHOOLS***
>
> *A. To organise gram sabhas by summoning the panch, the villagers and their leaders.*
>
> *B. To identifying the issues involved in education & to sort out their solution from the people.*
>
> *C. To make the parents understand the values of education through literacy campaigns.*
>
> *D. To associate the villagers in the various cultural functions (Pujas, national celebrations, children's fairs, meetings).*
>
> *E. The parents should also invite the teachers to join in the various festivals organised in the villages.*
>
> *F. The educational and the developmental responsibilities of the school should be entrusted to the villagers.*
>
> *G. To organise Mahila Samities to increase literacy among the women and to enhance the attendance rate among the girls.*

5. The training programmes for teachers should highlight more of tribal problems.
6. Consciousness should be created among the VEC members and parents to check teacher's absenteeism.
7. Special incentives and allowance should be provided to the teachers working in tribal ares. They should be transferred to plain areas after serving 3/4 years in tribal areas.
8. Special training to tribal teachers and special coaching to tribal students.

9. The teachers should have knowledge about the tribal environment and local tradition.
10. The teachers should be given tribal language training. The Academy of tribal Dialect and Culture, Bhubneswar is imparting a tribal language programme.
11. Social source book for teachers may be prepared to develop the tribal knowledge such as folk songs, tales, proverbs, riddles, play songs, traditional games, dance, music etc. to impart joy of learning through the folklore and bridge the gap of home culture and school atmosphere.
12. The teachers should use the colloquial native language while teaching the tribal children.
13. The school time table be co-opted with the agricultural and social necessities, which will facilitate the parents in economic development and educational development of the child.

Tribal Students

In order to bring the children of 6-14 age groups to the pale of primary education, the following measures are to be taken:

1. To open up ECCE centres in tribal villages.
2. To open up NFE centres (where there are no schools).
3. The teachers should establish a healthy rapport with the tribal students and create a positive environment for them.
4. The authorities should take care to supply the books at the proper time.
5. The parents should provide scope to their children to learn their lessons at home.
6. Instead of teaching the students about world view or national issues, ample scope should be given to them for local visits.
7. To provide free of cost health services.
8. To keep harmony between school timings and daily routine work and agricultural work.
9. The teachers should command love and affection from the students.
10. The children should organise their traditional games, folk dance and music in the schools.

Study Materials and Books

1. The study materials needed for class room teaching should be provided in time. The materials and the textbooks provided under Operation Black Board Schemes and Welfare Department should be properly utilised. Services of the local architect, painters, artists should be utilised to build up required study materials.

2. Preparation of the text books and supplementary readers: The text books should be based on the traditional knowledge and folklore of the tribals. The Chart on page 287 shows the linkage that can be established between the tribal folklore and MLL text books.

Conditions of the Educational Institutions

1. More number of residential ashram schools are to be opened in tribal areas.
2. Constructing houses for the teachers.
3. VEC to take up the responsibilities of the school.
4. To open NFE Centres in the scattered tribal habitations.
5. To decorate the classrooms with the art of tribal girls.
6. To increase dignity of labour in the minds of the children by creatings green gardens in the school compound.

Social and Cultural Issues

Communal life forms a basic parameter of the tribal society. It finds manifestation through the various festivals and cultural celebrations. If the teachers can participate in these occasions by giving due regards to the tribal culture, then She can build up a good educational centre in the village. In the tribal village, the teacher should be a learner, more specifically a 'seeker' of local knowledge from the tribal culture, which would ultimately turn into a global knowledge. The oral tradition in teaching must be an important device to develop the personality of a tribal child from its own cultural environment, instead of creating an artificial blurred personality dissociated with home and school environment. To bridge the gap of the socio-cultural environment with that of the school curriculum exploration of rich tribal folklore can be helpful in the promotion of tribal education.

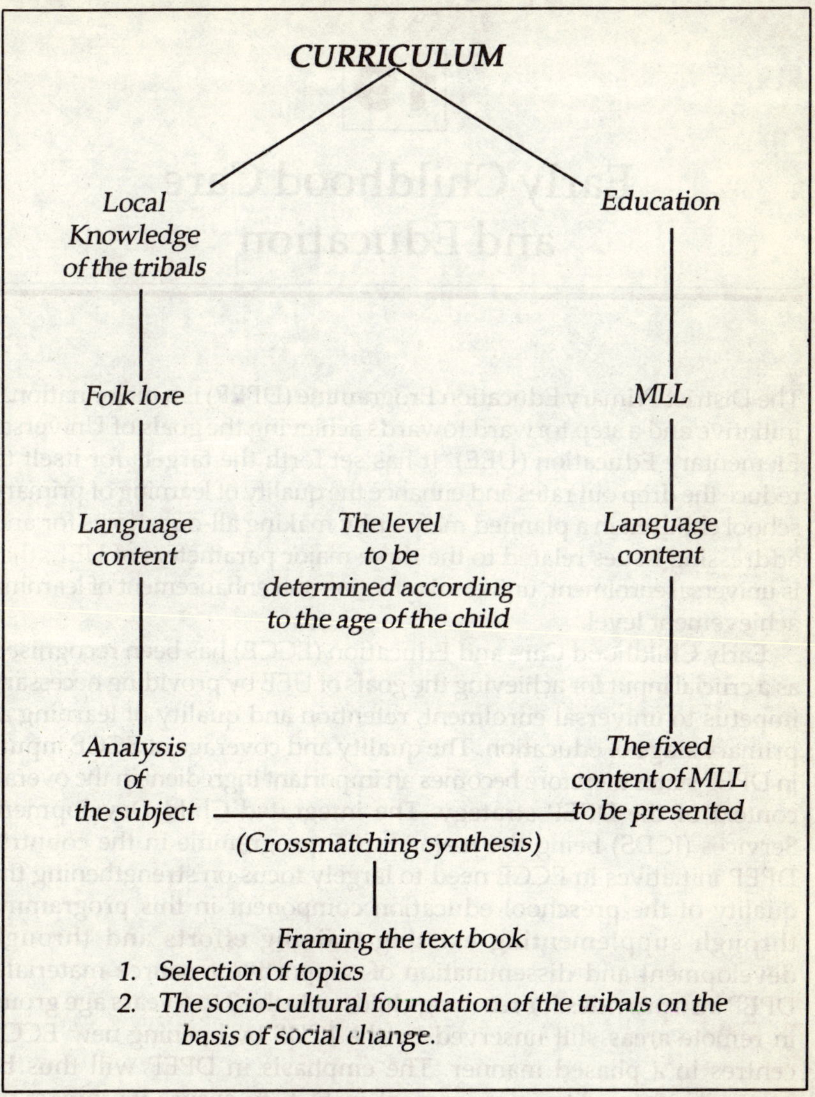

Source: DPEP Calling, September 1996.

19

Early Childhood Care and Education

The District Primary Education Programme (DPEP) is a major national initiative and a step forward towards achieving the goals of Universal Elementary Education (UEE). It has set forth the targets for itself to reduce the drop out rates and enhance the quality of learning of primary school children in a planned manner by making all-out efforts for and addressing issues related to the three major parameters of UEE, that is universal enrolment, universal retention and enhancement of learning achievement level.

Early Childhood Care and Education (ECCE) has been recognised as a crucial input for achieving the goals of UEE by providing necessary impetus to universal enrolment, retention and quality of learning at primary stage of education. The quality and coverage of ECCE inputs in DPEP states therefore becomes an important ingredient in the overall context of the DPEP strategy. The integrated Child Development Services (ICDS) being the major ECCE programme in the country, DPEP initiatives in ECCE need to largely focus on strengthening the quality of the preschool education component in this programme through supplementing existing training efforts and through development and dissemination of supportive resource materials. DPEP also provides for reaching children in the 3 to 6 years age group in remote areas still unserved by the ICDS by opening new ECCE centres in a phased manner. The emphasis in DPEP will thus be primarily on quality improvement in ECE to ensure its impact on attainment of goals of UEE.

To facilitate the planning and implementation of ECE interventions in the DPEP states a two days orientation programme was organised by the Department of Preschool and Elementary Education, NCERT, New Delhi on September 18 and 19, 1996 under the aegis of DPEP with the objective of discussing the following:

- the crucial significance of ECCE in the context of Universalisation of Elementary Education (UEE);

- the status of ECCE programmes in the country including ICDS and issues that need to be addressed for effective qualitative improvement; and
- in the light of state level experience, areas requiring special attention with a view to establishing/strengthening linkages between ECCE and Primary Education in the context of UEE.

METHODOLOGY

The orientation programme was conducted essentially in the participatory mode. In view of the short duration of the programme visits to ECCE centres could not be possible. Alternatively, participants were requested to visit *anganwadis* in their respective states/districts prior to participation in the programme. This was expected to provide the necessary baseline to participants for relating the programme inputs to their respective state specific issues and conditions.

The participants were also requested to communicate any five major issues/questions of priority to them with regards to ECCE. The programme schedule was thus planned in a flexible way to accommodate all these queries and make modifications where necessary.

The sessions were well supported with video film presentations on various themes related to ECE to highlight issues and stimulate discussion and sharing of experience. The participants were also exposed to a variety of resource materials in the area of ECE which could facilitate their planning in this area. The material was also made available to them on request. The material included:

1. Early Childhood Care and Education Programme
2. ECE Trainer's Handbook
3. Minimum Specifications for Pre-schools
4. School Readiness Programme
5. Pressure on Pre-School Child
6. ECE-CML Kit
7. Handouts on session themes
8. Minimum kit of play materials
   - A Guide

The programme commenced with welcome address by Prof. Venita Kaul, Head, Department of Preschool and Elementary Education, NCERT. She gave a brief introduction to the programme in terms of the objectives and scheduling of sessions Shri R.S. Pandey, Joint Secretary (DPEP) MHRD, Government of India in his opening remarks

ECCE IN DPEP

The concluding session of the programme was on Developing a Framework for District Level Planning for ECE. This session was conducted by Ms. Vrinda Swarup, Director (MS) MHRD. In this session she presented an action plan for ECCE in DPEP states longwith guidelines and financial provisions. Under broad categories of what can be done under DPEP and how can it be done she informed that DPEP will finance (i) expansion of ECCE centres in villages not covered by ICDS (ii) construction of ECCE centres next to primaray school (iii) developing of improved pre-school materials through SCERT/DIETs/ NGOs (iv) training of workers appointed in DPEP (v) joint training of AW/Primary teacher/health workers (vi) testing innovative models in ECCE (vii) documentation (viii) convergence with ICDS, with community etc. She also clarified that DPEP will not finance (i) nutrition (ii) duplication of ICDS (iii) norms other than ICDS except innovations.

Ms. Swarup briefly also highlighted some salient points for ECCE planning. These included:

- *A Programme Officer should be appointed to coordinate gender and ECCE related issues.*
- *Constant linkage with SCERTs/DIETs/NGOs will need to be maintained for resource support.*
- *Liaison will be required with the state level ICDS nodal department.*
- *The planning will have to be done in coordination with the DPEP planning processes and Annual Work Plan and Budget formulation.*
- *Prior planning, necessary data and information with respect to ICDS status and expansion plans and coverage will need to be procured and used as a basis for planning.*
- *DPEP financial parameters will have to be considered and conformed to.*
- *The executive committee approval will be required for the plans.*

Ms.Swarup also stated that in Annual Work Plan & Budget (AWP&B) information about the activity, funds required, agency that will execute and time frame to conduct activity should be clearly incorporated. She gave broad areas where monitoring of the programme will be of crucial significance. These were: (i) development of ECE related performance indicators for effective monitoring (ii) monitoring opening of centres (iii) monitoring training inputs (iv) monitoring resource support (v) monitoring convergence and (vi) conducting evaluation.

highlighted the crucial importance of Early Childhood Care and Education (ECCE) programmes in the context of Universalisation of Elementary Education (UEE). He attempted to demystify the meaning generally attached to constitutional Directives for free and compulsory education of children upto the age of 14 years by stressing that children below 6 years of age are also implicitly covered under the Constitutional provision which unfortunately has been generally interpreted as referring to children from 6-14 years only. He further emphasized that the programme for pre-school children has to be joyful, play-based and activity oriented. He opined that while there is a need to open more and more IEC centres to facilitate universalisation of ECE services, the quantitative expansion must be linked with quality as well. In this context he endorsed the modern economic theory which postulates that quality of supply creates demand, as against the traditional belief that demand decides supply and quality. Elaborating this concept further, Shri Pandey stressed the need to provide good quality pre-school education to children so that the community perceives its importance and comes forward to demand and support the programmes. He felt that the materials and methods used at this stage are most crucial to the quality of the programmes and its impact.

Prof. A.K. Sharma, Director, NCERT, inaugurated the programme. In his inaugural address Prof. Sharma noted that ECCE which was not given much attention in phase I of DPEP implementation has now been accorded a prominent place in the overall strategy of DPEP implementation and has become an integral part of it. He cautioned that ECCE should not be made a replica of primary education. ECCE should have its own personality interms of its content and methods which are directed towards a child's development in a holistic manner. In this connection he opined that a training of functionaries involved is of crucial significance for ensuring use of content and methodology appropriate to a child's development needs. ECCE therefore should make extensive use of audio-visual materials/play materials and toys and local specific low cost materials such as those generated in the Annual Toy Competition held earlier by the Department of Pre-school and Elementary Education. He also stressed that ECCE should be viewed in the overall context of universalisation of Elementary Education (UEE), as a very significant input.

At the end of the inaugural session a vote of thanks was proposed by the Programme Coordinator, Dr. G.C. Upadhyay.

The session following the inaugural was essentially devoted to getting to know each other through the play way method. Three introductory games were played with the participants by Ms. Romila Soni. The first game elicited the names of each participant in a rhythmic mode. This was followed by 'Zip Zap' a game which helped each participant to get to know his/her two neighbours. The third game taxed the memory skills of each participant by making him/her recall the names sequentially of all the participants of the programme present at the time. Following these games which helped to establish report between the faculty and the participants, the latter were given an opportunity to share some games, they knew with the others. The session concluded with a discussion on the significance of such games not only for any training programme but also in the early childhood education programmes with children.

Significance and Issues of ECE

Prof. Kaul highlighted the two-fold significance of ECE i.e. its direct influence on the overall development of the child and its potential contribution to achieve the goals of universalisation of elementary education (UEE). In this context she gave the basic rataionale for investing in ECE. The concepts of ECCE, ECE land Early Childhood Development were deliberated upon and the shift towards the concept of ECE as broader, all encompassing and holistic approach was highlighted. Some of the crucial issues concerning ECE were discussed. These included a) the low priority given to ECE in the Education sector despite its accepted and proven significance; b) the lack of even minimum essential material, human and financial resources; c) dearth of experience and capacity for ECE at present at state and substage levels in many states; d) inappropriate community perceptions and expectations; e) miseducation in the name of ECE by introducing formal teaching of the 3R's.

The role of NCERT/SCERTs/SRCs in promoting ECC programmes was highlighted. Prof. Kaul also gave an account of researches done in this area at National level and State level.

Methodology of ECE Programme

To make participants aware of the kind of curriculum (content) and methodology used in Early Childhood Education Programme a film *Meri Pyari Anganwadi* was screened for the participants. Some charts were also put to clarify to the participants both major objectives or goals of a good ECE programme as well as the specific principles of planning the daily, weekly and monthly programmes. A discussion was conducted by the resource person Ms. Sushma Singh, ECE Consultant, UP after viewing the film so that participating states get an opportunity to have clarity with regards to the content, their sequencing, material used, organisation of outdoor/indoor activity and methodological issues. The concept of programme planning and its principles were also highlighted in the discussion. For evaluation of children's progress, indicators developed in each area of child development i.e. physical motor, personal-social, language, cognitive and creativity were shared with the participations. Similarly indicators developed for assessing school readiness of children were also discussed. A major point of discussion was the observation that despite all training and emphasis on play and development oriented programmes the field reality indicates that most *Anganwadis* are functioning as little primary schools and teaching children alphabets and number when they are developmentally not ready for this. The adverse effects of this practice were discussed and the need for advocacy and community education in this context was stressed.

Training

Training is one of the most vital components in the overall context of the quality of ECE programmes. The facilitator for the training session in the afternoon, Dr. Adarsh Sharma, Addl. Director, NIPCCD gave an overview of the shifting focus in training of functionaries of ICDS in the context of ECCE. She informed that the training package (sandwich courses) now being adopted is focussed more on (1) increasing access to services (2) improving utilisation, quality, impact and sustenance. The training would lay emphasis on reducing the burden of *Angan Wadi Workers* (AWW) on the one hand and lay emphasis on improving the skills, and reorienting the training content with the life cycle approach with an emphasis on a holistic perceptive.

The holistic perspective will be translated into actual practice by reconceptualising the training content in terms of different blocks of training based not on different service components like health, nutrition, ECE etc. as done at a present but on different age groups targeted i.e. 0-2 years, 2-3 years, 3-6 years with all services considered as relevant to each in a holistic manner. One of the strategies highlighted to clear backlog in training was to expand institutional capacity. At the same time alternative non-institutional district training teams/ mobile training team approaches should be concerned. Dr. Sharma suggested possible DPEP intervention in this area. The possibilities and benefits of joint training of functionaries from Department of Education and Department of Women and Child Development as well as of AWWs and primary teachers were also discussed.

Linkage

Establishing linkage between Early Childhood Education and Primary Education is the top priority at present. Most of the participating states had raised queries bout the ways and modalities to bring about convergence/coordination, of efforts between different departments.

Dr. K. Lakshmi, Director ERC, Andhra Mahila Sabha covered various components which would be necessary to establish both horizontal and vertical linkage. The efforts which have been initiated by Department of Education and Department of Women and Child Development, Govt. of India were mentioned in this context. These included establishing linkages through ensuring that AWs are located in the premises of the primary schools or in their proximity and their timings are synchronized with AWs starting 15 minutes earlier to facilitate girls participation since they can leave their younger siblings in the AWs. It was also opined that school linkage has to be seen and operationalised in local specific perspective, keeping the working patterns, lifestyles etc. in view. The training needs for effective linkage programmes were also highlighted. The need to extend play based/activity based/child centered approach to class I & II for programmatic linkage was stressed and the advantage of organising joining training of AWWs/ECCE workers and class I teachers particularly from the point of view of continuity and mutual understanding of the programme objectives and roles were discussed.

A film on school linkage entitled *"Ek Sarthak Shuruaat"* was screened for the participants. The viewing of the film was followed by a discussion under different aspect of school linkage, and the issues involved in it. The need to explore alternative models was also emphasised. In this context the concept of feeder centres to primary school was introduced which can be taken up under innovations in DPEP. This model envisages extension of AWs/ECE centres into AW+ grades 1 and 2 in an ungraded way. This model has advantage of providing a more child-friendly environment in the crucial first two years of school through proximity, familiar worker/teacher, space for bridging the gap between home and school language etc. This could ascertain mastery of self learning skills in children prior to entry into primary school.

Status of Pre-School Education Component of ICDS

The second day of the programme was devoted to a presentation of the findings of a study on "Status of Pre-School Education Component of ICDS and its Perception and extent of Utilisation by the Community" by Dr. G.C. Upadhyay, undertaken in 10 UNICEF-assisted ECE project states. Based on preliminary data available from some states it was found that only about 50% children in the 3-6 age groups are registered in AWs and out of the registered children only 60% were found attending AWs on the day of observation. Thus from the total population the percentage of children benefited was only about 30%. Various other dimensions of the study e.g. i) timings of AW; ii) activities conducted in

AWs (PSE programme); iii) extent of programme planning for PSE component; iv) material availability v) availability of outdoor/indoor space and other facilities like drinking water/toilet; vi) parental perception of AW as a pre-school centre; vii) school linkage and viii) skills/knowledge and attitudes of AWWs/AWHs/Supervisors were discussed as per the trends available in the study. The presentation which highlighted gross inadequacies in terms of resources available and quality of the programme opened up issues related with promotion of quality of preschool education. It was again reiterated that it is good quality ECE and not ECE per se that will have an impact on the goals of UEE or on the individuals child development.

AWWs load of work, AWW's job responsibilities also figures in the discussions. The question of gap between children's language at home and in school, single parent families and first generation learners were some issues raised in the context of children's retention in schools, and the scope to counter these through ECE.

After this presentation participating states were requested to share their experiences in the area of ECE. States of Karnataka, Tamil Nadu, UP and Maharashtra presented briefly the status of Pre-School Education in their respective states. One of the important references made during this session by the participants from Maharashtra was about the Ram Joshi Committees' recommendation on ECCE, which are being considered for implementation by Maharashtra Government.

School Readiness Programme

In the next session a film *"Nanhe beej ootho"* made on the theme of school readiness was screened for the participants. Activities appropriate for reading, writing and number readiness were demonstrated in the film. A discussion was organised after the film, which was initiated by Mrs Kanta Seth. The discussion emphasized the need for School Readiness Programmes in the initial stage of class I curriculum since almost 75% children enter class I without any pre-school education experience with the specific deficits in terms of competencies and attitudes required for readiness for 3 R's. This has been demonstrated in a recent research study conducted by NCERT. It was pointed out that the six weeks to two months programme helps children adjust better to the demands of primary curriculum.

Dr. Prerna Mohite who implemented the school readiness programme for class I children and brought out a book called *"Tarang"* in Gujarat highlighted the implementation of the programme in the state. She informed the participants that in order to increase enrolment, retention and learning achievement of children, children's needs and readiness levels should be considered before formal teaching in class

I begins. It was therefore decided to give children school readiness experience till September (the first three months in class I) through play-way, activity based joyful learning. She also informed that till September children continue to register themselves and as such there cannot be any formal teaching. The period from July to September is suitable for school readiness activities.

After September Class I curriculum is transacted in such a way so that children acquire competencies as prescribed under Minimum Levels of Learning (MLL) through activity based joyful learning extended to class I and class II. Training of teachers to implement "*Tarang*" is done by district level resource teams already in position. "*Tarang*" therefore as the name suggests aims to create ripples in the community teachers, children and parents. The setting up of Balmitra Varg i.e. class I classrooms made colourful and attractive by teachers as a part of *Tarang* training was also referred to by her in the context of making education child friendly.

Community Participation

The next session organised was on community participation and reaching the community. Majority of participating states had raised issues of community participation and involving of parents. In the first half of the session Dr. A.C. Lal discussed the concept and process of community participation and presented before the participants experience gained under Area-Intensive Education Project (AIEP) implemented in six states. Dr. N. Lalitha gave an overview of experiences of community participating in AIEP project in Tamil Nadu state. It was revealed that the community participation experience under AIEP were found positive and parents and communities have been able to sustain the programme even after the impending closure of the project.

In the latter half of this session on community participation participants were oriented to Participatory Learning and Action Approach by Ms. Deepika Srivastava of UNICEF, Delhi Office. She highlighted the basic tenets of Participatory Learning and Action Approach by suggesting reversal of present approaches towards interaction with communities and the paradigm shift to bottom-up rather than top-down approach.

It was emphasised by her that the essential elements for participatory learning and action approach are learning together, learning from each other and learning by doing. To achieve this end it will be necessary to have local issues analysed, understand how community views different institutions i.e. AW, Primary School, Panchayat, Health Centre etc. in order to work with these institutions effectively. It would also be important to have resource mapping done for planning an effective strategy for community participation.

Minimum Specification for ECE Centres

A document entitled Minimum Specifications for Pre-School was given to each participant which describes the minimum requirements for a pre-school centre. These requirement, however have been presented at two levels: 'essential' and 'desirable'. Alongwith this document one more title ***Users manual for minimum Play Material Kit*** was demonstrated before the participants by Ms. Kanta Seth.

The material developed by the Department of Pre-School and Elementary Education in the area of pre-school education was also presented and discussed with the participants by Ms. Romila Soni. One set of this material was given to each participant. The material includes a copy of ECE programme, Trainers' Handbook, Cards, Charts, Picture and Story Books for children, Instructional Material Series for teacher educators and pamphlets for parents awareness. The participants were informed that similar material has been developed in regional languages as well by some states.

The concluding session was chaired by Prof. A.N. Maheshwari, Joint Director, NCERT. Prof. Maheshwari in his valedictory address laid emphasis on different aspects of school readiness in children entering class I. In this context he highlighted the studies conducted in five states by the NCERT. He was optimistic of the gains which will accrue to primary education out of expansion of ECCE coverage and enhancement of quality of ECCE programme in DPEP states. The programme ended with a formal vote of thanks.

Source: DPEP Calling, November 1996.

20

Interventions for Children with Disabilities

India's Constitutional and successive policy commitments to achieving the goal of 'Education for All' remains elusive due to certain disadvantaged groups remaining out of the fold of the formal education system. One such group is the 'disabled' who have received inadequate attention so far. It is a well-recognized fact that Universal Elementary Education (UEE) cannot be achieved unless all children are brought into schools and provided education that is equitable.

This stance has been emphasized in the National Policy on Education (NPE) 1986 and was strongly reiterated by the Report of the Committee for Review of National Policy on Education (NPERC) 1991 and revised Programme of Action (POA 1992. These policy resolutions have introduced enormous challenges at the implementation level for both educationists and practitioners. Mobilising the general education system and making it responsive to the educational requirements of children wit special needs, has been highlighted repeatedly. By implication, what is being advocated either directly or indirectly is 'inclusive schooling' both as a means and an end of integrating the disabled child population into normal classroom settings.

Ending segregation and moving towards integration was considered to be a viable approach for the realization of UEE, and the Government implemented a centrally sponsored scheme - Integrated Education for Disabled Children (IEDC) - in 1974. This was followed up by the Project Integrated Education for the Disabled (PIED) in the GOI-UNICEF Plan of Operation for 1985-89, to strengthen the implementation of the former scheme. The aims were to increase enrolment, improve retention and achievement of disabled children in general schools through context specific delivery modalities.

India's commitment and subsequent movement towards 'inclusive schooling' gained further momentum with the World Declaration on Education For All (1990) wherein it was emphasized that 'the learning needs of the disabled demand special attention' within the framework of 'Education For All'.

However, inspite of all the above efforts even today a large majority of the school population with special educational needs are either not enrolled on schools or do not receive an appropriate need-based education, finally dropping out of the school system, adding to the already sizeable out-of-school population.

If any measure of success is to be attained by the year 2000 A.D., it is imperative that the movement towards inclusive schooling is given the much needed boost that it requires. An apt vehicle for giving impetus to this movement is through the on-going District Primary Education Programme (DPEP), a major multi-faceted scheme seeking to overhaul the primary education system in the country. Intertwining of integration of the disabled in an evolving programme such as the DPEP, seems to be a befitting solution for a number of reasons. The 'essence of the DPEP is decentralized planning that is highly flexible and contextual in nature. These features are crucial to the implementation of successful integration of the disabled population who have a wide variety of specific needs, requiring continuous support from all sources. The existing infrastructure available in DPEP districts if utilized to its optimal capacity will definitely serve to give a boost to inclusive schooling in the country, which is still in its embryonic stage.

Magnitude of the Problem

Planning and implementation of educational services for the 'disabled' school going population is no simple task. A tremendous challenge faces planners, administrators, educationists and practitioners at all levels due to a number of major constraints discussed briefly below.

The first step towards effective planning and management is estimation of the size of the target group. Ironically, this is one of the hindering blocks due to non-availability of accurate information, incompatibility of various organisations, geo-scatter of the disabled and difficulties in their identification and categorization. Other problems that further aggravate the situation are:

- lack of awareness and acceptability within the community;
- lack of resources-financial, trained manpower and equipment in schools;
- inadequate school infrastructure and support systems;
- lack of special support or absence of flexibility in the conduct of examinations according to the needs of different disability groups;

- lack of appropriate staff development programmes amongst others.

The major premise on which all the drawbacks can be dealt with is availability of an accurate, comprehensive date base. Exact numbers of disabled in and out-of-school children are not available, although surveys have been undertaken periodically by various governmental and non-governmental organisations. The National Council of

Table 1

Projected Population of Children with Disability

(Figures in Million)

Projected Population of Children with disability in the age-group 5-14 YEARS(*)		3.19
Locomotor Handicap	1.48	
Hearing Handicap	0.65	
Speech Handicap	0.91	
Visual Handicap	0.15	
Mentally retarded children in the age-group 5.14*		3.60
Children with learning disability in the age group 5.14		3.60
Children with disability in the age group 16-18 years		2.20

@ The 1981 figures of the survey by NSSO have been extrapolated on the assumption that population with disabilities would have grown at the same rate as the general population.

* Estimated at 1% of the population in the age group 5-14 years.

Education Research and Training (NCERT) has proposed to undertake such as survey in 1996-98 but the data may not be immediately available, especially if the DPEP is to be used as a vehicle of change. Therefore, in this particular case, planning will have to be based upon the National Sample Survey Organisation (NSSO) surveys 1981 and 1991 and estimates provided in the Revised Programme of Action (1992).

Table 2

Comparative Prevalence & Incidence (Disability Wise)

Sector	1981			1991		
	Male	Female	Persons	Male	Female	Persons
Visual disability						
Prevalence rate						
Rural	444	670	563	471	548	525
Urban	294	425	356	263	346	302
Incidence rate						
Rural	32	45	38	22	28	25
Urban	23	38	30	15	25	20
Hearing disability						
Prevalence rate						
Rural	595	510	573	498	435	467
Urban	386	395	390	325	355	339
Incidence rate						
Rural	20	18	19	16	14	15
Urban	14	15	5	11	14	12
Speech Disability						
Prevalence rate						
Rural	379	228	304	333	208	273
Urban	342	207	279	285	182	237
Incidence rate						
Rural	6	2	4	6	4	5
Urban	7	3	5	5	4	5
Locomotor disability						
Prevalence rate						
Rural	1047	597	828	1345	784	1047
Urban	500	544	679	1170	728	962
Incidence rate						
Rural	64	42	53	64	42	53
Urban	61	47	54	65	39	52

Figures are for per 100,000 persons in all the tables above.

Source: Pandey & Advani, 1995, pp. 21-22.

Since our main concern is primary school age children, the number of children in the educable 5-14 year age group can be estimated as above. Recently, Pandey and Advani 15 have presented a comparative chart of prevalence and incidence of different disabilities based on NSSO 1981, giving some indication of the stupendous task ahead. (See Table 2 on *p*. 301.)

It was found that "the prevalence in 1991 has marginally gone up as compared to 1981. In 1991, the prevalence in rural areas is 1.99 percent as against 1.84 percent in 1981. The prevalence in urban areas in 1991 is 1.58 percent as against 1.42 percent in 1981".

From the above, it is obvious, that the task ahead is phenomenal and requires immediate attention and priority. To facilitate the process of planning, it is imperative that at the outset the target group be defined in clear terms, as this will reflect on the identification, planning, assessment, development and implementation of strategies for the group in question.

The Target Group

The target group comprises five disabilities - visual, speech and learning, mental retardation, learning disability and orthopedic. These are being operationally defined for the purpose of this proposal.

Visually Handicapped

(I) Blind - are those who suffer either of the following conditions:

- (a) Total absence of sight;
- (b) Visual acquity not exceeding 6/60 or 20/200 (snellen) in the better eye with correcting lenses;
- (c) Limitation in the field of vision subtending an angle of 20 degrees or worse.

Low Vision

(II) Low vision children mean children with impairment of visual functioning even after treatment or standard refractive correction but who use or are potentially capable of using vision for the planning or execution of a task with appropriate assistive device.

Hearing Handicapped

Totally deaf children are those in whom the sense of hearing is non-functional for the ordinary purposes of life.

Hard of hearing or partially deaf are those in whom the sense of hearing, though defective, functions with or without a hearing aid.

Speech Handicapped

Speech impairment refers to those problems of speech which hamper communication.

Mental Retardation

It is a condition of arrested or incomplete development of mind of a person which is especially characterised by sub-average functions of intelligence manifested by two or more applicable adaptive skills such as communication, care of self, social health and safety, etc.

Learning Disability

"Specific learning disability means a disorder in one or more of the basic psychological processes involved in understanding or in using language, spoken or written, which may manifest itself in an imperfect ability to listen, think, speak, read, write or spell or to do mathematical calculations. The term includes such conditions as perceptual handicaps, brain injury, minimal brain dysfunction, dyslexia and developmental aphasia.

The term does not include children who have learning problems which are primarily the result of visual, hearing, or motor handicaps, of mental retardation, of emotional disturbance or of environmental, cultural or economic disadvantage". (Federal Register, 1977, p. 65083).

Orthopaedcally Handicapped

Orthopaedically handicap is one's inability to execute distinctive activities associated with moving, both himself/herself and objects, from place to place, and such inability resulting from application of either bones, joints, muscles or nerves. (Pandey and Advani, 1995, p.10).

Objectives

Keeping in view the various target groups and the goals of ILD in DPEP the following objectives are sought to be achieved:

1. to improve the enrolment, participation and retention of disabled children in general primary schools;
2. to provide support services to general primary school teachers, to meet the educational needs of all categories of disabled children in integrated settings;
3. to enhance the competencies and skills of general teachers to meet the educational needs of children with special needs;
4. to prepare multi-category trained resource room teachers to deal with all types of disabled children in general schools.

The Plan of Action

Based on the objectives, it is apparent that realization of integrated education implies the delivery of a comprehensive package of services at the primary school/village level. The stress is on development of capabilities of general schools and teachers to meet the educational needs of those wit disabilities/impairments. The major areas identified are as follows:

- *early identification*
- *assessment (functional and formal)*
- *orientation of and awareness generation in the village community*
- *mobilization of local resources and community*
- *development of linkages and networking between different agencies*
- *identification of special inputs/aids/assistance required for children with specific impairments in the examination process*
- *planning and implementation of an effective system of monitoring and evaluation*

All the above mentioned areas are inextricably interlinked and crucial to the overall progress and realistic integration of children with special needs into the general school system.

The key to successful implementation lies in the delivery of strong inputs in teacher development to meet the special needs of the target in question. Two models are being presented for consideration.

5. to develop instructional materials and suitable strategies for promoting the education of children with special needs through general school teachers;
6. to supply aids and appliance to the disabled child for promoting learning in integrated setting and in evaluative process.

Teacher Training Models

MODEL I - The PIED - 3 tier Cascade model

Level 1

At the first level all primary school teachers will be imparted an intensive 5 day training on special education inputs. In addition a 2 day training programme will be organised for identification of various disabilities. This will be provided by the State at the district/block level. The major focus will be on identification procedures and functional assessment. Orientation will also be given on the need for curriculum adjustment, adaptation of teaching strategies to special requirement of children with different disabilities, classroom management and use of aids and appliances.

Out of these teachers, some motivated teachers will be selected and provided a six week training at the second level.

Level 2

At the second level, daily living skills, plus curriculum areas, orientation and mobility, speech and language training will be focused upon. The DIET along wit the State will be responsible for imparting this training. Observation of disabled children in IED and special school settings will also form part of the training pragramme.

Level 3

Finally, at the third level is the multi-category training visualised to create an effective support mechanism in the overall structure and functioning of the integrated education scheme within the DPEP districts. This training input will make the cluster area/BRC self-sufficient in terms of trained manpower to meet the special needs of visual, hearing, orthopaedic, learning disabled and mentally retarded children within general schools. It is felt that with advances in training technology, materials and aids it is possible to train a single person to deal with special needs arising out of more than one disability. It is more viable to have multi category training (MCT) teacher providing resource support than a team of single disability teachers.

The 9 months MCT programme in the PIED has been underway in the four Regional Institutes of Education (RIEs) with NIE support. The programme can be adapted to suit the specific requirements of districts in consultation with States. Considering the DPEP objectives and infrastructure, the States may decide to conduct training at the State/District/Block and Cluster levels wit NGO and academic/ technical support from the RIEs and NCERT.'

In addition, a number of issues need to be examined and considered if the nine month long training is to be imparted to selected teachers in DPEP districts. They are:

- The resource room will become functional only when the teachers are trained and appointed either at the block or cluster levels. Thus the support will be delayed for nearly a year.
- Teachers who are to be sent for nine months MCT training will be drawn from the existing teacher strength in DPPE districts. This will obviously affect the teaching-learning in schools and quality of education which is a major concern of the DPEP.
- Feasibility of training: The required number of teachers per district at one time for a period of nine months needs to be viewed in relation to availability of infrastructural facilities, trained staff, finances.
- Once the training has been imparted the entire structure may become redundant or partially redundant.
- MCT training organised at the Regional Institutes as part of the PIED raises issues related to language, comprehension and medium of examination for teachers at the primary level.

Besides these issues the State/district authorities will have to consider the more general ones of:

i) creating MCT posts in DPEP districts

ii) recruitment of fresh candidates for MCT posts, or appointment of new teachers to replace those withdrawn from the existing system for MCT training/appointment.

Keeping in view all the above issues and spirit of decentralisation and flexibility in the DPEP an alternative model is given below:

MODEL II - Spiral Capacity Building Model

This model advocates recurrent short term training, so that capacities are built up over a period of time, with ample opportunity for practice, feedback and mid-course correction at the district level itself. The programme can be supplemented by the interactive distance mode, materials/techniques, which are already being planned for at the national level by NCERT and Indira Gandhi National Open University (IGNOU). A component can be included accordingly, specifically suited to the requirements of training all primary school teachers.

The capacity building exercise is based on an initial one-month course. Subsequently training is to be imparted through 4-5 refresher courses of 10 to 15 days duration each, focussing specifically on each disability i.e. visual, speech and hearing, mental retardation and learning disability.

The obvious advantage of this kind of a model is that it can be organised at the district level with academic support from the State. It is recurrent, on the job training and can be held in manageable batches of 30-35. Besides this, teachers will not be away from their schools/resource rooms for a very long period of time, encouraging continuous participation and upgraduation of both knowledge and skills, with opportunity of continuous feedback and problem-solving.

Instructional material for the basic and refresher courses will be prepared in a manual form. This exercise will be undertaken jointly by involving suitable persons/experts from all levels/disability areas. Care should be taken to include people directly involved in teaching at the primary level.

The major strength of this model lies in preparing all teachers and thus every individual school in handling children with special needs in integrated settings. This is achieved without disturbing the regular functioning schools in DPEP districts. The operationalisation of this model is subject to the establishment and functioning of the resource room/rooms.

The desirability of in-service or pre-induction training is left to the State/districts concerned.

The establishment of a 'Training Resource Group' (TRG) at the State level would be a very useful structure for strengthening teacher development at all levels. The TRG should have persons from DIETs/District Resource Groups (DRGs)/Block Resource Groups (BRGs) working together as equal partners in the exercise of teacher development. The focus of attention of the utilization of the TRG should be on making DIETs/BRGs viable support structures. Therefore, the TRG should concentrate on developing DIETs, DRGs and BRGs.

The resource persons attached to the SCERTs and RIEs may form a close network with the TRG, exchanging ideas and developing strategies/materials. This will help in promoting effective training in developing the DPEP districts in teacher education and pedagogical improvement with a focus on IED.

TRGs could thus be established with SCERT as nodal point and made functional with support from the national level institutions. An activity plan for staff development and course delivery for the various levels envisaged in the teacher training programme should be prepared based on teacher training requirements/needs in primary schools.

Training Needs

Broadly, training needs have been classified as specific to three categories:

I. Primary School (general) teachers

II. Resource room teachers

III. Administrators (general and school)

I. Primary School (Genral) Teachers

- Observation and identification, functional assessment and screening of children with special needs
- Understanding the needs of impaired/disabled children
- Evolving teaching strategies for all groups of disabled children
- Operation and maintenance of specialised aids and appliances
- Development of orientation, mobility and daily living skills.
- Development, monitoring and evaluation of individualized educational plans
- Counseling and guidance of disabled children, students, parents and community members
- Creating awareness amongst the other children regarding needs of disabled children.

II. Resource Room Teachers

- Development of co-ordination skills-teaching of braille: reading and writing
- Development of daily living, auditory, speech and reading skills
- Preparation of teaching materials through the multisensory approach
- Operational skills in planning/time scheduling and transaction of resource room support
- Adapting teaching-learning material according to various needs of disabled
- Development of guidance and counselling skills
- Conducting awareness programmes and providing information for stimulation of the child to parents, community members, students and teachers.
- Providing guidance to general and school administrators, parents, teachers and community.

III. Administrators (General and School)

- Planning and management of integrated education
- Mobilisation of resources
- Generation of community awareness.
- Identification and functional assessment
- Curriculum and examination adoption
- Architectural consideration
- Monitoring and evaluation of integrated education.

It needs to be mentioned at this juncture that the course design and materials to meet the requirements/needs of the various groups will have to be developed keeping in mind the following criteria:

i) educational level of primary school teachers

ii) previous exposure to IED, if any

iii) specific roles and responsibilities of various personnel involved in IED

iv) level at which they are to function : BRC/CRC/Village) other duties and responsibilities

vi) language ability

A necessary input is continuous resource room support to be provided either at the BRC/Cluster Resource Centre (CRC) level.

On providing level-1 training the first step of identification can commence in the village. This is to be followed by assessment, delivery of suitable education along with monitoring and evaluation.

Step 1 - Identification

i) identify out-of-school children with special needs so that they can be brought into the regular schools;

ii) identify in-school children within ordinary school in order to retain them as they are the potential drop outs of the system;

iii) identify children within existing special schools that can be integrated into general schools.

This will be done by the school teacher along with the VEC/ Panchayat members at the concerned village.

Step 2 - Assessment

The first step in the assessment process will be functional assessment to be done by the teacher in the school. This will aid the teacher in beginning classroom teaching and management. This should necessarily be followed by formal assessment which can be done by a group of experienced medical/para medical personnel located at the block level or a mobile team of experts.

The level and degree of integration of the disabled child will depend upon the individual child's needs and potentialities. Thus this step is extremely crucial if further success is to be attained. It would be a continuum of needs and corresponding services wherein follow-ups and frequent reviews are crucial. This can be facilated by the resource room teacher in collaboration with the general school teacher.

Techniques for assessment along with relevant material will need to be developed by the State Resource Group in SCERT/TRG/BRC/CRC in the local language.

Monitoring support from trained faculty at the SCERT, DIET, district and block level should be provided in the identification and assessment of children with special needs. DRCs and NGOs in the area can also be involved in this exercise.

Step 3 - Development of individualised education plans

This automatically flows from the above two steps. Integration of any child with special needs will depend on how effectively the teacher in the primary school can plan his/her work. This is dependent to a large degree on individual needs, curriculum adaptation, teaching strategies, use of aids and appliances in providing the same experience as is available to other children in the class. Training, will, thus, have to be imparted to the general teacher in the above mentioned areas. This is already envisaged in the training models discussed earlier. Besides training, development and upgradation of material should be a continuous activity. Resource room support is central to the success of total integration.

Step 4 - Monitoring and Evaluation

Monitoring and evaluation is to be an inherent part of the entire exercise. Feedback provide by different personnel at different levels in the DPEP structure will provide feedback to strengthen and improve all aspects such as:

- Planning
- Implementation
- Material development
- Training
- Developing linkages
- Assessment procedures
- Provision of resource room support

- Enrollment, participation and retention

Steps taken must ensure that the drop out rates of children with special needs is not more than that of the normal children in the school system. Role of parents and community members must be highlighted in order to strengthen monitoring and evaluation.

Internal monitoring and valuation can be done by the teachers, resource room co-ordinators, SRCs, TRGs, DIET personnel, DRCs depending on the level and areas of monitoring and evaluation.

External evaluation may be done by the RIEs/NIE/Ed.CIL/NGOs/ University Deptt./DPEP Bureau amongst other agencies.

It is imperative that training be provided to all those involved in the exercise and suitable tools developed for the same.

Besides these four areas, it is equally important that the district level authorities establish contact and create awareness within the community through community contact programme for VEC/ Panchayat/Anganwadi/Balwadi members amongst others.

- effectively utilze all available local resources/materials for meeting the needs of disabled children.
- collaborate, coordinate and establish linkages with all agencies working in the district, i.e. ICDS, DRCs, NGOs.

Suggested Models for the Development of Resource Room Support

Acknowledging that the distinctiveness of the DPEP lies in achieving IEE in a contextual manner with emphasis on participation and capacity building a number of alternative models options are outlined for implementing resource room support in districts.

Alternatives have been provided as t will further the flexibility, viability and decentralization process keeping in focus local specific needs and variations regarding numbers/type of identified disabled children.

The alternatives are as follows:

Alternative A - Block Resource Based Model

The model envisages that the resource room will be located in the BRCs of a district. Support to primary schools within that particular block will be provided either by: (i) A team of specialists - one for each disability, or (ii) 2-3 MCT teachers keeping in mind the size of the block in question and numbers and type of disabled children to be provided resource room support.

Arrangements will have to be made to bring the disabled children to the BRC from the different schools in that particular block.

Number of members in the BRC team will depend on the size of disabled child population at the primary level; it is recommended that special teacher/MCT be appointed for 8 to 10 children with special needs.

Alternative B - Mobile Peripatetic Service Model

This type of a model visualizes that a mobile team operates from either the BRC, or the CRC travelling from school to school providing educational support to children with special needs.

However, variations may be made in the constitution of the team depending on the training model opted for by the State/district. These variations are:

1) A team of specialists - one for each disability
2) A team of MCT teachers depending on the size of he lock, number and type of identified disabled children
3) A team of teachers selected after receiving the refresher courses according to the spiral capacity building model; selection of these teachers should be cautiously made depending upon back up support from other regular primary school teachers.

This necessarily implies the need for detailed planning of visits and a vehicle or vehicles to facilitate movement of the team members from school to school. The vehicle will also have to have space for storing of aids and appliances and teaching-learning material.

Training of teachers (resource room) in single disability will also have to be organised as a pre-requisite to establishing a team at either the BRC/CRC.

Alternative C - NGO Supported Resource Room Model

In this type of a model a major role is played by an NGO in providing resource room support to disabled children in primary schools. This can be implemented in two ways:

1) The NGO team is located at the BRC and through the CRC level which has either MCT teacher or provides support to all clusters of schools.
2) The NGO team is located at te BRC level and provides direct support to all primary schools within that block. This may be implemented where the CRC structure is still not viable in DPEP districts.

Alternative D - Cluster Resource Room Model

This particular model highlights the role for the CRC as the location for the resource room and staff will be located therein.

A MCT teacher/refresher course trained teachers will manage the implementation of this scheme. Either the children with special needs will come to the CRC or the teacher at times may have to visit the schools to provide guidance and support.

This seems to be viable especially in clusters where the numbers of children with disability are more and commuting is a problem to a great extent.

These various combinations are only outlined to provide a guideline to the DPEP State/districts in choosing a suitable model and resultant strategies for implementation of the IED scheme.

Establishment of a Resource Room

Central to the adoption of any of the above mentioned models is the establishment of a Resource room, which can be located with either at the block or cluster level. The materials required for the resource rooms will depend upon the type and numbers of disabled children identified in the concerned block/cluster.

While constructing new resource rooms it is essential that architectural barriers be avoided. On the other hand it may be necessary to remove these barriers from the existing schools/Resource rooms so as to facilitate the disabled child's access to equipment and free movement within the school/Resource room premises, construction of toilets suitable for them etc.

Based on the operational framework described above, the roles and functions of agencies at the cluster/block, district, state and national level are given below:

1) **CLUSTER/Block level:** The Resource room may be set up at the cluster/block level depending on the number of identified disabled children and existing DPEP infrastructure in the district/block in question. The BRC/CRC will be responsible for the following activities:

- training of cluster/village level personnel - teachers, VEC members, panchayat members, etc.
- data collection on IED and needs assessment of teachers/students
- provision of continuous resource room support
- planing and implementation of all activities related to resource room support
- identification and assessment of in/out of school disabled children
- establishing linkages with anganwadis/balwadis/PHCs, etc.

- awareness generation amongst parents, administrators and community members

2) **District level :** A district resource group should be set up with one person specifically assigned the responsibility of planning and implementation of integrated education for the disabled in each district. This person will be a part of the district project team for DPEP.

Their responsibilities will be to:

- impart training at block/cluster levels
- coordinate various activities at the district levels
- establish Management Information System (MIS) at the district level for IED
- monitor and evaluate IED work in blocks/clusters and schools
- develop action work plans for each district
- assess needs of teachers periodically for effective implementation of the scheme
- maintenance of aids and equipment
- act as a catalyst between the state project office and BRC/CRC

3) **State level:** A State resource group will have to be set up for planning and implementation of IED activities in DPEP districts. The major functions of this group will be to:

- provide academic/technical support to district/block/cluster level
- provide training to district/block level personnel
- provide funds for the implementation of the scheme
- monitor, supervise and evaluate progress of integration of disabled children
- develop material in regional language
- act as a clearing house
- establish linkage and networking with various departments and NGOs
- conducting research in DPEP districts.

4) **National level :** A national resource group will be responsible for the following:

- training of master trainers at the State/district level
- providing academic/technical support to the DPEP States

- development of examplar material involving persons from State/district levels
- institutional capacity building
- providing assistance in monitoring and evaluation of IED in DPEP districts with the State
- setting up a national coordination committee
- providing guidance in planing and implementation of IED in districts to the DPEP States.

References

Govt. of India, MHRD. National Policy on Education 1986.

Govt of India, MHRD. Report of the Committee for Review of National Policy on Education 1986, Final Report 1990.

Govt of India, MHRD. World Declaration on Education for All, 1990. Jomtien Conference.

Pandey R.S. & Advani, Lal, Perspectives in Disability and Rehabilitation, Vikas Publishing House, New Delhi, 1995

U.S. Office of Educational Federal Register, 1977. p. 65083

Source: DPEP Calling, May 1996

21

Interventions for Inclusive Schooling of Children with Disabilities in DPEP Districts : National Conference Report

The Conference was inaugurated by Shri P.R. Dasgupta, Education Secretary, Ministry of Human Resource Development, Government of India. Welcoming him, Professor A.K. Sharma, Director, NCERT highlighted the importance and need for bringing the disabled child into the fold of elementary education. Professor Sharma stated that the efforts of DPEP would remain incomplete till all children with special needs are attended to by educational agencies whether of the government or of the NGOs. He expressed his sense of satisfaction at the earnest and sincere efforts of the Government of India in this direction and assured all possible academic and technical resource support from the NCERT.

Professor N.K. Ambasht, Head of the Department of Education of Groups ith Special Needs, NCERT, highlighted the purpose of the Conference. He briefly alluded to the background paper generated by the Department making a mention of varieties of models reviewed and developed therein, and the possibility of their adoption/ adaptation and development according to the needs of the local area. He higlighted the Spiral Capacity Building Model of training and pointed out its advantages in the light of the requirement of large number of trained manpower, recurrent nature, cost effectiveness, etc.

In his introductory remarks, Shri R.S. Pandey, Joint Secretary, MHRD and Bureau Head, DPEP Bureau, higlighted the urgency of the coverage of the disabled child. Out of all such children, he pointed out, only one per cent were being provided schooling whereas to achieve the goals of Universal Elementary Education (UEE) and of Education for All, 100 per cent such children must be enrolled and retained in the scool system, whether regular or alternative, formal or non-formal. He appreciated the comprehensive and thoughtful background paper and congratulated the NCERT for having produced it. He expressed hope that tis Cnference would be a harbinger of a new deal for the children with impairments. Shri Pandey explained the DPEP structure from village to national levels and urged the Conference to think and suggest as to how special education strategies and structures could be meshed in with those of the DPEP to make it comprehensive, viable and effective.

Inaugurating the conference, Shri P.R. Dasgupta stressed the need to converge the support systems of various Ministries like HRD, Health and Family Welfare. For example, the School Health Programme could be effectively integrated with identification and assessment. He further stressed the need for providing early childhood education and care to disabled children so that they were ready to enter the primary schools and continue schooling. He also emphasized that the need for educating disabled children could not be ignored in the programme of 'Education for All' (EFA), and this would be possible only if the disabled children were caught young right at the pre-school stage.

He state that the Government of India was very keen on making the DPEP a success and expressed satisfaction that the DPEP was proving innovative in nature and as such would certainly success in providing integrated education to the disabled children.

He further said that to make inclusive schooling a reality, it would require strong linkages and networking between various Government departments and agencies such as Health and Family Welfare, Women and Child Development, ECCE and NGO's working in DPEP districts. Besides this, training of regular and special resource room teachers was an extremely crucial input for making the integrated education programme a success. The inaugural session concluded with a vote of thanks proposed by Shri C.D. Tamboli.

After the inaugural session, the Conference met in a plenary. The participants discussed the general issues. It was emphasised that PIED experimentation and IEDC experiences should be taken advantage of and adapted to the situation wherever applicable. It was also pointed out that the IEDC experiences should be taken advantage of and adapted to the situation wehrever applicable. It was also pointed out that the IEDC scheme, which is not being fully utilized in all States, should be linked with DPEP efforts for the benefit of inclusive schooling in DPEP districts. This sould be further reinforced by the optional involvement of NGO's at all the levels within the programme. The Conference stressed the need to develop awareness in the community and ensure its involvement n inclusive schooling, particularly at the primary level.

Other important areas of intervention identified we Research and Development and Capacity Building. Finally, it was unanimously agreed that inclusive schooling was important, especially if EFA was to be attained by the turn of the century.

After the plenary session, the participants met separately in five groups as follows:

Group I Identification and Assessment
Group II Interventions
Group III Resource-Room Support
Group IV Teacher Training
Group V Structures, Linkages and Monitoring.

The salient recommedations of the Conference are as follows:

Identification and Assessment

Identification of children with impairments even before they enter school is a necessary condition for detecting and locating such children who have to be covered for inclusive schooling at a posterior date as envisaged in the DPEP guidelines. The convergence between elementary education, ECCE, School healt, and ICDS etc. could be fruitflly utilized for this purpose. For children already enrolled in school, similar exercise is necessary for obvious reasons. It may be necessary to provide short training to the functionaries of these agencies in the skill of identification through tools and materials developed by various agencies like the NCERT, National Institutes of Handicapped, etc.

Since this task involves census approach a large band of workers needs to be trained. Naturally at the village level the functionaries are the primary school teachers, the ICDS/ECCE & village health workers. All of them need to be covered under the training programme.Identification is just a preliminary bench mark to plan strategies for education coverage, extension of specialized services and remediation if possible. Therefore, the extent of impairment needs to be assessed.

Two types of Assessment are visualized: Functional and Formal. The first type of assessment can be done by the primary school teachers who can then refer children for formal assessment to the district level, which falls in tune with the DPEP structure as envisaged in DPEP structure guidelines. For the second type however, a group of specialists comprising of doctor, psychologist, pediatrician, ENT/Eye, Orthopeadic specialist, and others would be required for purposes of medical and psycho-educational testing of identified children.

Training in regional language is a necessary input required to prepare teachers for functional assessment. Tools developed by the

NCERT and other National Institutes could be used. Periodical assessment is crucial in order to facilitate effective teaching learnign within Primary Schools.

Immediate feed back of the formal assessment should be communicated to the concerned resource room teacher and class teacher for developi individualized educational plans.

Interventions

As mentioned above, the need for coordinated intervention should be possible through existing DPEP structures. Needless to emphasize, interventions at the pre-school stage are as important as in-school interventions. Whereas enrolment of all children is the DPEP goal, it is essential to remind ourselves that enrolment, retention and achievement are intrinsically related to all children including children with impairment/disability. Therefore, there is a special need to make educational functionaries not only aware but conscious about special efforts required to bring all such children in the fold of inclusive education.

The Conference felt that there should be a greater emphasis on bringing out the latent potential of children with impairments and their interactive nature with environmental resources should be recognized in planning any strategy aimed at ameliorating the needs of these children. The Confernece also felt that these children cannot be denied education for want of resources whether manpower, material of financial. With technological development, it is possible to acquire various kinds of aids suitable for different types of disabilities, single or multiple. This should not be given a back seat for want of funds. At the same time, it was recognized that there is a great need for research and development activities - both hardware and software.

Specific interventions for children with impairments can be classified into pre-educational/preparatory and educational.

Pre-educational services, for example orientation, mobility and daily living skills, are considered as absolutely necessary to prepare the child for inclusive schooling. This would require interventions for ensuring an integrated service delivery system involving ICDS, ECCE, WCD and other agencies available at the grass root level besides family and community members. This has been categorically emphasised in the DPEP guidelines.

Adequate inputs in terms of media awareness programmes, aids and appliances, allowances, guidance and counselling and rehabilitation services would not only serve to prepare but facilitate effective integration of the impaired child into primary schools.

Removal of architectural barriers is a basic prerequisite so as to provide access to all children with disabilities. Provision of transport and physical assistance are also envisaged as crucial inputs to maxmize their attendance and participation in primary schools.

The educatinal interventions could be considered in terms of introduction of a plus curriculum for children wit differentiated needs. Curricular adaptations, teaching-learning materials and strategies and training for optional and appropriate use of teaching aids is of equal importance in the context of teaching a disabled child.

This implies intensive curriculum research and development in terms of objectives for achievement of given Minimum Levels of Learning (MLL) competencies, adaptation of instructional material, teaching-learning proceses, assessment and evaluation techniques according to the specific needs of each impaired child.

In addition, as envisaged in recent Persons with Disabilities (equal opportunities, protction of rights and full participation) Act, each disaled child has to be provided free of cost reading materials adapted to suit his/her special needs.

While it is necessary to provide inputs in educational activities, it is also necessary that children with impairments are provided special services like physiotherapy, speech therapy etc. for which DPEP structures will have to link up with agencies providing these services. The *modus operandi* to put such a programme into action at the door step of each child could be considered by providing mobie support units.

It is realized that vocationalisation of education is not possible at the primary stage because of policy imperatives. At the same time it is felt necessary that work experience activities may be introduced and adapted to suit the specific needs of the impaired child.

Resource Room Support

Resource room support is central to the success of inclusive schooling.

The four models mentioned in the background and issue paper namely Block Resource model, Peripatetic model, NGO supported Resource model and Cluster Resource model have their utility. Any or a combination of these could be considered in various geographical and DPEP structural contexts. In order to keep the spirit of flexibility and local relevance as the prime concern the Conference felt that it would be in the interest of the programme to keep applicability of these models according to the local needs. Depending on the need of the area, any one model singly or in combination with oters can be selected. However, transportation facility is a must irrespective of the model selected by district/block. The ultmate goal is that Resource room facilities should be available to all children who need it.

Obviously the person who manages the resource rooms should have proper training in dealing with various kinds of impairments, single or multiple.

The function of the Resource room teacher could be:

- Special educational assessment with the help of para medical team, NGOs, VEC members, Panchayat members and other administrators.
- Development of special teaching learning materials and aids.
- Planing individualised instructions.
- Meeting the counselling and guidance needs of the child and the family.
- Monitoring and operating the aids and equipment.
- Providing form for exchange of ideas and teaching strategies.
- Organize remedial interventions.

The overall coordination of the resource room should be the responsibility of a special coordinator at the district level as envisaged in the structures discussed later in this report.

Aids and appliances which form an intrinsic part of the support services at the resource room could be as per the lists given in the appendix of the background paper developed by the NCERT.

Teacher Training

The Conference felt that no single straight jacket model can be visualized for training of the personnel because of the local specific character of the DPEP. Yet, it is necessary that every functionary connected with education must have proper attitude and appreciation of the need of the disabled including the primary school teachers. For this, short term training programmes could be devised which may include awareness, appreciation of the child's needs, counselling, curriculum adaptation, simple techniques of identification and functional assessment, handling of children with single and multiple disabilities, amongst other aspects that might be considered necessary. It may be considered worthwhile to integrate these components with the general training programme of the primary school teachers in the DPEP districts. Since it is proposed to integrate tese components with the general training, the modalities are not being separately suggested.

Special educational services to such impaired children are of prime importance and, therefore, a support system for the primary school teachers to function effectively is envisaged. In this connection the existing models of PIED and the proposed model of the 'Spiral Capacity Building' may be considered for adoption/adaptation by the concerned districts as per their requirements. It needs to be underscored that these are not the only models or are sacrosanct but it is necessary to note that the need for such trained manpower is absolutely essential.

Each DPEP district could consider the structure and organisational pattern of the training programme in the light of their own specific structure and possible linkages taking cognizance of available trained manpower and projected manpower needs.

It may be worthwile to review the existing training programmes and adapt it to the local needs and environment. The proposed Sprial Capacity Building model described in the background paper could als be considered in the context of local needs of manpower requirements, available resources, time frame, cost effectiveness, etc.

Linkages, Structures and Monitoring

The first level of operation envisaged under the interventions is of the Child and Family, Community. For this, linkages need to be established with the existing structure of Village Education Committee (VEC) as envisaged in POA (1992) and DPEP. It may be worthwhile to mention that the Gram Sabha could also be involved in the process althoug it is imperative that involvement of VEC implies involvement of Gram Sabha. This is necessary in view of the 73rd Constitutional Amendment.

At the second level of operation Child Welfare and Rehabilitation Services available in the Panchayat Samiti/Village through the Health and Family Welfare Programme, WCD agencies, Rural Development and ECCE need to be harnessed and dovetailed at the Child-Family-Community level.

The third level at which the programme should operate is the Primary Teacher-Primary School. The teacher training as indicated above could be effected through the mode opted for by the DPEP in the concerned district. However, linkages with the resource teacher (at the cluster/block, Panchayat Samiti or any other such level decided by DPEP) and the VEC, Parents, Mother-teacher Counsel, Mahila Mandals and alternative schooling system operating in the village like NFE, pen school infrastructures will have to be established and networking ensured.

It is envisaged that the fourth level will consist of a cluster resource room, in case the DPEP has a Cluster Resource Centre (CRC). A trained multicategory teacher should be made available if this exists. The Resource room could be a part of CRC. It is expected that at the cluster level consisting of 8-10 villages, there will be Panchayat Samiti as per the 73rd Consitutional Amendment, which would imply that the networking between the Panchayat Samiti, Cluster Resource room would be necessary.

The fifth level, that is the Block Resource Centre (BRC), as envisaged in the scheme of operations connected with the inclusive schooling of the disabled child, is a crucial level for organizing training if Spiral Capacity Building model is to be adopted. In any case, close linkages between the Block Samiti, BRC and paramedical/medical team as well as the trainers or resource persons will have to be developed. These would in turn draw expert advice from the District Institutes of Education and Training (DIETS) and referral centres for different kinds of disabilities at the district level.

The district unit of the DPEP should acquire total responsibility of implementation of this component and may devise methods and means of establishing a District Resource Group (DRG) as art integral part of the District Resource Centre. This resource centre will have to establish linkages with the district hospitals, special schools and medical experts specializing in different kinds of disabilities in order to become a comperhensive and functional Resource Centre. The regular functioning of this Resource Centre is of extreme importance and its function would include awareness generation, advocacy, liaison, coordination, production and distribution of materials, training, monitoring and evaluation and consolidating the needs of each village, cluster, block, in the form of district plans. The DRC will be the prime mover of the entire scheme and, therefore, it needs to have experts in different areas either pooled from various agencies or apponted if necessary. It would be advisable to link the DRC with the existing DIETs keeping in view the nature of functions it has to provide.

Looking at the dimensions of the work involved and path breaking that needs to be undertaken, DPEP may consider nominating/appointing a senior and experienced person in this area as Project Incharge Special Education, like that of Officer Incharge Girls Education.

Deriving from the nature of support that the district requires, the State will have to build a State Resource Group (SRG). This State Resource Group will function in close coordination with the State Project Dierctor. It would ensure uninterupted supportive mechanisms through the Project Director, undertake monitoring and evaluation work, provide training at the State and district levels, establish networkign with NGOs, organize mass media campaigns at the State level and perform clearing house functions in the shape of documentation. In case the State decides to locate this group in SCERT or wherever IEDC Cells are located it would be advantageous. However, if this is not possible, even then the need of establishing strong linkages with concerned SCERTs cannot be over emphasized.

At the national level, the DPEP Bureau may establish a National Resource Group (NRG) on special education. Looking at the resources and the expertise available at the NCERT it may be advisable to locate this National Resource Group in the Department of Education of Groups with Special Needs. It may have other experts from outside the department and the Council depending on the requirement of specializations.

It is also felt necessary to co-opt all the Diretors of the National Institutes as members of this National Resource Group. The Ministry of Welfare, Health and Family Welfare, Department of Women and Child Development besides the Department of Education should also find representation in the NRG.

The NRG will undertake research and development activity, monitoring and evaluation function inter-institutional coordination and policy planning.

Source : DPEP Calling, May 1996

Teacher Training Designs : A Quick Appraisal

Prof. G.L. Arora
Dept. of Teacher Education and Extention, NCERT.

Dr. Ajit Singh
Dept. of Teacher Education and Extention, NCERT.

Dr. S.K. Yadav
Dept. of Teacher Education and Extention, NCERT, New Delhi.

In-service education of teachers is undoubtedly one of the most important strategies to improve the quality of education. Researchers have very often emphasized the importance of the link between the quality of education and the adequacy of opportunities for the professional development of teachers. However, recent reviews of research on in service education converge in their findings with regard to ineffectiveness of in-service education available to teachers. There are a number of reasons contributing to ineffectiveness of in-service education. For instance, training content is generally decided by people other than the teachers for whom in-service education is meant. As a result, in-service education programmes rarely address their individual needs and concerns. Further, in the planning and implementation of in-service training programmes, sound conceptual basis is very often absent which is essential to ensure their effectiveness. In-service education a training of teachers, to be effective, therefore,needs to be designed appropriately. In-service training to primary teachers and their trainers is a significant intervention in the District Primary Education Programme to improve the quality of primary education. DPEP states have, therefore, developed designs for the training of primary teachers and their trainers heads of Cluster Resource Centres (CRCs), Co-ordinators, Block Resource Centres (BRCs), DIET/SCER & T faculty. A need was, threfore, felt to appraise the training designs developed by different DPEP states for which a study was undertaken by the NCERT with the following objectives:

- to assess the strengths and weaknesses of the training design developed by different DPEP states;
- to provide forum to the states to learn from experience of others and
- to suggest ways and means to improve the quality of training.

The study was delimited to the states of Assam, Haryana, Maharashtra, Madhya Pradesh, Karnataka and Tamil Nadu.

Main Findings

Main findings of the study with regard to different aspects of training design are given below:-

Need Assessment

The study revealed that training needs of different functionaries primary teachers, head-teachers, and trainers-heads of Cs, Coordinators, BRCs, DIET/SCERT faculty were identified by the states on the basis of i) experiences of SCERT/DIET faculty while working with primary teachers and other functionaries; ii) findings of the baseline learning achievement studies conducted by the NCERT and the NIEPA, and interaction with wazzu concerned personnel. States have however, not identified training needs of the these functionaries by conducting research systematically. This may be due to the reason that they were in a hurry to launch in-service training programmes.

Training Objectives

State had not delineated explicitly objectives of training for different functionaries as revealed from their training designs. There is enough research evidence to suggest that the failure to clarify intended goal(s) of the programmes is one of the major pitfalls which threatens the success of an in-service training programme. Therefore, it is essential that training programmes must reflect explicitly the objectives of training. These should further be negotiated with trainees at the commencement of the programme.

Training Content

The content of training of different functionaries has been identified by the states. The content delineated by the state of Tamil Nadu for primary teachers teaching classes III to V comprises topics such as DPEP objectives; mobilisation of community resource; role of Mother

Teacher Councils (MTC), Parent Teachers' Association (PTA) education of the disadvantaged, Village Education Committee (VEC), gender sensitization, teaching learners with disability, methods of preparing low cost and no cost teaching aids, organisation of co-curricular activities, learner centred approach, evaluation etc. The training content delineated by the state of Kerala for primary teachers constitute topics like of primary education, DPEP minimum levels of learning in Mathematics, Malayalam, Environmental studies, preparation of teaching aids, evaluation etc. The study further revealed etc. The study further revealed that enrichment in the content of school subjects has not been given due emphasis in all the states.

Training Periodicity

Most of the states have planned to provide recurrent training to primary teachers and other functionaries. For instance the state of Tamil Nadu has planned to provide training to primary teachers for six days followed by here days training every year. Similarly the state of Kerala has planned to provide five days training to primary teachers followed by training of the same duration every year. The state of Haryana has planned seven days training of primary teachers every year.

The states of Karnataka and Maharashtra which have not so far planned recurrent training of teachers need to reshape their training design. This is because staff development and in-service education is more effective when it is part of training that continues over an extended period of time in comparison to 'one shot' training.

Transactional Approach

Activity approach, discussion, demonstration are the transactional approaches planned to be followed in the training of teachers. This is a healthy sign because lecture/lecture-cum-discussion has heretofore, been the predominant transactional approach. This approach makes the participants passive listeners and erodes the effectiveness of the programme to a great extent.

Monitoring and Evaluation of Quality of Training

Most of the states have been drawn up plans to monitor and evaluate the quality of training by seeking trainees' perceptions at the end of the programme either through a questionnaire/and / or interview. This is inadequate to ensure quality of training. Training programmes can yield desired dividends only if the training is of appropriate quality. To ensure the same a comprehensive monitoring and evaluation mechanism needs to be evolved. The indicators of the quality of training could be participants gain in knowledge, refinement of requisite skills, desirable effort on their self-concept, attitude towards work, pupils and the school. Participants satisfaction with the programme and the desired changes in their instructional behaviors are some other indicators. A monitoring and evaluation system developed on the basis of indicators mentioned above shall have to address to the training inputs, processes and outcomes.

Follow-Up

The review of training designs developed by different states revealed that states have not yet paid adequate attention to the follow-up aspect of the training.

SUGGESTIONS

- State DPEP offices need to evolve strategic plan to provide recurrent in-service training to different categories of personnel.
- Training needs of different categories of personnel should be assessed through research.
- In some states the training package is the same both for primary teachers and trainers. States need to consider additional inputs for trainers in the light of their responsibilities / role as trainers.
- Training designs did not specify explicitly the objectives of training visualized for different categories of personnel. These need to be spelt out precisely so that their atainment is monitored effectively.
- States need to develop mechanism for monitoring and evaluation of training quality.
- Content of training of primary school teachers as visualized by DPEP states reveals that content-enrichment of teachers in different school subjects has been given due emphasis. There is a need to assess teachers' content enrichment needs through research.
- Presently training input is the same for all teachers working in different contexts. Local specific needs of teachers working different contexts are not being taken care of. There is a need to identify local specific content training needs of teachers working in different contexts.
- Monthly meetings of teachers at the cluster level have been

visualized. To ensure that these meetings enrich teachers' competencies, there is a need to structure the content of monthly meetings and to develop suitable material for the same. DIETs should take up the responsibility of developing material and should oversee the effectiveness of these meetings.

Source : DPEP Calling, December 1996

23

Competency Based Teacher Training Programme

The Constitution of India provides for free and compulsory education for all children upto the age of 14 years. Educational reformers and researchers planned so many schemes to achieve the goal of Universal Primary Education (UPE). Besides this, developing and developed countries recently joined hands and pledged to have 'Education for All' before the turn of the century.

Yet today, even after a lapse of more than 45 years after Independence, much still remains to be done, particularly in rural parts of India.

Literacy does not stop with acquiring the three R's but goes further in developing the innate talents of children. Both qualitative and quantitative aspects of education, especially in a densely populated country like India, should get equal stress in all the efforts.

One cannot be compromised at the cost of the other. The major focus in education for the masses needs to be on the teacher and the taught.

Children have to be moulded and guided for proper development of their innate talents and for that purpose, the teacher must possess the required competencies, skills and the bent of mind.

Of the many projects implemented with the aim of achieving UPE through improving teacher competencies and skills, the innovative and home grown District Primary Education Programme (DPEP) is the latest.

A lot of research/survey work has preceded the launch of this holistic programme. Further research on the effects, outcomes of this comprehensive national programme is indispensable for chalking out further strategies to achieve the cherished goal of UPE.

The research proposal entitled "Effectiveness of District Primary Education Programme in improving the teacher competencies through in-service training programmes", is a small venture in this direction.

The aim of the research proposal is to study the impact of various in-service and pre-service programmes in relation to those designed in the DPEP.

To assess the impact we have to analyse the meaning of competencies as applied to the teacher and the strategies for developing those competencies through various means of training. The competencies have to be categorised according to the place of applicability and classified as per the accepted norms.

Competency Defined

Competence is nothing more than an improved modern term applied to an ancient human value; for example, the right way of doing things is the competent way; the right way to perform a job, the right way to live and work in association and cooperation with others. In other words it means a desired quality of job performance. The qualities of competency are enthusiasm, fluency, industry, neatness, originality, adaptability and thrift. The training for competency has always been and still is largely training for creating abilities or qualities that are placed in actual job situation/context. Competence does not result from possession of great amount of knowledge. It must become functionally operative at the appropriate time. Knowledge must be integrated into a pattern of behaviour to serve a useful purpose.

Applied to teachers, competency means the right way of conveying units of knowledge, application and skills to the students. The right way includes knowledge of contents as well as the processes, methods and means of conveying them in an interesting way, involving the activities of students. In short, a competent teacher makes the teaching-learning process a joyous experience for children and also to himself/herself.

Identification of Competency

The teacher has a role to play as a friend, philosopher and guide and secure the cooperation of society, co-workers, officials and so on in the discharge of his/her duties and for the achievement of the desired results. As such the competencies can be classified as under:-

(1) Classroom competencies;

(2) Competencies related to administration and management;

(3) Competencies in relation to school, society co-workers and pupils;

(4) Competencies in relation to content and curriculum;

(5) Motivational and value based competencies.

Classroom competencies deal with classroom situations and are mainly devoted to the actual interaction in the class with the pupils.

Further, the management of the class requires skillful handling of the situation in imparting the desired qualities and abilities to the students. Classroom is a miniature society.

The teacher must develop the required talents in children so that they will discharge their duties as members of the future society.

As an able administrator, the teacher must posses a variety of competencies to enable him/her to perform the role of a leader dedicated to tasks assigned. The administrative capacities will enable the teacher to run the school on smooth lines securing 100% cooperation both from co-workers and members of society. As a role model s/he impresses upon his colleagues and pupils the salient features of a good administrator.

Public related comprehencies play a pivotal role in maintaining a cordial and conducive environment and to secure the maximum cooperation and assistance. To secure maximum mobilisation of resources and to have a convergence of various maxims and services, the teacher must have an open mind, taking cognizance of the views of different sections of society to which s/he belongs and to which s/he is responsible.

To secure 100% enrolment and retention the curriculum must have a direct bearing on the life and livelihood of the society from where the pupils come. The content provides only the base and the teacher must have a mastery over the content for developing the required competencies aimed at.

The method adopted must be suitable to the age and mental ability of the pupils, social mores and the available resources. The method and mode of approach must lessen the burden of learning and increase the eagerness and happiness of school life. Activity based participatory process of teaching and research oriented techniques, will make learning interesting and joyful.

By being a teacher s/he must inspire his/her pupils not only by teaching but also through behaviour and activities. By direct contact and through his word the teacher reaches members of society and influences them towards the accepted ideas of perfect behaviour. By being a role model he influences his fellow teachers and is in turn influenced by the role model of other teachers.

Consolidation and Classification of Competenecies

The empirically identified competencies are consolidated by synthesising the overlapping items. Competencies for defined and specific areas have been arrived at thus. Further, competencies are classified under 5 major categories as detailed overleaf.

- Cognitive based competencies define knowledge and

intelligence skills and abilities that are expected of a learner. They are content based and help enlarge the sphere of activities.

- Performance based competencies: Instead of mere knowledge as stated above the learner demonstrates that he/she can perform some activity rather than simply being aware of facts. Performance based competencies are skill based and overt action oriented.
- Consequence based competencies : To demonstrate this competency a person is required to bring a change in others. The level of success is not measured by what one knows or does but by what one accomplishes. The achievement of pupils is a standard measure of consequence based competency.
- Affective competency: A great emphasis has to be laid on this type of competency rather than the previous categories. What one know is not important but what one is able to teach and so bring a change in the pupils is important. The affective competencies define the expected attitudes and values and tend to resist specificity. These competencies are expressed in terms of behaviour rather than by precept.
- Exploratory competencies: This type of competencies are those that cannot be fitted into any of the above four types in competency based teacher education. The activities provide opportunity to students to learn, but specific nature of outcome cannot be desired. They are also referred as experience objective or expressive objectives. The Competency Based Teacher Education (CBTE) does not depend on exploratory competencies. The specific outcomes are yet to be explicated.

Training Programme

A way to develop the various competencies has to be assessed and programmes organised to develop them. The following programmes are suggested for the development of the above mentioned competencies.

(1) Seminar

(2) Workshop

(3) Training

(4) Discussion

(5) Symposium

(6) Buzz

(7) Brain storming and

(8) Ice Breaking

A competency can be developed by different programmes and one single programme can develop more than one competency. Hence, two kinds of classifications, namely programme based and competency based are arrived at. Out of the different programmes, those which inculcate more number of competencies will be selected for giving suitable training. Modules depicting the salient features of the programme and the results to be secured will be clearly indicated in the content to derive the maximum advantage. Trainers will suitably be trained to inculcate the competencies in teachers.

Preparation of Questionnaire

Questionnaire in selected schools in the 4 DPEP districts will be issued to teachers for obtaining their views and requirements regarding the competencies to be developed, the programmes they require as well as the duration of the programmes.

Mode of Analysis and Assessment

The entire programme is aimed at improving the achievement levels of children as well as their enrolment and retention. So to assess the impact of training and importance of the competencies to be developed a test will be conducted before and after the training to teachers. This test will measure the achievement of children in DPEP districts where the trainings are given and in non DPEP districts where teachers do not have the opportunity of undergoing the training.

Workshops on Identification of Competencies and Training Programmes

Two 2-day workshops - one at DIET Krishnagiri and the other at DIET Vadalur were held wherein the Principals, the DIET faculty members, Headmasters and teachers. Headmasters and teachers participated for identification of the required competencies and assessing the training needs of teachers.

On the first day in the first session a general outline about the expected outcomes of the workshop was given as a prelude to the participants.

Ample opportunities were given to the participants to express their opinion freely and frankly.

The DIET faculty members contributed in no small measure in guiding the deliberations of the workshop. The participants were divided into groups and made to discuss in detail the various components of the workshop.

From these exercises it was possible to assess the real picture of the present set up and the model as desired by the participants.

Conclusion

The study is to find a solution for increasing the competencies which will make teachers discharge their duties efficiently for achieving success in providing quality education. It will also enhance the teaching skills of teachers. It will formulate the various inputs for providing effective training programmes to teachers. In short the study will analyse the maladies prevalent in the education system and suggest ways and means to eradicate the outdated, illogical and dull teaching practices.

Findings will enable the Department/Educationists to frame and conduct such of those training programmes which improve the competencies of teachers for qualitative education. It will also assess the impact of in-service training in providing Education For All. The findings will help the replicability and sustainability of the in-service training programmes of the project.

Teacher Competencies in Relation to Raising Achievement Level

I. **Class Related Competencies**

1. Lesson Planning and Instructional Management
2. Evaluating and Remedial Skill
3. Innovating and Experimenting.

II. **School Related Competencies**

4. Development of Positive Attitudes
5. Administration and Management
6. Inter-school Relations
7. Image and Morale Building.

III. **Pupil Related Competencies**

8. Identification of Pupils Talents
9. Identification of Pupils' Characteristics
10. Identification of Pupils' Needs
11. Developing Non-Cognitive Skills among Pupils
12. Guidance and Counselling Skills

13. Helping Pupils to Develop Personality.

IV. **Community Related Competencies**

14. Awareness Building
15. Ensuring Participation
16. Mobilization of Resources and its Utilisation
17. Public Relations.

V. **Curriculum**

18. Initiating
19. Planning
20. Developing
21. Implementing
22. Evaluating Skills.

VI. **Motivational Competencies**

23. Motivating Pupils
24. Motivating Colleagues
25. Motivating the Society.

VII. **Value Related Competencies**

26. Playing an Ethical Role Model
27. Developing Values Among Pupils
28. Developing Values among Members of the Society.

VIII. **Leadership Role Model**

29. Developing Leadership Qualities for Self
30. Developing Leadership Qualities among Colleagues
31. Developing Leadership Qualities among Students
32. Developing Leadership Qualities among Societal Members.

Knowledge/Cognitive

1. Lesson Planning and Instructional Management
2. Evaluation and Remedial Skill
3. Identification of Pupils' Talents
4. Identification of Pupils' Characteristics

5. Identification of Pupils' Needs
6. Initiating Curriculum
7. Developing Curriculum
8. Implementing Curriculum.

Feeling/Affective

1. Development of Positive Attitudes
2. Motivating Pupils
3. Motivating Colleagues
4. Motivating the Society
5. Playing an Ethical Role Model
6. Developing Values among Pupils
7. Developing Values among Members of the Society
8. Developing Leadership Qualities.

Doing/Performance/Psychomotor

1. Administration and Management
2. Fostering Inter-School Relations
3. Developing Non-Cognitive Skills among Pupils
4. Guidance and Counselling Skills
5. Helping Pupils to Develop Personality
6. Ensuring Participation
7. Mobilization of Resources and its Utilisation
8. Implementing Curriculum
9. Evaluation of Curriculum
10. Developing Leadership Qualities among Colleagues, Students, Societal Members.

Consequence

1. Image and Tone building
2. Fostering Public Relations.

Explorative

1. Lesson Planning and Instructional Management
2. Innovating and Experimenting.

Symposium

1. Lesson Planning and Instructional Management
2. Identification of Pupil's Talents
3. Helping Pupils to Develop Personality
4. Public Relations
5. Developing Leadership Qualities for Self
6. Inter-school Relations
7. Guidance and Counselling Skills
8. Developing Values among Pupils and Society.

Seminar

1. Playing an Ethical Role Model
2. Image and Tone Building
3. Identification of Pupils' Characteristics
4. Ensuring Participation
5. Initiating Curriculum
6. Developing Leadership Qualities among Colleagues, Students, Members of the Society.
7. Identification of Pupils' Needs
8. Developing Values among Pupils and Society
9. Instructional Management
10. Administration and Management.

Workshop

1. Lesson Planning
2. Inter-School Relations
3. Identification of Pupils' Needs
4. Mobilization of Resources and its Utilisation
5. Planning Curriculum
6. Implementing Curriculum
7. Developing of Non-Cognitive Skills
8. Developing of Positive Attitude
9. Motivating Pupils
10. Motivating Colleagues

11. Motivating the Society
12. Developing Values among Pupils
13. Developing Values among Members of the Society

Discussion

1. Remedial Programme
2. Image and Tone building
3. Awareness Building
4. Crisis Management
5. Playing an Ethical Role Model

Brain Storming

1. Guidance and Counselling Skills
2. Innovating and Experimenting
3. Identification of Pupils' Talents
4. Helping Pupils' to Develop Personality.

Training

1. Planning and Instructional Management
2. Administration and Management
3. Evaluation and Remedial Skills
4. Development of Positive Attitude
5. Mobilisation and Utilisation of Resources.

Ice Breaking

1. Awareness Building
2. Motivating Pupils', Colleagues and Society
3. Development of Positive Attitude.

Buzz

1. Public Relations
2. Identification of Pupils' Talents and Characteristics
3. Playing an Ethical Role Model.

Competency	*Programme*
Lesson Planning and instructional Management	Symposium, Workshop, Training, Seminar
Evaluation and Remedial Skill	Training, Panel Discussion
Innovating and Experimenting	Brain storming, Training
Development of Positive Attitudes	Ice breaking, Training
Administration and Management	Training, Seminar
Inter-school Relations	Workshop, Symposium
In age and Tone building	Seminar, Panel Discussion
Identification of Pupil's Talents	Symposium, Brain storming, Buzz
Identification of Characteristics	Buzz, Seminar
Identification of Pupil's Needs	Workshop, Seminar
Developing and Non-Cognitive Skills among Pupils	Workshop
Guidance and Counselling Skills	Symposium, Brain Storming
Helping Pupils' to Develop Personality	Symposium, Brain Storming
Awareness Building	Panel Discussion, Ice breaking
Ensuring Participation	Seminar, Workshop
Mobilisation of Resources and its Utilisation	Workshop, Training
Public Relations	Symposium, Buzz
Initiating Curriculum	Workshop, Seminar
Planning Curriculum	Workshop
Developing Curriculum	Workshop
Implementing Curriculum	Workshop
Implementing Curriculum	Workshop, Panel Discussion, Seminar
Remediation, Evaluation	Training, Panel Discussion
Motivating Colleagues	Ice breaking, Workshop
Playing an Ethical Role Model	Buzz, Seminar, Discussion

Developing Values among Pupils	Seminar, Symposium, Workshop
Developing Values among Members of the Society	Seminar, Symposium, Workshop
Developing Leadership Qualities for Self	Seminar, Symposium
Developing Leadership Qualities among Colleagues, Students, Societal Members	Seminar, Symposium
Crisis Management	Discussion

Source : DPEP Calling, April 1996

24

District Planning Training Programme for Officers

Introduction

DPEP was extended to selected districts of Andhra Pradesh and West Bengal in 1994-95. These districts are in the process of preparing and finalising their plans and programmes. At present, the programme is being extended to the selected districts of Himachal Pradesh, Gujarat and Orissa. These states are in the initial stage of preparing district plans and state intervention strategies. The present training Programme was organised to extend professional support and help to the district and state level officers from these states to prepare their DPEP plans.

Objectives

The specific objectives of the programme were:

- to introduce them to the planning methodology;
- to train them in the techniques of plan formulation; and
- to acquaint them with the process of plan preparation under the DPEP.

The programme was organised from 29th August to 1st September, 1995 in New Delhi.

Participation

The participation of the programme consisted of state and district level officials and faculty members from the resource institution who are associated with the DPEP planning activities from the states of Himachal Pradesh, Gujarata and Orissa. A total of 33 officers participated in the programme.

Methodology

The training methodology in the remaining part of the programme essentially consisted of classroom interactions followed by group work. The themes for interactions were identified on the basis of the requirements to prepare plans under the DPEP.

Resource Persons

Resource persons for the programme were drawn from the MHRD, NOS, Ed. CIL and NIEPA.

Inauguration

The programme was inaugurated by Professor Kuldeep Mathur, Director, NIEPA. In his inaugural remarks he drew the attention of the participants to expansion of the system in terms of enrolments, institution and teachers which is very impressive. However, drop outs continue to be high and learner achievement levels of primary school graduates are rather low. Therefore, in the recent past, the policy intervention measures are increasingly focussed on these dimensions. Similarly, it is observed that a substantial proportion of the non-enrolled are girls and children from the deprived sections. Hence, decentralised planning and targetting becomes essential to bring these groups to school and to retain them in the schools.

The effort, in the recent past, is to encourage and promote decentralised planning in education. At present, the district is considered as the viable unit for decentralised planning in India. The District Primary Education Programme (DPEP) is one of the major interventions initiated by the Government of India of facilitate decentralised educational planning in India.

Drawing up of district level plans requires developing planning competencies at the district level. For a very long time, NIEPA is actively involved in helping the state and district teams to develop plans. Our experience in this process has shown that there is a need to professionalise educational planning and management in India. Over the years, NIEPA has gained considerable experience and expertise in planning education at the district level through its involvement in research and plan formulation exercises. This training programme is one of such efforts to professionally support the district and state level officers to develop district plans within the framework of the DPEP.

Planning Methodology and Process

The District Primary Education Programme (DPEP) is an exercise in decentralised planning at the district level. Very often, it is noted that district planning exercises in India have two major limitations. First, even when plans are prepared at the district level, the resource allocation decisions used to be taking place at the state level. Second, there is the relative absence of planning competencies at the district level to draw up district specific plans. Due to these reasons, it was difficult, if not impossible to draw up realistic district plans to the district level.

The DPEP provides an opportunity to overcome these two limitations. Under this programme, resource availability to the district is ensured and plan formulation process itself is seen as an exercise in developing planning competencies at the district level. Apart from the technical and professional aspects of drawing up plans, the DPEP also equally emphasises the process as an essential step in the planning process under the DPEP. With the recent constitutional amendments and activisation of local level bodies, decentralised planning exercise involves detailed participatory process and consultative exercises. This participatory approach ensures more realistic plans and better conditions for their successful implementation.

One of the first steps involved in any planning exercise is to make an assessment of the present situation. An elaboration of the existing programmes,an assessment regarding the achievements made and an identification of constraints and problem areas form an essential part of assessing educational situation in any district. Very often one has to depend on various indicators to arrive at realistic assessment regarding the present status of education. Developing and using such indicators give a better professional input to the planning process.

The targets are almost given to any district level. Based on the present levels of achievement, the planners have to clearly identify the task involved to achieve these targets. This is true in case of almost all targets in the context of EFA. Then the planning effort is to seek ways and means to reach these targets. The ways in this context mean strategies to achieve targets.

Strategies to achieve plan targets may vary between districts and localities. A strategy which is successful in one location need not be totally applicable in another location. Therefore, the effort needs to be to identify local specific strategies. How do we identify strategies?

In the past we have relied more on experience than on expertise and empirical evidence to evolve strategies. Consequently, many strategies are uniform across localities with very little local specificity. The DPEP envisages to generate empirical evidence on what can work better in a given situation. The district specific studies initiated under the DPEP is an effort to clearly identify local specific strategies.

The programmes and activities to be initiated in the district should follow from the strategies envisaged to achieve the targets. Specification of the programmes and an elaboration of activities under each programme become an essential part of the planning exercise. In fact, for purposes of monitoring, specification of activities is very important. The DPEP does not prescribe any particular programme of activities to be initiated at the local level. It is left to the planners to identify the programmes and activities which are most suitable to their own areas of operation.

The next step in plan formulation is drawing up the implementation

Data Base for Educational Planning

The first stage in the planning process is the diagnosis of the present system of education. It is helpful in identifying the strengths and weaknesses of the system in the area for which the plan is to be prepared. The importance of database for planning is such that without appropriate, timely and reliable data/information no planning exercise can properly be undertaken to any level. The most important data that are needed for planning purpose are the demographic data specially the size, age and gender composition of population as the database has a lot of implications for education. Further, proper data on various indicators of quantity, equity, efficiency and quality of education are required. It includes data on items like number of institutions, teachers, enrolment, promotion, dropout and repeaters rates, age-grade data forgetting the idea of non-enrolment ratio. Data on all these items are required for various regions, groups as well as for males and females separately, and educationally backward castes like SC, ST and OBC etc. separately.

Looking at the data system that is prevalent in various states for education one comes across some problems which include not only non-availability of data on certain items that is important for planning purpose but also problems like reliability of data, the timeliness as well as proper utilisation of the data that are collected. It is to be ensured that reliable data on all items are made available for purposes of planning. It is therefore needed that appropriate data base is created to develop not only for the planning purpose but also for developing educational management information system that helps in taking proper decisions at various levels.

Since the process of planning is in decentralised mode under the DPEP, it should be ensured that reliable data base at the district level where programme is being launched is developed. It is the responsibility of the district level personnel who have the responsibility of developing district plans to ensure that data on all items are collected and available in time so as to make use of it for developing the district plans in a proper way.

plan. An implementation plan has to identify the agencies responsible to carry out the activities elaborated and the time when each of these activities will be completed.

Many of the activities specified may have financial implications. The cost implications of these activities need to be clearly spelt out for purposes of funding. Annualisation of the total expenditure on account of the planned activities provides an yearly budget for plan implementation. The items included in the project budget should correspond to the activities and their implementation schedule.

Any change in the activities will automatically change the budgetary provisions. The DPEP envisages drawing up of medium term plans for the whole project period and elaboration of annual work plans which will be reviewed every year.

The DPEP initiates various programmes and activities. Many of these activities are to be continued even after the project period is complete. Therefore, it is essential to ensure that the state government will be in position to sustain the activities even after the project period.

This session was followed by group work where the participants were given plans prepared by some of the districts which were covered under the first phase of the programme. The participants presented their observations on their plans and tried to relate them with the planning exercise they have to undertake in their own districts.

Enrolment Projections

Planning is bout taking decisions for actions to be initiated in future. The actions to be initiated in future depends on the likely scenario that we develop for the future. For example, if one has to make educational plans for the year 2000, it is necessary to develop a scenario with respect to the absolute six of population and school age population for year 2000. Similarly, an idea regarding the size of enrolment in the year 2000 will help us to plan for educational facilities to be provided.It will be on the basis of this enrolment size that we can decide about the number of schools to be additionally opened, the number of teachers to be recruited, as well as other infrastructural facilities to be provided.

The projection exercise enables us to give future information on all the variables that are necessary for planning purpose. These variables are population, enrolment, institutions, teachers, Infrastructure etc. For making enrolment projections various techniques such as rate of growth method, enrolment ratio method and methods based on student cohort technique are very useful.

The enrolment projection techniques can be broadly categorised into two groups, namely mathematical techniques and analytical techniques.

The mathematical methods are quite simple but are not useful if we want to project grade-wise enrolment. So, for grade-wise enrolment projection grade transition method nag grade ratio method are used. The applicability of these methods depends upon the availability of data on grade-wise enrolment and number of repeaters. So the precondition for using the grade transition method for projection purposes is the availability of repeaters data. But in case repeaters data are not available we can use the grade ratio method.

For undertaking the enrolment projection exercise, it is important to have the data on transition ratio, dropout rates, promotion rates and repeaters rate. Further, it is also necessary to have data on the present and past entry rate or promotion rate which is also known as admission rate. As far as dropout rate, retention rates and promotion rates are concerned generally the data at primary and elementary level of education are not available grade-wise, i.e. for various grades of primary school/sections.

By taking different assumption in flow rate and single age population of 6 year, i.e. the entry age in education system different scenarios can be generated and the planner can retain one of these scenarios according to its present situation on enrolment ratio, entry rate, dropout and repetition rate.

The lecture-discussion in this session was followed by group work on projection techniques and methods.

Costing of DPEP Plans

Activities to be initiated under the DPEP is to be costed. The DPEP guidelines provides a separate chapter on financial parameters indicated in the DPEP guidelines. As per the guidelines:

- the DPEP funds should be an additionality; in other words, the DPEP fund should not be substituted for activities or funds which would have been available otherwise;
- the DPEP does not fund incentive schemes;
- financing of salaries would be on a declining basis; (iv) civil works expenditure is limited to 24%, and (v) each school will be provided Rs. 2000/- and Rs. 500/ per teacher annually. These are some of the considerations based on which costing exercise is to be initiated under the DPEP.

Each of the activities elaborated in the plans is to be costed. While costing it is better to indicate the unit cost and total expenditure estimated. The unit can be a student, a school, a Programme or an item.

DISTRICT INFORMATION SYSTEM ON EDUCATION

For the success of multi-level planning in a large country like India, it is necessary that not only the vital data for planning and management are available in time but also that appropriate information flows should take place between various administrative hierarchies to facilitate the process of decision-making. A survey of present status of data collection, collation, analysis and use for decision-making does not present a satisfactory picture. Besides the time delays, most of them are not used in decision-making defeating the very purpose of collecting large amounts of educational data.

As a part of the DPEP implementation, NIEPA was entrusted with the responsibility of developing a standardised proforma for data collection and also to develop a software for computerisation of institutional level data. The district/state and national level flows of information were also identified for monitoring the progress of education in the states/districts. A simple and core set of data elements were identified in consultation with the states and the Department of Education, MHRD, Government of India. The software development for setting up district level database has been completed and training of all EMIS staff at the state and the district level was completed by December, 1994. The development of the software was guided by the following considerations:

- *to create an institutional level database at the district level which will be updated annually;*
- *to develop software that is simple and can be operationalised at the district level;*
- *to prepare standard output format reflecting the salient features at the block and the district level indicators with flexibility to generate additional reports on ad hoc basis;*
- *to build a simple proforma containing key information about each school so that it could be shared with the school authorities and the Village Education committee, and*
- *gradually to extend the software for creation of state and the national database.*

The states have already started the implementation of DISE at the district level. The data collection for the year 1995-96 will soon begin with September 30, 1995 as the record date.

The unit cost estimations provide useful insight to make cost comparisons between different districts for a particular activity.

Once the cost estimations are made, it is better to classify the costs under different heads like civil works, furniture, equipment, vehicles, salaries, maintenance, consumables etc. However, each one of them may be clubbing different activities. For example, civil works may include new school to be opened, additional rooms to be constructed in the existing schools, toilets to be constructed in the existing schools, repair work of major or minor variety, water supply, electrification, new buildings like SIEMT etc. Same is the case with other heads also. Therefore, it is better to cost the activities and then categories them under different heads.

Some of the project expenditure may be of recurring nature while others may be of non-recurring nature. For example, expenditure on account of civil works, furniture, equipment vehicles etc. are generally non-recurring whereas expenditure on salaries, maintenance etc. are recurring. It is always preferable to classify the total expenditure by recurring and non-recurring components. The share of recurring expenditure provides an idea regarding the extent of liability to the state to continue the activities after the project period. In other works, the sustainability of project activities depends on the states, commitment to bear the recurring expenditure after the project period.

Another important point to be noted is that allocation of funds is on an annual basis and hence the cost estimations are to be divided between years. This yearly budget should correspond to the activity schedule developed as part of the implementation plans.

The fund flow mechanism envisaged under the DPEP clearly indicates that funds would be released from the Government of India to state-level societies. The contribution of the Government of India is 85% and the remaining 15% is to be contributed by the respective state governments.

The DPEP guidelines also provides detailed account of items that can be funded and that cannot be funded from the DPEP funds.

It is better to cross check at every stage whether the cost estimations made are with the guidelines of the DPEP. Needless to add, there is ample scope to initiate various innovative programmes at the district and state level. The plans need to innovative activity envisaged under the programme.

Lastly, it is necessary to give detailed cost indicting unit cost, quantity, total cost, distribution of expenditure by years and classification of expenditures by recurring and non-recurring components. Similarly, summary cost tables indicating major heads and cost components also to be provided in the documents.

This discussion costing was followed by a practical exercise to help the participants to undertake costing exercises under the DPEP.

Scheduling and Sequencing

Specification of activities to be undertaken under the DPEP forms only part of the planning exercise. Equally important is scheduling and sequencing of activities are complete. For example, teacher training programmes can not start unless teacher trainers are trained. Perhaps, the teacher trainers cannot be trained unless and until training modules are developed. This involves sequencing of activities. One of the task involved is to identify activities which can start simultaneously and those activities which are necessarily to be sequential in nature. This sequencing may have to be done for activities envisaged under any particular programme or activities envisaged under different programmes. Once the sequencing of the activities are complete, then one can develop schedule of activities indicating when these activities will be commencing and when they will be completed. Such detailed scheduling of activities facilities proper monitoring of the programme. In general, for purposes of monitoring it is better to identify agency or individuals who will be responsible for implementing each of the activities. This gives task specification to different functionaries.

The DPEP envisages to develop project monitoring data base. Therefore, district and sub-district level officers and functionaries are supposed to send periodic report on the progress of the project. Development of such detailed implementation schedules not only helps in proper monitoring of project activities but also reduces the burden involved in sending periodic reports to the district and state implementation societies. The budgetary allocations to the DPEP should correspond to the scheduling of activities. While preparing the annual Plans, such implementation schedules my be of much help. Some state implementation societies are in the process of developing formats for project monitoring. At time it may happen that there may be delay in release of funds or administrative sanction to initiate an activity. If activities are sequenced and scheduled properly, one can initiate remedial actions as and when funds are made available. This may help to compensate for the delay in implementation of the DPEP plans.

Source : DPEP Calling, October 1996

25

Micro Planning and School Mapping

Universalising provision of educational facilities is one of the essential steps towards universalising primary education. India has made considerable progress in primary education. As per the Sixth All India Education Survey, nearly 95% of the rural habitations are provided with a primary school within a walking distance of one kilometre. A majority of those who now remain outside the orbit of the educational system are, perhaps, the most deprived groups living in the most backward and remote regions of the country. Target oriented local specific plans are required to make educational provisions to attract and retain them in schools. Micro-planning and school mapping are useful planning techniques/tools to develop local-specific plans.

School mapping exercise attempts to provide equal educational opportunities by levelling off of the existing inequities in educational provisions. Micro-planning exercises help to ensure that the provisions are optimally utilised by bringing more children to schools and their alternatives and by retaining them here. In other words, school mapping helps to prioritise educational investments across geographical areas and micro planning helps to improve the institutional performance and efficiency.

The District Primary Education Programme (DPEP) is a serious effort in decentralised planning of education in India. It focusses on planning from below to make plans more local-specific and to ensure local participation in planning and management of education. Needless to add school mapping and micro-planning are an integral part of the decentralised planning effort initiated under the DPEP. The involvement of local bodies and community at large is very important for initiating and implementing school mapping and micro planning exercises. Experience in India shows that local capacity building is an important step to make plans decentralised and local specific.

NIEPA continues to provide professional support to such district and local level efforts by developing required capacity and competency in local level planning. As part of our continuing efforts in local level capacity building a five day Training Programme was organised at NIEPA from 9th -13th September 1996.

Objectives

The objectives of the training programme were:

- to orient the participants to decentralised and local level planning;
- to introduce the participants to the concept and approaches to school mapping and micro planning;
- to train them in school mapping and micro planning activities; and
- to equip them to undertake micro-planning and school mapping exercises.

Participants

The participants of the programme consisted of state and district level officers from Orissa and West Bengal. 12 officers from these two states participated in the programme.

Themes

(i) Concepts and linkages between decentralisation, school mapping-planning;

(ii) Methodology of school mapping and micro-planning

(iii) Participatory process in local level planning

(iv) Opertionalising school mapping and micro-planning activities.

Training Methodology

The training methodology consisted of classroom lectures and discussions followed by groupwork and practical exercises. A major share of the time was spent on practical exercises and groupwork.

Management of the Programme

The programme was organised by the SNS unit of the Institute. A taskforce under the chairmanship of the Director provided the overall guidance for the conduct of the programmes.

The organising team consists of Dr. N.V. Varghese, Dr. Arun Mehta, Dr. Jayashree Jalali, Dr. S.M.I.A. Zaidi, Dr. Bijoy Panda, Shri K. Biswal and Ms. Ranjana Agarwal. The day-to-day management of the programme was carried out by a team consisting of Dr. N.V. Varghese, Dr. Bijoy Panda and Ms. Ranjana Agarwal.

Professor Kuldeep Mathur, Director, NIEPA, New Delhi, inaugurated the programme. In his inaugural address, Professor Mathur highlighted the expansion of the educational system and management challenges therein. He emphasized the need for professional educational planning and management to improve efficiency of educational institutions.

The priorities and concerns of educational planning have been changing over a period of time. NIEPA at the national level has always been closely scrutinizing these changing priorities and concerns of educational planning. Through its research and training activities NIEP has always played significant role in facilitating educational planning.

From the eighties onward NIEPA has been making serious efforts to facilitate district planning in educataion through development of planning competencies at the local level. Needless to add, DPEP is one of the recent efforts to facilitate district planning. NIEPA has played a significant role in conceptualizing and concretising this programme also. One of the areas of emphasis under district level educational planning is local level planning through a participatory process. How to draw local specific micro plans is one of the major concerns. Experience shows that this required development of planning skills at the local level.

Unfortunately, such skills are not yet developed. NIEPA's efforts have always been towards helping the state and district level educational authorities to equip them to undertake responsibilities of local level planning. The skills required for developing local level planning are different from that at other levels. Therefore, one has to concentrate on problems of capcity building for a large range of areas through a larger number of functionaries.

Educational planning in India had an input orientation and was fucussing more on the provision of facilities. However, now it is increasingly realized that provision of facilities does not necessarily ensure achievement of the targets. Very often these facilities remain under-utilized. For example many of the science kits and other teaching learning materials distributed under the Operation Blackboard scheme remain unused at the school level. How to make better use of the facilities provided is another area which needs priority attention. Micro level planning exercises help substantially to optimize utilization of resources at the local and institutional level.

The focus of the training programme was on two important dimensions of local level planning, namely School Mapping and Micro Level Planning. It was expected to develop local level skills in these two specified areas which will help in developing local level educational plans.

Prof. Kuldeep Mathur hoped that the participants shall be better equipped after the seminar.

Dr. Bijoy Panda proposed the vote of thanks towards the end of the opening session.

Decentralisation of Educational Planning

Educational planning in India is an integral part of the overall economic planning. In the initial phase, expansion of the system was the major focus of educational plans. The expansion that resulted was not shared uniformly across regions and segmetns of populations and hence equality or reduction of disparities in educational development became an areas of priority action. Consequently targeting became an unavoidable feature in educational investment decisions. Targeting in the Indian context focussed on three dimensions:

- targeting the regions;
- targeting the deprived groups; and
- targeting the girl child.

Regional targeting in the context of educational planning in India meant according priority to educationally backward locations. In the seventies, it was found that more than three-fourths of the non-enrolled children belong to nine states and these were categorized as Educationally Backward States. Discussions on universalizing primary education mostly centered around strategies to be adopted in these states.

Further disaggregated analysis of relative levels of educational development in the eighties revealed that intra-state disparities are as important as inter-state disparities. It was found that there are educationally advanced districts even in educationally backward states and similarly, there are educationally backward states and similarly, there are educationally backward districts even in educationally advanced states. Hence, the argument for considering district as the unit for planning and prioritizing investment decisions got further strengthened. Consequently district is recognized as the spatial limit for decentralized planning in education.

India has a multi level planning framework and planning efforts are initiated at the national, state and district levels. Decentralized planning at the district level is an area based sub-state planning and it is based on the detailed examination of the resource problems and potential of the local areas so as to prioritize investment according to local specific requirements. Although decentralization of the planning process is widely welcomed and endorsed at all decision making levels as a desirable objective its implementation is rather slow.

The District Primary Education Programme (DPEP) is the most recent effort to operationalise decentralised planning in education. District planning in India did not get operationalised due to various constraints. The major constraints are:

- absence of an organizational arrangement to carry out planning process in a systematic fashion; and
- lack of planning competencies at the district level.

The DPEP attempts to overcome these difficulties by earmarking resources for the districts, by creating planning groups to prepare district plans, and by providing professional guidance and technical support to prepare plans through the national state and district level resource organizations.

The planning process initiated under the DPEP is district specific and hence the plans should reflect local specificties. One may notice that the planning process under the DPEP envisages a technical and professional dimension and a participatory process of developing plans. The participation process helps in identifying local specific areas of intervention. The technical and professional support attempts to prioritise the local requirements within the constraints imposed by the resources and other national concerns. A plan prepared under the DPEP is therefore expected to have local specificity and technical rigour. The capacity building exercise under the DPEP is to ensure that the planning process is participatory, the targets and strategies reflect the local concerns and the plan document is technically sound.

The district planning process under the DPEP envisages a medium term plan for a period of 6-7 years and an annual planning exercise. The medium plan provides the broad strategies and areas for priority action. The annual plan provides details of operationalising district plans. In other words, the district plan unfolds itself through the annual plan by ensuring the necessary corrective actions when ever needed.

The districts selected under the DPEP are educationally backward districts. In most of them a large number of children remain non-enrolled and many schools functions at very low levels of institutional efficiency resulting in high rates of dropout and low levels of learning achievement.

The questions of non-enrolment may be partly related to paucity of schooling facilities while the question of low retention and institutional efficiency are related more to making best use of the available resources. School mapping and micro-planning are useful techniques to seek solutions to these problems.

School mapping focuses more on the input to the system i.e. provision of educational facilities. It attempts to reduce geographical inequities in the provision of facilities. Micro-planning attempts to ensure optimal utilization of facilities already provided by the public authorities. It is an effort to activate the local communities to ensure that educational institutions become functional.

School Mapping

Primary Education in India is pre-dominantly funded and manged by the government. Therefore, investment decisions by the state sector determine the pattern of expansion of educational facilities. Over a period of time it is noticed that certain areas are more endowed with school facilities than other areas. School mapping is an essential planning tool to overcome possibilities of regional inequities arising from the investment policies of the public authorities.

School mapping incorporates spatial dimensions into the educational planning process. The major question answered by the school mapping exercise is where to locate educational facilities. Location of educational facilities depends on the norms and standards developed by the public authorities. Even within the norms and standards developed by the public authorities. Even within the norms and standards, many geographical areas may be eligible for opening of new schools. School mapping techniques help us to identify the most appropriate location of schools or their alternatives so that more number of children can be benefited from the same level of investment.

The major objective of school mapping is to create equality of educational opportunities by leveling off of the existing disparities in the distribution of educational facilities. This techniques is useful to planning all levels of education. However, it is more widely used for plan for facilities at the compulsory levels of education. School mapping is not confined to locating formal school; location of alternatives to formal school are part of the school mapping exercise.

The methodology of school mapping envisages specification of norms, diagnosis of the existing educational facilities, projection of future population, deciding the location of school and estimates of facilities required in all the (existing and new) eduction institutions.

One of the first steps in school mapping is to select a unit for the exercise and diagnose the educational development in that area. The term 'diagnosis' in education refers to analyzing the present status of education in an area/region to identify the strength andweakness of the system. These weaknesses and strengths of the system are identified with the help of certain indicators.

For diagnosing the educatiaonal situation it is better to collect data on the selected items during the previous 4-5 years or a decade. We may require demographic data, literacy data, data regarding enrolment, teachers, building flow, rates of students, infrastructure etc. The population data is very important in school mapping exercises. Data on total popultion by sex, caste and age group for atleast two points of time are minimum requirements. We may also need to have data on population of age group 6-11, 11-14. Further single year age data is also required e.g. population of age 6, 7,8 and so on is needed sex-wise and caste-wise.

For diagnosing the educational situation data important indicators like literacy rate, enrolment ratios, retention rates and dropout rates are required. The present status of teachers positions is important and in this respect data on number of teachers by qualification, experience, training and sex are required. Similarly, teacher-pupil ratio is also important to assess the present situation. Another set of information required is on buildings and infrastructure facilities. Information on the condition of buildings and on other facilities in schools like blackboard, water, toilet, electricity, playground, etc. are useful to prepare school specific plans.

The next step in school mapping exercise is to assess the number of children to be enrolled. This estimate is to be made on the basis of the catchment area concept and it requires projection of total and school age specific population. There are various methods of population projection. Methods of population projections are classified into three categories namely Mathematical, Economic and Component methods. Keeping in view scant demographic data at the block and district level, it is not possible to undertake detailed population projection exercise. Therefore, growth rates and ratio methods of population projection are more commonly used at the district level.

Enrolment projections are important to decide on the opening of new schools, upgradation of existing schools and estimate the number of teachers required. The techniques of enrolment projections can broadly be classified into two - mathematical and analytical methods. Mathematical methods require aggregate enrolment data at least for five to ten years, and only total enrolment can be projected. On the other hand, analytical methods require promotion, drop-out, repetition and apparent entry rates. There are three simple methods of enrolment projections, namely rate of growth, enrolment ratio and grade-transition methods. The application of a particular method depends upon the requiremetns and the availability of data. At the lowest level, cohort method for grade-wise enrolment projections is more desirable. However, at the local level information required to make reliable projections are not available. Therefore, one may have to depend on the most probable approximations. For example, the projection method used to derive school age group children in this exercise is based on the assumption of a fixed proportion of the total population.

The next step in the exercise is to specify norms, standards and catchment area. Opening of new schools or their alternatives are based on the norms regarding threshold population which indirectly defines the potential number of children to be enrolled in a given locality. In India the norm that is followed is to open a primary school in areas which have population of 300 and above in plains and 250 or above in the remote or tribal areas. Similarly, after the 1986 Policy the norm adopted for the number of teachers is a minimum of two teachers in all the primary schools irrespective of the type of the enrolment.

The other important norm is regarding the maximum permissible distnace a child has to travel from home to school. This is the school mapping technology for definition of catchment area of a school. The catchment area of a school is the geographical area served by a school and is defined as the maximum acceptable distance a child can travel from home to school. Normally catchment area is mesured in terms of area of a circle or Hexagon. In India, especially in remote areas, the settlement is in habitations. One may frequently come across location where one may not find any household miles together in remote areas in India. And where habitations do exit it may have a cluster of households. Given this pattern of population settlement in India we have not adotped the traditional catchment area concept. What we have adopted alternatively is a distance matrix method whereby the distances between habitations are measured. Therefore, number of habitations and their distance from the school is taken to decide the catchment area of the school.

It is easy to locate schools based on the distance matrix method. As mentioned earlier location of schools is based on the norms and resources available. Due to constraint on resources schools are opened only in some selected locations and the norms form the basis to prioritise such decisions. Based on the distance norms and the resources available, decisions regarding opening of new schools, if required, can be arrived at.

The next question pertains to facilities to be provided in the schools. Based on the population growth and potential growth in enrolment, additional infrastructural facilities may be required in the existing schools. It may be important to incorporate not only the infrastructural facilities but also other requirements of teaching learning materials to be purchased in the school. Cost estimates can be made on the basis of these needs and proposals can be prepared for funding.

Micro Level Educational Planning

Planning at the smallest spatial unit can't be termed as micro level planning. In the Indian context micro level planning can mean planning carried out at the village level or even at the habitation level. While selecting a unit for micro planning one has to consider the availability of educational facilities like a school or a non-formal education centre. In other words, while we try to develop micro level planning in education we may have to select a unit centering around an educational institution. This may be a school or its alternative which is already existing or planned to be opened.

The objectives of the micro level planning are:

- to mobilize local community to prepare village level plans:
- to provide a support system to the schools and teachers so that schools become more functional; and
- to ensure that all eligible children from the locality attend the schools. The major objective of the school mapping exercise is not on issues pertaining to allocation of resources but on issues to better and efficient use of resources which are already allocated to a particular locality, area or school.

Micro planning should not be seen as a one shot exercise. It is a continuous process and it unfolds itself in the process of implementing and operationalising plans prepared either at the local level or at the higher.levels. Micro planning focusses more on the operational details of achieving a specified plan target.

Micro planning exercise can be undertaken by local people. In fact the object and subject of micro planning is local people.

- How to make schools community based?
- How do we ensure accountabilities of the school to the community it serves?
- What is the mechanism to channelise social forces towards education?

These are important questions in micro planning exercise.

Micro planning exercise involves less of technical skills and more of social skills.

- How to interact with the community for a common cause?

These are the issues which make a micro planning exercise a success or a failure.

- How to organize a micro planning exercise in a village?

The steps involved in operationalising or developing a micro planning exercise are the followings:-

i) Understanding the village: This may be a first step to identify the problems faced by the village so that basic intervention strategies can be clearly understood.

ii) Preparation of a village map: A village may be having many facilities and educational facilities may be one among such facilities. It would be better if these facilities are plotted on a map so that people of the locality can visually observe their village and allocation of the facilities in their village. A discussion based on such a map would be a meaningful exercise.

iii) Identification of non-enrolled and dropout children. Normally household surveys become a part of micro planning exrecise. Household survey provides details about the children to be enrolled, retained in the school or who dropped out from the school. This information can be very useful under the micro planning efforts.

iv) Village education register: Based on the household surveys one can develop a village education register clearly, indicating the households which are not sending children to the schools. This will help us to adopt corrective measures to encourage the parents of these households to send their children to schools.

v) The village may have a school. If the village has a school then one has to relate the efforts made during the micro planning exercises with the facilities available at the school level.

vi) The preparation of a village education plan : Once the community inputs and the school inputs are identified then it is possible to prepare a village education plan focussing on the specific educational problems faced at the household level and at the school level. Preparation of such plans and monitoring of activities thus identified in a village plan make micro planning exercise an effective tool in making the best use of the resources available at the local level.

One of the major questions in micro-planning is: who will initiate a micro-planning exercise? Unfortunately, these cannot be a single answer to this question. The pattern may be varying in different localities, given their specific features.

The co-operation from the elected representatives, functionaries and people at large is essential. Therefore the organizational arrangements need to evolve locally, rather than be super - imposed from outside. A common patteren found in areas where micro planning exercises are seriously initiated is to form a core group consisting of different segments of populations of the village, orient the group members to the idea and help them in the initial stages to organize some of the activities under the micro planning exercises.

Source : DPEP Calling, October 1996

26

Monitoring and Evaluation: An Urgent Need

—*Prof. G.L. Arora*
Dept. of Teacher Education and Extention,
NCERT, New Delhi
—*Dr. Ajit Singh*
Dept. of Teacher Education and Extension,
NCERT, New Delhi

Despite concerted efforts made since independence the goal of universalization of elementary education has so far remained elusive. No doubt, there has been unprecedented expansion of educational facilities and enrolment of children at different levels, but the appallingly high drop out rate has been the major handicap frustrating our efforts to achieve the goal.

Further the level of pupils learning achievement in mathematics and language in primary grades is very dismal as revealed by studies. This is a cause of concern and calls for steps to improve the situation. The District Primary Education Programme (DPEP) has been conceived as an intervention to reduce overall dropout rates for all students at the primary stage to less than 10 per cent; raise average achievement levels by 25% over measured baseline level; and to provide according to national norms, access for all children to primary education i.e. primary schooling where possible or its equivalent non-formal education.

Recurrent in-service training of primary teachers and their trainers-heads of Cluster Resource. Centres (CRCs), Co-ordinators, Block Resource Centres (BRCs), DIET/SCERT faculty is one of the significant strategies envisaged in the DPEP to achieve its goal. It improves instructional quality and productivity of teachers leading to improvement in the quality of education.

DPEP states have assessed training needs of their primary teachers and their trainers; and have developed materials for the training of these functionaries. A substantial amount, about 70% of the earmarked allocation for a district, is to be used for programme component-training of primary teachers and their trainers. A considerable investment in terms of time, money and energy is, therefore, being made in the in-service training of teachers but very little is known about the benefits which accrue from training in terms of changes in teachers classroom behaviour and improvement in pupils achievement. So there is need to ensure quality of training for which systematic monitoring on a continuing basis is essential.

The indicators of training quality shall obviously include trainees learning outcomes, gain in knowledge, refinement of skills, desirable effect on their self-concept and attitude towards work, pupils and the school. Participants satisfaction with the programme and the desired changes in their instructional behaviour are other indicators of the quality of training. Among the factors which contribute to the quality of in-service training, the important ones are adequacy of infrastructural facilities, availability of necessary equipment, appropriateness of training input, training materials, instructional approaches, competence of resource personnel, etc. To monitor the quality of training, the processes as well as output ends of training need to be appraised.

The institutions involved in the training of teachers need to develop appropriate mechanisms to monitor the quality of training of teachers and other educational personnel. The mechanisms may comprise compliance monitoring, diagnostic monitoring and performance monitoring.

Compliance monitoring attempts to ensure whether the required inputs have been provided or not. The assumption underlying the use of compliance monitoring is that adequate level of performance would follow if training centres meet specified standards on various input measures. The purpose of monitoring should be diagnostic i.e. to identify strengths and weaknesses of training processes rather than to make persons accountable for the weaknesses of the programme.

The performance monitoring aims at determining as to whether desired changes occurred in participants knowledge, attitudes and skills or not and to what extent objectives of training programmes have been realised.

The Department of Teacher Education and Extension, NCERT, has developed a framework and instruments for monitoring and evaluation of the quality of in-service training. These tools are Trainees reactions scale, Classroom observation scale for assessing quality of resource persons instructional behaviour, scale for assessing adequacy of inputs which contribute to the quality of training, interview schedule for resource persons, coordinators and directors of the course.

Trainees reaction scale has been developed to monitor the quality of training as perceived by consumers i.e. trainees in terms of their satisfaction with the training content, materials and the process of training. Further an observer's assessment of adequacy of training inputs, quality of instructional behaviour of resource persons has also been taken as indicator of the quality of training. Tools for assessing quality of training in terms of trainees gain in knowledge, desirable changes in their instructional behaviour are in the process of development.

The department will be organising a workshop at the NCERT Campus, New Delhi from October 28-30, 1996 to share these tools with coordinators of training in DPEP States and to design studies to monitor the quality of training. In this workshop, participants from the states of Haryana, Kerala, Tamil Nadu, Assam and Maharashtra are expected to participate and design studies to monitor the quality of in-service training of primary teachers in their states. The department plans to provide academic support to states for undertaking studies by training their investigators in the collection and analysis of data and writing of reports.

Source: DPEP Calling, October 1996.

27

Management Issues in DPEP

Policy Background

The National Policy on Education 1986, proposed to overhaul the system of planning and management of education with emphasis on development of a long term perspective, decentralization and autonomy, pre-eminence to people's involvement and accountability in relation to the given objectives and norms. The NPE further laid down that special attention will be paid to the training of educational planners and administrators and heads of institutions.

To operationalize this resolve, the Programme of Action (POA) suggested that in addition to specialized institutions at the national and state level for the training of educational administrators and heads of institutions, institutes of management and similar organisations will also be motivated and enabled to take up management development and training programmes as well as policy research.

The Chellenge in DPEP

DPEP lays a great deal of emphasis on planning and management in the programme. The success or failure of the directional changes pointed out by the National Policy on Education 1986 and as revised in 1992, critically depends on the response of the educational administration. The marked emphasis on quality and equity in planning and execution of education projects, poses great challenges for the management of education. The challenge lies in areas of demand management, community mobilisation and participative management systems which can make schools accountable to local communities. Promotion of quality and equity have been helped by a shift of resources towards elementary and adult education, but they need to be complemented by an ethos of cost-effectiveness, process-orientation and accountability throughout the education system.

An event which has had an important bearing on decentralized educational bearing on decentralized educational management is the 73rd and 74th Amendments to the Constitution of India, which lay down that the responsibility for taking decisions regarding activities at the grassroot, level should rest upon the elected members of local bodies themselves. It ensures that development planning is more responsive and adaptable to regional and local needs of the population. Thus Panchayati Raj/Municipal bodies will have an important role to play in the reconstruction of the educational system Implications are in that Village Education Committees would be set up; their role and functions defined; reorientation and training provided; and professional and organizational support be arranged.

Capacity Building for Planning and Management

In this context, DPEP seeks to build national capacity in planning and management with special focus on the following:

(i) Organise a network of technical resource support for DPEP through planning/management institutions experienced in management of public systems.

(ii) Strengthening of state-level institutional capacity for educational planning and management. Various modalities need to be explored such as setting up of State Institutions of Education Management and Training (SIEMT) or by entrusting the training task to existing institutions such as IIMs, Institutes of Public Administration etc.

(iii) Develop a research and development agenda and undertake studies in areas related to educational planning and management.

(iv) Strengthening of district planning through norm-based planning, and training of district educational planners.

(v) Develop prototype training packages for and organise training and orientation programmes for Village Education Committees (VECs) and other Panchayati Raj bodies, through district and state level institutions.

(vi) Effective use of MIS in planning and management. Use of reliable data for indicating project performance and as a statistical base for informed decision making.

(vii) Develop guidelines and basic instruments for micro-planning.

National Level

At the National Level, NIEPA has been directly engaged in research, training and consultancy in the area of educational planning and management. However, with the introduction of large scale educational projects in several states of the country and the consequent demands for inputs in educational management, the task of developing and organising training programmes for educational functionaries at different levels, orienting local self-government institutions and conducting research in the area of planning and management is too large to be managed by any one institute. In view of the enormity of the task, it is proposed to involve more and more institutions in this area.

Thus, DPEP envisages systematic institutional development and networking of professional institutions to build capacity for educational planning and management. In fact DPEP looks beyond mere educational management, and takes a more holistic view of management capabilities. DPEP seeks to build capacity in management of public systems. Education is not to be viewed in a compartmentalized manner but as a significant and dynamic fulcrum where convergence of health, early childhood care, rural development, etc.and primary education create a synergistic system of development.

District level structures (possibly DIETs) and state level institutes (SIEMTs, SCERTs) would need to link up with national resources institutions like NIEPA, IIMs, other social science institutions, to create a mesh of supportive structures, whereby management/planning training can be given and reiterated in a systematic manner.

State Level

With increasing recognition of educational management as a critical input for achieving. UEE, and the recently reinforced trend for decentralization and reactivation of the Panchayati Raj system, there is a need to provide facilities for educational planning and management in the states that are sustainable in nature.

The need for training of state and local level functionaries is recognised and there have been attempts to address this need through planning and administrative wings in SIE, through the SCERTs and even with State Institutes of Administration. However, none of these institutes have been able to provide the course content that was desirable or sustain the regularity of training and orientation programmes for the various levels of officials/non-officials involved. Therefore, most states are now thinking about new structures that can be created to address the particular needs of educational planning and management.

There are proposals to start State Institutes of Educational Management and Training (SIEMT) in several states. The functions envisaged for SIEMTs or other institutes selected for the same purpose are:

- to organise training programmes and workshops for educational planning and management in the state.

- to conduct and facilitate research on educational management issues.
- to provide technical support for educational planning and management.
- to create datable for monitoring, undertake assessments of learner achievement levels and evaluations.
- to provide technical and training support for district and micro level planning.

The major categories of persons who will require training and orientation are:

- education managers at the state, district and block levels including:
    - State level officers of Department of Education and Directorate of Education.
    - Divisional level field officials of Directorate of Education.
    - District level officials of Directorates of Education such as District Education Officers, AEOs, etc.
    - Block level education officers and education extension officers.
    - Project staff at the state and district, sub-district levels.
    - School Headmasters, Principals, Vice-Principals, Cluster Incharges.
- Other departmental officers who are closely related to educational processes at the state and field level. Some joint trainings would need to be organised along with field officers of Department of Women and Child Development; Social Welfare, Rural Development, Panchayati Raj, Public Health, Civil Works, etc.
- Orientation to members of state and district level elected bodies dealing with educational issues, e.g. Zilla Parishads, District Boards of Education, State Advisory Boards of Education.
- Elected representatives of the Panchayati Raj system at the block and village level and local bodies in urban areas.
- Members of Village Education Committees.
- NGO's and other institutions/agencies that play significant roles in achieving UEE.

The specific activities which Educational Management institutions would need to undertake to discharge their responsibilities for training and orientations would include the following:

For Training

(a) undertaking a training needs assessment for the various categories identified above;

(b) design and development of training and orientation programmes required by the various groups;

(c) identification of training resource materials available (background materials, resource persons, other institutions that can be linked, etc.), as well as those that need to be developed and produced;

(d) production of training materials;

(e) training of trainers;

(f) actual conduct of training programmes for officials and agencies at state and district level and technical support to agencies identified for conduct of training programmes and support to UEE;

(g) development of annual calender of activities and budgets as well as their monitoring and periodic evaluation.

For Technical Support

(a) formation, strengthening, and effective functioning of Village Education Committees;

(b) involvement of NGOs and other resource institutions in UEE;

(c) planning and implementation of comprehensive and effective monitoring, evaluation and management information system at block, district and state levels including computerisation efforts.

For District Planning

(a) help the Department of Education to work out details of the district planning process including techniques and methods to be adopted.

(b) preparing manuals and other details of processes to be used for district and micro-planning.

Objectives for Workshop on Management Issues

The objectives of organising a workshop for Management issues in DPEP are to:

- *explore possibilities of networking with management and research institutions for educational planning and management in the longer context of management of public systems.*
- *Identify areas in educational planning and management that need to be developed and locate existing capacities (micro planning; MIS usage for planning and management; models for training of educational administrators; models for training elected representatives, etc.)*
- *identify institutional linkages with state level institutions for delivery of management training and to assist in setting up/strengthening these facilities.*
- *identify areas for action research in educational planning and management.*
- *evolve modalities for addressing the above objectives.*

A Few Management Challenges

Promotion of quality and equity have been helped by a shift of resources towards elementary and adult education, but they need to be complemented by an ethos of cost-effectiveness, process-orientation and accountability throughout the education system.

With increasing recognition of educational management as a critical input for achieving UEE, and the recently reinforced trend for decentralization and reactivation of the Panchayati Raj system, there is a need to provide facilities for educational planning and management in the states that are sustainable in nature.

Source : DPEP Calling, September 1995.

28

Planning, Management and Monitoring Strategies for DPEP

—*Yash Aggarwal*

Background

The complexity of the multilevel decision making and control mechanisms in education increase due to wide geographical dispersion of institutional network representing a variety of school locations and endowments. Therefore, in order to improve the quality and effectiveness of educational management, not only a variety of data is required but is needed in a form and at a time that conforms to the requirements of user agencies operating at various geographical and administrative hierarchies. The pay-off from an improved, consistent and timely availability of data on key and simple indicators of educational health can be enormous. It will not only provide the right type of signals to educational administrators, but also help in more sharply focusing the scarce resources for areas/activities where these are most needed.[1]

As a result of recent efforts, a computerised EMIS system developed by NIEPA has been implemented in most of the DPEP districts.[2] The EMIS consists of two modules, namely District information System for Education (DISE) and Project Monitoring Information System (PMIS) covering primary schools/sections.[3] The former deals with school statistics and the latter with the monitoring of DPEP project activities.[4] Reports for 37 out of a total of 42 DPEP district are now available. These reports provide very valuable insight and base line data for more than 50,000 schools in the country. For 1996/97 data, reports for more than 100 districts covering DPEP I and DPEP II will be available by March, 1997. Quarterly progress reports are being generated by PMIS.

The EMIS database can be used as tool for multiple activities like perspective planning, monitoring of project activities, as a tool for research designs and for providing decision support service to educational administrators. Active involvement of policy planners, decision makers, educational administrators and researchers will be necessary to derive maximum benefits from the DISE database. The following discussion highlights various applications and the potential benefits that the new information system can deliver especially at a time when the focus of planning and management is shifting to local levels. It will now be possible to analyse spatial, gender and social aspects of equity and also provides a framework for temporal analysis in key performance indicators of educational development and school efficiency.

Summary of Indicators Generated by DISE

In addition to the data available from other sources, three type of indicators are generated by DISE;

- *System defined tables/reports for any academic year at the school, cluster, block and district level.*
- *System defined multiple year reports (time series/trends) on key performance indicators at the block and district level.*
- *user defined reports/listing or computation of new variables at the school level.*

As is clear from the above, the DISE software provides a number of system generated reports and countless possibilities for obtaining user defined variables and reports. For example, it is now possible to generate new indicators and use any type of selection criterion based on the computed indicators. For example, DISE can respond to complex questions like: share of SC girls in class I enrolment of the government rural schools in a given block. A more complex query could be to generate the list of Ashram schools under tribal welfare department, which have more than xx% of ST students and have not been inspected during the last academic session[6]. Government schools without facilities, equipment and buildings can also be identified using the DISE s/w.

There are many other sources of educational data. Besides the DISE and PMIS data, the following data sources may be consulted in order to improve the quality of planning, management and monitoring of the project. It is no doubt true that data obtained from different sources do not match and create further confusion for the user agencies. The planners and administrators will have to reconcile and use their experience and judgement about the data that must be treated as reliable. Some important sources of data for project planning, management and monitoring are:

- Staff Appraisal Report.
- Project inception report and pre-appraisal documents.
- Education and other statistics of the state directorate of education and/or the concerned district/block.
- Population data on children in the school going age group
- School census records at the village level.
- Social and economic data obtained from the state level economic and statistics bureau or any other equivalent agency.
- Report of the appraisal and supervision Missions.
- Reports of the baseline studies for the district.
- Evaluation reports/studies.
- Annual accounts and audit reports.
- All India Educational Survey Data.
- DIETs and other social science research institution in the state/district.

Areas of Concern for Educational Administrators

The educational planners, administrators, policy analysts, researchers and social scientists use the same type of data in many ways. Let us first examine the broad areas of concern for educational planner and administrators:

- to understand the historical growth patterns and past trends in the selected indicators of performance at various levels of spatial aggregation either through linear or non-linear transformation of data;
- To develop organisational designs for delivery of project inputs and monitoring of outcomes;
- design information systems so that macro and micro plans can be realistically formulated and their implementation monitored;
- to understand the nature of relationship, association, similarities and dissimilarities between the selected indicators cross space and/or time;
- to build models, undertake simulation and projection exercises

based on past trends and/or to evolve scenarios based on specified future targets/objectives;

- to monitor and evaluate the progress of certain schemes/ events through selected indicators so as to provide feedback and evolve suitable interventions consistent with the stated objectives. Monitoring offered flows, civil works, teacher training etc. is important for time bound project.
- to develop programmes for capacity building of resource institutions so that technical and professional support for programmed interventions is available at the local level.
- to provide decision support services to educational administrators and facilitate the provision of certain facilities by making information available in time.
- to share information among other users and interest groups through a network;

As will be seen in the following discussion, DISE provides considerable amount of data for undertaking the above exercises.[5] Nevertheless, additional data will be needed according the nature of analysis.

Primary Education: Management Issues, Response and Action Matrix

As mentioned earlier, DISE is now a principal source of data on school statistics and PMIS offers data on financial flows, civil works, teacher training and other important activities undertaken in the DPEP districts. Therefore, any planning, management, research or review application which requires the data on these aspects, can now have access to computerised database being maintained at the district and the state level.

While it is not possible to list all scenarios where the DISE data will be useful, an effort has been made to identify major areas of concern to educational planners, administrators, researchers and policy analysts. Corresponding to each question/issue, the precise element of data source from DISE/PMIS has been identified. Finally, guidance is provided to the users for possible action points. The nature and scope of the issues and actions will vary from district to district. Nevertheless, DISE data can be used at all levels including for micro-planning and school mapping.

The analysis of temporal changes in important performance indicators like enrolment, share of girls to total enrolment, % GER, NER, % single teacher schools, % schools not inspected for last three years if any, % schools without facilities and the trends in the condition of school buildings etc. can provide information on the likely impact of the project interventions. The fact that trends can even be studied at the block level, further increases the utility of data for long term planning and assessing the impact of project interventions.

There is always a concern for the qualitative impact of the project interventions, especially in areas like in-service teacher training, motivation, awareness generation, gender sensitization programmes, nature of classroom interaction, teacher motivation, inter-personal relationship etc. It is still not clear as to what is the impact of incentives on enrolment, retention and achievement of learners. Another area on which considerable research is needed relates to the utilization pattern of equipment and facilities in primary schools. These are very important research questions on which considerable amount of additional data will be needed and will have to be collected through specially designed studies. However, the DISE can assist the researchers in the scientific selection sample of the schools.

Darrange District: Some Issues for Planning and Management of Education

Darrang is one of the educationally backward districts of Assam and is covered under DPEP. Among other things, DISE was implemented in the district during 1995/96. The district consists of 6 educational blocks and four town areas. As on 30the September, 1995, there were 1499 primary schools. Three of the educational blocks and two towns were declared as tribal. The total estimated population in the 6-11 years age group of the district was 282,216.97% schools were located in rural areas. The TLC has not been launched in the district as yet. The management of practically all primary schools vests with the government as 1475 out of a total of 1499 schools were under government management. There were 13 private aided and 6 private unaided schools. Therefore, the major responsibility for educational reforms at primary stage lies with the government.

The district presents a unique educational scenario and the following issues were identified for reforming the educational system.

- Unrealistic annual work plans for the district had little relevance to their implementability.
- Plans were prepared even before the spade work for their implementation was completed resulting in a general slow down and under-utilisation of budgetary allocations.
- Over ambitious target setting. No concern for time and cost over turns.

- No proper assessment of the unit costs.
- Poor facilities and imbalances in the teachers deployment.

Table 1

Selected Educational Data, 1995/96

Block	Students	Teachers	Class Rooms	Sections	Pupil Teacher Ratio
Sipajhar	16301	760	268	883	21.5
Kaligaon	21515	764	344	1137	28.2
Dalgaon	16277	440	233	810	37.0
Majbat	17620	439	228	789	40.1
Udalgiri	24478	677	355	1276	36.2
Khaiarabari	25943	668	309	1238	38.8
Mangaldoi Town	2495	107	39	76	23.3
Tangla Town	1928	53	16	47	36.4
Udalguri Town	1299	44	23	40	29.5
Kharupetia Town	1975	33	22	44	59.9
Darrang District	129871	3985	1837	6340	32.6

- A major programme of school infrastructure rehabilitation is required.
- Predominance of small schools with multigrade teaching and distorted enrolement pyramid.
- Excessively large concentration of enrolment in class I and high repetition rates have serious implications for planning for school places.
- Low participation of women in teaching profession.

Priority Concerns

Low participation rates

The GER varies from 34.2% in Dalgaon block to 94.5% in Sipajhar block. What policies are needed to encourage additional enrolment in the blocks with low enrolment rates. Actual GER may still be lower as the population estimates appear to be on the lower side, as was revealed during discussions with the project staff. The problem becomes serious as 1981 population census was not conducted in Assam. Because of the problems with the population data, the estimates of NER are not correct. The district planning team should obtain more realistic population estimates for 6-11 years old children so that NER could be estimated.

Age structure of enrolment

It is strange that out of an enrolment of 5,300 in class I, only 2,800 students were new admissions and the rest were repeaters. Therefore, the share of overage children in total enrolment is high. This trend continues to be true for other classes as well. The following questions arise in this context:

- Why there are so many repeaters when the policy of no detention is in operation?
- The focus of planning for universalisation should be on six year old children. All six year old children should be enrolled and facilitated to continue in the educational ladder without dropping-out or repeating in the same class.
- Sample studies should be conducted to ascertain the reasons for high repetition rates? Is it a ploy to show higher enrolment or is a genuine problem?
- Implications of the increased enrolment at grade I are never worked out for other grades. Consequently bottlenecks may arise as the enrolment expands due to enrolment and special drives.
- Areas/social groups affected by high repetition rates may be identified.

Small schools

34% of schools of Darrang district were having an enrolment of 60 or less students. There were practically no schools having more than 300 students. What are the implications of this for planning for the universalisation of elementary education in the district.[7] The enrolment in grade IV was 5 or less students in 40% of small schools. Large imbalances in the location of schools were also discernible.[8] While it is expected that small schools is essentially a phenomenon in small villages, the evidence shows that small schools can be identified even in large size villages. In depth analysis of the locational aspects of schools will be needed to answer many of these questions.

Villages with multiple schools

Many villages were found to have more than one school. Four villages were having as many as six schools. Most of these schools are small. What are the planning implications of multiple schools in a village, all of which have little enrolment. This may either be justified on grounds of the dispersion of village but it may also be a result of unplanned expansion and provincialisation without any regard to the adequacy or the need for the new school? This is serious question which should attract the attention of researchers and planners.

Distorted enrolment pyramid

The classwise enrolment distribution shows that the share of class I enrolment to total primary school enrolment high and shows an abnormal behaviour. The distorted enrolment structure could be the result of the following:

- Rapid increase in enrolment of class I as a result of enrolment drive. This a positive sign and should be encouraged. If this is the case, the system should prepare for the rapid increase in enrolment in subsequent grades in the coming years. The efforts to sustain the rapid increase must be planned in time. It has serious implications for additional teachers, additional classrooms, facilities, equipment etc.
- The rapid increase in enrolment may also be spurious. Showing high enrolment at the beginning of each year and then at the end of the year, often showing high drop-out and high repeaters. In the case of Darrang district, the repetition rate for class I was 43%- a figure difficult to believe in the normal circumstances. Many policy options and planning issues are involved.

School buildings

Some schools (1.74%) were found to be without buildings/classrooms. Majority of the schools (86%) were having only one classroom. This shows that most schools are multi-grade. What are its implications for the in-service teacher training and the content of the in-service training courses?

The school buildings are in depressing condition. 62.4% of schools require major rehabilitation. This ratio was more than 70% in some selected areas. A large number of schools are more than 20 years old. Only 10% of schools were established in the last 10 years. About 40% of schools were more than 40 years old. As the schools become more old, the need for rehabilitation will increase exponentially. What type of civil works program is needed for large scale rehabilitation of dilapidated school buildings? The resource requirements may be more than the resources available from DPEP? What alternative sources can be exploited to meet the rehabilitation requirements.

Developing a maintenance schedule for the school buildings is an immediate necessity. The data on the condition of school buildings and classrooms is also available from DISE data. What strategies and allocations are needed to keep the existing schools in reasonably good condition?

School inspection

For the first time, data on school inspection of primary schools is being collected. Among other things, the quality of data supplied by the schools needs to be established. It also needs to be related to the availability of the inspecting staff and their workload. As many as 36% schools were not inspected during the academic session 1995/96. In certain educational blocks more than 50% schools were not inspected at all. The reasons for this needs to be ascertained. As the data base builds for subsequent years, it will also be interesting to know if the same school is not inspected for many years.

Working days

The average number of working days in many schools were less than the prescribed minimum. The reason for this needs to be ascertained.

Participatory Planning

None of the primary schools in the district has VECs constituted during 1995/96. What is the progress of constitution of VECs?

Rationalisation of teachers

The pupil teacher ratio was 32.6 for the district as a whole and varies from 21.5 to 40. Ideally the data for each school should be analysed to identify the demand/supply of teachers. The reason for low/high PTR may be the enrolment profile of schools and the teacher deployment policies. The teachers requirements can be estimated for each school and the rationalisation of teachers will be able to identify excess teachers in the system. It is expected that out of two teachers in a school, one will be female. The data shows a different ground level reality.

Policy towards single teacher schools

There are large number of single teacher schools in the district. Khairabari had 19.3% of its schools classified as single teacher schools. This situation prevails after the scheme of OBB was implemented in the district. The data shows that more than 87% of schools in this block were covered under OBB. Where is the problem? Were the teachers appointed under OBB shifted elsewhere or the teachers were not appointed at all. What is the policy regarding the single teacher schools and what are its planning implications?

High repetition rates

The repetition rate is extremely high in the district (28.6%). In one of the blocks (Khaiarabari) one in every two students is a repeater. What policies and programmes are needed to arrest the repetition rates?

Gender issues

Girls account for 46% in class I enrolment. The corresponding rate for SC girls to total SC enrolment was 44.3% and the similar ratio for ST girls was about 48%. Thus the disparities within SC, ST and other categories are not high. Therefore, the main concern is the overall low enrolment rate, a reference to which has already been made.

The share of female teachers in primary schools in rural areas was only 19% which is exceptionally low. Steps are needed to promote the women's participation in teaching profession especially at the primary level.

Equity and social concerns

The share of SC and ST enrolment to total enrolment in the district was 4.1% and 21.6% respectively. Since the population data was not available for SC and ST population, it is difficult to compare population share with the share of teachers.

School buildings

The school buildings programme is lagging behind. An ambitious programme has been chalked out. Nothing was taken up till the end of the second quarter in the state of Assam. At best some civil works could be initiated during 1995/96. This has serious planning implications for UPE. What will be the impact on enrolment, if the new schools are not opened in time? The training and other quality improvement programmes my suffer as the construction of BRC/CRC is delayed.

Fund utilisation for buildings is erratic. There is a bulge in expenses towards the end of the year. In 1996/97, for the first two quarters, the total funds spent account for about 8% of the funds spent for 1995/96. Does it indicate slowdown?

Availability of equipment and facilities

The following data suggests that there is a general shortage of equipment and facilities in the primary schools in Darrang district.

- Only 67% rural schools had blackboards in good condition. On an average one blackboard was available for nearly 120 students. This ratio is much lower than the desired ratio. Should this ratio not be equal to the average class size?
- Teachers guides were not available in about 77% primary schools.
- More than half schools were without globes, although OBB was implemented in 88% schools.
- Primary schools had no educational charts.

Many schools were found to have none of the above equipment. The list of such schools can be generated using DISE and other utilities. What can be done to correct these imbalances/ shortages in the availability of essential teaching learning equipment.

The analysis also shows that toilet facilities are practically lacking (6.3% rural schools had common toilets). Book banks are operational only in 19% primary schools. First aid kit was available in 25 schools.

While the above data presents a depressing picture, it is necessary to have an independent cross-check on sample basis. Discussions with project authorities indicated that some schools may not be providing the correct picture with respect to the equipment and facilities in the hope to get these from the project. If found correct, this tendency has to be stopped.

The above scenario is only indicative of the availability of equipment and supplies. The extent of utilisataion and the impact of these facilities on learning outcomes needs to be studied separately. The studies will have significant implications for the provision of facilities.

Furniture and benches and desks

A large number of schools indicated that mats/benches and desks for students were not available for all students. Adequate number of chairs and tables for teachers were also not available in more than two third of the schools. What is the DPEP policy for such a situation?

Fund flow analysis

Against a budgeted amount of Rs. 678.35 lakhs for 1996/97, an expenditure of Rs. 19.95 lakhs was incurred. The ratio of actual expenditure to total budget is less than 3% during the first six months of the year. Does it not reflect unrealistic planning which has no relation to planned targets. Can more realistic plans be developed? What led to such a steep shortfall?

The management expenses for the Darrang district accounted for more than 50% of the total expenditure incurred upto 30.9.1996 under DPEP. In many critical areas of intervention like women development programms, VECs, Media, CRC and DIETs, less than 1% expenditure was reported.

The above situation shows that no worthwhile activity has been undertaken in relation to what was planned for the year? Why? Is the planning process at fault or the plans are prepared without considering the ground reality?

A reflection on the district plan formulation

Whatever little data on project monitoring is available through PMIS points to a number of issues for planning and management of DPEP activities at the district level. A perusal of district plans indicate that no scheduling of activities is done and the feasibility of the proposed activities is never examined. The district plans should be more realistic and able to present a more consistent picture of the activities that can be accomplished.

- The plans must be derived by the real needs rather than the availability of funds;
- The districts must be given the flexibility to identify their own needs through participatory processes and in consultation with the experts from the DIETs and other resource institutions.
- The absorptive capacity is an important consideration and must be properly assessed at the time of annual plan formulation;
- The efficiency of district administration to undertake large scale reforms;
- The recruitment or redeployment of staff in critical areas;
- The target setting in terms of enrolment, retention and drop-out must be worked on the basis of scientific methods and their implications for the school places in various grades, teachers deployment, new schools etc must be worked out in detail;
- The existing PMIS is highly inadequate to meet the data requirements for management and monitoring of various project activities. It is emerging as more of an financial accounting package rather than a monitoring or a management tool. There is no analytical framework for the PMIS and is

likely to create considerable confusion as the coverage expands to more and more districts/states. There is an urgent need to review the PMIS and tune it to meet the projected needs for management and monitoring of DPEP.

Some Concluding Observations

The foregoing analysis was undertaken to identify the main issues that emerge from the primary school data for the Darrang district in Assam. The issues were identified to initiate a discussion on their implication for policy, planning and monitoring of the DPEP programme in the district. While an effort was made to highlight the important issues, an in-depth analysis and discussions with the state officials will provide further insight in to the functioning of primary education in the Darrang district. Some of the issues have ramifications for the state administration whereas the others can be addressed at the district level.

References

1. For a review of the source of data and the issues involved in the collection and analysis of educational data, see Aggarwal Yash (1996) Data base on Elementary Education in India : Scope, Coverage and Issues, NIEPA.
2. In some districts, the DISE could not be operationalised for want of proper computing facilities and the absence of professional manpower.
3. For operational purposes, the scope of the software is restricted to primary schools or primary sections in other type of schools. However, it can be easily extended to cover all levels of school education.
4. See User's manual for a detailed description of the scope, function and applications using DISE. DISE (1996), A User's manual for DISE 2.01, NIEPA.
5. It will be futile to assume that all data requirements will be met by DISE. But it is one of the source of educational data, particularly for the school districts. The advantage with the DISE data is that it is more exhaustive, data becomes available in time and, being in an electronic form, it can be readily shared and manipulated for a variety of purposes. The built in features like report generation provide comparable sets of indicators for all blocks and districts in the DPEP states.

6. For more details see User's Manual DISE 2.01 (1971), NIEPA
7. For detailed analysis of planning and management issues for small schools in Darrang district see, Aggarwal Yash (1996), Small Schools: Issues in Policy and Planning, NIEPA, NEW Delhi
8. Ibid

Source : DPEP Calling, December 1996.

29

New Features in Planning and Implementation

District Information System for Education (DISE) is a most comprehensive data entry and analysis software for establishment and maintenance of school level databases on personal computers. It includes many new features that will considerably facilitate the day-to-day management task of educational planners and administrators. It also provides a variety of decision support services to technical and professional staff engaged in the planning and implementation of DPEP in India. It is for the first time, in the history of independent India, that a detailed school database, forming part of an integrated national information system, is being generated and made available to users. The data for 1996/97 is being computerised using DISE 2.01. The important features of DISE 2.01, in addition to the ones given in the adjoining box are:

a) DISE is the only source of data on items like:

- Age grade matrix by caste, gender and class.
- Information on NER will be provided from Block level onwards.
- Enrolment pyramid (by classes, by SC/ST enrolment)
- Vital information on access (Villages without schools, school size)
- Indicators of internal efficiency like repetition rate, drop-out rate etc
- Type and status of school buildings/classrooms
- Formal inspection of schools
- Receipt and expenditure in respect of DPEP contingent fund
- Classification schools by selected attributes
- School working days in a year

- Establishment and meetings of VECs
- Classification of school data by management, school size, rural/urban character and many other important characteristics
- School level PTR are compared with the average for Block/Taluk.
- School summary report to be shared with VECs
- Block and cluster level reports for analysis of status and program interventions.

Some Important Features: DISE 2.01

DISE is designed as a national system of information for primary education to be implemented in all DPEP districts. Other levels of education can also be added subsequently. It should gradually replace the existing manual system in other districts also.

It overcomes most of the constraints of the manual system. Easy to install and maintain. Bridges gaps between the producers and users of data/information.

It is an integrated system and is designed to cut short time delays in the availability of database in the final form. It is expected that the reports would become available within 6-8 weeks of data collection.

The school database contains a minimum amount of data that will be collected from all recognised primary schools/sections covered under DPEP. It is consistent with the national system of educational data for primary education.

- School level information can be assessed from the district, state and even from the national level.
- Provides comparable information of key performance indicators across time and space. Key indicators include GER, NER, PTR etc.
- Comparative analysis of DPEP and non-DPEP schools.

b) While the district acts as a nodal centre for collection, storage, management and maintenance of primary database, it will be simultaneously shared ata the state and the national level.

c) Special controls and checks have been built in to make sure that duplicate records are not included and non-responding schools are tracked instantly.

d) The school database will form a common core of comparable data for all the DPEP District. The same formats will be used for the collection of core data.

e) There is a provision for data entry in multi-user mode so as to reduce the time required for data entry.

f) The software provides data aggregation multiple levels. Comparable reporting and analysis is possible at the school, cluster, block/Taluk/Mandal, district, state and the national level. It is thus possible to compare the performance indicators for two schools across different districts/states, a possibility that never existed before.

g) The software can provide on-line data for five years. The software contains provision for the analysis of the data for last five years. It would thus be possible to monitor the trends of key performance indicators at various levels of geographical aggregation.

h) Selected standard reports generated at the District level will flow from district to the state and the national level. Block and Cluster level reports will also be generated for sharing among the BEO/AEOs and other officials working at the cluster level.

i) For in-depth analysis and relating it to other social and economic data, the DISE data can be exported to other packages like LOTUS, EXCEL, Dbase, SPSS etc.

j) There is a provision for the bi-directional flow of data. The reverse flow of data is from the district to the Block/Taluk and to the school for verification and sharing among the members of the VEC. the report incorporates general information, enrolment data and a number of key indicators of school performance. Similarly the data can be transferred and shared with higher level of users at the state and the national level.

Indicator	*Gender*	*Caste*	*District*	*Block*	*Cluster*
Primary/upper primary schools	•		•	•	•
Enrolment (total/by classes)	•	•	•	•	•
Teachers	•	•	•	•	•
Classrooms			•	•	•
Number of sections			•	•	•
Average number of working days			•	•	
Schools without buildings			•	•	
Schools not inspected in last academic Year			•	•	
Schools covered under OBB			•	•	•
Schools covered under DPEP			•	•	•
Village with TLC completed			•	•	
Village with NEF facilities			•	•	
Data on tribal schools	•	•	•	•	•
Buildings by management			•	•	
Enrolment by single year age	•	•	•	•	
Underage/overage children	•	•	•	•	
% trained teachers	•	•	•	•	
Gross enrolment ratio	•	•	•	•	
Net enrolment ratio	•	•	•	•	
Pupil teacher ratio			•	•	•
% schools with VEC constituted			•	•	
% single teacher schools			•	•	•
% repeaters in primary classes	•	•	•	•	•
Schools by management			•	•	
Schools by enrolment category			•	•	
Student getting free textbooks	•	•	•	•	
Student getting other incentives	•	•	•	•	

Educational Management: Issues and Response Matrix

	Frequently asked question?	*Response (DISE/EMIS/PMIS)*	*Action points*
A	ACCESS		
A1	How many villages are without primary schools?	List of villages without schools is generated by DISE for each district/block	Examine the list with other data on size and structure of population. Options may be: • The village has a school within walking distance and no need for further action. • Open a new primary school/centre • Open an NFE or other learning centre, if not existing already.
A2	What is the status of Total Literacy Campaign in villages where schools are located?	DISE classifies villages according to: TLC completed TLC in progress TLC not taken up TLC suspended	• The available evidence suggests that successful completion of TLC leads to a spurt in primary school enrolment. • Check whether additional capacity needs to be created to meet the anticipated demand. • The cascading effect of demand mobilisation should become an intrinsic part of micro-planning.

	Frequently asked question?	*Response (DISE/EMIS/PMIS)*	*Action points*
A3	Does the existence of pre-primary facilities in a primary school affect access/participation?	DISE identified school with/without pre-primary facilities.	• It is more of a research question before policy interventions are made on a large scale. • If the Positive relationship is established, then the schools without pre-primary facilities can be identified for providing such facilities.
A4	Have the targets for the quarter/year been achieved for • Establishment of new schools, • reconstruction and rehabilitation of classrooms and other civil works in the selected schools?	PMIS provides the quarterly progress reports on these aspects.	• % targets completed/initiated should be an important performance indicator. Large gaps in the planned and actual outcome raise the following questions: • Was the needed preparatory work completed before the targets were set? • Were the targets realistically set? • Reasons for shortfalls or delays? • Implications and lessons for future work plans and target setting? • Effect of delays in terms of costs and time over-run?
A5	What type of targets can be realistically set for enrolment, retention and drop-out rate?	DISE provides time series data on most of these indicators.	• Can past growth be a guide for the future? • Is the district prepared to implement reforms at accelerated pace? • Is the educational administration responsive?

	Frequently asked question?	*Response (DISE/EMIS/PMIS)*	*Action points*
			• Is it possible to ensure high level of community/NGOs participation?
B	SCHOOL BUILDINGS/CIVIL WORKS		
B1	How many government schools are without school building?	List of such schools by block/district is identified by DISE.	• Develop a long term plan for providing school buildings? • Which school at what time should be covered. • Contributions from alternative source of funding, if any?
B2	How many classrooms are in dilapidated condition and require major repairs/ reconstruction?	Preliminary data is provided by DISE. Needs to be supplemented by other sources of data. Special surveys may be needed to assess the site plans and other requirements.	• Does a long-term plan for school rehabilitation exist? • What are the maintenance plans for the rehabilitated schools? • If not, develop such a plan based on requirements/availability of resources. • Balance new construction/maintenance? • What other sources of funding can be tapped for school rehabilitation?
B3	Progress of other civil works? This includes construction of toilets, BRC/CRC and other buildings?	PMIS provides quarterly data on planned, started and completed civil works.	• Was adequate preparation done? • Were the targets set realistically? • Based on the first two quarters of progress, can be current year targets be achieved?

	Frequently asked question?	*Response (DISE/EMIS/PMIS)*	*Action points*
		Also consult reports of the supervision Mission.	• What needs to be done to ensure that time and cost overruns are contained to the minimum?
C.	PARTICIPATORY PLANNING		
C1	How many schools functions without VECs?	DISE provides the list of schools without VECs.	• What are the impediments in the constitution of VECs? • Focus on the constitution of VECs on priority basis.
C2	Are VECs meeting regularly?	DISE provides school level data on the number of meeting of VEC held during the year. Supplement with data from other sources.	• Identify schools where VECs exist but are not meeting regularly. • Reasons for lack of interest may be ascertained? • What could be the negative effect of non constitution/participation of VECs in school management functions?
C3	Are any voluntary organisations active in providing NFE?	DISE provides the number of NFE centres run by the voluntary organisations?	• What additional role can be assigned to voluntary agencies?
D	PARTICIPATION RATES		
D1	What is the Gross Enrolment Rate?	DISE calculates GER for each category and for each Block/district.	• Identify blocks having low GER. Illustrative reasons for low enrolment could be: • Lack of facilities in the neighbourhood

	Frequently asked question?	*Response (DISE/EMIS/PMIS)*	*Action points*
	Is it possible to know the GER for SC and STs? Is it possible to know the differentials in GER between rural/urban areas?		• Difficulties in access to the neighbouring school. • Lack of awareness/isolation from main stream. • Special and economic deprivation. • Undertake further research. • Develop programs/ intervention for demand mobilisation to overcome identified constrains. • Activate VECs, if not functioning properly, • Consider establishing NFE centres for the drop-put/out-of-school children.
D2	What is the Net Enrolment Rate? It is possible to calculate separate NER for boys/girls and SCs and STs?	DISE calculates NER for each category and each Block/district.	• Identify blocks having low NER. These may be the same as those with low GER or different examine the reasons.
D3	Is there any improvement in the GER since the beginning of DPEP?	DISE provides a time series analysis of GER for each block/district.	• Is the improvement along the expected lines? • What interventions will be required to obtain the target of UPE.
D4	Can UPE (enrolment) be achieved by the projected date? Can separate targets be defined for SC/ST and others?	Time series data on NER for all students, SC and STs is provided by DISE. Yes, NER is available for all groups.	• Further consolidation of enrolment drives. Incentives and quality improvement programs may be necessary. • Need for shifting the target data (closer or further away).

	Frequently asked question?	*Response (DISE/EMIS/PMIS)*	*Action points*
		Supplement this data with school census.	• Equity can only be achieved by iniquitous allocation of resources?
E	SCHOOL EFFECTIVENESS		
E1	• What is the average school size? • How many primary schools are not viable? • How does the school size of government schools compare with private schools?	DISE provides the distribution of schools in various categories of enrolment at the block/district level. DISE also provides distribution of schools under different management. Query mode provides list of schools on selected indicators.	• The management issues in small schools are significantly different from those of the large schools. • Are Some of these issues addressed at the planning stage? • Will it be worthwhile to examine the implications during in-service training programmes. • Training for multi-grade teaching is vital for small schools.
E2	Are there any single teacher schools?	DISE tables provide this data for each block/district. The listing of schools having one or no teacher can be obtained using DISE. A high ratio of single teacher schools is a cause of concern.	• Was the district covered under OB? • Is it the state government policy to continue with single teacher schools with low enrolment? • Is the second post not sanctioned or is vacant? • Examine the implications for plans and policies of the government?

	Frequently asked question?	*Response (DISE/EMIS/PMIS)*	*Action points*
E3	How to reduce the incidence of overage children in the school?	DISE provides age distribution of children in each class by sex, caste and many other charac- teristics.	• Despite the limitations of age-grade matrix, the data can be used to plan for school places and evolve strategies to reduce the share of overage children. • Children in high age-group in higher classes are potential drop-outs. What can be done to prevent it or reduce incidence? • An important research questions is to study the learning curve vis-a-vis age and its implications for curriculum development, classroom transaction and teacher training.

E4	Working days?	DISE analyses the average working days for all schools in the block/district. Listing of schools having working days less than a user defined number can be obtained?	• Low working days may be result of
			  • Dislocation of teaching due to postings and transfers.
			  • General neglect of teachers.
			  • Administrative reasons like teachers being assigned other functions, etc.
			• Besides other measures, strengthening of inspection system will be necessary. Schools with low working days should become specific target of inspection teams.

	Frequently asked question?	*Response (DISE/EMIS/PMIS)*	*Action points*
			• An important research question is the relationship between school working days, achievements, drop-out and repetition rate in the school.
E5	Are schools beings inspected regularly?	DISE provides the list of schools not inspected during previous academic year?	• Lack of interest/motivation among inspecting staff. • Inadequate staff? • Problem with the inspection norms? • Problems with the style and process of inspection? • Strengthen self-appraisal?
E6	What is the performance of the school compared to the average for the Block where the school is situated?	School Summary report provides comparative information.	• Schools with adverse performance indicators like pupil:teacher ratio, repetition rates and drop-out need to be put on the watch list? Reasons for their poor performance should be examined and remedial measures suggested.
E7	Are there any schools without blackboards and teaching learning materials?	DISE provide the percentage of schools without blackboards and other essential items like syllabus, teachers guides, educational charts etc.	• Ensure that all schools have the minimum facilities.

	Frequently asked question?	*Response (DISE/EMIS/PMIS)*	*Action points*
F	SCHOOLS MANAGEMENT EFFECTS		
F1	Distribution of schools by management?	DISE provides the distribution of schools/by management category.	• It is more of a research question. Is there any difference in the performance of government and private aided/unaided schools? • Implications for planning include in-service training of school headmasters and teachers in pedagogy and administration. • Other reasons like facilities, teacher motivation and accountability etc. may also require specific interventions. • The decision making process and complexities of compliance with rule and regulations also need to be examined.
F2	How to rationalise the deployment of teachers in the district? Are there any surplus teachers who can be redeployed? Are there any schools facing chronic shortage of teachers?	DISE provides list of schools with exceptionally high or low pupil teacher ration. It is also possible to assess the requirement of teachers in each school and then identify whether the school has excess or shortage of teachers?	• Teacher rationalisation can result in enormous savings? • The need for additional teachers with projected enrolment can in some cases be met merely by teacher rationalisation.

	Frequently asked question?	*Response (DISE/EMIS/PMIS)*	*Action points*
G.	GENDER QUESTIONS		
G1	What is the difference between the participation rates of girls and boys?	DISE provides a wide spectrum of data to examine the gender related issues in participation, repetition, drop-out and age structure etc.	• Persistence of high differentials is an area of concern. • Special measures may be needed to bridge the gap. Improving access, generating awareness, promoting VECs intervention, improving the management of incentives and school facilities etc. may be necessary to promote equity. • Evaluate the effect of earlier efforts to reduce differentials?
G2	Are the girls likely to drop-out faster than boys?	Enrolment structure for various grades, repetition and drop-out rates for different groups by various geographical aggregations.	• Are there any special pockets/problems areas? • Are there any active NGOs/VA in the area? • Are incentives being delivered properly? • Are there any social taboos which prevent girls education? • Gender sensitisation programs. • Promote women's participation in VECs.
G3	Women participation in VECs	This data is not available in DISE but needs to be collected separately.	• Active participation of women members of VECs can lead to substantial improvement in girls enrolment.

	Frequently asked question?	*Response (DISE/EMIS/PMIS)*	*Action points*
G4	What is the share of women teachers?	DISE provides a comprehensive data on the number and distribution of female teachers by caste, management of the school and other characteristics.	• Teacher recruitment and deployment policies. • Special programs for women school heads, if need be.
G5	What is the share of women Headmasters/principals?	DISE provides this data at the school/block/district level.	• Need for special training? • Programs for capacity building of headmasters.
H	CONCERNS FOR SOCIAL JUSTICE & EQUITY		
H1	Are there significant differentials between the enrolment of SC/ST and other students?	DISE provides detailed enrolment data at block/district level for the SC/ST/others.	• Separate targets for reducing the differentials. • Special programs for improving participation of SC/ST in primary education. • Gender sensitisation programs. • Management of the incentives for SC/ST. • Need assessment for residential schools. • Special needs of nomadic and tribal population groups.

	Frequently asked question?	*Response (DISE/EMIS/PMIS)*	*Action points*
H2	What is the extent of differentials in enrolment of boys and girls within SCs and STs?	Data provided by DISE at various geographical levels of aggregations.	• Intra-caste differentials are as serious as inter-caste differentials. Generally within the SCs, it is the poor rural female which is most deprived. • What are the policies and programmers for reducing inter-caste (within SC and ST) differentials? • It is also a research question as little is know on this aspect.
H3	What is the share of SC/ST teachers in the total teaching workforce? Is it commensurate with their share in the population.	DISE provides the share of SC/ST teachers to total teachers. Comparing with population data will provide the necessary information.	• Implement state norms for reservation of SC/ST posts. • Special in-service teacher training needs assessment and programmes.
I	FUND FLOWS AND UTILISATION		
I1	How reliable are the unit cost?	No source/analysis of financial and other data. Sample estimates need to be worked out.	• Important implications for overall budgetary and resource allocation processes. • Reasons for differences in unit costs? • Examine differences between proposed and actual unit costs?

	Frequently asked question?	*Response (DISE/EMIS/PMIS)*	*Action points*
I2	Promises versus performance?	PMIS is the principal sources of data on fund flows and utilisation. % budgeted amount expended each year by type of activity.	• Degree of which planned activities are implemented? • Areas/activities of concern? • How long shortfall prevailed for each activity? • Lesson for the future? • Extent of re-appropriation? • Whether the ceilings are being maintained? • Implications for planning methodologies. • Time and cost over-runs?
I3	Did all schools get the contingent grant under DPEP?	DISE identifies whether a school received DPEP contingent grant during the last financial years or not?	• Shows the effectiveness of disbursement mechanisms? • Share of schools not receiving contingent grants is important indicator of its outreach. • Further sample studies may be needed to establish whether grants reach schools in time or not.
I4	What is the level of expenditure of contingent grant?	DISE provides the expenditure on contingent funds during the last academic year.	• Data provides important feedback for planning of next years activities. • Further research may be needed to assess the impact of the scheme.

30

Project Management Information System Workshop

—*R.S. Pandey*
Joint Secretary and Bureau Head, DPEP
Govt of India
New Delhi

Introduction

Project Management Information System under DPEP aims at emphasizing a fair degree of integration and holistic view of information, stressing on processed data in the context in which it is used by end users. It is meant to facilitate all management functions like:

- Planning
- Organising
- Control
- Co-ordination and
- Decision making

Work on developing a responsive MIS started simultaneously with the launch of DPEP in 1994. Keeping in view the requirements of the program two softwares have been developed. They are PMIS and EMIS.

PMIS is an acronym for Project Management Information System. It is basically meant for monitoring the progress of the DPEP project in terms of expenditure incurred and physical achievements (i.e. number of trainings, number of schools, number of additional teachers etc.) The information is collected from the states at quarterly intervals. The information flow is through floppies at present.

As of now the PMIS has been developed and tested by a private firm - Inter Continental Computer System (ICCS), New Delhi. Traditional MIS cell within the technical support group DPEP of Bureau is identifying the post implementation problems through the reports generated for the first time.

The MIS cell visited the concerned states for providing training. The state level team in DPEP have been trained in the use of software.

Need for the Workshop

In January 1996 the DPEP-I states were provided the software. Since the activities were state specific, states encountered problems in codifying action plans. This was due to the fact that each state had a different outlook for the activities provided in the software and there was no common understanding. Thus data compilation at the national level did not yield meaningful reports.

The software given to the states was DOS based and it was developed in clipper. It had the following shortcomings:

- It did not accept the spilled over activity of the previous year.
- Advances were not accounted.
- Reappropriation facilities were not provided.

This paved the way for modification in the software.

Features of the New Software

Based on the visit to six states earlier this year and the feedback received, the software was upgraded with the following additional features:

- Upgraded to Windows environment and it now runs on Windows 3.1 and above.
- Provides for prior year budget carry over. Surplus budget of prior year when expenses can be tracked in subsequent claim.
- Integrated with codes for reimbursement claim. No need to submit separate report for reimbursement claim.
- Provides for classification of budget and expenditure by the Quality parameters like Access. Retention, Quality Improvement and Capacity Building.
- Provides for tracking advance disbursed against the activity along with expenditure data.
- Provides for budgetary re-appropriation of funds from one activity to another.
- Provides for more detailed information on release and receipt of funds.
- Provides for additional reports.

The other problem in the earlier software was that, it was not generating statement of expenditure. So this was done outside the software which led to the following consequences.

- The state/district had the burden of duplicated work.
- The data showed some deviation from the actual expenditure which made the users rely more on manual accounts keeping and viewed PMIS as only a monitoring package.

To cater to the above needs the software was modified, activity list was freshly prepared. The software was also made more user friendly by using the least advances in the field (making it Window based). Then the need arose to discuss and find the additions and modifications required in the new activity list. To resolve these issues, a workshop was planned to introduce the new software to the DPEP-I states and to reach a consensus bout the activities coded in PMIS.

Objectives

The objectives that the workshop set for itself were:

- To draw an Integrated plan for PMIS to discuss coding and monitoring systems.
- To facilitate effective monitoring of the programme at the state and district level, a uniform list of activity codes was to be drawn.
- This would facilitate compilation of data at National Level.
- To present the enhanced software to the states.
- To introduce the revised package of the software to the states.
- To discuss and finalize further improvements in the PMIS, and feedback regarding the revised PMIS software.
- To remove the defects in the software and get it corrected on return to states.
- To coordinate in achieving systemised monitoring system.
- To inform them about the requirements of the Ministry.

Proceedings of the Workshop

The workshop was spread over three days. First came the introduction session followed up by an in-depth analysis of ways to overcome the shortcomings of the software. All others were a combination of theory (discussion of Activity Master/Code list) and practical sessions.

Shri R.S. Pandey, JS (DPEP), addressed the State Participants. In his comprehensive speech, he expressed his concern about PMIS. He said their main endeavour was to make PMIS success and he envisaged that the workshop would prove fruitful and beneficial. He remarked that the MIS was an important component of planning and implementation of DPEP. The innovative structure of DPEP-I states demanded a specific PMIS at the district, state and National level. Uniformity in coding and monitoring system were the basic requirements. This workshop would provide common platform for sharing expertise and resolving problems. A consensus had to be reached regarding the optimum number of codes common to all states. States was laid on these issues:

- Understanding the code for various items
- Input of code
- Abiding by the codes and make available the proper data and the fact that some solution has to be arrived at by the end of the workshop.

Ms. Vrinda Sarup, Director, emphasized that the basic exercise was to generate the correct data, which would facilitate compilation at the national level, which in turn had to be presented to the supervision mission. She said that the workshop was an anchor. After consensus was reached regarding the standardization of codes, accounts and the AWP would fall in line. She clarified that the states had a rolling budget i.e. the previous years grant could be carried over the next year. Thus any activity of 94 carried out in '95 will be booked against '94 AWP for monitoring but will be shown as expenditure in '95 for reimbursement. She told the State representatives to conclude and adopt optimum common codes by the end of the workshop.

The opening day of the workshop was devoted to reviewing the problems identified and demonstration of the upgraded PMIS software by ICCS by clearly defining the Government of India needs, followed by a question hour session identifying some of the state issues. This was followed by a discussion on Activity Master Code list.

Consultant (Disbursement) underlined the fact that cost codes have to be decided and categorized with reimbursement codes. The reimbursement code shows the nature of the expenditure. Reimbursement claims area to be prepared on the basis of standardized and approved codes.

Representative of ICCS said that as the DPEP project is in the evolving stage, the system requirements were not clear from the user point of view. So as and when input were recovered they would be incorporated in the software. It was clarified that the PMIS was not an accountancy voucher based software but only a monitoring one.

Source: DPEP Calling, July 1996.

31

Needs Assessment Mission

District Primary Education Programme is local and population specific in planning and implementation of interventions for contextual improvement in quality of primary education. Therefore capacity building in planning and implementation at all levels, specially the district and sub-district levels, has been an important thrust are for DPEP. It assumes greater significance in view of many States enacting Panchayti Raj Legislations in accordance with 73rd and 74th amendments to the constitution transferring powers to local bodies including primary education. The DPEP bureau organised an assessment of the capacity building needs at various levels, starting from the village upto the national level, from April 24 to My 10, 1995.

Information from all DPEP implementing states was collected and analysed. Institutions in Karnataka and Madhya Pradesh were visited on a sample basis. Four areas were identified for immediate capacity building requirements:

Planning & Management

Teacher training & pedagogy

Evaluation and Research

Organisational Development

Within the four broad categories, areas for specific skill development were identified. They are:

In Planning and Management

Institutional management and preparing annual work plan at school and VEC level;

Monitoring and information gathering at cluster level;

Programme evaluation, data collation and analysis at block resource centre level;

Project planning, outcome measurement and needs assessment at direct level;

Programme evaluation and supervision, Management Information Systems at state/national level.

In Teacher Training & Pedagogy

Primary education methodology (lesson preparation, transaction and assessment).

(Multigrade teaching, Dealing with overcrowded classrooms;

Competency based teaching (MLL) & assessment techniques;

Use of teaching learning aids;

Techniques for writing primary grade text books and supplementary material;

Designing training course, developing training plans, etc.

In Monitoring, Evaluation and Research

Techniques for action research and rapid appraisal method;

Basic research data collection, processing and research methodologies;

Test construction and interpretation;

Preparation of research designs and adapting evaluation instruments;

Assessing research/evaluation proposals.

In Organisational Development

Internal needs assessment of an organisation.

Analyses of skills and internal processes.

Organising and designing staff development plans.

The Needs Assessment Mission also suggested a strategy for meeting these capacity building needs.

Accordingly, professionals in respective areas would be identified from various institutions (and in exceptional cases, "individuals") and selected to undergo training's/skill development programmes. These professionals will then act as master resources/trainers for particular skill development at various levels. A set of guidelines will be developed to identify and select the professionals.

A resource inventory will be developed to select the institutions that will render the skill development/training programmes, largely in India but a few in Europe as well.

There will be another set of guidelines on use of these professionals after completion of their training/skill development by the DPEP bureau. The Bureau will set up secretariat (in Ed. CIL) to coordinate the resource use and their networking.

Suggested strategy for capacity building in the identified areas is development of professional resource groups in the area of teacher training (4), planning and management (40), monitoring evaluation and research and institutional development. The members for professional resource groups can be identified from institutions on the basis of a well laid down identification and selection criterion.

As a further follow up the DPEP states expected to identify the institutions with assigned responsibilities to work out the organisational development requirements; earmark individuals (a panel) from within these institutions & others for identification and training in respective capacity building areas; and start preparing a resource inventory for skill development within their state.

Source: DPEP Calling, July 1995.

32

DPEP Provides Basis for Judging School Quality

—*Prof. M.A. Khader*
Regional Institute of Education, Ajmer

Low school quality, particularly at the primary level, continues to be one of the major concerns in India. The thrust placed on achievement along with access, enrolment and retention by the National Policy on Education, 1986 and the updated version in 1992 demonstrates the magnitude of this concern. The prevailing school quality, measured in terms of achievement, is exceedingly low. The baseline study, for instance, undertaken as part of the DPEP strategy to assess the learners' achievement in language and mathematics presents a dismal picture (for details see NCERT, 1994). Learners attaining mastery level in word meaning and reading comprehension are too less in most of the districts and the size does not exceed 10 percent. The picture is in no way different in mathematics indicating an exceedingly low level of performance in addition and subtraction.

A related study undertaken in West Bengal points out that the percentage of learners attaining minimum expected score is certainly less, whether it is language or mathematics (Guha Roy, Mitra and Roy, 1995). These evidences substantiate the contention that the primary school classrooms are crowded by non-achievers. If we allow this trend, the gap between a few who achieve and the majority who do not gets widened and sharpened leading to what is often called Mathew effect. Obviously this trend needs to be arrested by discerning manipulable school conditions that are important for learner achievement.

In fact, central to any effort to improve the quality of education is teaching-learning process in a classroom setting (Scheerens, 1992). The premise is that the classroom transaction reflecting the nature and level of involvement of teacher and learner sets the context for learning and achievement. The process for involvement is set in motion by the teacher. However, the problem gets compounded when the teachers' knowledge level of subject matter is inadequate (Shukla, 1995).

Contradictory Early Researches

Early researches on student achievement formulated around input-output model have been contradictory and suggest weak organisational effects (Murnane, 1981, Rutter, 1983). The model has been criticised for its limited success due to emphasis on variables that are easy to define and measure (Williams, 1992) and its failure to suggest how to improve school practice (Levin, 1980). In the recent past there has been a shift towards school processes (Purkey and Smith, 1983, Good and Brophy, 1986) and the shift has tilted the researchers attention towards process components. What is important from policy perspective is the identification of process components that can be influenced through school policy, and practice. In fact, classroom transaction is a major process component that has important consequences for policy formation.

There is a linkage between school and classroom factors. For instance, most of the factors that have been identified as the indicators of effective school (Scheerens, 1992, Reynolds, 1993) are in fact reflections of the indicators of classroom process (Creemers, 1995). Evidence points out the importance of curriculum, grouping procedures and teacher behaviour (Creemers, 1995), questioning, eliciting and feedback mechanisms within the task, time and talk framework (Alexander; 1995), periodic learner assessment and feedback (Satvir Singh et. al., 1995), and possessing essential knowledge and skills, and performing such skills by the teachers (Chapman, 1993) in explaining the classroom level. Recognising the need for scaling down teacher's resistance for change and innovation, and encouraging them to support new classroom practices, Chapman (1995) suggests a set of strategies such as revising innovations, creating incentives and persuading teachers for their participation and involvement.

Classroom transaction in multigrade context continues to be a major concern. Observation reveals that though teachers invariably rely upon conventional pedagogy and students are seldom involved in the learning process (Sujatha, 1995), appropriate intervention strategies in multigrade teaching situations can make a significant shift in the pattern of achievement (Nagaraju, 1995). What is emerging is the need for formulating appropriate classroom transaction strategies specific to multigrade context (Mohan Lal, 1977, Khichi, 1986, Muralidharan et al., 1993). Whether it is multigrade or non-multigrade context, what goes on in the classroom mirrors the quality of teaching and learning.

Recognising the centrality of classroom transaction in judging the quality of schools, this paper tries to discern the pattern of classroom transaction in multigrade and non-multigrade schools. The evidences are based on a data system gathered from schools under the District Primary Education Project. Considering the thrust placed on improved teaching and learning competence in the DPEP, creation of a baseline data system on classroom transaction would facilitate in choosing the relevant academic inputs to the project.

The paper addresses the following questions:

- What is the level of classroom transaction in multigrade and non-multigrade schools?
- Which are the major variables that differentiate the two groups of schools?
- What is the pattern of difference in the classroom transactions between multigrade and non-multigrade schools?

Metodology

Sample

The study is operationalised based on a sample drawn from the DPEP district, Hissar, Haryana. Unit of observation is school and using stratified random sampling 10 multigrade and 10 non-multigrade primary schools were drawn for intensive observation of classroom transaction. Each category has school drawn from rural and urban areas. Thus, the sample consisting of 20 schools is grouped into four-rural multigrade, urban multigrade, rural non-multigrade and urban non-multigrade.

Classroom Transaction

The classroom transaction is conceived and identified in terms of the following variables:

- Instructional planning: refers to advance planning done by the teacher in terms of clarity of objectives and organisation of lesson. Clarity of objectives unit (COU), clarity of objective - lesson (COL) and clarity of objective - total (COT) where the first two are quantified on five point scale ranging from less clear to highly clear and the average of the two indicates the score of -COT. Likewise organisation of lesson consists of organisation of lesson - selection of activities (OLSEA) and organisation of lesson - total (OLET). The data on OLOC and OLSEA are obtained on a five point scale ranging from less appropriate to highly appropriate and the average of the two indicate OLET. Thus, instructional planning consists of 6 variables.

- Instructional strategy: refers to the strategies used by the teacher in the classroom including their effectiveness. It consists of 5 variables identified as instructional strategy - direct presentation (INSDIP), instructional strategy - learner centred approach (INSLECEA), instructional strategy - effectiveness (INSEFF) and instructional strategy -total (INSTO). The data on the first four are obtained on a 5 point scale ranging from low to high and the average of the four indicates the score of INSTO.
- Learner involvement (LIN): denotes the extent of involvement of learners in the learning process during the classroom transaction. The data is obtained on a single item on a five point scale ranging from less involved to highly involved.
- Time on task : indicates the extent of time devoted by the students on task. It consists of two variables: Time on task - teacher (TOTT) and Time of Task - Student (TOTS), and each is quantified on a 5 point scale ranging from minimum to maximum.
- Attention to individual learning (ATIL): means efforts of the teacher to promote learning and attainment of the identified competencies by each learner. It is identified in terms of grouping of students, remedial instruction, teaching to suit the level of learners and different levels of activities. Data are obtained on a 5 point scale ranging from never to always for four items and the average score indicates ATIL.
- Classroom management (CROMA) : refers to instructional management of classroom in multigrade situation and is identified in terms of peer tutoring, learning teams and group work. Each is identified on a five point scale ranging from never to always and the average score indicate CROMA.
- Effectiveness of classroom management (EFFCROMA): denotes the effectiveness of instructional management of activities, time and involvement of learners. Data is obtained based on a single item ranging from less effective to highly effective.
- Evaluation and feedback (EVAFE): refers to the pattern of evaluation practiced and the extent to which evaluation data is used for identification of learner deficiencies and remedial

instruction. The two items on learner deficiency and remedial instruction are quantified on a five point scale ranging from never to always and the average score indicates EVAFE.

- Innovative practice (INPRA): refers to the teacher's effort to use novel methods, experimenting new instructional strategy and searching for new ideas. Each component is quantified using a five point scale ranging from never to always and average score indicates INPRA.
- Resistance to innovative practice (REINPRA) : indicates teacher's resistance to practising innovative ideas and strategies, and is identified on single item using a five point scale ranging from low to high.

Observation

An observation schedule to gather the field data on the 20 variables specified above was developed. Prior to field observation, using the schedule two observers observed the classroom transactions at the primary level classes in the Demonstration school, RIE, Ajmer for 7 days. This exercise was done to try out the observation schedule as well as to orient the observers on the observation of classroom transactions. Based on try out data the observation schedule was revised. Field observation of multigrade and non-multi-grade schools drawn from Hissar was completed in two phases with a gap of 10 days in March-April, 1996. Each school was observed for a day by each observer. Among the two observers, while one observed multigrade schools, the other observed non-multigrade schools during the first phase. They exchanged the type of school during the second phase enabling each observer to observe all the multigrade (10) and non-multigrade (10) schools.

Each observer made two observations of classroom transactions per school and each school has 4 observations, except one school where the total observation is three. Observers also held discussions with teachers wherever precise and more detailed data were required.

Data Analysis

The obtained data were analysed to determine the inter-rater reliability. Using two-way analysis of variance the analysis was done. Results indicate no significant difference between observers on most of the variables except on four variables - clarity of objective -unit, organisation of lesson - ordering of content, time on task-teacher and time on task-student.

The data were further subjected to multivariate analysis at different levels as outlined below for answering the research questions. The data on 20 schools over 4 groups 20 variables are subjected to MANOVA. The analysis gives univeriate F-ratios for each variable over groups, group means for variables and correlations between variables. The data, as given under MANOVA are further subjected to canonical discriminant analysis giving results in terms of eigen values (Variances for extracted discriminant factors) factor pattern and group centroids in the CDA space. Using the above analysis schools nag groups are well differentiated.

Results and Discussion

Manova

Group and total means are given in Table-I . Mean score of the groups are compared on the basis of total means.

On clarity of objective -unit, total mean is 1.85 and both rural and urban non-multigrade groups have higher mean score than the total mean. On the other hand, both rural and urban multigrade groups have mean values lower than total mean. The highest mean score for clarity of objective-lesson is for rural non-multigrade. Except rural multigrade, multigrade, the remaining three groups have higher mean value than the total mean (2.25). Total mean for clarity of objective - total is 1.95, expect rural multigrade, the remaining 3 groups have been mean scores either same or above the total mean. It is important to note that in all the three variable rural multigrade group has the least mean values below the total means.

With regard to organisation of lesson-ordering of content, urban multigrade and rural non-multigrade have higher mean values than the total mean (1.89). Total mean of organisation of lesson-selection of activities is 1.59. Except urban-multigrade, the remaining three groups show higher mean value than the total mean. Rural non-multigrade groups have been values below the total mean (1.85). On the other hand, both non-multigrade groups have values above the total mean.

Groups means of the instructional strategy-direct presentation for both rural and urban multigrade groups are either same or above the total mean. However, the means of rural and urban non-multigrade groups are below the total mean (3.68). It is important to note that among the 20 variables direct presentation has the highest total mean value. Value of the total mean of instructional strategy - learner centered approach is 1.96. While both rural and urban multigrade groups have values below the total mean, rural and urban non-multigrade groups have values above the total mean. In the case of instructional strategy - material used the total men is 1.54. Among the four groups, only the rural non-multigrde has value above the total mean and the urban multigrade has the lowest value. With regard to instructional strategy - effectiveness the total mean 1.99. Among the four groups only the rural non-multigrade has the mean value above the total mean. Likewise, on instructional strategy - total only the rural non-multigrade has the mean value above the total mean.

What is strikingly visible among the instructional strategy variables is the observation that direct presentation has the highest mean values in both groups and total. It means that whether it is multigrade or non-multigrade groups all follow conventional textbook approach during instruction.

Value of total mean on learner involvement is 2.29. While rural non-multigrade has higher mean value than the total mean, the remaining three groups have values below the total mean. However, the values of the four groups are below average on the five point scale. This reflects the existing level of learner involvement.

Table - 1

Group and total means

Variable Groups	1	2	3	4	5	6	7	8	9	10
A	1.53	1.89	1.74	1.58	1.74	1.68	3.68	1.89	1.47	1.89
B	1.80	2.30	1.95	1.90	1.05	1.80	3.85	1.70	1.40	1.80
C	2.25	2.67	2.25	2.42	2.08	2.17	3.58	2.33	2.00	2.75
D	1.93	2.29	1.96	1.86	1.68	1.86	3.61	2.04	1.50	1.86
TOTAL	1.85	2.25	1.95	1.89	1.59	1.85	3.68	1.96	1.54	1.99

Variable Group	11	12	13	14	15	16	17	18	19	20
A	2.10	2.21	3.53	2.16	0.58	0.68	2.05	0.53	0.58	2.21
B	2.05	2.20	3.65	2.25	0.25	0.60	2.15	0.35	0.10	1.90
C	2.58	2.92	3.25	2.50	1.08	0.00	3.00	0.50	0.92	1.42
D	2.14	2.14	3.50	2.14	0.29	0.00	2.79	0.08	0.25	1.79
TOTAL	2.18	2.29	3.51	2.23	0.47	0.32	2.48	0.53	0.39	1.86

See Table 1A for list of Variables

Table - 1A

List of Variables

Variables

1. Clarity of Objective - Unit (COU)
2. Clarity of Objective - Lesson (COL)
3. Clarity of Objective - Total (COT)
4. Organization of Lesson - Ordering of Content (OLOC)
5. Organization of Lesson - Selection of Activities (OLSEA)
6. Organization of Lesson - Total (OLET)
7. Instructional Strategy - Direct Presentation (INSDIP)
8. Instructional Strategy - Learner Centered Approach (INSLECE)
9. Instructional Strategy - Materials Used (INSMA)
10. Instructional Strategy - Effectiveness (INSEFF)
11. Instructional Strategy - Total (INSTO)
12. Learner Involvement (LIN)
13. Time on Task - Teacher (TOTT)
14. Time on Task - Student (TOTS)
15. Attention to Individual Learning (ATIL)
16. Classroom Management (CROMA)
17. Effectiveness of Classroom Management (EFFCROM)
18. Evaluation and Feedback (EVAFE)
19. Innovative Practice (INPRA)
20. Resistance to Innovative Practice (REINPRA)

Group

A - Rural Multigrade

B - Urban Multigrade

C - Rural Non-Multigrade

D - Urban Non-Multigrade

The total mean for time on task - teacher is 3.51. The value is, certainly, tilted towards above average on the five point scale. Among the four groups both multigrade groups, show mean value above the total mean. Where as both non-multigrade groups are below the total mean. Well, the difference between both sets of groups is marginal. The mean scores reflect that the teacher's share of time on task is more. Total mean for time on task-student is 2.23 and it is well below the value of teachers time on task. While urban non-multigrade group has the lowest mean value (2.14), rural non-multigrade has the highest mean value (2.50). It is highly visible that the teacher's share of time on task as compared to students is substantially high.

Highest Mean Score

The highest mean score for attention to individual learning is for rural non-multigrade and the value of rest of the groups are much less. The total mean is 0.47 and it explains the prevailing low level of effort to provide for individual attention for learning.

In the case of classroom management the total mean is 0.32 and the value explains the prevailing low level of instructional management specific to multigrade setting whether it is rural or urban. The total mean for effectiveness of classroom management is 2.48. While both non-multigrade groups have higher values than the total mean, multigrade groups have values below the mean. Rural non-multigrade group has the highest value.

On evaluation and feedback the total mean is 0.53 and all the group means are below 0.70. Extremely low mean values mirror the prevailing evaluation and feedback mechanisms in multigrade and non-multigrade groups. These schools seldom use evaluation data either for identifications of learner deficiency or for remedial instruction.

Likewise the total mean for innovative practice is extremely low (0.39). Teachers of multigrade and non-multigrade groups seldom involve in using novel methods or experimenting new instructional strategy or searching for new ideas. It does not mean that teachers are highly resistant to innovative practice. The total mean for resistance to innovative practice is 1.86. The highest men is for rural multigrade group (2.21). The group and total means are at below average level. Though there is certain degree of resistance to innovative practice in multigrade and non-multigrade groups, this can be possibly, overcome by adopting suitable strategies.

Use of Evidences

These evidences are used to answer the question - what is the level of classroom transactions in multigrade and non-multigrade schools? The emerging evidence indicates that except on instructional strategy -direct presentation and time on task-teacher, the multigrade and non-multigrade groups maintain below verge or low levels on all other variables which have implications for active classroom transactions. What is striking is that selection of objectives and organising the lessons

Table -2

Among Group Correlation

Varia-bles	1	2	3	4	5	6	7	8	9	10	11	12	13	14	15	16	17	18	19	20
1	1.00	0.97	0.98	0.94	0.35	0.96	-0.44	0.71	0.75	0.70	0.77	0.68	0.68	0.69	0.40	-0.82	0.89	0.17	0.27	-0.99
2		1.00	0.99	0.97	0.16	0.93	-0.21	0.55	0.69	0.67	0.71	0.68	-0.54	0.76	0.35	-0.67	0.75	-0.06	0.17	-0.98
3			1.00	0.99	0.28	0.97	-0.31	0.65	0.78	0.76	0.80	0.76	0.65	0.81	0.47	-0.69	0.79	-0.02	0.31	-0.99
4				1.00	0.29	0.97	-0.26	0.64	0.83	0.83	0.84	0.84	-0.68	0.89	0.57	-0.59	0.71	-0.13	0.40	-0.59
5					1.00	0.48	-0.92	0.91	0.74	0.67	0.73	0.56	-0.10	0.29	0.74	-0.54	0.60	0.61	0.84	-0.33
6						1.00	-0.46	0.79	0.90	0.87	0.91	0.85	-0.81	0.83	0.63	-0.71	0.82	0.07	0.50	-0.97
7							1.00	-0.89	-0.58	-0.48	-0.59	-0.34	0.79	-0.07	-0.45	0.77	-0.77	-0.85	0.57	0.41
8								1.00	0.88	0.81	0.89	0.72	-0.97	0.51	0.72	-0.78	0.85	0.55	0.74	-0.70
9									1.00	0.99	0.99	0.96	-0.95	0.85	0.90	-0053	0.67	0.09	0.83	-0.75
10										1.00	0.99	0.99	-0.91	0.90	0.93	-0.42	0.58	-0,04	0.84	-0.71

11	1.00	0.96	-0.95	0.85	0.89	-0.55	0.69	0.10	0.82	-0.77
12		1.00	-0.84	0.95	0.92	-0.32	0.48	-0.19	0.81	-0.69
13			1.00	-0.65	-0.86	0.63	-0.74	-0.36	-0.86	0.67
14				1.00	0.78	-0.21	0.38	-0.43	0.61	-0.71
15					1.00	-0.16	0.32	-0.07	0.97	0.41
16						1.00	-0.98	-0.70	-0.15	-0.79
17							1.00	0.60	0.29	-0.87
18								1.00	0.09	-0.13
19									1.00	-0.27
20										1.00

Value of significance of r at 0.01 level of confidence is 0.287, DF = 78.

in advance for instruction by the teachers are not that common. Classroom transactions based on learner centred approaches and instructional support materials are rare features in these schools. It is quite revealing to observe that available instructional support materials are seldom used. Further probe indicts lack of skills in the use of such materials and highlights the need for training in this area. Well, the effectiveness of instructional strategies employed is low. Direct presentation based on textbooks and more time on task by the teacher imply the dependence on conventional instructional approach to classroom transactions. In the context of less active instructional strategies and more dependence on conventional strategy, it is natural for the students to involve less in classroom transaction. Likewise, the effort to promote individual learning and use of evaluation data for locating student efficiency and remedial instruction are too less. Certainly, classroom transactions take place but active classroom transaction are rarely visible in these schools, whether multigrade or non-multigrade.

Among group correlations are shown in Table-2 on the previous page. Important variables with high significant correlations are only discussed.

Group correlations suggest that clarity of objective unit has high correlations with clarity of objective-lesson (.97), clarity of objective-total (.98), organisation of lesson ordering of the content (.94), organisation of lesson-total (.96), instructional strategy-learner centered approach (.71), instructional strategy-materials used (.75), instructional strategy-effectiveness (7.0), instructional strategy-total (.77) and effectiveness of classroom management (.89). However, it has negative high correlations with classroom management (-.82) and and resistance to innovative practice (-.99). Clarity of objective lesson has higher correlations with clarity of objective-total (.99), organisation of lesson ordering of content (.97), organisation of lesson - total (.93), instructional strategy-total (.71), time on task-student (.76) and effectiveness of classroom management (.75). However, it has high negative correlation with resistance to innovative practice (-.98). Organisation of lesson-ordering of content shows high correlations with organisation of lesson-total (.97), instructional strategy materials used. (.83), instructional strategy effectiveness (.83), instructional strategy total (.84), learner involvement (.84), time on task-students (.89) and effectiveness of classroom management (.71). However, it has negative high correlations with resistance to innovative practice (-.59). Likewise organisation of lesson selections of activities indicates high correlations with instructional strategy-learner centered approach (.91), instructional strategy materials used (.74), instructional strategy materials used (.74), instructional strategy-total (.73), attention to individual learning (.74) and innovative practice (.84). Its negative high correlation with instructional strategy -direct presentation (-.92) is clearly visible.

It is striking to see that instructional strategy direct presentation has negative high correlations with instructional strategy-learner centred approach (-.89), effectiveness of classroom management (-.77) and evaluation and feedback (-.85) while it shows positive high correlations with time on task-teacher (.79) and classroom management (.77). Instructional strategy effectiveness materials used (.88), instructional strategy - effectiveness (.81), instructional strategy-total (.89), learner involvement (.72), attention to individual learning (.72), effectiveness of classroom management (.85) and innovative practice (.74). On the other hand, it shows high negative correlations with time on task -teacher (-.97), classroom management (-.78) and resistance to innovative practice (-.70). Instructional strategy - materials used shows high correlations with instructional strategy-effectiveness (.99), instructional strategy total (.99), learner involvement (.96), time on task student (.85), attention to individual learning (.90) and innovative practice (.83). It shows negative high correlations with time on task-teacher (-.96) and resistance to innovative practice (-.75).

Instructional strategy-effectiveness too shows high correlations with instructional strategy-total (.99), learner involvement (.99), time on task-student (.90), attention to individual learning (.93) and innovative practices (.84). However, it has negative high correlations with time on task teacher (-.91) and resistance to innovative practice (-.71). Learner involvement has high correlation with time on task student (.95), attention to individual learning (.92) and innovative practices (.81). But it shows negative high correlation with time on task teacher (-.84). Time on task teacher shows negative high correlations with attention to individual learning (-.86), effectiveness of classroom management (-.74) and innovative practices (-.86), effectiveness of classroom management (-.74) and innovative practices (-.86). On the other hand, time on task-student shows high correlation with attention to individual learning (.78) and negative high correlation with resistance to innovative practice (-.71). Attention to individual learning shows high correlation with innovative practice (.97).

F-ratios in Table-3 point out that 3 variables have significant (P 0.05) variation over 4 groups. The highest differences among the groups are seen in classroom management followed by effectiveness of classroom management and organisation of lesson-selection of activities. As compared to these variables the remaining variables are less powerful in discriminating the groups. Values of F-ratios of these variable are in decreasing order, higher the value of F, more the power to discriminate the groups.

Canonical Discriminant Analysis

Results of Eigen values and related statistics in Table 4 reveal that three discriminant functions have the ability to discriminate the 4 groups 100 percent. Eigen values and their associated canonical correlations indicate the relative ability of each function to differentiate the groups. Eigen values for the three functions are 3.03, 1.34 and 0.83 respectively. The first three functions together explain 100 percent variance among groups. The first function explains maximum variation to the extent of 58.29 percent while the second function accounts for 25.82 per cent and the third function accounts for 15.89 percent of the variation.

Results in Table 5 show the emerging factor pattern for discriminant functions. Factors/functions are characterised by the variables which are highly correlated with them. These are indicated by plotting the factor pattern scores and showing them as vectors (See figures 1, 2, and 3).

Table 5 and the related figures suggests that classroom management and effectiveness of classroom management have highest contributions to the first factor. The factor is loaded heavily on the negative side by classroom management and with effectiveness of classroom management on the positive side. While classroom management implies instructional management of classroom in multigrade situations, effectiveness of classroom management denotes the effectiveness of instructional management of activities, time and involvement of learners in general. These two variables have high negative correlation (Table 2). Since both variables reflect the classroom management from two perspectives the first factor is termed as classroom management with the emphasis on multigrade situation on the negative side and general on the positive side.

The data in Table 5 and the related figures suggest that the second factor is loaded positively by organisation of lesson-selection of activities, attention to individual learning and innovative practices. Organisation of lesson-selection of activities has the highest contribution to this factor followed by innovative practice and attention to individual learning. It is important to note that the contributions of latter two variables, as compared to the first variables, are much less in second factor and their contributions are more towards the third factor. Besides organisation of lesson - selection of activities has significant high correlations with attention to individual learning and innovative practices (Table 2). Organisation of lesson-selection of activities implies

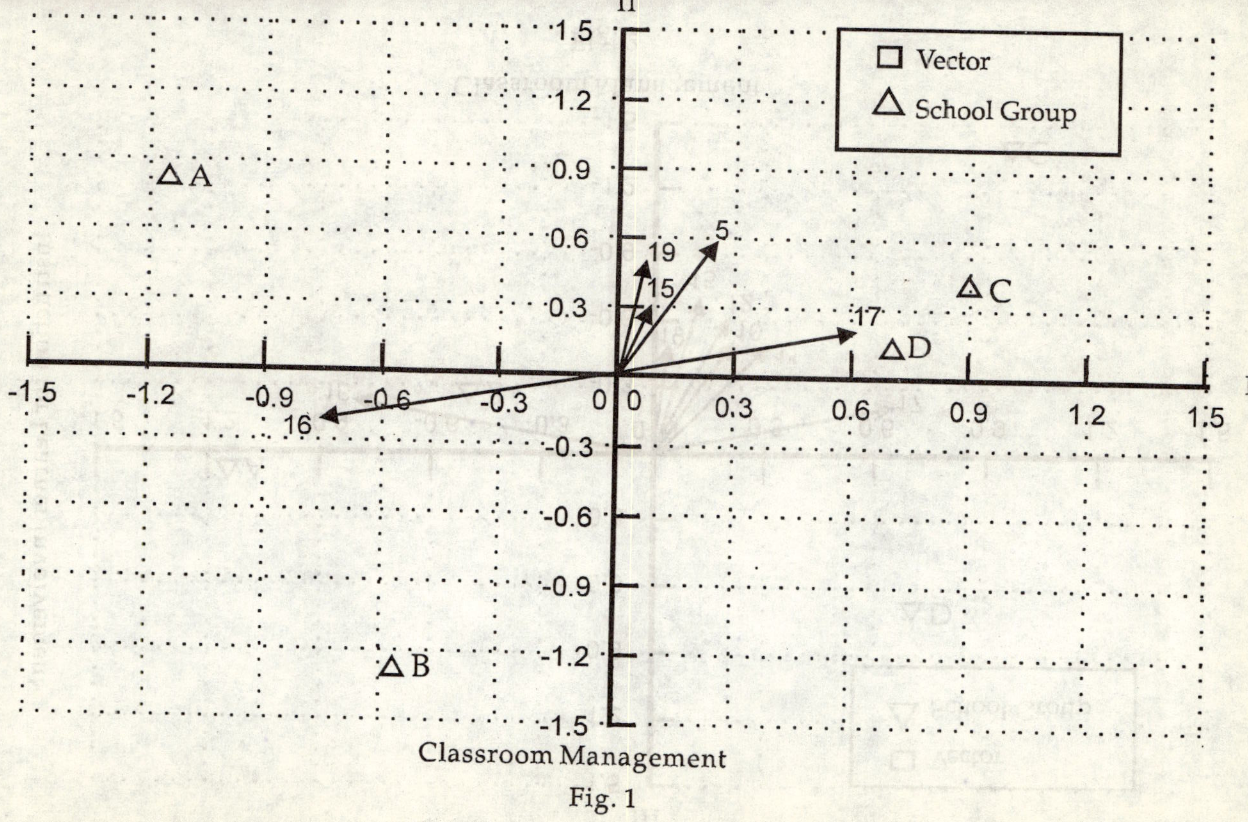
□ Vector
Δ School Group
ΔA
ΔB
ΔC
ΔD
5
19
15
17
16
I
II
1.5
1.2
0.9
0.6
0.3
0
-0.3
-0.6
-0.9
-1.2
-1.5
Classroom Management
Planning Instructional Activities

Fig. 1

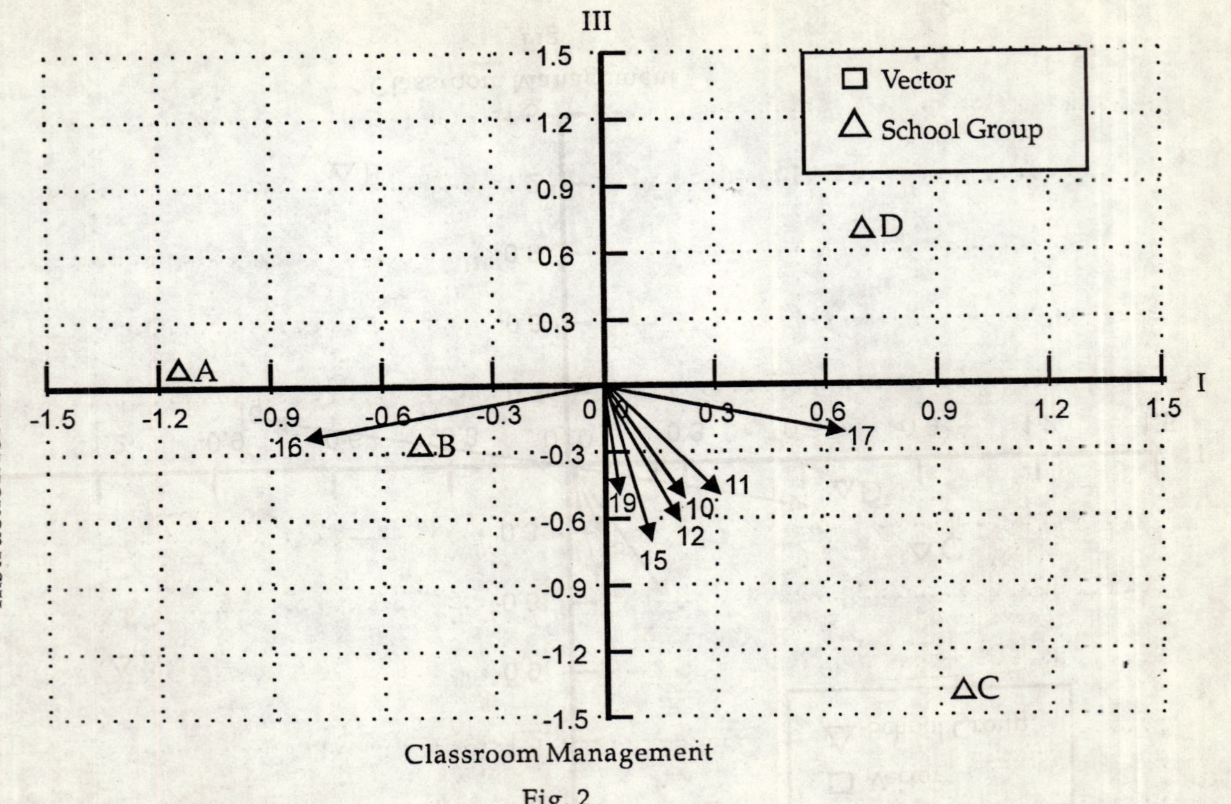
Vector
School Group
III
I
ΔA
ΔB
ΔC
ΔD
16
17
11
10
12
15
19
Instruction for Learner Involvement
Classroom Management

Fig. 2

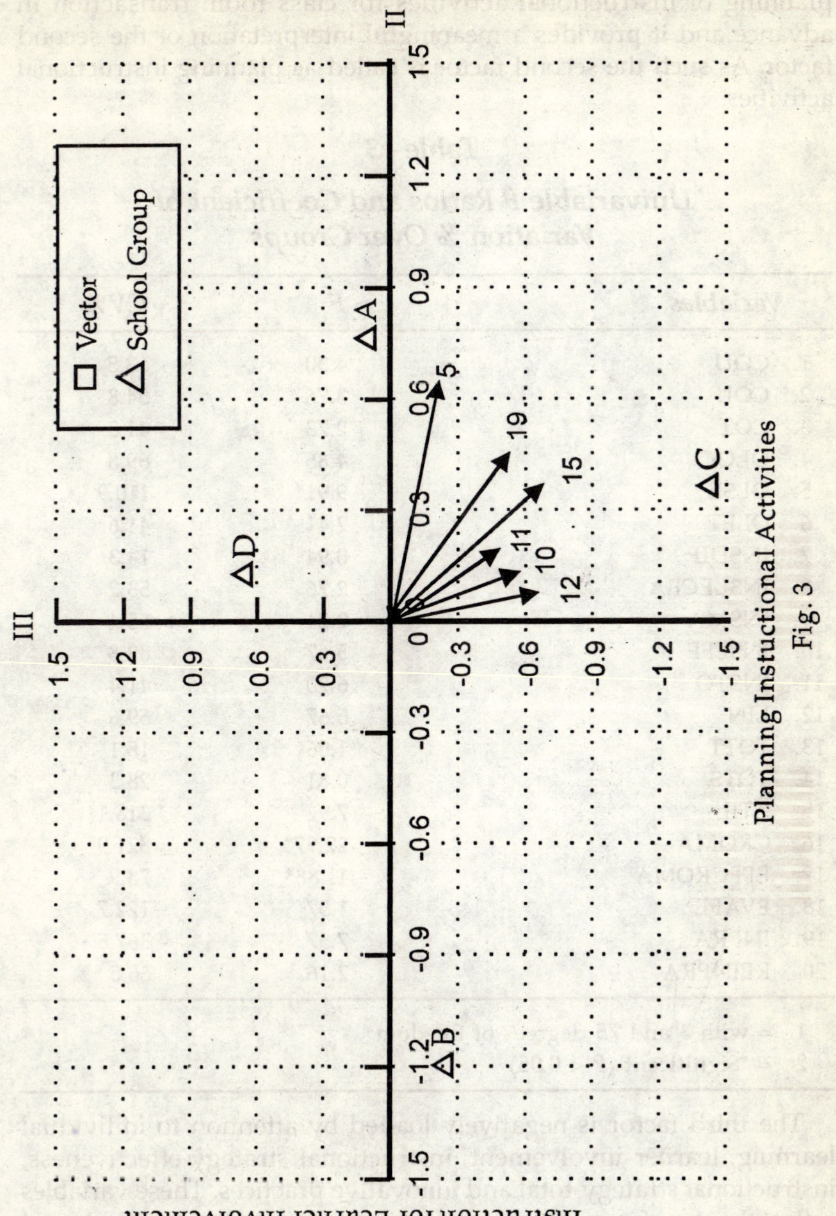
Vector
School Group
II
III
ΔA
ΔB
ΔC
ΔD
5
19
15
11
10
12
1.5
1.2
0.9
0.6
0.3
0
-0.3
-0.6
-0.9
-1.2
-1.5
Planning Instuctional Activities
Instruction for Learner Involvement

Fig. 3

planning of instructional activities for class room transaction in advance and it provides a meaningful interpretation of the second factor. As such the second factor is called as planning instructional activities.

Table - 3

Univariable F Ratios and Coefficient of Variation % Over Groups

Variables	F	CV%
1. COU	4.30	63.5
2. COL	3.76	54.8
3. COT	2.73	41.3
4. OLOC	4.85	69.8
5. OLSE	9.91*	110.9
6. OLET	2.41	41.6
7. INSDIP	0.94	14.3
8. INSLECEA	2.76	53.2
9. INSMA	2.21	65.4
10. INSEFF	5.67	83.8
11. INSTO	6.70	41.4
12. LIN	5.67	59.6
13. TOTT	1.06	18.1
14. TOTS	0.81	28.3
15. ATIL	7.92	318.1
16. CROMA	22.97*	521.9
17. EFFCROMA	11.88*	78.9
18. EVAFE	1.57	122.7
19. INPRA	7.57	367.5
20. REINPRA	2.16	68.5

1 = with 3 and 75 degrees of freedom
2 = *Significant ($P < 0.05$)

The third factor is negatively loaded by attention to individual learning, learner involvement, instructional strategy-effectiveness, instructional strategy-total and innovative practices. These variables reflect the use of instructional strategies specific to learner needs and ensuring their involvement in classroom transaction and learning. As such the third factor is called instruction for learner involvement.

Further evidences about the groups- A (rural multigrade), B (urban multigrade), C (rural non-multigrade) and D (rural non-multigrade) and D (urban non-multigrade) - differences are derived from the group centroids reported in table 6. These are the mean discriminant scores for each group on the respective functions. The centroid summarise the group locations in the space defined by the discriminant functions I and II, I and III, and II and III. The differences can be visualised with ease after plotting them on graphs (figures 1, 2, and 3).

Table - 4

Eigen Values and Related Statistics

Roots Removed	Canonical Correlation	R-Square	Eigen Value	Chi-Square	NDF	Lambda	Trace %
0	0.87	0.75	3.03	148.17	60	0.11	58.29
1	0.76	0.57	1.34	56.18	38	0.43	25.82
2	0.67	0.45	0.83	0.00	18	1.00	15.89

It is important to note that the mean values of the variables contributing to the functions I, II and III are, in general below average on a five point scale (Table I) and it reflects the level of prevailing classroom transaction. Locations of groups on the planes of discriminant functions are discussed as high or low within the existing level.

Figure I illustrates that the plots divide the four groups depending upon their locations. Groups centroids are plotted in the canonical discriminant space defined by the first two discrimanant functions - classroom management (I) and planning instructional activities (II). Locations of rural non-multigrade (C) and urban non-multigrade (D) groups on the positive sides of classroom management and planning instructional activities explain their district nature. The two non-multigrade schools form a cluster indicating that they are relatively high in the classroom management and average in planning instructional activities. It means that non-multigrade rural and urban groups plan instructional activities to a certain extent and manage instructional activities, time and learner involvement relatively well.

On the other hand, the emerging pattern is entirely different for rural multigrade (A) and urban multigrade (B). Rural multigrade group as compared to urban multigrade group is high in the management of classroom specific to multigrade situations. The two groups difference is further sharpened by planning instructional activities. Rural multigrade group plans instructional activities relatively well. On the contrary, urban multigrade group is below the level of rural multigrade group in the management of classroom specific to multigrade situation and is extremely low on planning instructional activities.

Table - 5

Factor Pattern for Canonical Discriminant Functions

Variables		***Factors***		
		I	***II***	***III***
1.	COU	0.39	-0.07	-0.25
2.	COL	0.32	-0.16	-0.28
3.	COT	0.28	-0.09	-0.27
4.	OLOC	0.32	-0.10	-0.42
5.	OLSEA	0.24	0.61	-0.22
6.	OLET	0.26	-0.00	-0.28
7.	INSDIP	-0.14	-0.19	-0.01
8.	INSLECEA	0.26	0.25	-0.18
9.	INSMA	0.17	0.13	-0.33
10.	INSEFF	0.21	0.17	-0.55
11.	INSTO	0.29	0.21	-0.52
12.	LIN	0.17	0.11	-0.59
13.	TOTT	-.13	-0.16	0.17
14.	TOTS	0.06	-0.02	-0.25
15.	ATIL	0.07	0.34	-0.61
16.	CROMA	-0.78	-0.17	-0.06
17.	EFFCROMA	0.64	0.15	-0.10
18.	EVAFE	0.16	0.20	0.20
19.	INPRA	0.04	0.45	-0.50
20.	REINPRA	-0.28	0.06	0.19

Location of groups on the plane of classroom management (I) and instruction for learner involvement (III) differentiate the multigrade and non-multigrade groups further. Though rural and urban non-multigrade groups (C and D) have some level of classroom management they differ considerably in providing instruction for learner involvement. While rural non-multigrade group (C) makes relatively higher effort to provide instruction for learner involvement, the effort of the urban non-multigrade group (D) is extremely low. Though rural multigrade group (A) maintains higher level of classroom management specific to multigrade situation than the urban multigrade group (B), both groups are low in providing instruction for learner involvement. If providing instruction for learner involvement is a major component of classroom transaction, then rural non-multigrade as compared to the remaining 3 groups, makes relatively high effort in providing instruction for learner involvement. Among the remaining three groups while both rural and urban multigrade groups are low, the urban non-multigrade group is extremely low in providing instruction for learner involvement.

Table - 6

Group Centroids in Canonical Space

Groups	Factors		
	I	II	III
A	-1.19	0.84	0.04
B	-0.50	-1.21	-0.13
C	0.89	0.37	-1.38
D	0.78	0.13	0.66

A = Rural Multigrade
B = Urban Multigrade
C = Rural Non-Multigrade
D = Urban Non-Multigrade

Location of groups on the plane of planning instructional activities (II) and instruction for learner involvement (III) provides further insights into the differences between groups. Though rural multigrade group (A) make relatively higher effort as compared to the rest in planning instructional activities, they are weak in providing instruction for learner involvement. Urban non-multigrade group (D) attaches importance to planning instructional activities to a minimum level but the group is extremely low in providing instruction for learner involvement. On the other hand, rural non-multigrade group (C) stands apart from the rest in the sense that the group shows relatively high degree of effort in planning instructional activities and providing instruction for learner involvement. However, urban multigrade shows entirely a different picture. The group is low in both planning instructional activities and providing instruction for learner involvement. In fact, these evidences substantiate the earlier findings highlighting the teachers needs for subject specific training with the focus on child centred activity based interactive mode of transaction based on a data from the DPEP district, Hissar (Khader, Rath, Shrimali and Arya, 1996).

The above evidences explain the answers to the research questions two and three. With respect to the question on major variables that differentiate the multigrade and non-multigrade groups, the evidences suggest that classroom management, effectiveness of classroom management and organization of lesson - selection of activities are the significant and most powerful in discriminating the various groups. Though less powerful variables such as instructional strategy effectiveness, instructional strategy-total, learner involvement, attention to individual learning and innovative practices have important consequences in differentiating the groups. With regard to the question on the pattern of differences in classroom transaction among the groups, explanation is based on the factor pattern derived from canonical discriminate analysis. The groups are well differentiated on the planes of derived functions/ factors - classroom management - planning instructional activities, classroom management - instruction for learner involvement and planning instructional activities, classroom management - instruction for learner involvement and planning instructional activities instruction for learner involvement. What is emerging is that it is more appropriate from strategic planning perspective to differentiate the groups based on functional dimensions or characteristics. Each group, rural multigrade, urban multigrade, rural non-multigrade and urban non-multigrade shows distinct pattern of differences on the planes of discriminant functions. The planes of the functions reflect the context of the group. In fact, each group has a distinct context.

Evidences for Policy Planning

The emerging evidences point out that the prevailing level of classroom transaction in multigrade and non-multigrade schools is below average. If we consider the mean values of the variables contributing to the three functions, then all the groups - rural multigrade, urban multigrade, rural multigrade, urban multigrade, rural non-multigrade

-are all below average level. This mirrors the existing level of classroom transaction in these DPEP schools. Rural multigrade, urban multigrade, rural non-multigrade, and urban non-multigrade are differentiated well on the planes of classroom management and planning instructional activities, and instruction for learner involvement. Rural and urban non-multigrade group makes effort to provide instruction for learner involvement. Certainly urban non-multigrade is extremely weak in providing instruction for learner involvement.

Among multigrade groups, rural multigrade maintains relatively high classroom management specific to multigrade situation and plan instructional activities. Though urban multigrade maintains classroom management to a certain extent, the group is considerably low in planning instructional activities. However it is highly visible that both multigrade groups are weak in providing instruction for learner involvement.

These evidences point out that identification of the context of school is essential for strategic planning. Location of groups on the planes of derived functions explain the context and suggests the strength and weakness in relation to the existing level of classroom transaction.

From strategic planning perspective urban non-multigrade groups require training inputs to promote instruction for learner involvement to desirable level. Equally important is to provide training inputs to strengthen the existing levels of classroom management, planning instructional activities and instruction for learner involvement in rural non-multigrade group.

Both rural and urban multigrade groups need training inputs to build the capacity to provide instruction for learner involvement. Training inputs on planning instructional activities is a major need for urban multigrade. However, training inputs are needed to strengthen the existing level of classroom management and planning instructional activities in rural multigrade as well as the classroom management in urban multigrade. The evidences mirror the quality of training programmes received by the teachers of these DPEP schools. What they require is need specific training programmes if the objective is to improve the classroom transaction.

Source: DPEP Calling, August 1996.

33

Alternative Education in DPEP

—Subir Shukla

Within DPEP, there has been an awareness of the shortcomings of the existing NFE scheme running across the country. Some of these are:

- The scheme is far too rigid and does not really allow for variations according to the situation. By and large it has got reduced to 'night school' in most places.
- There is really very little of the 'non-formal' element in the scheme; it is not much more than the condensation of the formal curriculum into a shorter duration. This is also reflected in the kind of material used.
- Training of instructors has been very poor, as has supervision. As a result, no appropriate teaching methodology has been really made effective in the field.
- The incentive to the instructors for each student passing out at class V level tends to create a situation where many instructors (who are also formal school teachers) make their formal school students appear in the NFE examination.
- Many of the above elements have led people to term NFE as a second grade education meant for those who cannot afford to go to formal school.

A more detailed and objective analysis may be found in the evaluation study commissioned by the MHRD and undertaken by the Operations Research Group.

It was in order to avoid the kind of shortcomings listed above that the idea of Alternative Education was emphasised in DPEP. By this was intended not merely a change in nomenclature, but in the concept itself. However, as of now the concept of Alternative Education has not been formally defined in great detail. Perhaps this explains why, despite intentions reflected in the AWPs many states have not been able to go very far in this area.

This article attempts to put together the various thoughts about Alternative Education that have emerged till now.

Emerging Features

Some of the features of Alternative Education as emerging in DPEP are as follows:

Clientele

By and large, Alternative Education would be required in areas where there are small and scattered habitations, remote and inaccessible areas, where population size is not large enough to enable formal school to be opened. It could also be required in areas where high drop out rates are observed, primarily due to aspects such as child labour or social taboos (in case of girls). Finally, it would also be required to serve the needs of special communities such as nomadic tribes or migrant labour.

What this implies is that Alternative Education tends to be crucial input towards the education of the most disadvantaged sections of society. The larger proportion of out-of-school and drop out children tend to be girls. Scattered and remote habitations are often populated by tribal communities, and children here who cannot tend formal school due to economic reasons are disadvantaged by poverty.

Equity being a major focus of DPEP, Alternative Education assumed the role of a key intervention towards fulfilling the needs of special focus groups in the programmes.

Special needs

Given the nature of the clientele, Alternative Education would, while ensuring broad parity with elements of the formal school curriculum, need to emphasise special needs. Some of the questions that have been raised,but not yet really answered are:

- How can really remote and small habitations be served? Would any teacher be willing to stay there?
- If larger proportion of out-of-school/drop out children are girls, would different focus be needed?
- In tribal areas, and in most remote areas especially, the language of the home tends to be fairly different from that of the textbooks. What are the implications of this?
- The world view, or the range of familiar experience, of children attending Alternative Education classes tends to be different (and rich in its own way). How can this be taken into account?

- If there are communities that are nomadic, how can their children be educated?
- When needs and situations vary so greatly, is it possible - and desirable - to create a 'standard' Alternative Education package?
- Mainstreaming of children passing out from alternative education centres.

Assessing the Needs

The nature of the micro-planning exercise initiated in areas where Alternative Education is likely to be undertaken, would need to be able to identify all the elements considered important in determining the nature of Alternative Education most suitable for that area / habitation. The school mapping exercise should provide indications such as likely candidates who would be suitable as teachers, the kind of community support likely to be available and the possible links between the Alternative Education and the nearest formal school (which could be seen as the nearest resource institution).

Community Involvement

While community involvement is important to primary education in general, in the case of Alternative Education it becomes even more crucial. Apart from the micro-planning exercise, selection of the teacher and often provision of the site for the school, the role of the community is particularly required in sustaining Alternative Education, both through local supervision as well as ensuring that children who enter the Alternative Education centres remain there till their course is over.

Flexibility

The key aspect of Alternative Education is that it would be *a system adapting itself according to the needs of children* rather than expecting children to adapt their lives according to the needs of the school. Hence, the most obvious characteristic of Alternative Education would need to be that of flexibility. The *timing* of the alternative school would vary from place to place, being adapted to the needs of the children. The *entry point,* too, would naturally vary, depending on age and previous schooling experience of the child. The *duration* of the course too could vary according to the needs of children,some being able to complete it in perhaps three years and others even taking five years, once again according to the amount of time they are able to spare. (The 'normal' duration of the course would be arrived at after an understanding of the needs of children as emerging from a collation of the micro-planning exercise).

Curriculum and Materials

A certain degree of flexibility would also be expected in *curriculum* and *materials.* While the curriculum would provide a broad direction, it would facilitate a teacher adopting different paces according to the varying ages, experience and background of children. The curriculum would also need to keep in mind that regular attendance is not really possible for many children due to domestic and economic activities. Hence, a key aspect would be that of *sequencing.* At present, curriculum tends to be linear in sequence, i.e., if a child misses, say, units 5 & 6, she will find units 7 & 8 difficult to understand. Alternative Education curriculum and materials would attempt to overcome this problem by weaving in an element of constant revision, so that every unit would contain elements of earlier levels as well. There would thus be a back and forth movement and sort of helical movement would be adopted.

As mentioned earlier, there would be need to create material that permits greater local *specificity.* (For example, instead of giving names of 4 birds, a lesson might ask: name 4 birds in your area. The lesson could then go on asking many other questions which children would be required to answer on the basis of their own observation in their own area.) Such material would facilitate greater adaptation.

Support Material and Activities

Given that Alternative Education would be more likely to be implemented in remoter areas where children's exposure to material other than textbooks would be limited, one possibility worth exploring is that of a school library programme or a mobile library programme. Occasional activities such as *bal melas* could also provide high points in the educational life of children, and facilitate retention.

Language and Culture

While efforts would be made to void cultural biases as well as give place to a child's natural and social environment in the education process, of particular importance would be the issue of language.

At present, a large number of children tend to grow up feeling that their home language is inferior. If a child uses her home language in the school, she is even called *ganwaar* or uncouth! In Alternative Education, an effort would be made to accord respect to a child's language in the classroom. Children would be free to use their own language and would not be made to feel that it is wrong.

The teacher would, however, slowly start using the language of the textbook and ensure over the course of alternative Education that the child becomes adept in both languages without feeling that her own is inferior.

Teachers and Teacher Training

An effort would be made to recruit local teachers. The recruitment norms would be different from those for formal schoolteachers. It should, in the interest of obtaining local persons, be possible to recruit high school and even middle school pass candidates.

The help of the community could be taken to identify suitable candidates, which will facilitate a greater degree of acceptability. This, however, should not be a facile exercise, but a fairly rigorous one, and perhaps linked with the school mapping exercise as well.

The key element would then be that of teacher training and motivation. For these recruits a longer term training plan would be required. An *initial training,* ranging from 4-6 months would prepare them to initiate the Alternative Education centres in their habitations.

Subsequently, every year they might be required to undergo Al training of3-6 weeks for the next 2-3 years.

It would need to be kept in mind that Alternative Education centres would be, by and large, multi-grade as well as multi-level in context. Hence, teacher training would take this as a working assumption.

Teacher Support/Supervision

One way of follow up from the training might be to supply these teachers with some relevant reading material periodically and then organising peer group meetings to facilitate learning and development. However, it is not yet clear whether Alternative Education centres should be linked with the nearest CRCs or whether a separate arrangement should be worked out to provide on-site support or opportunity for peer interaction.

Evaluation

In view of the flexible nature of Alternative Education, perhaps it would not be advisable to undertake periodic evaluation. On the other hand, more informal ongoing assessment could be utilised, with something like a 'credit' system, *where on accumulation of the requisite number of credits* in a broadly specified period, a child could be considered as having moved on to a next class. This would facilitate greater flexibility, and also allow each child to find his/her own pace.

Innovation

The diverse requirements from Alternative Education, the challenges posed by the difficult conditions in which Alternative Education will usually need to function,and the dire need of the special focus groups imply that a degree of innovation is required in order to overcome the odds. What is needed, therefore, is willingness and the availability of capable personnel to try out innovative ideas. This is all the more urgent in light of the fact that despite all efforts,universalisation of primary education will not be possible through the formal school which, by its very definition, is not likely to be flexible and would tend to leave some children out of its ambit. Alternative Education then would be the key link leading to UPE.

Source: DPEP Calling, April 1996.

34

Priorities for Alternative Schooling

A four day workshop on Alternative Schooling (AS) was organised recently in Gurgaon, Haryana. The workshop was planned to share with states different attempts as well as issues connected with the education of children who remain out of school. This issue has gained special importance in the context of universalisation of primary education. A large number of persons having experience in this area from across states worked as Resource Persons for this workshop. This large number was necessitated by the attempt to share with the states a variety of possibilities. Also it was felt necessary to examine these issues from different perspectives and in all its dimensions. This workshop was preceded by a workshop in Udaipur in which a background note listing issues for the Gurgaon workshop was prepared and sent to the states. Participants from the states were expected to have discussions around these issues in their respective states. The workshop was designed to give states opportunity to work in small groups and articulate their views. The expectation was that, at the end of the workshop the states would be able to move towards developing a tentative plan.

Objectives

In summary, the objectives of the workshop were:

a. To share different experiences with the participating states and give inputs in terms of ideas regarding possibilities and dimensions of issues pertaining to the subject.

b. To have the states clarify their own idea of AS and develop tentative plan(s) that they can take up.

c. To give feedback to the states on their plans and programmes of AS.

d. To provide them an opportunity to discuss with Resource Organisations and individuals possibilities of collaboration and working together for the state programme.

Participants

A total of 68 participants from the states under DPEP - I and DPEP - II participated in this workshop. State Project Directors of some of the states also participated in this workshop in varying degrees. While some of them could be there for more than two days others could only spare half a day. State Project Directors were briefed by some members of the core team about the discussions in the workshop.

The following states participated in the workshop:

Andhra Pradesh, Assam, Gujarat, Haryana, Himachal Pradesh, Karnataka, Kerala, Orissa, Madhya Pradesh, Maharashtra, Tamil Nadu, Uttar Pradesh and West Bengal.

Issues Discussed

The workshop began with the address of Shri R.S. Pandey, Joint Secretary, DPEP Bureau, Department of Education. Shri Pandey highlighted various issues concerning AS and its importance in the context of efforts for UPE. The workshop was divided into different sessions covering some important issues such as:

- What is AS? essential features, assumptions about education, about children, curriculum, material and participation.
- Goals of AS and curriculum expectations from S.
- Knowing the clientele (children), their socio-economic conditions.
- Varieties of efforts possible under AS.
- Teacher - child relationship, Teacher training.
- Importance of community participation.
- Need for decentralised participatory management structure and importance of micro-planning and other issues of planning and management.
- Issues related to materials development.

The work experience of various organisations in this area was shared with the participants. In the last session feed back from the participants was invited. Participants expressed their satisfaction with the outcome of the workshop. The participants acknowledged that they got an opportunity to understand new ideas and information. They felt that many of their own beliefs need to be examined in the light of the discussions. DPEP states are preparing new action plans for AS activities for 1997-1998. They also agreed that in the light of the workshop discussions they would amend their state plans.

Some of the important conclusions which emerged from the

workshop are as follows:

- Our commitment is to provide quality primary education to all children in the age group of 6 to 14. AS should not be seen as a low cost inferior quality education provision for children who did not join school or dropped out from the school.
- Our first effort should be to bring change in the school situation, so that children get attracted towards the schools and they do not get pushed out from there. The teaching learning process in the schools should be activity based, and joyful.
- Necessary improvements in TLM, and training, need to be initiated to make learning joyful and socially relevant.
- Every effort should be made to ensure community participation in the planning and management of education.
- We should have village-wise assessment of every child. Whether they are in school or not? If they are out of schools, then the reasons therefore.
- Reasons for remaining away from schools will be varied and therefore varieties of efforts would be required under AS which should suit local specific conditions.
- AS should be innovative, flexible and a vibrant system responding to local needs of the society. It is not enough to plan good modules by just picking up appropriate ideas. The structures created must have antennas to receive feedback from the ground and allow changes accordingly. The system must be a living organisation, interacting, feeling and modifying itself. No sundry collection of ides that are good but out of context would help to ensure quality.
- Lack of access to the school is not merely because of distance or geographical barriers. There are many other barriers which keep children out of school. AS would require studying the reasons and developing structures and processing that attempt to remove these barriers.
- Equivalence with school and quality education cannot be achieved with investment of 2 hours a day for 2 years. We must have AS running for longer hours and for longer duration.
- The school/AS must provide free space for learning to learners.
- All different institutions created for learning must mutually strengthen each other and there should be co-ordination

between the schools, the AS and the NFE centres etc. If possible there should also be a linkage with other systems including health in particular.

- Making it possible for the girl child to attend school is very important. Apart from designing AS specially catering to their needs, the question of gender sensibility in all aspects of our effort must be seriously addressed.
- Language of dialogue between teachers and children is a crucial issue. It must be made possible to have dialogue in the mother tongue of the child.
- The children and the community must feel that something relevant is being learnt in the school. There must be a place for and methodology to include their traditional knowledge base and their culture. It should have space for developing life skills (if possible) useful for the community.
- The qualifications of teachers instructors are not as important as their having sensitivity to the children and respect for the community from where they come.
- The effectiveness of the school programme depends on the teacher. He/she must feel cared for, have opportunities for participating and contributing to the process, and have possibilities of academic and professional growth. The system must respect her value and her ideas.

Important Element of School/AS

School is like a human being; it may have all its components like kidneys, hands, legs but yet may not be alive. Physical facilities, material, technically right pedagogy, teacher may fail to make a lively dynamic school. What gives life to school is the relationship of programme planners and implementers including teachers with children and the community and also the relationship, attitude of the community towards the school.

In a lively school, important aspects of relationship with children are:-

- Freedom from fear and punishment
- sense of developing self discipline rather than imposing it on them
- Respect for child's understanding and world view
- The teacher and the school must give - freedom to learn at their own pace

- School should not lower but should enhance the self respect of the child
- Teachers should treat children as partners and the running of school should be a joint venture. Teacher should be unbiased and impartial in dealing with children and the teacher child relationship should be democratic and children should be able to question the teachers and they must feel equal
- The teachers and the children should trust each other, care for each other and feel secure with each other. The children must have a sense of freedom
- The idea that the school also belongs to children and they are partners in maintaining it, cannot be explained by words; it has to set reflected in actions
- The children and teachers should be able to participate in pranks jointly
- Children are thrilled when they learn something on their own. Schools should organise events where children get the thrill of learning. (Thrill and joy of learning is distinct from entertainment; learning seriously can be a very thrilling activity)
- There should be very few but well chosen fixed principles in the orgnisation and functioning of a school. The school should be able to respond to specific situations immediately.

Source: DPEP Calling, February 1997.

The DPEP Route in Madhya Pradesh

Amita Sharma
Mission Director
TLC & DPEP
Madhya Pradesh

If the status of literacy is an index to the development of a society, then the largest state in India - Madhya Pradesh represents an area of challenges to development initiatives particularly those that are societal in nature since the state has a literacy rate that at 44.20% is lower than the national average of 52.21% and the female literacy rate stands at just 28.85%. The problems are aggravated by factors distinct to this state - 23.27% tribal populace, the widespread afforested land, large tracts of remote and inaccessible habitations that by the very nature of logistical difficulties persist on the periphery of development and distinct regional cultural identities that defy standardised homogeneous solution. Inevitably, any development process to be effective here needs to acknowledge these intrinsic challenges and to forge approaches that distinctly address their individual and complex character. The foremost implications of such a scenario for development planning are : decentralized and disaggregated planning; an integrated vision sensitive to the inter relatedness of issues; and above all an empathy with those whose lives and circumstances are being planned. In fact, if the start off point is the last factor viz. empathy with those whose condition is the is raisonne de' etre of action then the other development prerequisites - decentralization, micro level disaggregation, integration become inevitable partly as process concomitants and partly as process consequent. beginning with the people as and where they are, proves to be an effective way of beginning, unfolding, as it does new vistas of perceptions, developing new insights often surprising and often quite at variance with commonly assumed planning maxims.

Initiating Participative Process

Such an experience in development planning is evolving in a rich and fairly complex manner in education planning in M.P. The immediate stimulus for this has been DPEP. DPEP, an internationally aided project has been formulated precisely with a view to initiate participative processes at different levels all relating together as a complex but educational reform. The emphasis on decentralized participative processes had manifested through the Total Literacy Campaign (TLC) targeted at adults. In TLC the thrust is on grass root mobilization and an attempt to draw up the TLC strategies through capturing the aspirations and sentiments of the community and developing motivated persons who emerge as literacy activists voluntarily shouldering the responsibilities of developing and sustaining a literacy campaign. The effort is to create a sense of commitment to a cause that motivates people to participate volitionally in the Literacy movement. The whole TLC strategy is designed in a way that its multiple components aim at mobilising such volitional participation from the village level survey and contact with community, to training of workers; to development of literacy primers and evaluation. The ways in which this is attempted constitutes detailed subjects of study and analysis of how participative processes at the grass root levels shape and permeate an entire movement and how this is manifested in diverse ways such as the emergence of a large corps of volunteers, people's groups involved in determining the content of literacy primers and above all the transformation of conventionally hierarchical structural relationships and functional modalities into collective processes and democrative reciprocal interactions. It is this spirit that renders each literacy activity into an event of collective action and differentiates it from the routinised top down adult education centres. In fact, when successful, a TLC really becomes an occasion where the community participates to teach and to learn together. In M.P. currently about 5 lakh volunteer teachers have been mobilised at the grass root level teacher adult non literates; and energetic district academic groups have emerged developing local academic materials - peoples primers in a way.

Inevitably, the experience of such mass mobilization and the evidence of the possibilities immanent in such participative processes, creates a base supportive of more elaborate educational planning, fraught with an understanding of the implications that an effective TLC has for initiating other educational programs and processes, particularly the nuances of community participation. This is proving to be particularly pertinent for primary education planning. And a large scale complex programme like DPEP identifies a successful TLC as an important criteria for selecting a district for DPEP initiatives.

A large scale and complex programme for improving primary education, the major issues of DPEP are those that have over the years concerned educationists and planners - better facilities for better access, improved materials for teaching and learning; improved teacher training and effective class room transaction; institutional strengthening for better resource support academically and managerially. What differentiates DPEP from any other large scale Govt. sponsored primary education programme is its perspective and approach to these problems since DPEP like TLC perceives the strength of educational planning to be in the ability to generate meaningful participation of all those involved in the programme. Building on the experience, wherever possible of the experience of TLC, the basic project prerequisite of DPEP is to enlist the participation of those for whom the programme is meant.

Tapping Resources and Forging Synergies

Confronted with the task of initiating participative planning, sometime in July '94, the DPEP in M.P. has had to identify and tap all available relevant resources; forge synergies wherever possible and evolve creative solutions to initiate even the preliminary stages of participation of primary education.

- The first step was to analyse the immediate implications of participative planning in the context of primary education so that the amorphous issue of participation could be broken into identifiable groups, specific tasks and focussed strategies. For this purpose, a State planning group was setup comprising of government officials and educationists of academic resource institutions; NGOs' and teachers. This provided a consultancy forum to discuss and analyse the major issues of participation and develop appropriate strategies for reaching out to them.

The reference points of participation were understood as indicating primarily the participation of:

- Community, parents/guardians, of children who went to/did not go to school, local educated youth/local leaders/opinion makers, with special emphasis on disadvantaged groups, SC/ST, women.
- Teachers of primary schools.
- Key management personnel.

These were distinct and yet organically interrelated groups and so required strategies that were differential and also mutually well coordinated.

- The objective of enlisting the participation of these groups was defined as:
- Stimulating public debate on education
- Generating awareness about the need for schooling - as a prelude to starting a major school education programme.
- The strategies for stimulating participation were drawn up determined by a candid acknowledgement of **existing constraints** and analysis of possible strengths. The constraints were in the nature of:
- Inadequate time : 7 year DPEP project for M.P. had to be revised by end of November '94, to be ready for appraisal by the Appraisal Mission visiting India in Dec. '94. Also the stipulation was that the project revision should be through participative process. Since the implications of this were still being analysed in July '94 - a monsoon period causing logistical difficulties, the time available for this process was just about 3 months - to plan, orient, initiate the process and capture the feedback for project covering Madhya Pradesh - 19 large districts with about 28,000 villages. This seemed an impossible schedule.
- Interactions with the community particularly in backward rural areas tend to be open-ended, unstructured, informal where the best seen agendas can get disturbed by the free unprecedented reactions and demands of the community. Community participation is not really meaningful unless the people feel that what they say is being heeded seriously, that they have the freedom to exercise options and determine the nature of decisions concerning them. A project with preset parameters cannot really be discussed with the community because it rules out the exercise of several options. Its grooves are defined and genuine participation does not run on predetermined grooves. In fact the damp response to all initial effort at participative planning was the standard refrain of the field level educational functionaries "why ask the people" when we will give them what the project allows; not always what they really want.
- Lack of sufficiently trained and motivated manpower to initiate participative processes at different levels.
- Cynicism among the government personnel about the value and need for participative planning.

"Strength" Factors

Some of the strengths that could be identified where:

- The experience of TLC in most districts in some form or the other.
- The emergence of an effective and animated teacher motivation programme called the teachers empowerment programme or Shikshak Samakhya.
- Newly elected panchayats offering a host of non-officials from the local community, who could bridge together the government and the community.
- A political climate in favour of community mobilization, administrative decentralisation and empowerment of local bodies.
- A manifest commitment at the state level to social sector programs such as health, primary education and literacy.

The strategies for initiating participative process attempted to capture the positive emerges of the "strength" factors and either to turn around the constraints into advantages or else to deal with them in a tactful pragmatic way.

The time constraint was used to chalk out a clear and highly structured calendar of well defined activities. This also lent a sense of urgency to the exercise - that conveyed the important message that conveyed the important message that this was a carefully planned task that had to be completed on time. This proved useful in organising initially diffused resources into focussed time bound activities.

Design of Strategies

The essential design of the strategies adopted included:

i) Creating an appropriate environment

ii) Identifying responsible groups that would manage participation.

iii) Developing simple instruments of participative planning that could be easily understood at every level, and would not be distorted or diluted through a transmission process.

iv) Developing a cascade model for orienting identified groups in "initiating", and facilitating participation.

v) Developing mechanisms for feedback, capturing and organising data thrown up through participative interactions and sharing it at each level and transmitting it upwards.

vi) Formal involvement of local panchyat bodies so that the documented outcomes of participation are consciously deliberated and decisions taken through formal competent structures.

A beginning was made by turning the time constraint to advantage by initiating planning through a high profile mobilization campaign consciously structure to evoke an enthusiastic atmosphere surcharged with the sense of education as a "cause " and so to endow primary education with positive images at grass root levels. The idea was to arouse the people's minds from their apathetic and in fact quite often, negative attitude towards education.

To do this TLC strategies of evolving dramatic symbols that capture people's imagination and create a sense of mass movement were adopted. At the state level a high level function presided over by the Chief Minister of the state was organised in which children and teachers from the 19 DPEP districts participated. The messages of the function were: formal launching of the District Primary Education Programme, visible commitment of the highest political and administrative will in the programme and floating an imaginative mobilising symbol to arouse people's interest in education to make education a community issue. The Shiksha Jyoti or a symbolic torch of education was lit by the Chief Minister in a public function and 19 similar torches were lit and carried to each district by the district teams; then from there the torches travelled down to the block H.Q. and from there to the villages, at each level being welcomed with considerable enthusiasm in public ceremonies involving officials and non-officials. This event proved extremely successful in creating an exhilarated atmosphere for education so much so that in certain areas where the local administration had indeed been able to organise the whole event effectively, visually by using local cultural forms and by using reinforcing social messages with education such as health and environment and organising effective rallies and public functions the expectations of the people were roused to such a pitch that they were extremely critical of the DPEP inputs not being introduced directly. This was the experience for example in some districts like Betul and Bilaspur - both tribal, forested districts.

Strategy for Mobilising Primary School Teachers

While the "Shiksha Jyoti" strategy aimed at generating a general positive ambience for education, a more focussed and carefully structured strategy was used for mobilising primary school teachers. For this an innovative Teachers Empowerment Programme being implemented in selected districts of the state - by the State Council of Educational Research and Training (SCERT) with UNICEF assistance - described as Shikshak

Samakhay, was used. The power of Shikshak Samakhaya is it's motivational impact on teachers. Under this programme, one day teacher workshops in a camp mode are held; in which field level educational functionaries also participate. The workshop modalities are it's main strength, since they tend to be highly interactive, democratic and allow the teacher centre stage space. This facilitates problem solving sessions which are a necessary catharsis to attempting any serious orientation of the teachers. This is followed by an active demonstration of how to make teaching joyful and child centered and the classroom an attractive place. An interesting range of devices such as music, dance, pictures are used to transform teaching into an animated experience exciting the teachers. Using a few forms to catalyse activities, an effort is made to stimulate the teachers to create their own child friendly activity based pedagogies with the freedom to use their own language. In this participative workshop, the teachers rediscover their own creative instincts, and in that their childhood. In this lies the immediate motivational power of the Shikshak Samakhaya. Effectively organised, the programme has been able to motivate teachers in a big way. Analysing this, the Shikshak Samkhaya methodology was used as a way of addressing and mobilising the teachers' using the Shikshak Samakhaya Resource Persons, single day workshops were organised at Block head Quarters in each DPEP district, in a continuous series. This was done almost simultaneously with the Shiksha Jyoti Programme, so that the teachers were clearly addressed at the very outset of the programmed. In districts where the local administration timed the two events carefully, they had remarkable positive reciprocal influence on each other, creating bands of enthusiastic teachers joining hands with the community for the cause of EFA as in the districts of Rajgarh and Raigarh - the former a district with a literacy percentage of 31.81% below the state average and the later an interior tribal district.

'Precursor' Activities

These two mobilising strategies - use of popular emotive symbols and public function for environment building and teacher targeted motivational workshops covering 19 districts, 198 blocks and approximately 30,000 teachers in a space of a month and a half - from mid August to September end, constituted the two major precursor activities to starting participative planning at the grass root level. The consequences of these activities were:

- Making education a "live" public issue.
- Generating information about the DPEP programme.
- Throwing into relief active, interested persons from the

community and among teachers.

- Giving a leadership role to panchayat bodies by making education a subject for collective action.

Main Instrument of Participative Planning

The time taken for these precursor activities was also spent at the state level in developing instruments of participation and orienting key resource persons.

The main instruments of participative planning that were developed were:

At the Village Level

- An interactive questionnaire to be used at the village level by the local teacher to carry on a dialogue with the local community. Care was taken to maintain a conversational sequence; and a balance between direct educational queries and general systematic observations and to avoid leading questions.
- A format for organising, arranging, classifying and quantifying wherever possible the information thrown up and recorded in the questionnaire. This format also served as rudimentary village level education plan, since it was meant to be prepared in a collective forum of panchayat, teacher and VEC representatives and to document village educational needs and priorities.
- Simple instructions on how to use the questionnaires, and the format, how to organise community meetings and develop simple educational plans at the village panchayat level.

At the Block Level and at the District Levels

- Format for compiling and classifying information received from the lower level.
- Format for recording basic relevant block/district level data (educational and related); so that the perception of needs thrown up by community can be critically analysed.
- Suggestive lists of issues and subjects specific to education for discussions and decision - making.
- A simple framework for developing block and district level educational plans indicating status, needs, resources - available and required, an attempt to define the resource - source and to differentiate between financial and non financial resource

input to indicate priorities and to phase the required input.

- Instruction to the educational functionaries to convene meetings, facilitate discussions, record and document and to help develop plans.

Orienting Resource Persons

Resource persons were identified at different levels-state-district-block and oriented in one day orientation sessions. The resource teams consisted at the state level of management personnel and educationists and the district and block level of district administrative heads - district Collector, educational functionaries and teachers.

All necessary documents and a calender of activities were shared and finalised at these orientation sessions. The districts were given the freedom to modify and evolve new instruments, based on the principles of participation and keeping intact minimum essential information required.

Care was also taken to use a language that was familiar to the people in rural areas. While reference was made to the new DPEP programme, discussion was in no way confined to it; and the resource persons were oriented to encourage participants to discuss all that seemed relevant to them to improving education.

The resource persons were also cautioned against "forcing" participation since, there would be instances where the community would be totally averse to any discussions. In such cases efforts would have to be made but if nothing availed then reasons for participation failure should be understood, and no false accounts were to be rendered; and that there was no competition of "figures".

A clear emphasis was spelt out on eliciting participation of women, disadvantaged groups, parents whose children did not go to school.

Participative Meetings

The micro unit of participative planning was the village. Along with participative planning in most villages, the village education committees comprising of official and non-official persons also began to crystallise. A typical participative meeting in a village consisted of the panchayat representatives; community elders, parents, local leaders, and the local teacher who was responsible for convening, facilitating the meeting and for documenting its outcomes. Wide publicity was given to the meeting a day prior to it to ensure wide participation. The discussion outcomes after being recorded by the teacher were deliberated upon in a formal panchayat meeting and simple village education plans were drawn up. The teacher was responsible for submitting all the village level documents to the block education officer.

A similar process was invoked at the block level with the help of the block resource person; under the guidance of the block education officers and eventually at the district level with the help of the district education officer. At each level, the educational personnel with the help of the teachers who were responsible for organising theft received from the lower level and presenting it along with other relevant district data to a participative representative forum for discussion. The final block level education plan and the overall district education plan were drawn up with the active involvement of and the endorsement of the panchayat bodies at these levels. This was necessary because of a considerable devolution of administrative powers to the panchayats by the government.

The district plan that so evolved became the DPEP 7 year project for 'hat district. The whole exercise from resource persons orientation, micro level planning upto the district level took about 30 to 40 days depending on the size and resource capabilities of the district. Based on figures recorded at the village level meetings, a quantitative profile of village level participation is presented in Appendix 1.

Achievements

What this entire process, wherever successfully carried out, achieved was:

- Intense awareness about educational issues.
- Involvement of local community, specially local bodies in local educational planning - to creating a sense of ownership of the plans.
- Provide a realistic basis for formulation plans.
- Highlight people's perceptions about a number of issues such as school - timings, holiday - calendar, educational curriculum, providing thereby important and relevant social data for consideration and decision making including policy formulation. For example, the demand for local determination of school timings and holidays subject to a minimum number of school days has prompted the government to consider decentralising these powers to the district level. Similarly the response to school as a dull unattractive place where no teaching took place has prompted the state government's decision to focus consciously on pedagogue reform; and to experiment with academic decentralisation at the regional level by developing locally relevant teaching/learning materials; using the opportunities offered under DPEP for text book reform.
- By involving the local self-government bodies compel a

"holistic" view of local educational arrangements. The people were discussing not just DPEP, but in fact assessing their own constraints and strengths, and so attempting to plan for alternative resource mobilization in areas where DPEP funds were not forthcoming or else insufficient. Thus alternative government programme funds were committed to a number of needy areas where DPEP funds were not sufficient to meet the requirement such as for school building and repairs. This district perspective on education rather than a programme groove was possible as a result of multilevel interactive discussion involving people from a wide cross section of community, government and local bodies.

The entire process of participative planning had been monitored at the state level through diverse formal and informal means. The formal monitoring measures were built into the planning exercise - such as periodical progress report and feedback sessions at the district and state level. Informal information channels included discussions with volunteer activists; panchayat representatives and spot visits.

Effective Participative Planning

Factors critical to effective participative planning were:

- Motivated teachers and educational functionaries
- Active leadership of panchayat representatives.
- Commitment of the district administration reflected in the sensitivity and interest of the district Collectors.
- Efficient management and scrupulous attention to detail and time and vigilant field monitoring at the district level.
- Effective mobilization process under TLC.

Wherever this process was weak and "participation" had not been possible, the reason really had been either inefficient management or lack of motivation or insufficient empathy among the administrative personnel/teachers with the entire philosophy of participation - handicaps that may have been overcome with repetitive cycles of orientation, had more time been available.

Implications of Participative Planning

The implications that emerged of such a process of participative planning were:

- Participation could not be a one time, pre-project exercise.

It was a continuous process that needed to be strengthened. A participative process was essentially dynamic, hoping to move from an initial consultation process to a spontaneous and empowered participation. This required:

- Developing local participative structures and developing adequate powers and responsibilities in them. In M.P. this had been possible through panchayat bodies and VEC.
- Constant sensitization and training of such structures:
- Conscious remaking of conventional relationship between "government" structures, and orienting government functionaries to their new roles.

Facts ...

DPEP - District Primary Education programme, being implemented in M.P. with assistance from European Community channelised through the central Govt. is a 7 year primary education project (1994-2001) covering 19 districts with low literacy rates aiming at improving access, retention and achievement. The project is based on district level planning and community participation.

TLC - Total Literacy Campaign, a centrally sponsored scheme for imparting functional literacy to non literates in the age group of 15-35 in time bound campaign mode lasting about 12-18 months. The programme is managed by autonomous registered district literacy societies and mobilises volunteers on a large scale to manage the programme and teach non literates. The volunteer teachers, in the ratio of 1:10 (teacher : pupil) receive no remuneration and represent voluntary community participation in the highest form. In M.P. all the 45 districts have TLCs.

In M.P. the Annual Work Plans for DPEP are also being developed through participative micro planning, which also permits opportunities to the people to review and rethink their priorities and options in view of the experience gained through the implementation of the programme. This review opportunity is also an essential aspect of an evolving participative process, showing it's sensitivity to people's needs and choices.

- As far as possible, prompt response by decision makers in addressing the genuine problems thrown up through such processes of local collective self reflection was essential to sustain the seriousness and relevance of participative planning and not to stultify it into decorative gesture. This was vehemently expressed by all participants at all levels.

- Participation cannot be confined to just a formal consultation but will have to be carried through to its full incremental implications. In M.P., under DPEP, the logic of participation has been carried forward to include management and implementation - beginning with community construction of 1300 school buildings and 198 teacher training centres through local community groups involving teachers; and panchayat representatives responsible for managing resources and taking all relevant decisions about constructions. Similarly in managing diverse programme components like alternative school systems, early childhood care and education centres, the VEC and the panchayats have been given a central role.

The implications of participative planning are being analysed for pedagogue reform under M.P. DPEP. Selective areas have been identified for developing local specific teaching learning materials on an experimental basis. And this exercise has begun with community discussions at the village levels with the initiatives of NGO's and academicians. This is a major academic venture in terms of academic decentralisation and significant because it begins with grass root community participation.

M.P. has taken a step in the direction of initiating and understanding participative processes at multiple levels of educational reform. DPEP comes as a major opportunity to evolve meaningful interventions responsive to people's articulation of their needs and based on the insights yielded through this continuous and complex process of peoples participation in improving the quality of education for their children.

Appendix - I

DPEP Participatory Planning

District	Persons Participation		
	Male	Female	Total
Betul	143695	18849	162544
Raisen	3367	700	4067
Rajgarh	135395	31910	167305
Sehore	81550	1500	83050
Bilaspur	12927	2100	15027
Raigarh	186634	41990	228624
Sarguja	116457	16100	124557

(Contd.)

Appendix - I *(Contd.)*

Guna	108457	16100	124557
Dhar	55022	8341	63363
Rajnand Gaon	86843	2827	89670
Rewa	191207	22902	214109
Satna	206476	22587	229063
Sahdol	199827	43034	424861
Sidhi	130113	29649	159762
Chhatarpur	82502	6492	88994
Panna	42701	4936	47637
Teekam garh	93206	18943	112149
Mandsaur	24666	6594	31269
Ratlam	98305	5304	103609

Source: DPEP Calling, July 1995.

36

Community Participation in Civil Works: A Reality in Haryana

S.C. Girotra
Executive Engineer
HPSPP, Chandigarh

Civil Works are generally executed either through Contractor/ Contracting Agencies or by employing departmental labour and purchasing departmental material.

While planning DPEP Works, concept of community participation was introduced. This was a new concept particularly in construction of Civil Works in Haryana.

At the first instance it was thought that execution of Civil Works through community participation may create serious problems of quality control and financial control. However, in the month of September, 1995 a beginning was made in Haryana and drive for forming Village Construction Committees was launched. The idea was to have a compact and suitable team for execution of simpler and small works by involving local people.

Formation of Village Construction Committees

District Primary Education programme is primarily meant for improvement of status of females, whether in education or social status. With this idea in mind the Village Construction Committees were formed with the constituents as under:-

1. Pardhan : Woman member from Village Education Committees.
2. Member Secretary : Head Teacher of the Primary School, who is also Secretary of Village Education Committee.
3. Active Members : 3 Nos
   - (a) Member of the Village Education Committee who is retired Govt Servant or Ex-Service or a social worker.
   - (b) A Member of Village Education Committee who is from Scheduled Caste.

(c) Any other Member of Village Education Committee or a member/personnominated by Village Education Committee.

Workshop / Training

Number of Workshops were held at District level and block level and these Workshops were addressed by State Project Director, Executive Engineer and District Project Coordinators.

In fact all BRCs, CRCs and School Teachers and members of the Village Construction Committees were called to participate in programme of construction of Civil Works. A comprehensive scheme i.e. Workshops in all the 28 blocks of Kaithal, Jind, Hisar districts was launched on 8th December where all members of the Village Construction Committees, all primary school teachers, Cluster Resource Coordinators and Block resource Coordinators participated. The Workshops at Block level were addressed amongst others by a Senior Member of either HPSPP or DPIUs. The Workshop at Pundri was inaugurated by Honorable Education Minister, the Workshop at Tohana (Hisar) was addressed by State Project Director and the Workshop at Bhuna (Hisar) was conducted by Executive Engineer HPSPP and so on.

Production of simple literature in Hindi

Many doubts were raised by members of the Village Construction Committees, Cluster Resource Centres and Head Teachers regarding the role of VCC in execution of Civil Works. In fact there was a lot of enthusiasm in the members of the Village Construction Committees to participate in the drive. After intensive consultation and interaction with VCCs, Head Teachers and CRCs etc, it was decided/transpired that there should be some comprehensive simple literature available with the members which should indicate the following :-

(a) The role and constitution of VCCs.

(b) Simple Drawings.

(c) Quantity of material required for each component.

(d) Simple details about construction.

(e) Simple details regarding maintenance of accounts.

The components of Civil Works which were thought to be executed by VCCs were:

1. Construction of Toilets.
2. Installation of Hand pumps.
3. Repair to School Buildings.
4. Construction of Boundary walls.

Keeping the above in mind, efforts was made probably for first time in Haryana and a booklet called 'Gramin Nirman Smiti' was prepared in Hindi giving the constitution of Village Construction Committees, the works to be constructed by Village Construction Committees, responsibilities and roles of VCCs and material required for each component. In addition to above simple form of drawing were prepared and attached in the booklet. It also indicated some important facts to be remembered while execution of Civil Works. These facts and details were not only applicable for construction of Civil works through VCCs but could help the Villagers in day to day construction of their own houses and other construction in the village.

Capacity Building

To help the VCCs a team of Technical Resources Persons (TRPs) who were either retired Junior Engineer, Head Draftsman or qualified Junior Engineer (Diploma holders) having four to five years experience and residing preferably in the same block were, recruited.

The main aim of these Technical Resource Persons was to impart technical guidance and not to act as Supervisors/ Inspectors. These TRPs were trained by Sub - Divisional Engineers and by the Executive Engineer. They will visit at least 2 to 3 VCC per day, they will tour the countryside 15 days in a month and will spend five days in the DPEP office to report their progress to the Sub - Divisional Engineers and DPCs. They were employed @ 150/- per day for 20 days in a month. This process helped lot in imparting technical guidance to the Village Construction Committees and Head Teachers.

Final Assault

A specially designed format called MOU for VCCs by Ed. CIL, which had the approval of World Bank was supplied to all District Project Coordinators. The money for construction was distributed to VCCs through Bank Drafts in stages.

In all, Rs. 159.13 Lacs were distributed to VCCs during the period.

Third Joint Supervision Mission visited Haryana between 24th June 28th June, 1996. The Mission applauded the role of Village Construction Committees by saying that small works implemented by communities arc progressing well and at an acceptable level of quality. At the same time Mission encountered several examples of good construction especially where the community had been actively involved in the process. Encouraged by the progress and quality involved in the process. Encouraged by the progress and quality it has been decided that in addition to smaller works mentioned above, the construction of additional one classroom should also be entrusted to VCCs. Recently, the construction of additional classroom has been started by Village

Construction Committees in all the four districts in addition to other components mentioned above.

Table 1 The magnitude of Civil Works in as under:

Name of Component	*Completed*	*In Progress*
Toilets	1137	338
Hand Pumps	395	56
Boundary Walls	-	53
Repair of Primary Schools	198	

Conclusion

It is felt that if confidence is imposed, and community is inspired, it can create wonders and can execute works by inculcating sense of involvement.

1. The Village Construction Committees were given free hand in purchasing the required material from open market.
2. Mahila Village Pradhan advocated everywhere that they will not allow pilferage of material at any stage and will see that work is executed as best as possible.
3. Some of the VCCs even contributed from their own resources where the Government money fall short of the Project cost. This was particularly so in case of providing drinking water facilities and toilets.

Source: DPEP Calling, December 1996.

37

Implementing Dream Designs for School Buildings in Kerala

Meant to assure the child into the threshold of knowledge, primary school buildings are intended to lure the child to the folds of education and give him his first exposure to life and the world. Sadly, it all remains a dream; or a nightmare! It is noticed that at least 50% of children joining the primary classes at the age of four develop a deep rooted aversion to education and are reluctant to go to school. Such is the effect schools have on the average Indian child. Why this child reluctance to go to school? What intimidates him? What makes his experience so frightening? Does the teacher, the text book or the classroom itself frightens him? Social experts feel that it is the heavy work load faced by the young ones that blunts the child's desire to go to school. But it is unfortunate to note that the whole educational system itself is the culprit.

DPEP Kerala, recognising this urgent need to re-vitalise the entire fabric of our education has started restructuring the curriculum in schools. Teachers' training goes along with this. But sometimes a 'small part' could ruin the 'whole' system moving towards perfection. This happens when we neglect the fact that the design of the school building or the class room has a bearing on what is being taught in the class.

The concrete monstrosities that stand today for schools help promote only a rigid, inflexible kind of education. This has to be changed if the classrooms are to be activity oriented, and child-friendly. It was in this context that DPEP organised workshop on Possible Design Guidelines for Child-friendly Classrooms. The workshop conducted in association with the Indian Institute of Architects, Trivandrum chapter on 5th November, 1996, at Mascot Hotel, Trivandrum was aimed at exploring (1) modern trends in the design of classrooms (2) the cost-effective methods in construction (3) the principles of traditional architecture. Sri K. Jayakumar, Secretary General Education, Government of Kerala in his inaugural address emphasised the need " to change the whole philosophy of approach and attitude of education". He stressed the fact that you cannot have a new kind of education in the old style of classrooms. After his speech ten teachers selected from different parts of the state gave their views and suggestions as to what they thought is required in a classroom. Teachers know best and their suggestions were:

- Designers should keep in mind an activity based classroom with sufficient space for storing teaching-learning materials.
- The room should be sufficiently ventilated and light weight furniture (which can be handled by children) should be used.
- Classrooms should be separated so that disturbance from adjoining classes will not be affected.
- Electricity and potable water should be made available.
- The whole design should be eco-friendly.
- Staff room should be airy, sufficiently spaced and should contain material for academic interaction.
- Separate kitchen has to be provided.
- Space for wall hangings, bulletin boards etc. should be provided.
- Children's park as well as open air auditorium are desired.
- Asbestos should be avoided.
- Classroom should be round (circular) or hexagonal in shape.
- It would be good if some space is provided for children to do experiments.
- The position of the teacher is very important. He should be accessible to front seaters as well as back seaters
- Urinals should be near the classrooms.
- Since parents come to school, a separate area for them to interact with the teachers is welcome.
- The children should have reading corner in the class.
- A writing space for children should be provided in the class.
- Emphasis should be made on hygiene and cleanliness of the students.
- Since some activities have to be done outside the classroom, provision should be made for that too.

It was in this background that the resource persons listed below spoke in the workshop on various aspects required for child-friendly, eco-friendly class room.

Mr. Roger Bonner : First Secretary (Infrastructure), British Council Division.

Laurie Baker : Noted Architect

Dr. A. Achuthan : Former Vice-Chancellor, Cochin University and Executive Director, Vasthuvidya Prathishtan, Calicut.

Mr. Balagopal T.S. Prabhu : Head of Department, Civil, REC, Calicut.

N. Mahesh : Architect, Trivandrum

T.M. Cyriac : Engineering College, Trivandrum

Mr. Roger Bonner, First Secretary British Council, spoke on Modern Concepts in School Building Construction, Mr. Laurie Baker on Environment and Cost-effective interventions and Dr. AA. Achuthan and Mr. Balagopal, T.S. Prabhu on Principles from Traditional Architecture relevant to classroom design. Mahesh and T.N. Cyriac gave additional papers in the workshop. The experts identified six major things that are essential or in a classroom. They are:

1. Abundant natural light
2. `Proper ventilation
3. Space for circulation
4. Display facilities
5. Storage facilities
6. Instruction board/Chalk board

A brief sketch of the experts vision of an ideal classroom:

A single class room that extends to a verandah and on to an outdoor garden facilitating free movement for the children from the completely closed to the completely open space. A single wall of the classroom having two windows to allow natural light and nature to come in. 'Jalees' all around the bottom wall upto 2 ft. to provide ventilation or 'EARS' at the top of the roofs as in Kerala Traditional Architecture which also allows free passage of air. Pin-up boards to display children's work which is the greatest thing to persuade them to work. Little cupboards, pigeon-holes or boxes around the room to keep both playing and teaching materials safely licked up at night and easily swung open in the morning. Another idea is to improvise old tin trunks and build into wall as cupboards. They are ant-proof, rat proof and even child-proof, if locked up. Chalk boards or black boards below the window for access to children as well as teachers. The room painted in red or green also helps to attract the child into the classroom. All these are not be enclosed in huge compound walls but hedged in by fruit bearing trees, flowering trees and medicinal herbs making the school interesting to look at and interesting to sit in.

Following the presentations of the experts, the participants of the workshop divided into three groups and discussed design guidelines for child-friendly class rooms incorporating modern trends and principles of traditional architecture. The group discussions centered around the idea that teaching and learning trends have undergone a massive change and therefore designs for classrooms should cater to these informal trends. The recommendations that evolved out of these discussions are given below in detail:

1. No wet lands/reclaimed lands should be selected as portable sites.
2. Deep cutting/fitting to be avoided as far as possible.
3. Trees more than 5 years old should not be cut to accommodate the building.
4. Discourage the use of compound walls. Instead hedgings should be resorted to.
5. The location should not abound busy bus routes, railway lines etc. yet it should not be more than 500m away from the bus routes and 1.5 Km. from the community.
6. The minimum width of the access road should not be less than 5.0 meter.
7. Minimum area should be 1.0 Acre for LP school.
8. The plot should have access to potable water and other service facilities.
9. Aspect ratio of the plot (Width: Length) should not be less than 1:3.
10. The total design concept is to conform to the land profile. Single storeyed buildings are preferred for primary school buildings.
11. Efforts should be made to prepare a master plan to include future expansion possibilities before the commencement.
12. Local peoples' participation and representation both in the design and execution process should be ensured.
13. Use of locally available materials which are cost efficient and durable should be encouraged.
14. Large openings should be provided for each class room to ensure maximum natural lightings and ventilation. Perforated walls could be one of the solutions. At least 20% of the floor area should be reserved for window.

15. Hard wood should not be used for joineries. Instead promote the use of wood substitute like MDF or treated wood like rubber etc.
16. Cost efficient roofing systems incorporating clear storeys area to be adopted. Tiled roof over concrete trusses is a preferred model.
17. The class room should be so designed as to cater to the new informal trends of teaching and learning. For instance, the design of activity areas needs critical attention. Form should follow function. The design should incorporate the possibilities of closer group interaction.
18. The class room should have enough storage spaces. The craft materials and products as well as charts and other teaching materials are to be stored inside each class room.
19. The storage space should be as secure as possible.
20. The spaces around the children including the class room should be visually stimulating to the children. The rigid rectangular boxes should be avoided as far as possible.
21. The colours for walls, doors etc. should be selected in such a way as to cater to the stimulant needs. As per Vastu principles red represents energy and green, intellectual activities.
22. The design of the buildings should follow the dictates of the micro climate of the area. This should reflect not only in the design but also in the selection of technology and materials for the school building.
23. Spaces should be reserved for parents to come and interact with the children and their teachers.
24. Teachers should have enough quiet areas to enable them to prepare their lessons and teaching materials.
25. The use of light weight and movable furniture should be encouraged. It should cater to the new trends in informal education. Also ensure that walls can be one of the solutions.
26. Each class room must lead to semi open spaces which in turn should lead to open spaces. This relationship is to be maintained for all class room.
27. Area per student should not be less than 0.7m2/pupil plus 10% for storage etc.

28. Windows/openings should be so designed as to ensure maximum comfort for the child like lowering of sill height etc.
29. As per Vastu principles, the teacher should face west/south during the lecture session.
30. The recommended forms as per Vastu principles for a class room are octagon, circle or a square. But the roofs can be in any shape/form.
31. Open to sky urinals and wash spouts are recommended for dwarf walls. The toilets should be easily accessible from the class room. The finishes should be so specified to ensure proper maintenance. As per Vastu traditions, urinals should not be in NE.
32. Hard and scape components like garden seats/benches, pavements etc. can be introduced in the open spaces.
33. Provision for mini amphitheatres for outdoor teaching can be thought of.
34. Also the provision for pet animal enclaves and small botanical gardens to initiate the child into a world of flora and fauna can be thought of.
35. Enough spaces should be reserved for flower gardens.
36. Plant as many flowering and fruit bearing trees in the site. Fast growing varieties like wild cherry, medicinal plants like Thulasi, Neem etc. can be some of the potential choices.
37. Energy efficient systems like solar panels etc. are to be introduced for lighting/cooking etc.
38. Use of high energy materials like cement and steel should be minimised to the limits possible.
39. Use of asbestos cement room to be banned for health reasons.
40. Use of systems like bio-gas cooking system should be encouraged.
41. Cost effective construction techniques in walling roofing, finishes etc. are to be introduced into the construction phase after ensuring the structural safety.

In the light of the above discussions DPEP Kerala ahead initiated steps to follow the above guidelines in the design and construction of 200 school buildings and 800 additional classroom. It is also proposed to hold a competition to get new cost effective designs from architects and novel ideas from the public which includes school children. It is hoped that children would be 'WANTING' to go to school on a regular basis and would be happier, more attentive and also retain much more of what the teacher is talking about in these new surroundings. The teacher too will do better job if he/she has this comfortable, interesting surroundings to work in.

Source: DPEP Calling, December 1996.

38

The Maharashtra Experience

The DPEP (District Primary Education Programme) experience of Maharashtra in 5 districts of the State has been visions and visionaries. There have been fortresses that have been conquered.

One of the objectives of the DPEP programme was to bring a new outlook in achieving the objective of universalisation of Primary Education.

In the 5 DPEP districts 100% enrolment has been achieved in 1996-97 from a rate of 92% enrolement in 1994-95. This has been possible through various innovative steps which were taken up in addition to the normal programmes. Enrolment drive was organised in each district from May to September, 1996. This enrolment drive includes programmes like Letter of Appeal, Slogans, Akshar Yatra, Cultural Activities, Display of Stickers etc.

Enrolment Drive

1. A letter of appeal

In Aurangabad district, Education Officer and Dy. Project Officer, DPEP appealed to teachers to utilise their summer vacation time; in reaching every family in the district. Propaganda material and banners were prepared by teachers in their vacation time. Teachers conducted padayatra in their village announcing the importance of education. Similar practice was adopted in other districts too.

2. Adoption

The educationally backward villages where VEC were not adequately activated in the progress of the school were adopted by educational organisations for continual support and monitoring. In Aurangabad, 50 such educationally backward villages were adopted by educational organisations during 1996-97. Some clusters were also adopted by district and block administration officers.

3. Rani Lakshmibai Brigada

This was a brigade of educated women in the villages of district Parbhani. Their interest in providing leadership in different welfare activities in the village was fully used by motivating them to fight against illiteracy among girls. All these educated women were mobilised, groups were formed and they were entrusted with the responsibility of monitoring enrolment and regular attendance of the girl child.

Community Mobilisation

1. Participatory rural appraisal (PRA)

Participatory rural appraisal was conducted in Aurangabad district especially in the remote village of Jangaltanda. This innovative PRA exercise helped in developing better understanding in the villagers about their participation in the schooling of their wards.

2. Village Education Committees

For effective supervision of day to day work of the primary schools the Village Education Committees with at least 50% women members have been set up in these districts. The committee is expected to supervise the following:

A) Regular attendance of teachers in the school.

B) Improvement of educational environment in the school.

C) The village community has an important role to play in providing local help in cash or kind for improvement of physical facilities like water tank, tedadpatris (mats) etc. in the school.

3. Grants to VECL

To ensure active involvement of VEC's in DPEP it was made mandatory for the VECs to raise local contribution of Rs. 500/ Rs. 2000/- under DPEP for school infrastructural development.

All the VECs have raised their local contribution and have been disbursed the infrastructural grants. From this grant, the schools in the project have undertaken painting of walls, making display charts, pictures, block boards, games, equipment, furnitures, stores facility and other physical facilities.

4. Training to VEC Members

A detailed schedule of orientation to the VEC members is being organised to cover them effectively. An effective model is being designed for this purpose.

Special training programme for the women members of VECs has also been organised in 95-96.

A folder and handbook has been published and distributed to BECs members to orient them regarding DPEP activities.

5. Training and Orientation of GP and VEC Members in Construction Activities

A 2 day orientation cum training workshop was held for the GP and VEC members to orient and involve them in the evolving construction design and implementing the toilet construction activities.

Focus on the Children

1. Free Text Books

MPSP has provided free text books to all the girls studying from standard 1st to 4th as a special intervention for the girl child.

From 1996-97 this activity has been taken up through the regular state funds in nearly all the books of the DPEP districts. Only the remaining blocks which are not covered through the regular Primary Education Programme are now covered through DPEP funds.

2. Rani Lakshmibai Brigade

As special intervention for the girl child Laxmibai Brigade were organised in Parbhai 11 years attend the school regularly.

3. Mahila Probodhan Prakalp

The Mahila Probhodan Prakalp Programme MPP of MPSP is proposing and formulating special strategy for ensuring 100% enrolment and retention of the girl child.

MPSP has recruited 320 field level Mahila Shyoginis (women field workers) to ensure universalisation of primary education for the girl child.

A) The main objectives of MPP are: (I) Bring all girl children in the education system either formal or non-formal in DPEP district. (II) Organise Programme to retain girl children in the school system upto Std. 8th (III) Design and implement innovative schemes to ensure regular attendance of the girl children in the school (IV) Emphasise role and importance of girl child for equality.

B) The objectives of the project with regards to field officers and works are as follows: (I) Prepare training material for administrators, trainers to ensure universal enrolment and retention of girls in school. (II) Undertake environment building campaign to emphasize gender equality upto grass root level through community participation. (III) Disseminate information on different schemes and scholarships for women and girls education. (IV) prepare training material for training in cleanliness, hygiene, social cleanliness and nutrition for parents, specially mother parents.

C) For effective implementation of MPP the State has constituted an MPP Core Group which meets regularly and advises MPSP on different aspects under the project.

D) Survey : A survey of children (boys and girls) in the age group of 6 to 14 years was conducted in DPEP districts to understand the nature of difficulties and problems faced in bringing the girl child in the main stream education system. This survey was conducted in October, 1994.

E) A second survey was undertaken during 1996 to find out aspects in which the girl child is differentiated in the school environment. A questionnaire was circulated. A questionnaire was circulated and information was collected with the help of District Mahila Sanchalikas from 100 schools. On the basis of this a 10 points action plan was developed to bring in gender equality in schools.

F) Environment Building : For environment building activities like the orientation workshops, Mahila Melawe and Kishori Melava, gatherings, collaboration of special days have been taken on a large scale under this programme. International Women's Day 8th March, 8th September : Literacy Day, Palak Shikshan Din -3rd January - Savitribai Phule Balika - Din have found special significance under the programme.

G) Production of Learning Material: Under MPP special efforts were made to dismount information on government schemes, new developments regarding women and girls education at all levels. It was therefore, necessary to produce learning material for field workers and facilitators, MPP posters, charts, folders small booklets,wall charts, planners were developed and distributed.

H) Training and Workshops : Series of training programmes and workshops were organised under MPP during 1995-96 and 1996-97 (12 workshops) for preparation of the above learning material.

I) MPP Centres : Every MPP centre organises special programmes for women's empowerment and education of the girl child. In the 325 centres in the 5 districts, women are invited once in a week regularly. They are oriented on different subjects like nutrition, hygiene, environment, law, facilities for education of the girl child, government schemes, economic savings, etc. At every centre a group of 15-20 women attend these gatherings regularly. Subject experts speak on various subjects. A lot of exposure is given through such regular interaction.

As a result of all this in 1996 DPEP districts have attained 100% enrolment. Pre-school education activities and ECE activities are also monitored through the Mahila Sanchalikas.

Alternative Schooling

4 types of alternative schooling have been provided in the DPEP districts:

1. NFE centres for the working children / children involved in agriculture or other wage earning activities.
2. Sugar schools for the children of migrant labourers who work seasonally in sugarcane factories.
3. Contract schools for children for non-accessible or remote areas.
4. Summer schools for migrant labourers in the rural areas.

In 1995-97, 832 NFR centres and 17 contract schools have been started in the DPEP districts. 20 summer schools have been planned from December, 1996 to May, 1997 in district Parbhani. These schools will run for a duration of 2 months. The instructor will be a local teacher working on an honorarium basis of Rs. 150/- per month + a contingency of Rs. 300/-.

5. A detailed syllabus and curriculum has been developed of the NFE centres and the ECE programme. The curriculum defines the competencies to be covered the duration in which to be covered, and the methodology for covering the same.

Teacher Motivation and Capacity Building

1. Tejaswini Award

In Nanded district, this award is given to the most outstanding lady primary teacher. Her work is evaluated on the basis of the enrolment achieved by her in the primary school. The felicitation ceremony takes place once a year and a silver medal is presented to the teachers.

2. Dnyanratna Puraskar

This award is given to talented and devoted teachers who render their services for the cause of philosophy. Teachers with outstanding performance are awarded this award. This award is given at two levels; a candidate who is ranked first at BRC level is awarded "Gyanbhushan" award. These Gyanbhushan awardee teachers again appear for district level exam and the teacher ranking first at the district level is awarded "Gyanratna Puraskar". She is felicitated with a gold medal, a certificate, and a shreephal.

Besides the concept and content competency, the teacher is also encouraged to develop his/her talent in sports and cultural activities.

Every year sports and cultural activities are arranged for primary teachers and the successful candidates are awarded shields. Like teachers, the best cluster head i.e. the best cluster co-ordinator is also awarded on the basis of the cluster performance in enrolment, retention and quality education.

3. Competition

Teaching competitions are held every year for primary teachers in Nanded district. Teachers present their demonstration lessons and the best demonstration is awarded. This competition has a strong bearing on the capacity building. Teachers are encouraged to develop their teaching skills through such efforts.

Innovations

1. Alternative designs and cost effective construction technology

A. MPSP through its design team and a Wardha based NGO (Centre of Science for Villages) has evolved cost effective, environment friendly technology based on local material for construction of BRCs and school rooms. All the 34 BRCs and a few demonstration schools will be constructed using this technology.

B. MPSP through its design team has also worked out an alternative design and technology for the schools and the BRCs.

C. MPSP conducted a 2 days training programme for the members of the Gram Panchayat, the VEC members and the masons in all the 5 districts to train them on the technique of constructing cost effective and hygienic toilets with low water requirements. The workshops were conducted in the 1st week with help of Centre of Science for Villagers, an NGO in Wardha well versed with the technology. The innovative technology has allowed MPSP to provide for additional items within the same costs.

2. Interactive selection process to recruit Sahyoginis(Women field workers)

A. The Mahila Sahayoginis will supervise regular attendance of every girl child through mobilisation of women in the village. She would constantly interact with members of the VEC Grampanchayat Mahila Mandal to follow up the probable dropout of the girl child. The selection of Mahila Sahayoginis is done in a very careful manner through a 2-day participatory selection workshop.

B. Innovation in selection of Mahila Sahayoginis:

At the state level, the MPP Cell interacted with district Mahila Sanchalika and Taluka Sanchalika and evolved areas of general intervention at the village level and identified role of Sahayoginis (Woman Activists).

After carefully examining crucial roles, evolved a recruitment module with the help of Mahila Arthik Vikas Mahamandal, Mumbai was evolved.

A 3 days training programme was organised at Aurangabad between 6th September to 8th September, 1996 for Mahila and Taluka Sanchalikas, Project Officers and Dy. Project Officer from 5 DPEP districts.

These participants were expected to quality analysis of leadership cooperation, mental stamina, attitude towards social problems, awareness and level of conscientisation. In order to ascertain quality selection, each team of the district was assigned the responsibility of selecting Sahayoginis in the adjacent district. 320 Sahayoginis were selected through this process.

3. Special intervention with regard to media campaign:

A. Video Cassette: At the state level, MPSP, Mumbai has prepared a 161/2 minutes video cassette high lighting the DPEP interventions in the districts. This cassette was immensely appreciated by the wife of the President of the World Bank during her visit to MPSP in October, 1996.

B. Folder : MPSP has prepared a folder on MPP programme and a 10 point action programme for gender.

C. Display of Gender Charts in the ST buses: MPSP, Mumbai has given contract to the State Transport Corporation to display messages about gender equality and promotion of education of the girl child.

D. News Bulletin : Every district issues a news bulletin (Vidyawarta) for interaction with teachers in the district. This bulletin is circulated to all the teachers and their innovative ideas, experiments, success stories are widely encouraged.

Research and Evaluation Strategy

A Workshop was held at the State and the District levels to formulate Monitoring, Research and Evaluation (R & E) strategy for the DPEP programme. The workshop was coordinated with the assistance of experts in the field of R & E including Dr. Denzil Saldanha from TISS, Mrs. Vijay Chavan, UNICEF representative and Smt. Padmaja Bhang from Chetna Vikas. The participants were drawn from all the 5 districts of DPEP-1, in which they expressed their expectations and concerns regarding the evaluation. Thematic areas were also identified. There after, a consensus was reached on the thematic priority areas and finally a strategy was prepared on how to operationalise evaluation in the identified thematic areas.

Strategy paper was thereafter evolved which is being further detailed for actual operationalisation at the School level.

Monitoring Strategy

As a first step of evolving monitoring strategy, the SPD felt it necessary to activise and orient CPS Coordinators on community involvement and pedagogical aspects of teachers training and Classroom Transactions. For this purpose a 2-day workshop was conducted with the help of Mr. Subir Shukla, Ed.CIL. The participants were drawn from BRCs and the District education machinery including CPS Coordinators. The objective of the workshop was to train master Trainers in conducting similar programmes to orient and enhance the capacities of the CPS Coordinators in their respective districts.

The workshop was an eye-opener for all the participants. The inputs given by Mr. Subir Shukla revealed to the participants how teaching can be made interesting and how training methodologies can be developed to ensure internalisation of the training in the participants. All the participants in the workshop were made to apply their mind in each and every session so that all the participants were actively involved in all the sessions. This was a unique feature of the workshop since it gives a window on how similar processes if repeated in the classrooms can ensure the involvement of all the children in the classrooms can ensure the involvement of all the children in the classroom teaching. DPEP in the State is picking up momentum with each passing day and as the programme mount, so also the agonies and the ecstasies.

Source: DPEP Calling, December 1996.

39

The Year that Was

R.S. Pandey
Joint Secretary and Bureau Head
DPEP, Department of Education
Government of India

Are we doing right? The introspective question impulsively reverberates within as the year passes by.

To bring about educational change, pedagogical renewal and transformation of the milieu that impact educational achievements and outcomes would be tall order by all standards. But it would take nothing less to help realise the cherished vision of universal primary education. Despite stray proverbial silver linings dotting the horizon, the primary education system - the second largest in the world - is shrouded in dark uninspiring clouds prompting many to call it insipid, moribund wasteful. The task of turning the primary schools, which, thanks to enormous improvements in infrastructural expansions, now cover 94 per cent of the habitations, into lively, vibrant, joyful, institutions is challenge - colossal and daunting.

DPEP, during its incessant course of meeting the challenges, completed its second year towards 1996 end with a sense of accomplishment and fulfilment. It has been a year of consolidation, a year of substantial expansion, a year of realisation of significant milestones, a year of accolades and encomiums which, I pray, does not go to our head. A year which flew by with amazing speed, has been full of activities and events at the national level and in all the project states. All Central Government Departments have lent a willing and helping hand. The Planning Commission has described the programme as one which "needs to be supported fully". The Expenditure Finance Committee headed by the Department of Expenditure has approved the project proposals without demur. Two significant agreement have been signed with IDA and ODA of U.K. providing for financial support for expansion of the programme. The programme has expended by nearly 200 per cent during the year gone by and is now set to cover 121 districts in 13 States as against 42 in seven states when it began. Process of introducing the programme in 27 revenue districts of Bihar has also begun with the IDA Identification Mission having visited the State during the year. The States concerned have mustered sufficient enthusiasm and energy to provide vibrancy to programme planning and implementation. The pedagogical renewal processes which are crucial for all aspects of educational reform continued intensively. The new pedagogic infrastructures envisaged under DPEP, namely the Cluster Resource Centres (CRC) and Block Resource Centers (BRC) have been largely completed in all project districts. Visioning exercises at all levels and teacher training activities which have a strong component of motivation and competence have been intensified. Textbook and other teaching learning materials have been completed up to class 2. The International Research Seminar organised in the middle of 1996 focussed attention on class-room innovative practices. The process of strengthening of National Resource Group and its replicas at State and district levels continued. The teacher training strategy is being further intensified with the introduction of a new element of distance education.

Equity Issues

Equity issues in matters of enrolments, retention as well learning achievements are of paramount concern in our efforts towards universalisation. DPEP with a strong interface with the Mahila Samakhya Programme provided wide ranging interventions to promote education of girls. A mechanism of quarterly get-together of all State Gender Coordinators provided a focussed forum for cross state learning, review and follow-up. Similarly, tribal interventions based on situational needs and backed up by studies and research inputs continued throughout the project districts. Widening the scope of addressing the equity issues, guidelines have been issued for providing integrated education to disabled children. A strategy for addressing the educational needs of working children has been adequately discussed in a get-together of all the project States.

Community support which is the basis of contextuality got further fillip with the introduction of micro planning exercises. All project States engaged themselves in their own unique way in the process of building and improving upon the environment - a gradual but decisive step towards community ownership of schools.

An Elaborate MIS

Expenditure incurred is a rough and ready, though crude, way of measuring achievement of any project. Given the nature of DPEP which is essentially a process project, expenditure alone can never be a reliable indicator of progress. In this respect too, however, during the year that went by, the cumulative project expenditure went upto around 65 per cent of the target as compared to 12 per cent in the first semester of the project. Given the momentum, we should catch up fully with the target in another year's time. A fairly elaborate Management Information System became operational by the fall of the year. An exiting monitoring tool is now in place.

All project States made use of lessons learnt in DPEP Project districts to replicate interventions in non-DPEP areas. These included the textbooks and teacher training strategy.

DPEP has now, very recently, got its national logo. With the logo and signature, further harnessing of media to serve the cause of universal primary education should be further facilitated.

Indeed the reward for work well done is the opportunity to do more. DPEP, taking strides of progress and surging ahead, will have to turn from looking at the year that was to the year that will be. A long agenda awaits 1997. All functional aspects, pedagogical interventions, interventions to promote equity issues, researches, capacity building, convergence, widening the partnerships will have to be pursued with an even greater sense of urgency. Horizontal as well as vertical expansion is on the anvil.

Super goals

All the Super goals of the programme - enrolment, retention and learning achievement - are dependent on the quality of education. The key lies in quality of education which has to be perceived as joyful by the children and useful by the parents. All the interventions have to converge on the schools and the class-rooms to make it happen. But learning achievement is not a function of teaching in the school alone. Researches have conclusively established that socio-economic status, with its diverse attributes, is also its key determinant. The overall socio-economic development of the community will also have an influential bearing on the programmes of universalisation. The working of the Panchayati Raj institutions in the aftermath of the Constitutional Amendments of the Constitutional Amendments in this regard will be watched with interest. DPEP's success will, in a large measure, be dependent on vibrant functioning of the Village Education Committees and Panchayati Raj Institutions. Promotion of school effectiveness will have to be relentlessly pursued making full use of convergence of the various programmes of socio-economic development.

Mid-term evaluation of the programme is due by the new year's end. A number of evaluatory and exploratory studies and researches by individual and institutions would begin soon.

One looks with excitement to the association of a wide range of apex educational and management institutions and NGOs in this endeavour.

The inherent strength of the programme stands confirmed with the promises revealed during two years of implementation. The States are increasingly asking for more and further expansion. The programme has acquired visibility even internationally. Two most outstanding International Educational Conference during 1996 - The Mid-Term Review of EFA at Amman, Jordan and the International Conference on Education in Geneva, Switzerland - evinced considerable interest in DPEP in India. A steady stream of international enquiries and visits has been the result thereafter. The World Bank President having made a personal assessment of the programme implementation has commended it copiously. It has indeed emerged as a flag-ship programme in the whole world.

The Challenges Ahead

The challenges ahead are indeed enormous. But with the fine band of workers at all levels - districts, state and national and given the commitment which is available to the programme politically and from various institutions in Governmental and non-Governmental sectors, the path and the goal are clearly visible.

Will Durant said, "Truth always originates in a minority of one and every custom begins as a broken precedent". DPEP began as a programme two years back. The promises seen and the responses received are beginning to make it both the programme and the strategy to universalise primary education. Having been in and with DPEP for over a year now, nothing echoes my feelings better than the words of Archimedes-'`Eureka!' (We have found it).

Source: DPEP Calling, December 1996.

40

Invitation to Individual/ Institutional Researchers to Participate in DPEP

Under the National Research Component (NRC), DPEP announces two schemes, PROMOTE (Promoting Individual Research in Primary Education) and INSPIRE (Institutional Projects in Primary Education). Research studies pertaining to the areas identified below will be sponsored through these schemes.

Priority Areas for Research

Curriculum Analysis and evaluation of curricular materials (especially textbooks) with reference to learning load and gender sensitivity

Longitudinal research on language development in school curriculum with reference to reading, vocabulary development and socio-linguistic concerns

Longitudinal study of impact of curricular interventions

Curricular adaptation to needs of disadvantaged learners

Curriculum transaction in different social contexts

Curriculum policy

Rationale and empirical validation of MLL

Use of mother tongue in primary school teaching

Teaching of mathematics concepts in primary school

Translation of curriculum into specific learning tasks

Alternative approaches to early reading in Indian languages

Defining concept of readability in different languages and incorporation into language and subject textbooks

Longitudinal studies to test levels of reading readiness

Analysis of curriculum (based on information, skills and values)

	Evaluation of instructional materials (objectives, continuity and content) Interaction between learner and curriculum When should textbooks be introduced? Methodology for evaluation and validation Curriculum in action/curriculum implementation Role of language in subject matter teaching Curricular change

Priority Areas for Research

Teacher and Education Training	Curriculum components of teacher training and training courses Duration of teacher education courses Learning possibilities between teacher peers Multi-grade teaching methodologies Development of graded instructional materials for training courses Longitudinal studies on impact of different training courses. Strengthening of practice teaching in classrooms Efficacy of training in classroom situations. Assessment of teacher knowledge of content area and pedagogy Design of training programmes to develop research skills and motivation in teachers to find answers to specific problems Teachers' abilities to handle children with identified learning disabilities Extent of on-the-job support required by teachers Needs of teachers in dealing with special groups Effectiveness of gender-sensitive teacher training
Society, Economics and Education	Demand for education (both quantity and type) among different socio economic groups. Manner in which learning experiences of different socio-cultural groups is contextualised in schools Learning style of girls and boys Effect of panchayati raj on teacher accountability Development of gender-sensitive materials Educational needs of different tribal groups

Socialisation patterns in tribal communities and schools and implications for curriculum and teacher training
Use of tribal languages and dialects in primary education

Priority Areas for Research

Planning and Management	Link between policy pronouncements and planning for all children and specifically for girls, and children of SC/ST community etc.
	Unit cost studies and financing of education.
	Federal framework and impact on educational planning and financing
	Mix of public and private sectors in education
	Estimation of resource mobilisation from different sources
	Institutional planning (e.g. DIET, SCERT, etc.)
	Inter-ministry co-ordination with respect to education
	Micro Planning and Participation of Community
	Cost-effectiveness of alternative delivery mechanisms (e.g. distance learning).

The Schemes

Details of the schemes, their applicability etc. are provided below.

PROMOTE (Promoting Individual Research in Primary Education)

This scheme is for promoting research in elementary education by established individual research scholars from national educational institutions, universities, reputed non-government institutions and established freelance researchers with proven expertise and experience. In order to avail support under PROMOTE, individual researchers have to first submit a Concept Paper on the research theme. See Annexure for formulation of Concept Paper. For all individuals who are employed, the Concept Paper should carry a no-objection certificate from the head of the institution allowing the researcher to conduct the study on a full time basis during the mentioned period.

Time and Financial Limits

It is expected that individual researchers will take up few specific aspects of the problem they want to research and which could be analysed and solved in a 12-18 months period. Maximum financial limit for Research Studies under PROMOTE will be Rs. 3,00,000/-. No provision for purchase of furniture or equipment will be entertained through this scheme.

INSPIRE (Institutional Projects in Primary Education)

Under this scheme, Research Studies by institutions and universities will be promoted. Institutions having interest and experience in conducting research in education, socio-economic or other developmental issues will be given preference. In order to avail support under INSPIRE scheme, institutions have to first submit a Concept Paper on the research theme. See Annexure 1 for details about formulation of a Concept Paper.

Time and Financial Limits:

It is expected that institutions will take up research themes which can be analysed within 1-2 year period. Maximum financial limit for studies under INSPIRE will be Rs. 5,00,000. The funds will be used to meet expenses on execution of the project including payment of honoraria and salaries. No provision for purchase of equipment/assets will be entertained through this scheme.

Documents to be furnished:

Following documents should be furnished along with concept papers for consideration under INSPIRE Scheme:

(i) Endorsement from the Head of the Institute in the prescribed proforma (given at Annexure 3),

(ii) Registration Certificate, Memorandum of Association and Rules and Regulations of the Institution,

(iii) Details about the institution,

(iv) Bio-data of the Investigator(s)

Submission of Concept paper

Concept Paper can be submitted any time during the year to Deputy Secretary (DPEP) or Head, RESU, Ed. CIL's TSG. Addresses are:

The Deputy Secretary (DPEP)
Deptt. of Education
Min. of Human Resources Development
Shastri Bhavan, Gate No. 6, C Wing, New Delhi - 110 001.

The Head
Research Evaluation and Studies Unit,
Ed. CIL's Technical Support Group
A-264, Defence Colony New Delhi - 110 024.

All envelopes containing Concept Papers should be superscribed Concept Paper for DPEP Research Support under PROMOTE/INSPIRE Scheme".

Shortlisting and Communication

All Concept Papers will be shortlisted on the basis of: (a) their relevance to elementary education; (b) expertise and exposure of the individual/institution; and (c) background and experience of the Principal Investigator. Shortlisted Concept Papers will be further evaluated and researchers whose Concept Papers are found suitable will be intimated for submission of detailed proposal.

Annexure 1

Format for Submission of Concept Paper

The concept paper should be submitted in English in about 8 pages, types in double space, in the following format:

1. Cover page
   (a) Project title (descriptive, but not longer than two lines),
   (b) Applicants' names and full addresses, telephone and fax contact numbers,
   (c) Period of the proposed study in months, and
   (d) Approximate cost estimate in rupees.
2. *Statement of Problem and its Relevance to Elementary Education*
3. *Objectives*: Provide elaboration of each objectives in 1-2 sentences.
4. *Outputs*: Statement of all outputs expected of the study. Establish links with objectives.
5. *Scope of the Investigation and Methods to be Adopted*
6. *Work Plan and Calendar of Activities*: The tentative time-frame for the study should be provided.
7. *Project Team*: List the names of Principal Investigator and other key staff with their full addresses and contact phone and fax numbers. Attach brief resumes.

Annexure 2

Format for Submission of No Objection Certificate from the Head of Institution

(To be given on Letter Head and submitted for availing support under PROMOTE Scheme)

PROJECT TITLE: ______________________________

1. Certified that the Institute welcomes the participation of Dr/Prof./Mr./Ms. ______________________________ for the above project. Institute has no objection for his/her undertaking this project in the committed time schedule.

Name and Signature of Head of Institution

Date: __________ Place: __________

Annexure 3

Format for Submission of Endorsement from The Head of Institution
(To be given on Letter Head and submitted for availing support under INSPIRE Scheme)

PROJECT TITLE: ______________________________

____

1. Certified that the Institute welcomes the participation of Dr/Prof./Mr./Ms. ______________________ as the Principal Investigator and Dr/Prof./Mr/Ms. ______________________ as the Co-Investigator for the project and that in the unforeseen event of discontinuance by the Principal Investigator, the Co-Investigator will assume the responsibility for fruitful completion of the project.
2. Certified that the equipment, other basic facilities and such other administrative facilities as per terms and conditions of the research support, will be extended to the investigator(s) throughout the duration of the project.
3. Institute assumes to undertake the financial and other management responsibilities of the project.

Name and Signature of Head of Institution

Date: __________ Place: __________

Source: DPEP Calling, December 1996.

41

Landmark Conference of State Education Ministers

A conference of State Education Ministers was held in New Delhi on 10th August 1996 under the chairmanship of Sri S. R. Bommai, Union Minister of Human Resource Development. Hon'ble Prime Minister Sri H.D. Deve Gowda also addressed the Conference.

The Conference was attended by 25 Education Ministers from different States/UTs, Lt. Governor, Andaman & Nicobar Islands and Advisers to Governors of Jammu & Kashmir and Uttar Pradesh and Education Secretaries of all States/UTs. The Ministers discussed at length the overall scenario for school education in the country and the specific issues relating to earmarking 6% of GDP for education by 2000 A.D., amendment to the Constitution to make free and compulsory primary education a fundamental right and the Government's resolve to achieve full literacy by 2005 A.D.

A Conference of State Education Ministers was held at Vigyan Bhavan, New Delhi on 10th August 1996 under the chairmanship of Shri S.R. Bammai, Union Minister of Human Resource Development. Hon'ble Prime Minister Shri H.D.Deve Gowda also addressed the Conference. This Conference of Education Ministers was preceded by a meeting of State Education Secretaries on 9th August at the same venue. The Conference which was attended by 25 Education Ministers from different States/UTs, Lt. Governor, Andaman & Nicobar Islands and Advisers to Governors of Jammu & Kashmir and Uttar Pradesh and Education Secretaries of all States/UTs discussed at length the overall scenario for school education in the country and the specific issues relating to earmarking 6% of GDP for education by 2000 A.D., amendment to the Constitution to make free and compulsory primary education a fundamental right and the Government's resolve to achieve full literacy by 2005 AD.

Welcoming all the participants, Hon'ble Minister of State for Education Shri Muhi Ram Saikia said that increase in our literacy rate compared to what it was at the time of Independence was a positive development in our effort to achieve universalisation of elementary education. He also spoke about the Government's commitment to make the nation fully literate by the year 2005, allocation of 6% of GDP for education by 2000 A.D. and spending of 50% of this enhanced allocation on primary education. Referring to the decisions of the Chief Minister's Conference held on July 4-5, 1996 regarding Basic Minimum Needs which included primary education and literacy, he urged the State to step up their financial allocation for education.

What is required to make UEE a reality by the turn of the century is proper democratic decentralisation at the Panchayat level, due attention to education of girls, education of SCs/STs, disabled, minorities and other disadvantaged groups of society and acceleration of NFE programme for out of school children.

In his inaugural address, Shri S.R. Bommai said that a befitting way to celebrate the Golden Jubilee of our Independence was to make a united resolve in a true spirit of concurrency to address the unfinished task of universalisation of elementary education. The United Front Government has resolved to amend the Constitution to make UEE a fundamental right for which he urged all the state Ministers to be ready to fulfil the needs that education as a fundamental right would create. Touching upon the subject of making learning a joyful experience, he stressed the importance of implementation of various educational programmes and policy. What is required to make UEE a reality by the turn of the Century, he said, is proper democratic decentralisation at the Panchayat level, due attention to education of girls, education of SCs / STs, disabled, minorities and other disadvantaged groups of the society and acceleration of NFE programme for out of the school children. The Government intends to extend the Mid-Day Meals Programmes to the local body and private aided schools he announced.

Enough educational infrastructure and facilities were not enough to satisfy the people if we can not ensure quality teaching to our pupils, he added. Turning to the national literacy scene, he said the United Front Government was committed to making the whole of India literate by 2005 A.D. In order to make vocationalisation of education a success, he focussed on the importance of skill orientation in vocational courses instead of imparting mere bookish knowledge. Reiterating the Government commitment to invest six per cent of GDP on education by 2000 A.D. of which 50% would be spent on Primary Education, he referred to decisions of the Chief Ministers Conference on Basic Minimum Needs regarding transfer of the Centrally Sponsored Schemes to the States except the priority programmes in Elementary and Adult Education and sought concrete suggestions of the State Ministers.

Shri. P.R.D. Dasgupta, Union Education Secretary appraised the State Education Ministers of the decisions reached in the State Education Secretaries' Meeting held on the preceding day and sought their approval of the same. He said that the proposal to amend the Constitution to make free and compulsory primary education a fundamental right which was approved in the meeting of State Education Secretaries required careful consideration of its financial, administrative and legal implications and need for wide spread consultation at political level and also with the educational experts. He further added that the State Secretaries were of the view that the responsibility for harnessing necessary financial resources for translating constitutional commitment would have to be primarily that of the Central Government.

Shri. B. Durga Prasada Rao, Education Minister of Andhra Pradesh, mentioned that 90% of the rural habitations in the state are having primary schools within a walking distance of 1 km and 75% of the habitations are having upper primary schools within a distance of 3 kms. He urged the Ministry to extend the Mid-day Meal Scheme to the Non-formal Education System too. Andhra Pradesh has evolved "School Proformae" for monthly monitoring of enrolment, retention and quality of education of all the primary, upper primary and high schools in the state, he said, and requested for central assistance to the tune of 135.45 crores for supplying text-books to pre-matric students, maintenance of hostels, ashram schools and residential schools. Reiterating the state's commitment to total literacy, he sought for Rs. 418 crores central assistance for TLCs and PLCs.

The proposal to amend the Constitution to make free and compulsory primary education a fundamental right which was approved in the meeting of State Education Secretaries requires careful consideration considering its financial, administrative and legal implications....

The Central Government should also help the state in its endeavour to provide quality education in secondary schools and vocationalisation of secondary education, he added.

Shri. Lijum Ronys, Education Minister of **Arunachal Pradesh**, expressed difficulty of getting adult education instructors for adult education programmes with the existing honorarium of Rs. 100/- per month for which he sought an increase of honorarium of Rs. 200/- per month. He also said that Arunachal Pradesh had introduced compulsory vocational education because only vocational education could give opportunity to acquire knowledge for self-reliance thereby making students socially useful.

Shri. Jatin Mali, Education Minister of **Assam**, said that the state had accorded due priority to vocational education schemes in secondary education sector and vocational courses had been introduced in 150 schools. Steps are being taken to achieve 10% of the target set up by the Programme of Action (POA), 1992.

Shri. J.P. Narayan Yadav, Education Minister of **Bihar**, endorsed the Government of India's effort to make compulsory primary education a fundamental right. He referred to the State's target of enrolling 70 lakhs of students of the primary stage in next two years and need to recruit 1 lakh primary school teachers and establish 30,000 primary schools. He also mentioned that the Saksharta Abhiyan which was running in 25 districts out of 55 districts in the state had now taken a shape of mass movement and reiterated his government's commitment to extend the total literacy campaigns to whole of Bihar.

Shri Nalin Bhatt, Education Minister of **Gujarat**, lamented that 928 primary schools in the state had no classrooms while 4741 schools were having only one classroom. He referred to the launching of "**Bal Mitra Varg**" for joyful learning in the state. While endorsing Government of India's proposal to make education a fundamental right, he requested extension of Mid-day Meal Scheme and sharing of conversion cost by the Government of India. He also requested for removal of local contribution of Rs. 10000 in non-tribal areas under Operation Black-board. He further mentioned that the states should be given adequate funds for implementing the transferred Centrally Sponsored Schemes.

Shri. Ram Bilas Sharma, Education Minister of **Haryana,** referred to importance of Girls Education for which the state government had opened 536 primary schools exclusively for girls during the last four years and provision of free education till graduation level. While endorsing the proposal of making education a fundamental right, he stressed the importance of decentralization in education. School buildings in Haryana are being built by the Village Panchayats by using the funds of the education department. He requested for Rs. 11 crores central assistance to be provided under Operation Blackboard (OB) for construction of school buildings.

Prof. Narain Chand Parashar, Education Minister of **Himachal Pradesh**, spoke about his state government having introduced an innovative scheme of cash award of Rs. 20,000/- to any school where drop-out rates became zero. He sought central assistance for opening of 1100 new middle schools and annual requirement of Rs. 95 crores for providing cooked meal under the Mid-Day Meal Scheme. He also favoured making education a fundamental right and revealed his State's plan to achieve UEE during ninth plan period. Similarly, to improve access to secondary education, Himachal Pradesh is opening more and more senior secondary schools. He further mentioned that the state has set up a State Advisory Board of Education and Culture on the pattern of CABE to make appropriate recommendations for implementation of NPE, 1986 and POA, 1992. Referring to Vocational Education, he said state council of vocational education and a district vocational education committees for effective implementation of the vocationalisation of education has been constituted.

Shri A. Mohandas Moses, Adviser to Governor, Jammu & Kashmir, endorsed the proposal to make education a fundamental right. He said that there were 950 "school-less" habitations in the state where primary schools were to be opened and another 744 school buildings gutted by the militants to be reconstructed and for this he sought additional central assistance to the tune of Rs. 110 crores. While indicating about the removal of poverty line condition for supplying of uniforms in government schools in the state, he also sought Rs. 8.14 crores towards the 50% cost of conversion for providing hot cooked meals under the Mid-Day Meal Scheme. He also spoke about special measures needed for the disabled. TLCs are ready in 3 districts for which Government of India should provide necessary funds, he added.

Shri. H.G. Govinda Gowda, Education Minister of **Karnataka,** referred to the landmark decision of his government to reserve 50% of the posts of primary teachers for women and provision of school bag and note-books for girls belonging to SC/ST at higher primary stage. He requested for increase of central allocation for Operation Blackboard and enhanced transport subsidy under the Mid-day Meal Scheme. While concurring with the proposal regarding making education a fundamental right, he requested the Ministry to take up the state's proposal to spend 25% of the funds under Jawahar Rojgar Yojna (JRY) for construction of school-buildings with the Ministry of Rural Development. The Minister further assured that the state would make special efforts to rejuvenate the TLCs with the participation of Gram Panchayats in those districts where the programmes are lagging behind. The Government of India should support the scheme of continuing education in the Ninth Five Year Plan also, he suggested.

Shri. P.J. Joseph, Education Minister of **Kerala**, stated that the entire state had been made literate in a mass campaign with the participation of the community. He requested for release of funds to Sikshaka Kendras which were renamed as Gyan Vigyan Kendras.

Shri. Mukesh Naik, Education Minister of **Madhya Pradesh**, welcomed the proposal to make education a fundamental right and sought central assistance for building 2300 primary schools and recruitment of 71,000 primary school teachers. Referring to the innovative programmes called "School Chalo Abhiyan" and "Lok Sampark Abhiyan" for increasing enrolment, he suggested that Yoga and meditation should be made at all levels of education.

Shri. C.B. Morak, Education Minister of **Meghalaya**, informed that 13,000 habitations were yet to be provided schooling facility at primary level while there were as many as 307 "school-less" villages in the states as per norms. He requested for an increase in the subsidy for transportation cost under MDM and launching of a Centrally Sponsored Scheme on distribution of free text-books to primary school children.

Shri Ksh Irabot Singh, Education Minister of Manipur, spoke about the difficult terrain of the state which made it extremely difficult to access the habitations by motor-cars and other means of transport. Therefore, he requested for enhanced allocation for implementation of MDM scheme in the state. He urged the Central Government to give special consideration to the North-Eastern States.

Shri Nillo Rengma, Education Minister (school Education) of **Nagaland**, informed that 242 habitations with a population of 87,000 were still to be covered by primary schools. He agreed with the proposal to make education a fundamental right and requested for increased central assistance under the MDM Scheme due to high transportation cost in the state.

Shri Jayadav Jena, Minister of School and Mass Education of **Orissa**, recommended the organic unit of early childhood education, primary schooling, Non-Formal Education, Adult Education and Post-Literacy Campaigns and ensuring quality in education. He proposed to cover the entire state by 2000 A.D. and provide vocational skills during Post Literacy Phase. While agreeing with the proposal to make elementary education a fundamental right, he highlighted the need to extend DPEP to 7 more districts in the state having literacy rate from 8% to 23% in hilly and backward areas. Noting the positive impact of MDM scheme in school enrolment and retention, he called for additional assistance towards transportation charges and conversion cost. He also sought central financial support for providing free text-books in primary schools, provision of toilets and hostels for girls and drinking water facility in all the primary schools. He also called for strengthening of DIETs and setting up of an effective mechanism for monitoring the progress of Centrally Sponsored Schemes being implemented by the NGOs. The Minister lamented about the poor infrastructure for sports and games in Orissa for which he sought special financial assistance from the Government of India.

Shri Mohinder Singh K.P., Education Minister of **Punjab**, sought assistance from the World Bank for improvement of the primary education in the state. Punjab has set up a state level expert committee on vocational education to evaluate and monitor the programme. While agreeing with the proposal to make education a fundamental right, he observed resources were the major constraint for providing the adequate infrastructure.

Shri Gulabchand Kataria, Education Minister of **Rajasthan**, said that his government planned to provide at least one upper primary school in every Panchayat by 1997 - 98. Rajasthan would introduce compulsory education in selected districts as an experimental measure, the result of which should be deliberated upon in a specially convened meeting of CABE, he suggested. Seeking an increase in transportation cost to Rs. 50 per quintal under MDM scheme, he urged for launching a Centrally Sponsored Scheme exclusively for Girls' Education.

Shri Kedarnath Rai, Education Minister of **Sikkim**, suggested that pre-primary sector should be included for Central assistance and food-grains under MDM Scheme should increased to 5 kgs. per child for all. He also sought an increase in the transportation charges and additional financial assistance for cooked meals. He appreciated the adult education programme as it showed the rights of the women and weaker section people.

Prof. K. Anbazhagan, Education Minister of **Tamil Nadu**, said that his government had adopted an innovative approach to make learning a joyful experience. However, to provide at least one teacher for each class, his state required 54825 teachers additionally and hence the need for increased central assistance.

Shri Anil Sarkar, Education Minister of **Tripura**, spoke about his state's commitment to UEE. However, the impediment to achieve UEE in his state is that 40% of the habitations are yet to be covered by primary schools while 1661 primary schools have no class rooms. He sought full reimbursement on account of MDM scheme and asked for special central assistance to the tune of 8 crores on account of reconstruction of school buildings damaged due to floods and other natural calamities.

Shri R.C. Jain, Advisor to the Governor of **Uttar Pradesh**, agreed in principle regarding raising the financial allocation on education to 6% of State Domestic Product (SDP) but considering the competing claim for more funds in priority areas, he suggested for developing a differential scale of financing of educational schemes in backward states who had a commitment to basic education. He endorsed the proposal to make compulsory elementary education a fundamental right and indicated the State Government's commitment to open 4257 more primary schools in 38 districts of the state. He was of the view that Village Education

Committees (VECs) should supervise distribution of scholarships and foodgrains under the MDM scheme and share the responsibility for construction of school buildings. The process of serving hot meals would be tried on a pilot basis in villages for active community participation, he added.

Shri Kanti Biswas, Minister-in-Charge School Education of **West Bengal**, requested the Government of India to include all blocks and municipalities within the purview of MDM scheme in the second phase only. He endorsed the proposal to make compulsory elementary education a fundamental right. Seeking Rs. 71.40 crores for providing cooked food under MDM scheme, he suggested that while implementing the MDM in schools there should not be any differential treatment amongst the students of the school. He said that a Commission, namely Burman commission was set up in the state to decide the admission criterion of SC/ST students in institutions.

Dr. Rajendra Kumari Bajpai, Lt. Governor of **Andaman and Nicobar Islands**, spoke about the establishment of 27 centres for integrated education of the disabled and highlighted the need for construction of 900 teachers' quarters in the remote rural areas and relaxation of norms of primary schools from 200 population to at least 150. She also endorsed the proposal to make compulsory primary education a fundamental right. She expressed that the main hurdle in achieving the total literacy in the territory was due to the perplexing growth rate of the population of 4% per annum following the influx of migrant labour from the poorer mainland states. She also mentioned that there was a separate Senior Secondary Schools for girls at Port Blair and informed that Ashram School had been established in the UT. She reiterated her government's commitment to achieve the target of UEE by 2000 A.D.

Participating in the valedictory session of the Conference, Shri H.D. Deve Gowda, Hon'ble Prime Minister of India explained that education could not get the attention it deserved during the early years of independence due to some other pressing socio-economic demands. The Conference of the Chief Ministers called by him on July 4-5, 1996 had recognized Universalisation of Primary Education as one of the basic minimum services which should be achieved by 2000 A.D. as resolved by the Chief Ministers, he added. He also announced the Government's decision to raise allocation on education from the current year itself so as to achieve the target of 6% of GDP by the turn of the century. For the success of Primary Education he stressed the need for opening one school in each village with at least two teachers. In this context, Prime Minister stated that 100 Residential primary schools in rural areas meant for the poorest of poor will be operationalised soon.

The Prime Minister underlined the importance of decentralized management of education and assured all support to the states for achieving UEE. Referring to the promotion of Girls Education, reduction in drop-out rates, he suggested formation of a small group of Ministers to devise guidelines for protecting the educational interests of educational and religious minorities. Turning to the deterioration in the standards of education, he asked the Minister of Human Resource Development to examine the possibility of introducing a comprehensive Education Bill in the Parliament in this regard. He said the newly launched Centrally Sponsored Scheme of Residential Primary Schools meant for the poorest of the poor would complete the unaddressed tasks of Navodya Vidyalayas. At least one school in each district of the country would be built under the scheme. Even though it was intended to be operated by the NGOs, the State Governments could also avail of its benefit, he added. He solicited cooperation of all concerned for making UEE a reality.

Conclusion

The Chairman summed up the decisions of the Conference in his concluding remarks. Ministers welcomed the new initiatives taken by the Central government for

- (i) Provision of Rs. 10 crores for Residential Primary Schools for the Poor
- (ii) Teacher Housing schemes with a provision of Rs. 50 crores
- (iii) Exemption of Excise Duty on writing and printing paper to be provided to State Text Book Corporation
- (iv) Raising public investment on education in Centre and States together to 6% of GDP
- (v) Continuation of Mid-day Meal Scheme.

The Ministers were of the view that at least 50% of the cost of serving hot meals to children should be shared by the Centre. The Conference considered the follow-up action on the decisions of the Chief Ministers' Conference on 4th and 5th July, 1996 with regard to the importance of the new identified thrust areas and the decisions regarding the future of the Centrally Sponsored Schemes. The Conference decided that the Schemes of Operation Blackboard, Teacher Education, Non-formal Education and Nutritional Support to Primary Education (Mid-Day Meal) Scheme in the elementary education sectors and the schemes of the National Literacy Mission should continue as the Centrally Sponsored Schemes in keeping with the decisions of the Chief Ministers' Conference.

Spotlight

Participating in the valedictory session of the Conference, Shri H.D. Deve Gowda, Hon'ble Prime Minister of India explained that education could not get the attention it deserved during the early years of independence due to some other pressing socio-economic demands. The Conference of the Chief Ministers called by him on July 4 - 5, 1996 has recognized Universalisation of Primary Education as one of the basic minimum services which should be achieved by 2000 A.D. as resolved by the Chief Ministers, he added. He also announced the Government's decision to raise allocation on education from the current year itself so as to achieve the target of 6% of GDP by the turn of the century. For the success of Primary Education he stressed the need for opening one school in each village with at least two teachers. In this context the Prime Minister stated that 100 residential primary schools in rural areas meant for the poorest of poor will be operationalised soon. The Prime Minister underlined the importance of decentralized management of education and assured all support to the states for achieving UEE. Referring to the promotion of Girls Education, reduction in dropout rates, he suggested formation of a small group of Ministers to device guidelines for protecting the educational interests of educational and religious minorities. Turning to the deterioration in the standards of education, he asked the Minister of Human Resource Development to examine the possibility of introducing a comprehensive Education Bill in the Parliament in this regard. He said the newly launched Centrally Sponsored Scheme of Residential Primary Schools meant for the poorest of the poor would complete the unaddressed tasks of Navodaya Vidyalayas. At least one school in each district of the country would be built under the scheme. Even though it was intended to be operated by the NGOs, the State Governments could also vail of its benefit, he added. He solicited co-operation of all concerned for making UEE a reality.

However, it was decided that some of these schemes will provide for greater flexibility in implementation and allow a much greater autonomy to the States to make local contextual modification. In the secondary education sector the three major schemes viz. i) Computer literacy and studies in schools ii) Vocationalisation of secondary education and iii) Promotion of Yoga would be transferred to the state sector.

It would be, however, ensured that after the transfer to the State the basic idea behind these schemes is not lost sight of. it is expected that the schemes would play a more relevant role in the education sector in the States after such transfer.

In this regard it was decided that the funds of education sector will not be utilized for other sectors and particularly for vocationalisation of secondary education, funds would be earmarked and committed.

The Conference also constituted a group of State Ministers under the Chairmanship of Shri Muhi Ram Saikia, Minister of State for HRD, Government of India to identify the resources required to achieve universalisation of elementary education and total literacy and also to lay down the steps required to achieve these objectives within the time-frame laid down in the recent meeting of the Chief Ministers held on 4-5 July, 1996.

The Group will consist of education Ministers of Andhra Pradesh, Bihar, Haryana, Karnataka, Kerala, Madhya Pradesh, Maharashtra, Manipur, Orissa, Rajasthan, Tamil Nadu, West Bengal, Adviser to the Governor J&K and the Member (Education) Planning Commission.

The conference ended with a vote of thanks to the chair as well as to the Hon'ble Prime Minister.

Courtesy: DPEP Calling, September 1996.